Circling Four Corners

Re-Viewing Native American Indiens

Jay Miller, PhD

© 2017

Contents

#1-393

Foreword

Providing these overviews, published and drafts, in one place helps to clarify my own thought processes as well as address larger Americanist issues. It alsoenables my correction of typos, faulty data, and a title ~ restoring Cultural Amnesia. Before I became a *talwa* member, I relied on John Swanton and Southeastern ethnography to identify Breath Holder as the Mvskoki Creek high god. That is its Christian expression, which stomp grounds refer to *Ohfunka* = 'Above'. My text has now been amended based on my later lived experiences.

Throughout, a tilde ~ shows equivalent, same, alike. A convention much in need.

Thanks

Many people have helped me to understand the complexities of Tsimshian culture. In particular, at Hartley Bay, these were Chief John and Helen Clifton, Ernest, Lynne, Cameron, and Jodie Hill, Ernest and Margie Hill, Sr, and Mildred Wilson. At Klemtu, my teachers were Violet and Peter Neasloss, Chief Tom Brown, and others. Other colleagues include John and Luceen Dunn, Susan Marsden, Marjorie Halpin, Margaret Seguin, Carol Sheehan, Bill Holm, Robin Wright, Viola Garfield, Amelia Susman Schultz, Jean Mulder, Marie-Lucie Tarpent, Bruce Rigsby, Dale Kinkade, Jay Powell, Vickie Jensen, Guy Gibeau, and Stanley Newman.

Students in the Simon Fraser University, Native Language Teacher Program at Prince Rupert clarified and expanded my thinking: Cameron and Eva-Ann Hill, Nadine Robinson, Mel Tait, Maureen Yeltatzie, Beatrice Skog, Isabelle Hill, Pansy Collison, Deborah Schmakeit, Marilyn Bryant, Karla Gamble, and Shani Heal. Mary Tomlinson, Mercedes de la Nuez, and Thomas Perry helped me smooth out complications with Canadian bureaucracy.

For aid with Salish research, it is a pleasure to thank Vi and Don Hilbert for all their help and encouragement, along with their family of Lois, Ron, Jay, Bedelia, Jill, John, and all the grandchildren. Within the larger Lushootseed family, thanks go to Peggy Dunn, Alf Shepard, Robbie Rudine, Janet Yoder, Pam Cahn (*wiw'isu*), Carolyn Marr, Brad Burns, Carolyn Michael, Barbara Iliff Brotherton, Dean Reiman, and many more.

Among other degreed members, appreciation goes to Drs. Thom Hess, Pam Amoss, Dale Kinkade, Laurel Sercombe, William Seaburg, Dawn (*ɬup*) Bates, Andie Palmer, Robin Wright, Bill Holm, Greg Watson, Bob and Laura Dassow Walls, Mary Laya, John Adams, Sally Anderson, Astrida Blukis Onat, Ann Bates, Carol Eastman, Fr. Patrick Touhy, Fr Mike Fitzpatrick, Viola Garfield, and Erna Gunther.

Among the native community, while they cannot all be named, or wish to be, I single out the late Isadore Tom, Ed Davis, Lawrence Webster, Martin Sampson, Susie Sampson Peter, Morris Dan, Theresa Willup, Helen Ross, Lottie Sam, Walter Sam, and Dewey Mitchell. Younger members include Lona Wilbur, Dobie Tom, and the families of Andy Fernando and Jack, Deborah, and Fiander family. Blue, Sherry, and Sanger Clark provide strong support.

At the beginning, support came from James and Charlotte Toulouse, Carmie Lynn, Laura Lee, Charlotte Mary, Jeremy Alan, Tamaya Lynn, Trent, Marie, Ella Mae, and others. As an undergraduate at the University of New Mexico, Stanley Newman, W.W. "Nibs" Hill, Philip Bock, Bruce Rigsby, and, especially, Florence Hawley Ellis and Mary Elizabeth Smith set my academic course. Outside the classroom, Cynthia Irwin-Williams and the Anasazi Origins

Project gave me first-hand experience as an archaeologist on Sia Pueblo Land. Later as an advisor at Salmon Ruin, I was introduced to Chaco outliers and reoccupations.

As a graduate student at Rutgers and Princeton, my teachers were Robin Fox, Yehudi Cohen, Warren Shapiro, and Mark Leone. Margaret Bacon, Jane Lancaster, and Martin Silverman gave encouragement. Alfonso Ortiz, Esther Goldfrank, and Karl Wittfogel, Elizabeth Brandt, Wick Miller, Tom Windes, Anna Sofaer, and John Stein provided insights.

My parents and siblings aided as needed, as did fellow students Janet Pollak, Michele Teitelbaum, Cheryl Wase, Edward Deal, Nina Versaggi, Nancy Trembly, Kenneth Wilkie, Corinne Black, Karen and Tom Reynolds, John and Luceen Dunn and family, Glenn and Dorothy Williams and family, Andrew and Nancy Core and family, and Roland Wildman. Support also came from Marilyn Richen, Ann Schuh, Bob and Christine Keyes-Back, Tom and Donna Steinburn, Nancy Griffin, and, especially, Monday Nite.

At JONA, Darby Stapp, Kara Powers, Julia Longenecker, and ?? have been brought it all to fruition.

High-Minded High Gods in North America

In his Manchester College lectures at Oxford in 1932, Wilhelm Schmidt (1933) considered the ethnographic evidence for the belief and cults concerned with the notion of a (monotheistic) High God in Native North America. While his interpretations of the relative antiquity of his three ethno-linguistic groups are no longer tenable, the ethnographic reality of a High God for each of these groupings remains confirmed. According to Schmidt's argument, Yuki of California with their singularity as an unaffiliated language ~ isolate group were the oldest stratum; Algonkians represented an intermediate stage that was individualistic since they "no longer practice collective tribal initiation of boys, still less of girls" (1933: 63); and Interior Salish (whom he called "Inland Selish") were the most recent with the belief but no cult.

Through the succeeding years, other High Gods have been reported for Amerind tribes either without further comment or with the parenthetical remark that they may have originated under the stimulation of Christian missionization. The fact of the matter is that no one, except theologians, has presented a plausible explanation for the existence of the North American High Gods. Because I have recently been involved in fieldwork [917] among many of the tribes discussed by Schmidt and I have surveyed the Americanist literature to locate other High Gods, I feel that this background enables me to present a structuralist explanation for High Gods as an ultimate projection and personification of the symbolism of Mind (Intellect) so basic to many Amerind cultures. I see in the High God phenomenon an empirical vindication of the theoretical importance which Claude Levi-Strauss has placed on the Mind as the apical mediator for all human societies. The occurrence of the High God in North America, thereby, represents a particular example of the more general phenomenon. The personification aspect derives from the prevalence of anthropocentrism, the Precopernican perspective (Douglas 1970), in Amerind cultures. The usual explanation offered throughout Native North America as to the nature of the world is that everything (animal, plant, spirit, celestial bodies) is at base a Man or a Woman who assumes the "cloak" of their species or identity when trafficing with the Human World.

With this précis of the argument, we can now consider the ethnographic data before summarizing this new understanding of the role of the High God as mediating Intellect, as mindful master. We will first review evidence from the Yuki, Delaware, and Sanpoil before assessing data from the Naskapi, Creek, Pawnee, Keres Pueblos, and Lakota Sioux.

According to Yuki mythology, the Creator *Taikomal* ~ The One Who Walks Alone first appears as down, floating on the primal water, which changed into himself to the accompaniment of an all-pervading song Foster 1944). After he had created the world and travelled around to inspect and improve it, he rose into the sky where his continued existence is known because thunder is his voice, wind his breath, lightning his punishment, and wild tobacco smoke his preferred offering. Because of his ubiquity, *Taikomal* can be equated with all-pervading thought or consciousness. Since he remains in the sky, his appearance to the candidates of the highest ranking degree of Yuki shamanism, the sky shamans, must take place through the medium of thought. The young boys being initiated into the Creator Cult must remain silent, fasting, motionless for four days; again presumably to facilitate mental contact with the Creator. Now that *Taikomal* has physically left the earth, therefore, his essential intellectual quality has emerged with particular clarity.

The Delaware Creator is *Kishalamukong* ~ The One Who Created Us By His Thoughts so his cerebral asset is blatantly emphasized (Miller: ms).[1] He entrusted the care of the world to the Atlantean Cosmic Turtle, who is also believed to be sapient by the Delaware (Miller 1974). The Creator is visualized as eternally sitting in the twelfth or highest heavenly tier above the earth. If and when he communicates with these earth, it is by means of his thoughts, or what some modern Delaware prefer to call the "astroprojection" of his mind. His worship in the Big House rite, summarized by Schmidt (1933: 94-102), was specifically explained to me as involved with the Delaware sending their good thoughts and prays up to him.

During research with the Sanpoil division of Interior Salish, I had occasion to note the emphasis which they place on the mind or consciousness. When probing the memories of various elders, each of them could recollect events back to the time when they "came to." In American English, "to come to" usually refers to regaining consciousness after some traumatic experience. For the Sanpoil, however, "coming to" means to gain mental awareness as a distinct individual sometime about the age of two years old (Miller 1977-78).[2]2 In Sanpoil belief, their version of the Interior Salish High God is called Sweat Lodge. He was once a Man during the Myth Age, but near its terminus he decided to become eyeless, armless, and legless by transforming into the first [918] semi-hemispherical Sweat Lodge (Ray 1932: 179).[3]3 Since that time, people who seek continued health or solution to a quandary have entered the sweat lodge to clarify 'their minds and commune with the Creator. In the Sanpoil case then, too, the creator has become a quintessential embodiment of the mind. Moreover, as part of the origin myth. Coyote receives the charge from the Creator to modify and transform the world because Coyote was the first character to think for himself. In addition to these examples initially discussed by Schmidt in some detail, additional High Gods provide further support for my argument.

At nearly the same time that Schmidt was examining the data discussed above, Father John Cooper was probing the belief in a High God in the eastern subarctic of Canada along the west coast of James Bay. There he found an unquestionable belief in a High God in addition to a trinity composed of the Master of Food, the Master of Life, and the Master of Death. The High God is equated with *Manitu*, the source of supernatural power. This is an important equation because Cooper (1934: 38) cites the word *sokadis'u* as meaning either someone "has supernatural .power or mind power" as distinct from mere physical strength.

Among Christian Mvskogee Creeks, the Creator is called Breath Holder and breath is equated with life (Swanton 1928: 481). Creek shaman-priests frequently use techniques of blowing and breathing in their cures and rituals. As life was equated with breath so the essence of life was equated with "clear thought and vision." In one account of the origin of the world, seven people were able to expand the parameters of dry land "by extending their thoughts" (same: 487). Similarly, although all Creek are endowed with life-breath, the most important men, those who are the foundation of the most complex religious ceremony, the Green Corn or

---

[1] This and other data derive from my fieldnotes taken during over six years of research with Delaware-Lenape now living in the state of Oklahoma.

[2] These data are drawn from my 1977-78 fieldnotes concerned with Sanpoil and other tribes collected together on the Colville Reservation, Washington State.

[3] The legend of Sweat Lodge is still told by Sanpoils, as I personally can attest.

Busk rite, are respectfully called the "brains ~ mind" of the Busk (same: 302) and God is known as *Ohfunka* "Above".

The Pawnee High God is called *Tirawahat* ~ Expanse of the Heavens ~ *Tirawa* (The One Supreme Power In The Heavens Who Created The World (Golla 1975). Here the data are not entirely clear and the example may be spurious in terms of monotheism since he was a wife called Vault of the Heavens; however, Weltfish (1971: 16) does note that for the Pawnee "the primary level of reality is thought ... the Pawnee deity ... began the process of creation with thoughts and so created the universe and the stars, and they in turn were to create man in their own image ... In the Pawnee context, the thinking man was the essential human being."

The Keres example is especially instructive because here the Creator is a Woman rather than a Man and she created and articulated the world by the sheer power of her thoughts. For this reason, her name *Tsityostinako* is often translated as Thought-Woman (Boas 1928: 276), but careful probing of the meaning of *Tsityosti* (-*nako* indicates a woman's name) leads me to suggest that this term indicates full consciousness or complete mental awareness.[4] 4.

Out of deference to the Sioux, whom Schmidt (1933: 60) unjustly characterized as blood-thirsty, warlike, sun-worshippers, I feel compelled to also add the Great Mystery (*Wakan Tanka*) of the Lakota division to the listing of High Gods (Hassick 1964: 205 ff.). According to the holy men, the great mystery is simultaneously formless yet tetradic (quartered along various axes), not identifiable yet everywhere, and incomprehensible yet worthy of serious reflection by analogy to a universal intelligent sentience.[5] 5.

Based on these eight examples, I find support for my assertion that the role of the High God is a projection and personification of human thoughtful intelligence, of Mind. Other examples might also be cited if the data were more complete and conclusive. For the present, however, these eight will do nicely. A corollary of my assertion is that [919] the personification is necessary because these and other tribal cultures live with an anthropomorphic world view. This corollary is also supported most strongly by the Keres example of a Woman Creator. In other words, while almost all High God Creators are personified as men, the underlying rule of anthropomorphization rather than straight masculinization permits the occasional Woman Creator to appear. Since both are projections of human thought, the Precopernican world view exists without challenge from some other strategy such as zoomorphization or deification.

This projection and anthropomorphization also provides support, at least in terms of Native North America, for the assertion by Levi-Strauss that the Mind serves as the ultimate mediator between Nature/Culture. As all-pervasive, monotheistic personifications, these High Gods indeed do mediate the culturally-constructed natural world of their adherents. Until now, Levi-Strauss has provided us with such examples of the importance of the mind as the incest taboo, cooking, classification systems, and language. As suggested by the eight Amerind cases summarized above, we may now add an even more potent if intangible metaphor for the mind: The pre-existent High God ~ Creator who has both baffled and intrigued Americanists for so long because no one was properly mindful of the role he/she plays in human thought and expression.

---

[4] My research on the Keres Pueblos occupied 1968-69, 1972, and sporadically since.
[5] More support for equating *Wakan Tanka* with Mind ~ knowledge is Powers 1977: 172, 182.

The Matter of the (Thoughtful) Heart:
Centrality, Focality, or Overlap

Abstract
Throughout Native North America, and elsewhere in the world, the heart is often considered to be the locus of thought. After examining interpretations for this phenomenon as centrality or focality, the paper concentrates on an explanation of overlap as redundancy in order to discuss the main quality of mediators and the emic objectivization of the Levi-Strausian concept of Mind as mediator between Nature and Culture.

THE ULTIMATE TEST of any scientific explanation is its ability to integrate, or account for, more data than any alternative attempts. The most salient characteristic of this integration is its redundancy throughout the data, its organization of diversity. For this reason the most powerful anthropological explanation generally available at present is the structuralism of Claude Levi-Strauss. The notion of structure enables the recognition of the redundancy of the opposition of Nature and Culture as mediated by Mind throughout all human enterprise.

This redundancy is not limited to straight parallels, however, but can take other forms of relationship. Levi-Strauss has shown that data is never only what it seems; it is more, intricately more. Behind the intricacy is the process of transformation, code switching, that can occur as equation, reversal, segregation, and neutralization. Equation is the straightforward relationship of direct parallels between the terms involved in the relation, e.g., A : B :: C : D. Reversal inverts this relationship, generally reversing the most frequent association, eg, A : B :: D : C. By segregation, the relationship between the terms is extended or overdrawn, eg, A : B :: Y : Z. Alternatively, neutralization narrows the relationship between the terms, eg, A : B :: A_1 : B_1. This explication is necessary because structuralism is often accused of being a mentalistic exercise, without any empirical basis. This is patently false, because as part of anthropology, structuralism must be empirical: "That anthropology is first of all an empirical science is obvious: each culture that we approach confronts us with an entirely new situation which can only be described and understood at the cost of the most concrete and painstaking scrutiny" (Levi-Strauss 1972).

Nonetheless, structuralism parts company with the rest of empirical anthropology because its goals are "understanding" rather than "proof." It recognizes the primacy of form over content, so that concepts and ideas are given precedence over behavior and events. While the focus of analysis is upon relationships, the understanding emerges from inductive rethinking of the ideas represented by the data. As Levi-Strauss (1945: 528) has said explicitly, quoting Durkheim, "if sociological phenomena are just objectivated systems of ideas, to explain them is to re-think them in their logical order and this explanation finds in itself its own proof; at most, a few examples could be added as confirmation."

The constraints on this rethinking are those imposed by universal features of human thought processes and by localized factors of the techno-environment of a given human community. Every culture selects from the range of meaningful relationships and expresses them in terms of available signs and symbols derived from common human experiences and from the local ecology. [339]

4

Rather than apply this theoretical background to particular cultural data, I will use it to explore one of the most fundamental aspects of structuralism – Mind. If ideas are to have anthropological relevence they need objectivization in social pheonomena; their currency and redundancy rests on their empirical representation. In an earlier paper I explored the objectivization of Mind in terms of the so-called high gods widely reported from Native North America. There I argued that these high gods, bereft of all attributes save intelligence, serve as personifications of the ubiquitous, cosmic mediation of Mind for these cultures. In the present paper I would like to focus more intensely on the widely reported emic interpretation from all over Native America that the heart is the locus of thought, and sometimes also of emotions. First I will present a brief survey of such ethnographic reports from throughout the continent, and then I will individually examine three alternative explanations for the thoughtful heart as based on the recognition of centrality, focality, or overlap. This examination will lead us into the works of Aristotle, who also glimpsed the importance of this problem.

Ethnographic Reports

The broad spread of this phenomenon, regardless of linguistic, cultural, or geographical differences, can be seen from the following representative sample, organized for convenience from the Atlantic to the Pacific coasts of North America. This phenomena is actually much more widespread, probably once quite explicit even in Indo-European (Miller 1977), so the Native American examples are also indicative of global ones.

My initial experience with the thoughtful heart occurred during fieldwork with Delaware people, whose ancestors once dwelt along the Atlantic slope of the eastern United States. The Delaware believe that the heart is the source of thought and of emotions (Miller 1977: 147). Farther west, in the Plains culture area, the gestural lingua franca usually called the sign language represented the words "to think" or "thought" by pointing to the heart before bringing the hand forward "to gesture thought coming forth from the heart" (Uniker-Sebeok and Sebeok 1978: 120). For the American Southwest, we have the report of Carl Jung (in Hillerman 1976: 38) that members of the pueblo of Taos in New Mexico believe they think with the heart. In Arizona, Spier (1933: 33) found that "the Maricopa believed that one thinks with his heart," and that one's emotions were registered by the heart beat.

In the Northwest, the widely used trade pidgin called Chinuk WaWa jargon expressed the word for thinking as literally "to use the heart" (Gill 1933: 34). More specifically within this area, the word for 'heart' in the Salishan language of the Moses-Columbia is based on the root for 'think' (Kinkade 1975). Also in the Pacific drainage, the Kalapuya had many expressions relating the heart to thought and emotions. For example, the phrase, "Heart is not good" meant "I am angry" and "How is your heart" meant "What do you think?" (Jacobs 1945: 95, 137). Similar idiomatic usage equating the heart, thought, and emotions is reported for other areas, such as the Great Lakes (Kinietz 1965: 200). These few examples should indicate the ubiquity of the thoughtful heart; especially telling are the illustrations from such international means of communication as the Plains sign language and Chinuk jargon.

To initiate our discussion of the more general explanation of these occurrences, [341] we must revert to the classical roots of European intellectualism and follow the lead of Aristotle.

Alternative Explanations

The thoughtful heart is not only widespread, it is also ancient, attracting the attention of no less a figure than Aristotle. In discussing animal life, some of which is bloodless, he nonetheless observes (1931: 655b): "For in all animals there must be some central and commanding part of the body, to lodge the sensory portion of the soul and the source of life."

In the higher animals there was blood, and a heart in the commanding center of the body. Of all animals only humans stand erect, with the upper part of the body directed toward the upper realms of the universe. After arguing that the brain was a cold organ thickly covered with flesh and not the sensory center that some had claimed, Aristotle (1931: 669b) argued that the central location of the heart and its greater abundance of heat-generating blood explained the human upright stance:

"Heat ... tends to make the body erect; and thus it is that man is the most erect of animals."

Aristotle was led to disparage the brain because it was cold, bloodless, and enclosed. But the heart was the same as or analogous to organs in all animals; warm, full of blood, "in anatomical connection, through the blood vessels, with all the sense-organs," and "in a central position befitting the supreme organ" (same: 656a #3). Included within these attributes are glimpses of the three alternative explanations to which we will now turn.

Great reliance was placed on the central position of the heart, explicitly because such centrality provided a commanding position within the body. In more general terms, I view this argument as based on a synecdoche, having the part stand for the whole; in this case, the center of the body represents the entire organism. The difficulty with this explanation is that while the synecdoche accounts for the emphasis on the heart as a metaphor for the body, it does not explain why the heart should also serve as the locus of thought.

Therefore we might consider the heart as an example of focality, the condensation of a complex relationship around a fixed, central position in the body. Focality appears to be a better explanation, because it includes not only the location of the heart, but also its direct links with the rest of the body by means of the circulation of the blood. Similarly the circulation of the blood might be equated with the circulation of ideas and hence with thought. However, we are still unable to suggest a clear association of Mind and thoughts with the heart rather than with the more analogous blood. To complete the explanations and trace the relationships involved, we must carefully consider the process of objectifying ideas.

While the notions of centrality or focality have explanatory power for dealing with various signs as metaphors, they are inadequate for dealing with the relationships between Mind and heart. This relationship characterizes these objectivized ideas not as metaphors but rather as mediators. As I have written elsewhere (Miller 1978), mediators have special properties, which enable them both to synthesize the members of an oppositional pair and to bear an identity with other mediators recognized by a culture. Generally all mediators form an identifiable grouping, [341] because each shares the property of being a "permeating nexus." A mediator functions as a permeating nexus when it has a central point from which some tendril-like appendages emanate to permeate, engulf, and encompass everything else in the cultural realm. On this basis the frequent references to mediators such as spiders, crosses, and other nexi become understandable as variant or diverse permutations on this quality of mediators. More importantly Mind itself as a mediator is also associated with this shared property. Some ethnographic reports explicitly state that thought proceeds from a fixed point, such as a creator, to permeate the world.

This quality of nexal permeation is at the heart of the objectivization of Mind. It is neither centrality nor locality, because its characteristic is that of overlap into all cultural domains, and of redundancy throughout the culture. It is the organization of diversity, rather than some form of diminution through substitution of part for whole or condensation; the range of variation is organized, rather than simplified.

On the basis of this argument the identity of heart and Mind should be obvious. As Mind is the ultimate mediator, the permeating nexus, so the heart becomes its locus because the heart and circulatory system of blood vessels are a graphic objectivization of this mediator. The heart is the nexus and the vessels its permeations. Together they redundantly overlap through the entire body. In the extremely rational world that was Native America, logical consistency was an important adjunct to the entire world view. In this as in any other pre-Copernican universe – to use Mary Douglas's phrase (1966) – body symbolism played the crucial role in organizing a culture. Now that science has usurped the explanatory power of logical constructs for the modem world, we are less likely to grasp the satisfaction that derived from the equation of heart and Mind. They were isomorphic not only for understanding the cosmos, but also for rationally articulating an individual. As body is usually equated with house for the communal group, and with the cosmos for the entire realm of living things, the human form is usually the most powerful metaphor for a small-scale society.

The total integration of the world is accomplished by the isomorphism of heart and Mind. As the body articulated a metaphor that pervaded the cultural world, so did the heart and mind of an individual serve to mediate this world on three levels. First, at the level of sensory experience, heart and thought mediated the conceptualization of the individual. In some cultures centrality is given limited recognition at this level in that the concentric triad of center, inside, outside is usually expressed as heart, right side, and left side. Second, at the level of community interaction, the heart and mind together serve to integrate the individual members in terms of shared thoughts. Third, at the level of the cosmos. Mind as the ultimate mediator is directly linked with the heart of an individual, overlapping and crosscutting all other divisions.

The consistent reports situating the locus of thought at the heart are indicative more of certain universal characteristics of mediators than they are of any particular process or perspective revealed by these data. The heart as a nexus with the vessel system as its permeations serves as an objectivized idea for organizing diverse data in terms of a center and an infinitely expanding set of emanations. The thoughtful mind overlaps other phenomena, giving it a redundant, rational, and coherent unity.

In the last analysis, however, the only "improvement" science has made to our thought has been to replace the heart with its vessel tendrils by the brain with its neural lattice work. [342]

Basin Religion and Theology:
A Comparative Study of Power ~ *Puha*

THE Great Basin has been the focus of keen anthropological interest for some time. primarily because the efficient simplicity of societies indigenous to the region reveals much about the persistence, stamina, and ingenuity that people need to survive in a strenuous environment. The major concern of Basin studies has been with ecological theory, but these have all but ignored th e traditional ideology that was the basis of native lifeways. Aside from some important contributions to general ethnography, cultural ecology in the Basin has dealt with ecology to the virtual exclusion of culture.

Recently, with the possible deployment of the MX missile, the mining of subsurface minerals, and the expansion of energy transmission systems, Basin religious sites have been destroyed or threatened at an alarming rate, much as local food resources were destroyed over a century ago by settlers and livestock (Andrus 1979; Hartigan 1980; Inter-Tribal Council of Nevada 1976a, 1976b, 1976c). For this reason, an overview of Basin religion and theology has been greatly needed, one which treats the published information in a systematic fashion with the cooperation of native peoples. This study is a preliminary step in this direction.[6]

While there are many named groups in the Basin, on the whole it is a homogeneous area within Native America. Except for the [b] Hokan-speaking Washoe, all historic Basin groups belong to the Numic family of languages within the Uto-Aztecan language stock. Although there is some disagreement, it appears that Numic-speakers fanned out from the vicinity of Death Valley and diversified into three closely related branches (Lamb 1958). Southern Numic includes Kawaiisu, Chemehuevi, a dozen Southern Paiute (*Nuwuvi*), and Ute. Central Numic encompasses Panamint, Western Shoshoni (*Newe*), Gosiute, Northern Shoshoni, and Eastern (Wind River-Comanche) Shoshoni. Western Numic embraces Mono and several Northern Paiute (*Numa*) bands, distinguished by lake-based economies and the development of salmon fisheries in otherwise arid regions of Oregon and Idaho.

Today, most people live on reservations, often on or near their aboriginal territories or, in the interest of steady employment, they reside in colonies (reserved housing blocks close to ranches, towns, and cities). As was traditional, extensive visiting and travel between areas are the norms, but the need for wages has all but replaced foraging as a factor in the movements of individuals and families, except for some elders (Facilitators 1980).

Previous publications have been primarily concerned with ecology, subsistence strategy, and general ethnography, although fieldworkers collected data on a greater variety of subjects than their publications suggest. Sometimes, researchers were sent into an area to fill out a prior study. Thus, in 1935[67] Kroeber sent Frederick Hulse and Frank Essene to Owens Valley to collect folklore and other information lacking in the work by Steward (1933).

It was Steward who set the tone for Basin research with a "gastronomic orientation" that encouraged a disinterest in culture, ideology, and religion in their own right. The singular

---

[6] This article is based on material and thought assembled before, during, and after 1 was Principal Investigator on a contract between Ertec of Seattle and Facilitators of Las Vegas to prepare an overview of religious concerns in the Great Basin with particular reference to the MX impact area.

exception is the study of shamanism by Willard Park (1938), who also collected valuable information on Northern Paiute ritual and ceremony.

Some recent correctives to this functional view have been supplied by Hultkrantz (1966, 1976), working with data from Wind River Shoshoni. While they are located on the eastern margin of the Basin and adopted a heavy veneer of Plains features, Wind River people seem to have remained faithful to a generalized Basin theology. Nonetheless, Hultkrantz discusses it in terms of a religious ecology based on the subsistence technology, slighting the interaction of symbols with the total environment which lies at the heart of the ideological system.

Aside from Park (1938) and Hultkrantz (1966, 1976), discussions of Basin religion have been limited to unanalyzed treatments of the Circle, Bear, and Cry dances (cf. Fowler 1970), which are variations on the system rather than basic to it.

Culture, Society, Matrix

In all, previous research in the Basin has dealt with society rather than culture. Society consists of manifestations of behavior, subsistence, and institutions. It is the obvious empirical data shared among the social or human sciences, defined by time, place, and events. Culture, by contrast, is the semantic dimension that informs and renders meaningful all the experiences of a human as a member of a society.

While societies differ in terms of then-level of integration and complexity, all cultures are equivalent in that Culture is a distinctively human adaptation augmented by language and technology. Culture is sometimes used as a cover term for shared ideas or all aspects of a society, but this muddles its clarity. Cultures are basically the same; it is only their reflection and realization in society that differs, congruent with biology, habitat, ecological cycles, and population size.

Only in this manner can the Basin be considered at the lower end of any scale of complexity. While Basin cultures were as elaborate as any others, Basin societies display concern with practicality and efficiency. By ignoring this important distinction, Linton (1940: 117), commenting on the study by Harris (1940), made the absurd comment that "Aboriginal White Knife culture was so simple and amorphous that there was little to be destroyed by European contact."

Because cultures are subject to change over time, yet each seems to maintain some distinctive axiomatic principles, they have sometimes been likened to configurations with a stabilizer that keeps them on a given course. Such a stabilizer has been called an armature, ethos, paideuma, and so forth. Elsewhere, I have called it a *Struckon* (Miller 1979), an abbreviation for structural configuration, consisting of a reverberating axiomatic tension called an Echo and relationships called a Matrix.

The component relationships form a triad of exclusive, inclusive, and inclosive members. The exclusive/inclusive consist of a dialectical duality, with the exclusive as a special case of the inclusive. Hence, the exclusive is tightly defined, marked, and delimited, while the inclusive is indefinite, unmarked, and open. For example, many cultures regard both female and left as exclusive, in opposition to male and right as inclusive. In this case, females and the left hand are under various restrictions, such as negative evaluations that limit their range of activity or application [68] (Needham 1973; Miller 1979). Levi-Strauss (1978: 469) has identified these relationships in his sweeping mytho-logic of the Americas as disjunction, conjunction, and mediation.

The inclosive member is the most complex because it shares attributes both of the exclusive and the inclusive and of other members of the class of mediators. In addition to culturally specific attributes, all mediators have in common the image of a permeating nexus (Miller 1979). It is these mediators within a Struckon and culture which weave together all of the other dyads into a consistent whole.

While the Matrix occurs in all cultures, the character of the Echo sets each culture apart. Levi-Strauss has argued for a set of categories which I interpret to be the universal Echo of Human Culture. It consists of Culture as predictable and exclusive. Nature as accidental and inclusive, and Mind, reason and brain, as inclosive. For specific, cult-ures, however, these universals are subject to various combinations of internal developments, historical accidents, and external influences that assert the priority of a particular duality as the Echo. At present, about a dozen possible Echoes have been identified, with those of right / left, man / woman, and animal / plant playing significant roles.

An example of a Matrix in the Basin is provided by color symbolism. Although five is the pattern number and there seem to be five primary colors (white, red, black, yellow, and blue-green-gray), only the first three carry heavy symbolic loads. Powell (1971: 162) reported "Red paint signifies joy," with black "signifying war." Among the Gosiute, boys and girls were painted red at their puberty festivals, and white before embarking on a vision quest (Malouf 1974: 62, 53). Formerly, patients during a shamanic curing were painted white, as they still are among the Duckwater Shoshoni.

Because black was associated with war, a [b] male activity, and red with both males and females on joyous occasions, they are exclusive and inclusive, respectively. Its association with the sacred and spiritual links white with the inclusive. The associations of the other colors are not as well developed, although yellow sometimes substitutes for black.

In his composite model of the Southern Ute world, Goss (1972: 128) attributes white to the sky, yellow to the Upper Earth, blue-green-gray to the Middle Earth, red to the Lower Earth, and black to the Underworld. Apparently, symbolism varied through the Basin since Northern Paiute assign colors to the cardinal directions and black to the center. This matter is complex enough to deserve further study.

Recognizing the distinctions between society and culture, exemplified by Echo and Matrix, our concern is less with what people do and more with what they think, recognizing that the two are very closely related. In addition, the thoughts of some people are more helpful than those of others, much as the advice of an expert is more informative than that of a novice. In practice, these profound thinkers were or are often shamans, but sometimes they are people able to devote considerable thought to a subject. Often they are mentally curious but physically handicapped.

According to percentages reported by Whiting (1950: 28) for Northern Paiute and Reichel-Dolmatoff (1971) for the Desana of Colombia, only about 20% of a population possesses such informed knowledge, and less than 5% of these have a systematic overview of the valued information. Most often such adepts were supernaturally empowered by heredity and personal inclination, together with an arduous training period in self-discipline, empathy, esoteric languages, and special techniques (Handleman 1967). In the process, they perfect skills of mind-body control such as hypnosis, meditation, and [69] breathing exercises to induce trance.

10

Power ~ *Puha*

The intent of this training was the ability to control the supernatural power-energy-force after it was conferred by a spirit in a recurrent dream, which usually was due to the initiative of the spirit, either because it was familiar with the family or because it took a liking to the dreamer. This bonding took place without suffering, hardship, or mortification, although profound grief might bring out a power already lurking nearby. Often, power ~ *puha* ~ *buha* ~ similar variants in Numic languages or *wegeleyu* in Washoe) was inherited by shamans through family lines, while at Yomba it seems to skip alternating generations (Leiber 1964: 22). Once acquired power can be used either to benefit others, following sanctioned practice, or to advance personal desires, which is selfish and leads to sorcery. Power in and of itself is merely a significant gift to a human by one of the Immortal supernaturals, frequently the "boss", "owner", or "master" (large and beautiful progenitor of a species, who has existed from the dawn of creation, the first or a subsequent one, according to mythology (Park 1938: 16; Liljeblad 1969: 52).

Belief in this mana-like power apportioned by spirits was fundamental to all North American religions (Miller nd.a). Hence, this discussion of the Basin concept can be extended and amplified by occasional comparisons, which have the additional advantage of protecting Numic concerns for their own religion. Southern Paiute and Western Shoshoni advisors are sometimes reluctant with good reason to share their theology with outsiders, so in conformity with their wishes, I have used the expedient of citing close parallels to Numic practice from neighboring tribes. This enables my account to be reasonably full without violating confidences. It also places Basin religion within the larger context [b] of Americanist research into New World religions. While these belief systems are usually mentioned in the plural, my work across the continent has convinced me that there was and is a common system for North America, variously expressed by the acceptance, rejection, and differential emphasis of basic tenets. The appeal of Numic and Washoe religion is that it seems to be an elementary expression of the larger system.

In all. this unitary concept of power is most like the crucial concept of the Holy Wind where "Navajo naming of a particular aspect of the Wind does not thereby differentiate it as a kind of Wind having no relation to the whole of which it is a part, just as our naming of a sea does not imply that the waters referred to are distinct from the great body of water encompassing the whole Earth" (McNeley 1981: 17).

Further, continuing work on the concept of power has taught me much about the parallel concept of Culture, especially when used politically as in Red Power. Assuming that there is a Human Culture, with the boundaries differently drawn by different cultures, then each variant must be a selection from the whole adapted to local biota and landscape. Similarly, power seems to have a universal source or locus, abstractly phrased as the memory of the Creator, who knows everything from past, present, and future, and shares aspects of this with the other Immortals. The Creator, Immortals, and their interactions with humans are chronicled in the origin saga of the group, which also specifies the particular practices and commandments that a tribe had to follow. Each group respected both its own doctrines and those of other tribes, knowing that all of them were intermeshed to maintain cosmic balance. Thus, the whole was greater than the sum of its parts, and each tribe was only a portion of the pattern.

Discussions of power often overlook its [70] emotional aspects. Other groups felt a keen loss when another way of life became extinct, for it impoverished them all. The belief was that each life way was entrusted with a particular way of dealing with power, so the loss of any of them had philosophical and emotional sequences. These emotions were both communal and personal, in that the experiences of an individual had to be congruent with community expectations. Someone receiving the gift of power felt it immediately, often describing it as like an electric shock or jolt. Although the term in English also conveys something with a "pow," "jolt," or "charge," it has been toned down to agree more closely with the lack of affect in modern religions.

In the Basin version, the universal order that establishes power and its flow was the myth age "when animals were people" and everything was undifferentiated, having, a sameness based on full potentiality such that beings could take many forms with many abilities. According to Powell (1971: 73), the primal world consisted of the "original facts or primary concepts that there is a land and a sea, an abyss below, and a night above." Of these basic elements, night and water were among the most sacred.

Night was the universal condition until the stars, moon, seasons, and sun were created. It was a night of both time and space, with "the face of the night meaning the sky or apparent firmament" (Powell 1971: 73). Because it was of the very beginning, night remains the most appropriate time for curings, gatherings, and dances to capture power, especially around midnight and the blackness just before dawn. Northern Paiute personified night as the spirit who sent messengers and aid to the shamans. Olofson (1979: 13) was told that the spirit of night "is everywhere and sends animal messengers to the doctor; it is for this reason that shamans prefer to work at midnight when their power is strongest." [b]

Earlier, Park (1938: 17) heard at Pyramid Lake that night had two aspects: "Only shamans can see this second night. The people see only darkness. They cannot see the night under it." Because night is primordial, it is powerful and immortal. Among Kawaiisu, "supernatural beings are somehow associated with the sky and/or night" (Zigmond 1972: 133).

Stars are people who left the earth to dwell in the sky "where they are compelled to travel in appointed ways" (Powell 1971: 75). Stars are considered to be females or women. The song and dance by Whippoorwill (Powell 1971: 221) caused a Frog to rise into the air and become the moon, accompanied by his seven wives, the sisters of Wolf and Coyote , who became stars, and his son who became Venus (Powell 1971: 221, 229). It is significant for the argument below that stars are women and solitary planets are men, both obligated to travel in appointed ways.

The sun is the most important being in the sky. Among the White Knife Shoshoni, Sun Father was the source of supernatural power, distinguished from Ocean Woman, the creator in the southern Basin (Harris 1940: 56). Among the Chemehuevi and others, sun has a sky home (of crystal) surrounded by animals that include pet bears. He is also called Sun Spider, with the form of a black-widow. He was formerly much more brilliant and destructive, but some say that Cottontail shattered him into his present size and intensity, others that Coyote burned the old one up and made a smaller new one. As Powell (1971: 75) noted, the Numa have "a host of mythological stories giving the reason why the sun ... who should have a will of his own − is yet compelled to travel by a definite trail along the face of the night."

Southern Paiute mythology details the origin and development of the world under the direction of Ocean Woman, a creator who sprinkled particles of her skin upon the primal [71] sea to create a patch ut' earth, which she stretched out to present size by stimulating the process of birth with her body. Among the Chemehuevi, Ocean Woman was aided by Wolf, Coyote , and Cougar. Of these, Wolf is a wise and magical − also pompous and humorless − shaman using a *pooro*, the crooked rod that is the insignia of his calling. Coyote is innovative, sensuous, foolish, and selfish, an idea man who established the less than perfect patterns that humans now follow. Cougar is not well delineated, probably to avoid mentioning that he is dangerous, malevolent, and frenzied in that "the mountain lion and the rattlesnake ... conferred upon their possessors the power to do great harm" (Laird 1974: 22).

After Ocean Woman had made the flat earth disk and expanded it, humans were created by the union of Coyote as father and Louse as mother (Laird 1976). Coyote was given the task of carrying the basket filled with the forming humans from the island of Ocean Woman to the land emerging from the primal water. Laird (1976: 310) called this the Self-Mythologizing or Immortal Water, but I term it the Self Chartering Sea. To cross it, Coyote took the form of a water spider but, as always, his curiosity got the better of him and he opened the basket before he had reached the center of the world. Consequently, humans jumped out and scattered everywhere, thwarting the divine plan to have them radiate out evenly from this nexus. Moreover, humans have remained imperfect ever since because they "follow the way of Coyote." Similarly, they take after their mother because "her offspring have assuredly crept like lice over the beautiful body of the earth" (Laird 1976: 214).

While this southern creation is best known, there are others (Liljeblad 1969; Zigmond 1980). One is the Earth Diver motif where a series of water animals attempt to bring up dirt from the ocean floor until the [b] last one provides a tiny speck for the creation. In another. Wolf is the wise creator of a world in several, usually five, layers with the sun in the sky, people on the earth, and short giants in an underworld. Often, there is a shaft or *axix mundi* linking together the various layers. In all these versions. Coyote is the marplot instituting frailties.

From Jim Jones in Owens Valley, Hulse (1935: 150.3, item #29) recorded a modernized version of the creation of humans. Because it is an adaptation that nonetheless conveys important features of Basin tradition, I summarize it here.

The man who was to be the father of all Indians sat in his cave weaving a blanket from the skin of a rabbit he killed with his bow and arrow. His rock house was near the rock art site in Round Valley. When he looked up from his work, he saw a pretty girl ("Her hair shown like a spider web right after the rain") walking swiftly through the rocks up Pine Creek Canyon. He got up and followed her, but he could not catch up. Then he knelt and rubbed fine earth on his legs, praying to Mother Earth to grant him the life of wind so he could overtake the woman. They went up the slope until they reached Pine Creek Lake and he called to her to rest on a flat rock at the summit. She did so and he hurried to sit beside her as the sun set. They decided to make camp together for the night. By morning, they were married and moved down to camp at the mouth of the canyon. There the woman became the mother of many children, who grew up quickly. The father gave bows and arrows to the boys and baskets to the girls, sending the best looking of them away to choose the languages that they wanted. He kept the most homely and mean ones with him because they were the best warriors. Hence, the Paiute of today are not good looking but very strong. The woman eventually became a rock in the vicinity.

While this story is an updated version of [72] Coyote and Louse (Steward 1937: 365-368), the animal counterparts of the characters are not given. It is significant that the woman took the definite lead and the man pursued, following the path of a waterway flowing off a mountain peak. Also noteworthy was his attraction to her in terms of a glistening web. Among the Tubatulabal (Voegelin 1938: 53) and the Kawaiisu (Zigmond 1980: 47), myths make it explicit that men had an inferior position until they tricked the highly competent women into turning over control of society.

Mountains have an important role in Basin cultures, as they do in the areal ecology. Throughout the region, people can point out a particularly high or prominent peak as the sacred center where creation began or an Immortal lived. One such is Job's Peak in the Stillwater Range near Walker Lake, recognized by several Northern Paiute groups as center of the world.

Of all these centers, the most powerful in the south and central Basin is Charleston Peak in the Spring Mountains west of Las Vegas. Goss (1972: 128) argued from Southern Ute material that their model of the world most closely matched with the five biotic levels on this peak, although he could not be definite about this attribution. Yet, both Isabel Kelly and Alfred Kroeber earlier identified Charleston Peak as an important cosmic center. When I visited the peak, "physical evidence" of these mythological traditions was pointed out. Thus, not only is Charleston Peak the most significant center, but Ocean Woman left a memento of herself there as the wrinkled and reclining figure called Mummy Peak. A cave on a nearby slope marks the home of Wolf and Coyote before they wandered off to the north. Natives continue to visit these sites to pray, leave offerings, and meditate. Possibly, this peak was the initial central island, left high and dry after the primal sea receded. Its native name is Snow-Having, appropriate because its 12,000-foot elevation collects abundant snow which melts to feed many summer streams.[7]2

Other peaks of lesser altitude also function in the overall pattern since they are sacred centers meshing together into an overall network with Charleston Peak at the heart, at least for the southern Basin.

Allowing for variation, the beginning earth was everywhere flat and the same until many parallel sawtooth ranges and wide valleys were created. The Gosiute attribute these changes to Hawk slashing the earth with his wings (Malouf 1974). With "the origin of surface relief commenced the scattering of the nations, for there was now a diversity of country and each one chose for himself a special habitat" (Powell 1971: 77). Among the difficulties encountered by this diaspora was the loss of a common language and much of the accredited wisdom of the Myth Age. Coyote saw to it that life would be precarious and laborious, so it would not be easy or humans would regard it lightly. He also arranged that there be diversions and thrills to make life interesting at times.

In keeping with this mythic sameness, the population, while bearing the names of modern species, had no fixed forms, being simultaneously human, spirit, and biota. In her precise way, Laird (1976: 209ff) described these Immortals as constantly shimmering among the forms. This nicely describes the predominant characteristic of the Myth Age beings throughout the Americas, at the least. It also captures the great value placed on movement, the kinetic and dynamic, by Native Americans. It is qualitatively different from that of Europe, emphasizing stages and

---

[7] I venture to suggest that sacred mountains serving as cosmic centers all seem to consist of many smaller peaks around a summit. This is the case with Charleston Peak for the Paiute-Shoshoni, the San Francisco Peaks for the Hopi, Mount Taylor for the Navaho and Pueblos, and Moses Mountain for the Colville Salishans. In Salish, the name of the last peak means that it is a big brother surrounded by siblings. Given the communal ethic and sense of oblique responsibility so important to native America, such mountains are appropriate images for expressing these values in stone.

states, and so is frequently misunderstood.

Power as Kinetic Flow

Flux, action, and process are characteristic modes of the Americas, difficult to grasp because the English language best deals with [73] things and events, wliile they .ire assumed in the grammars of Amerindian languages. In his sketch of the American language stocks. Sapir (1929) indicated that verbs, are the most elaborated and complex component of these languages. Further, from time to time, attempts have been made to show that languages like Nootkan and Salishan lack a noun / verb distinction, relying heavily on abstract verbal steins. Nouns are almost always auxiliary in these grammars. Thus, people speak of living not life and moving not staying, implying ongoing interactions and reciprocities.

Similarly, power is not the best term for characterizing the life force-energy. It is not static or concrete, but rather kinetic, always moving and flowing throughout the cosmos, underpinning all facets of the universe in a way that a physicist could appreciate. Yet, convention and English usage place innate constraints on finding a more suitable term, aside from the classic treatment of *mana* in Polynesia.

The primary attribute of power is this processual dynamic affiliating it with life. Its quality of flowing is well represented in the tale of how Badger revived the wife and son of Owl after they were killed by the fatal fumes of an angry Skunk (Powell 1971; Laird 1980: 80). Further, it shows the importance of singing and dancing for controlling power by becoming attuned to it since all are rhythmical.

After Badger had his attention called to the lifeless bodies on his special plot of ground,

He painted himself and danced a dance and sang a song known only to himself. Then he dug a hole and burrowed along under the ground until he came to a point just under the bodies and there he emerged from the earth. Standing by the bodies of the woman and child, he pierced them with his medicine knife until the blood ran and they returned to life... [Powell 1971: 260].

Accordingly, once Badger was able to match his How of power with his song and dance, he moved through (lie ground to emerge beside the deceased and attuned them to the power by making their blood flow.

Since this flowing sometimes seems to be more like flying and hovering, Harris (1940: 56-57) reported that power was bird-like. Among the Columbian Salish, 1 know that the generic for bird also includes pet and guardian spirit, while among the Lakota, birds are messengers between earth and sky, humans and spirits, because they fly and are bipeds like humans. In addition to these avian qualities, supernatural birds conferred great power, such as the Eagle for hunting and the Hummingbird for healing by sucking. In all, birds are more an attribute of power than a source.

Women and Men

The flow of power influenced all of life, particularly humans. In the Basin lifeway, men and women scattered over their territory between strategic camps enabling them to hunt and gather particular resources. The basic social unit was the kindred composed of a married couple together with their children and a few other bilateral relatives. Bilaterality made for extensive kin networks, but the membership of functional kindreds remained small because foods, primarily seeds, were Ihinly spread and ripened precipitously, making it difficult to harvest efficiently. Also, animals and vegetation fluctuated from year to year because of variable rainfall. Large gatherings were only possible with a sudden abundance of some resource, occurring either naturally like pine nuts or socially via coordinated drives for grasshoppers, mudhens, rabbits, and antelope. A valley with a reliable water source had a larger population as a result and its leader was stronger, within the parameters of his title meaning "talker," a reference to his use of oratory alone to [74] maintain decorum. In addition, camps usually had a shaman with the supernatural clout to orchestrate communal drives and undertake curings. Sometimes, the talker and the shaman were the same person, but more often they had overlapping authority.

The wife of a talker seems to have had charge of female activities, which were especially cooperative (Steward 1938: 99; Kelly 1964: 29). If a chief had more than one wife, they apportioned the duties of house, children, gathering, and hospitality among themselves, under the guidance of the senior wife.

Among the Chemehuevi, "Everything to do with the gathering and preparation of seeds and fruits and with weaving belonged to the women's side. To the men appertained all that had to do with game, especially big game (except the packing of it into camp, when there was a woman available for the task). The hunter, using his awl, sewed or laced together buckskin clothes for himself and his family" (Laird 1976: 6).

More generally, "Both sexes usually made things used by both-houses, rabbitskin blankets, and clothing" (Steward 1938: 44). Men and women worked together during the pine-nut harvest and the hunting of small rodents. Most often, men engaged in solitary tasks, working and hunting alone (Steward 1938: 231, 236, 266; Whiting 1950: 68). Women shared their economic activities together, although they also divided any necessary labor among themselves since food gathering and child care, major female tasks, required different use of time and skills. It was not unusual in a camp to have two women divide up the routine so that the younger gathered food and the older, often a grandmother, tended children (Whiting 1950: 68).

While men and women cooperated for specific activities, they had different symbolic associations. For example, while both sexes worked on the house, women had primary responsibility for the covering, brush or [b] matting, and men set the inside supports. At Pyramid Lake, "Men and women cooperated in putting up the wikiup, the former erecting the framework, the latter making and tying the tule shingles" (Lowie 1924: 220). While both sexes worked harvesting pinyon trees, only men climbed the trees since modesty kept women on the ground (Lowie 1924: 203). Further, in terms of periodicity, the relation of time to activities, women were engaged in constant, continuous tasks, while those of men were intermittent.

A woman shared her food with coresident kin, but large game was shared with everyone present at the time, presumably because it was so perishable. If a woman gave food to other kin or neighbors, it was phrased as a gift, requiring a return (Steward 1938: 74), although Kelly (1964: 122) lists a term for a distant relative meaning "someone you feed." Nonetheless, the sexes did not contribute equally to the larder since women supplied most of the food eaten from day to day. Throughout the Basin, except during sucker runs at Pyramid Lake, plants provided the bulk of the food compared to meat, although hunting had a greater prestige value.

As Kelly (1964: 132) was bluntly told by the Southern Paiute: "Women dug roots and men ate them." Obviously, men were at a disadvantage since they were takers from women givers. "A man, then, is closely tied to and dependent on his mother and sisters" (Whiting 1950: 73), providing males with recurring frustrations that sometimes end in suicide. Primary loyalty goes to blood relations, so wives and affines were subject to suspicion and emotional outbursts. In all, women defined the quality of relationships and, even now, they are the mainstays and the buffers against economic and psychological uncertainty (Knack 1976).

In terms of the Matrix, therefore, the prominence of women in the Basin indicates that they are inclusive, reversing the more [75] common pattern. Men, engaged in solitary tasks and supplemental economics, are exclusive, a special case within the inclusive which contributes to male feelings of anxiety.

Such ambivalence toward females seems reflected in beliefs about Water Babies. Each Water Baby has a home in an artesian spring, and sometimes people will leave offerings there. The bubbling of the spring comes from their breathing, just as hot springs are caused by their cooking fires. Like any other resident of the Basin, they are seldom home, preferring to travel widely along all waterways, including irrigation ditches. They are powerful, dangerous, and closely associated with shamans.

Descriptions of them vary, but many people claim to have seen them. In general, each is about three feet high with long hair and a hard shell-like skin that makes them virtually impossible to kill. Some have wings or a mustache. They are feared because some draw unsuspecting people, especially women and children, to the edge of the water and drown them. Others take the place of a baby and eat the mother when she begins to suckle.

According to Hoebel (ms: 13) "These are small females standing about twelve inches high." The Washoe believe that Water Babies are a tribe, with members of all ages and both sexes, but like human societies, the women have the predominant role. One Washoe even saw tiny footprints indicating that one Water Baby has taken to wearing high heels.

Water Babies are also involved in the "ownership" of particular springs. Kelly (1964: 7, 22, 93) was baffled by reports from Kaibab that "Theoretically, watering places were inherited by the oldest child: in practice, they seem to have passed to the nearest male relative (either by blood or by marriage) who happened to be at hand and who continued to live at the site."

Her remark calls to mind the controversy over "family-owned hunting territories" in [b] the eastern Subarctic. Some anthropologists felt that they were aboriginal, while others argued that they were a product of the fur trade, a strategy to monopolize the pelts in a region. Tanner (1979) recently resolved the debate: these territories were aboriginal, but their religious basis was compromised by economic motivations. Traditionally, each plot was inherited on the basis of a combination of descent and of acquaintance with the terrain such that routine success at the hunt was taken to mean that the spirit responsible for the plot was pleased with that individual. Thus, a hunter, relative or not, who retains good relations with that spirit is regarded as "owner" of that plot, which is inherited by the hunter who best meets these same qualifications. In this context, "to own" means to know the terrain intimately while keeping good rapport with its spirit warden.

In the same way, spring "ownership" by male inheritance through coresidents suggests the same kind of special partnership between human and spirit, most likely a Water Baby.

Much as the "ownership" of springs was concerned with proper relations with spirits and power involved in the flow, so too was the possession of songs as an aspect of the rhythm of life. Laird (1976: 9) was told by her husband that Chemehuevi "owned" land because males inherited rights to it through either the song of the Mountain Sheep to "my » very own land" or the song of the Deer to "my very own mountain," depending upon the trail described in the song.[8]3

As power has a profound affinity for the living, some of it lingers as long as there is any vestige of life. Hence, there is always some power around graves, but by its nature it is less vital and so more likely to cause harm or be used in sorcery. It appears to be power that has been trapped and stagnated, only released when decomposition is complete. Therefore, graves were generally avoided, both from uncertainty about the power there [76] and the intentions of any lingering ghosts.

Because the protection of graves is specifically legislated in the American Indian Religious Freedom Act (AIRFA), people are being encouraged to speak about this reluctant topic. Throughout native America, life and death are aspects of a continuous process, such that community sentiment is intensified rather than severed after death. The dead merge into a vague ancestral group distinguished by a few famous leaders and they provide a subtle corporate continuity for the society and culture. Hence, a Yomba or a Moapa soul continues its identification with kindred and community long after the body dies, remaining loyal to those it can benefit and expecting the same from the living. Similarly, while graves are generally avoided, the location of family graves is taught to younger generations. In this way, recognized family and tribal claims to an area are marked by permanent residents in the ground, wliile the living were engaged in seasonal transhumance among the camps.

Some people received power from ghosts and some shamans kept vigil at graves, but these usually resulted in malevolent use of power. In some areas, graves occur in places also having religious import, concentrating much power in the vicinity because of the overlap of several sources. The best places for this are high mountains with caves, springs, rock cairns built during vision quests, rock art, and graves in close proximity. While such ties to ancestors and places are not well described in the literature, this is an oversight.

In the southern Basin, land and its attributes were created by Ocean Woman, reflecting the realities of the position of women in these societies. Women were the cooperative unit and the suppliers of most of the staples. Since the house is routinely viewed as a microcosm of the ordered world, it is significant that men supplied the inside posts and women the covering. [b]

Similarly, at festivals, "women are formed in a circle and dance in a slow shuffling manner, the men standing within dance on their toes with heels turned out and body bent forward leaping high in the air, and as they leap giving a yell and whirling a musical instrument [a bullroarer], which they hold in their hands and which gives out a curious shriek" (Powell 1971: 63). Sometimes only women dance in the Circle Dance, or men and women alternate in the ring with the center occupied by a post and a male song leader (Kelly 1964: 104). Note that because Woman is the inclusive category, associated with the outer ring, either women or men and

---

[8] The Chemehuevi had other song cycles, but recollection of them is dim. Some were named Salt, Quail, and Day Owl, with the Talking Song reserved for use in chiefly families (Laird 1976: 18ff), presumably because its rhythms were especially powerful. Notes taken by Van Valkenburg in 1938 also mention that "hunting grounds belonged to certain groups of people" and list songs and dances called Bird, Sheep, Deer, Quail, Salt, Cut Hair, and Coyote . In the notes, Charleston Peak is identified as Snow-Having, the home of one of the last two chiefs, Tecopa, who died near Mantz, Nevada (Museum of Northern Arizona Research Center Library, manuscript # 6315), published as Van Valkenburg 1976.

women can appear there, while the inside was exclusive to men. I have found no references to only men dancing in a ring and suspect it was highly unlikely.

During periods of fasting and abstinence associated with birth, puberty, and death, women are usually under restrictions for 30 days, and men for only 5 days. This nicely illustrates how the exclusive 5 is a special case of the inclusive.

In sum, Woman is associated with Outside and Man with Inside, with their interaction complementary and cooperative. In native America, an individual has oblique responsibilitibs such that he or she should be more concerned with the welfare of others rather than of the self. In the Basin and elsewhere, this takes the form of food sharing and motivates the few leading "old families" in each group to responsibly coordinate community activities for the greatest good. Hence, Ocean Woman shared the process of creation with Wolf, Coyote , Louse, Cougar, and others, instituting a network of reciprocity from the inception of the world. In native America, generally, the only people who work alone in disregard of others are both selfish and likely sorcerers. This was especially crucial in the Basin since survival depended on the intense cooperation of a few people. [77]

With this background, we can define the sexes more closely. Among the Southern Ute and others, stars and flocks of birds are considered to be females (Goss 1972: 124, 126). Similarly, lice are regarded as women. These share the characteristic of uniform size and diffuse distribution, appropriate metaphors for women of the Basin. The sun and large mammals, regardless of biology, are considered to be males because, like men. They are solitary and larger. In all, Man refers to pronounced parts of the environment and Woman to open, even expanses. By analogy, then, the relations between Man / Woman are those between figure / ground, inside / outside, taking / giving, concentration / dispersal, probing / spreading, promontory / plane, and exclusive / inclusive. The metaphors of promontory / plane are especially appropriate for Basin topography where rows of broad valleys are divided by sawtooth mountain ranges.

In addition, these genders also have graphic sexual references in that Woman spreads and Man probes or pierces, as exemplified by the awl of the hunter and the rod of the shaman. In a quasi-appropriate if neo-classical vein. Laird (1976: 216) also noted "That regenerating rod of power, by which those Immortals who had been killed in various ways were revived and by which in later times the shaman performed his curative work, is primarily the generative organ, the phallus .... Here is evidence clearer even than that afforded by Coyote 's partnership with his penis, of the existence of a phallic cult such as one would expect to find associated with the worship of the [*Mater Magna*] Goddess."

Harris (1940: 62, 104) reported that men could become ill or go blind by seeing female genitals. He underscored this with an account of a baby health contest which ended in disarray when "the nurses completely unclothed the female babies." This taboo applied only to men, specifically, since a jealous wife "might beat her rival and rip her skirt, expose her genitals and shame tier by spitting on them" (Harris 1940: 68). Quite explicitly, then, men are "kept in their place" in ways that women are not.

These associations are not unique to the Basin or the Americas, although they seem to occur infrequently. In Italian "the feminine is bigger because it embraces and envelopes while the masculine penetrates" (Ervin 1962: 256 #14).

All of these interpersonal interactions took place in a series of camps near resources across the landscape. Sudden abundances enabled larger groupings to appear who engaged in communal rituals, often Round Dances. The hub of all these activities was the winter encampment, usually located near pine-nut caches in the uplands. As Steward mentions again and again,

> Encampments tended to cluster with respect to mountain masses rather than valleys .... Mountain ranges not only capture but retain greater precipitation. As more than half of the annual precipitation generally falls in winter throughout most of the area, it is retained as snow on high mountain summits until well into summer (The Sierra of California even have small glaciers) and is released gradually in springs and streams. The run-off of moisture, however, depends upon mountain structure [Steward 1938: 232, 12, see also 14, 124, 141].

Therefore, while a balanced anticline waters the valleys on both sides of it, most Basin mountains are monoclines with sharp and sloping sides. Most often, drainage is best on the western side, making such valleys the usual population centers, such as the Reese River Valley of the Toiyabe Range rather than the Smokey Valley immediately to the east. As with any rule, there are notable exceptions, such as the Snake Mountains draining east into Snake Valley rather than west into Warm Spring Valley (Steward 1938: 126). [78]

Settlement pattern is influenced by the quantity as well as the location of water, so gathering areas are smaller near rivers than in the arid scrub. Of course, the amount of reliable water near these rivers significantly increased the diversity and density of local vegetation, enabling people to harvest more effectively in a smaller area. In all, camp sites were selected for the availability of water, firewood, seeds, berries, nuts, animals, and moderate temperatures (Steward 1938: 232).

Ultimately, water was the most important of all of these considerations, the most vital component of living successfully in the Basin. Hence, it is the keystone of Basin religion because power, with its affinity for life, was strongly attracted to water, "a purifying agent ... spoken of as being like the human breath" (Whiting 1950: 40). Whether as rain, snow, lakes, streams, or springs, water determined the location and movement of life in the Basin. As it fluctuated, so too did biotic populations.

Power is fundamental to all of these relations because it preceded them all. Close to the life force, it was the most cosmic of mediators, pervading the universe and symbolizing thought in its full expanse. In the southern Basin, it is the source for the immortality of the first beings, particularly Ocean Woman. For all of native America, the ultimate source of power is the mind of the focal being involved in creation, most especially the process of memory, which is crucial for imparting immortality (Miller nd.a). Memory is the basis for transmitting knowledge, particularly in elite families that supply consistently provident leaders. Their children were specially trained to memorize family, community, and tribal traditions, best encapsulated in mythology and rituals.

Memory was aided by many mneumonics, among which, although not usually considered as such, is rock art. Among Interior Salish, I have been instructed that rock art [b] was intended to communicate between humans and other "people" (spirits, animals, plants, rocks, and other sapients) of this and other times, aspects, and dimensions (Miller nd.b). Rock art serves to remind them all just what the appropriate activities are for certain areas for all eternity. Heizer and Baumhoff (1962) have argued that Basin rock art was deliberately located near ambush sites along game trails, but I would counter that such sites were selected to notify the Animal People about human intentions there, rather than to work some nebulous hunting magic.

In sum, power in Basin cultures, as elsewhere, can be traced to the memory of Ocean Woman in the south and to Wolf or Sun in the north because, like Merlin in the Arthurian legend, time is continuous in their minds as memory. Water both permeates the universe in a thin scattering and in definite concentrations with currents, generally where life is also clustered. Power has the same distribution, diffusely scattered everywhere and flowing along waterways. For example, Charleston Peak is called Snow-Having because it concentrates water and power, sending them down along regular routes.

All water is sacred, therefore, because power adheres to its reservoirs, as clouds, rain, snow, springs, seeps, lakes, streams, or the occasional river in the desert. Similarly, deep caves on slopes are sacred because they shelter life and collect water by seepage while remaining moist and dark like the initial world. They also are believed to open into the Self-Chartering Sea below the earth. In their formation, caves evoke the conceptual nexus, particularly if they consist of a main and branching chambers. Hence, caves are sacred, vital in the flow of power. In the same vein, salt is sacred because it was carried by water and deposited in caves and elsewhere, attracting human and animal life.

While power closely follows the flow of water, they are not identical because power is [79] definitely more significant. As in the Christian tradition of Lourdes and Fatima, power can manifest itself by producing a spring in a previously dry location. In myths, Coyote wills springs to appear on occasion, usually for his own convenience. Park (1938) reported that the springs of Water Babies never go dry, but I was told that if the Baby leaves or is (rarely) killed, then the water will go away, too.

In overall pattern, all these waterways are conceptualized as webbing linked to a peak with or without an alpine lake. In this way, the web is centered at the summit, with its radials moving out along slopes and valleys, all interlocking with the master web of central world peak.

Hulse (1935: 104.3, item 24) heard about a Water Baby with a spring in the Fish Lake Valley that connected by tunnel with a foothill along the road between Benton and Bishop. When someone came too close to this water hole, tiny fish would appear and Hash colorfully, keeping the observer's attention until the Water Baby arrived to drown him or her. The network of such tunnels must have been extensive since every Water Baby was supposed to have at least one for travel into other waterways. Among the Tewa, the underground is similarly believed to be honeycombed by a labyrinth of interconnecting tunnels (Ortiz 1969: 160 #10).

In theory, all of these linked waterways were considered animate in their own right and often personified. The situation is similar to the Navaho where, "Each mountain is a person. The water courses are their veins and arteries. The water in them is their life as our blood is to our bodies" (notes by Alexander Stephen, quoted in Reichard 1974: 20).

Like moisture, power is diffused everywhere in continuous flux and flow, which, however, is not haphazard because, as an aspect of memory, power is rational. From all available evidence, the routes of concentrated power within (lie generalized dispersion are weblike, moving both in radial patterns and in recursive concentric ones, out from the center and back again, like water in terms of a mountain top. This web image is obvious in population movement patterns so it is no accident that Coyote assumed the form of a water spider to carry humans to land and that Sun takes the form of a spider webbing the firmament.

People in the Basin were most successful when their movements followed those of power. Without recognizing its full significance, scholars have noted its web ~ net.

The temporary and shifting intervillagc alliances of this region, therefore, instead of consistently allying people to well-defined territories, entailed a linkage of village with village which extended net-like, throughout the area (Steward 1938: 247).

Communal hunts and ceremonies, reciprocal economic obligations, seasonal residence, intermarriage and transient membership of both camp and winter communities wove a loose net or linkages which spread throughout Western Shoshonean society (Harris 1940: 55).

This network of moral-mystical interdependence among people, with the pact between shaman and spirit at the center, probably did much to define the limits of Northern Paiute society (Olofson 1979: 247).

While the partnership of shaman and spirit was important in the Basin, it was not the only one because humans identified with the landscape through links to its spirit residents. These partnerships and linkages were, of course, more in the nature of mental or psychic ties than of physical contacts. Yet, they did produce concrete expressions, observable in terms of personal health, success, and rewards. Shamans and others kept in contact with their spirit helpers by means of a process called mind (*sonıminı*), involving telepathy and more (Olofson 1979: 17). [80]

By close cooperation, humans were able to work for the support of all, merging all of the important features for amassing and attuning power within the Round or Circle Dance, "concentrating power within the circle, by heightening the religious and empathetic feelings of the people" (Olofson 1979: 19). After leaving the dance, people take some of this power with them in other directions, giving behavioral form to a web of power.

More recently, other religious events have come into the Basin from other areas, but each of them has been fitted into the web pattern and associated with water flow.

The mourning ceremony of the Colorado River Yumans has been spreading in the Basin as the Cry Dance. In its origin story, a council was held in a far western country that resulted in the dance. "That place where they had danced turned to stone, and then from it trails arose in all directions. It is in this way that the Cry has come to be" (Sapir 1930: 347).

Northern and Eastern Shoshoni have adopted a version of the Plains Sun Dance, using a framework of outer posts and a center post with radiating roof poles. Within the enclosure, dancers form a circle but each moves separately towards the center. Here again, the pattern is like a web. At a Fort Hall Shoshoni Sun Dance, a bison head hung atop the center post. "The symbolism of the buffalo is associated with his ability to withstand thirst for long periods, as well as the fact that the bull leads the herd to water. Furthermore, it is maintained that the buffalo was the source of strength and life as the food-giver of the people and hence deserved a place of prominence in the worship" (Hoebel 1935: 576).

Similarly, during meetings of the Native American Church, members sit in a circle within a tipi, concentrating on the Grandfather Peyote in the center beside the fire. [b] Believers say there is a path between the center and each member, continuing beyond into life outside the tipi. All these paths lead to the universal center where all religions meet (d'Azevedo nd). In all, then, the peyote road has the pattern of a web.

This web is not static like that of a spider because the webbing actually consists of the flow of power, rather than filaments per se. Rather, the web is pulsating and multidimensional, even having aspects of a spiral, sometimes regular and sometimes erratic, intersecting with the radials from the center. This spiral movement is represented most graphically by an in-dwelling soul of a person, seen escaping the body at death as a whirlwind.

Belief in this universal web may have been esoteric knowledge in some regions, but it was widely distributed. For example, among the Yurok, "A character called ... 'world maker' fashioned the empyrean vault after the manner and pattern of a fish-net ... in an enormous circle" and when finished threw it up, "as it sailed aloft it became solid, and now stretches over us as the great blue sky" (Waterman 1920: 130).

The attraction of power for life is such that any gathering, particularly of humans, will concentrate it., while a closed dance circle contains it for a time. In the same fashion, rabbit, antelope, mudhen, grasshopper, or fish drives will encourage power to concentrate while some of it is transferred from the slain creatures to human beneficiaries, provided the former were treated with respect. Such a transfer of power is at the root of any type of sacrifice. After such a concentration, power apportions itself among the participants, going along with them as each takes separate trails radiating away from the central location.

For this reason, trails in the Basin are sacred. "Trails were regarded by Native Americans not only as highways for travel, but as sacred pathways which symbolize the cultural [81] continuity of ancient and modern peoples" (HDR 1980: 71). A century ago, Powell (1971: 39) also noted "with what tenacity an Indian clings to a trail." Each is considered immutable because of these associations with the ancients and the eternal flow of power. They arc never replaced by newer or more convenient ones because these lack the long bonds with power. All trails, whether human or animal, are sacred because all direct the flow of life. Moreover, some trails are not earth bound since rising tobacco smoke provides a trail between humans and spirits.

Support for the associations of power flow, water, and trails occurs in the closeness of the Shoshoni words for these: power (*puha*), water (*paa*), and path (*po'ai*) (Crapo 1976: 64, 71, 72). The association of water and breath has already been noted, but Shoshoni does this one better in the word *sua* = meaning "to breathe ~ think", bringing us full circle back to the overall mediation of the mind and memory (Crapo 1976: 77).

Invariably, throughout the Americas, the equipment of a shaman includes prismatic quartz crystals. Usually they are described as scrying stones, but beyond this, they represent crystalized thought and memory. The English word "crystal" comes from Greek meaning "solid water," so the Basin is not unique in associating crystals with water, power, and memory. Often they are the result of some life fluid. Among the Tohono O'otam ~ Papago, they are the solidified saliva of an Immortal; other tribes attribute them to tears. In his imporant article, Levi (1978) reports that some Yumans regard them as living rocks which are either male or female, depending on their inner tint. People are aware that crystals grow, and some say that each bed has a large central one that serves as leader. While the animate attribute of crystals is well reported, their function as cosmic mediators is not, nor is their association with memory.

All mediators have the quality of a [b] permeating nexus, reaching out from a center. Hence, many of the important animals mentioned in mythology are burrowers: Badger, Mouse, Rabbit, Bear, and Frog. Of course, burrowing is a typical adaptation to desert conditions, but it has been culturally recognized and elaborated. Animal burrows appear in myth as main rooms and side tunnels, like a permeating nexus. While Cottontail was trying to shatter the sun, he hid in such a burrow.

In addition to such herbivores, there were also prominent carnivores: Wolf, Coyote, Short Giants, and Water Babies. While some insects appear in stories, only Spider has a variety of roles, indicating his significance as a web keeper. Plants do not appear very often, presumably because they are not as active in the flow of power. In Northern Paiute, animals are called "movers" and plants are "bloomers" (Fowler and Leland 1967).

The listing of Frog among the burrowers relates to the fact that, in mythology, frogs dig the tunnels from the Self-Chartering Sea to the surface of the earth, creating springs (Powell 1971: 91). Among the Chumash, frogs are the source of fresh water since it is their urine (Blackburn 1975: 91). This is not distasteful because frogs have great power since they are both aquatic and changeable, from tadpole to amphibian, like the phases of the moon who began as a frog. Among tribes of the Pacific Northwest, Frog is a powerful shaman of the Animal World.

The animal mediators form a graded series based on their conceptual distance from humans. The sequence seems to be Spider, Mouse, Rabbit, Frog, Badger, and Bear. Spider is closest to humans because it weaves thought-like webs and lives with humans; Mouse moves between houses and desert; Frog lives in water around humans; Badger is a shaman because he roots around plants at night; and Bear is a humanoid animal living away from humans.

Another sequence seems likely for [82] carnivores, with Coyote, Wolf, and Cougar moving away from the human zone. Dogs were not often kept in the Basin − as with horses, they strained local resources − otherwise they would occupy the position closest to humans.

Another figure prominent in mythology is Bat, guardian of the land of the dead, probably because it is nocturnal and occupies an ambivalent position between animals and birds, calling it to the attention of thoughtful individuals.

Allowing for some slight local variation, these patterns and practices are remarkably uniform throughout the Basin. The only possible exception might have been Owens Valley, but after fieldwork there. I am convinced that the importance of sweat lodges, borrowed from the Yokut, and of irrigation (Lawton et al 1976) are merely intensifications of the Basin pattern. After all, both the *muusa* communal sudatory and the irrigated plots reflect a concern with power, water, and their advantageous flow.

Lastly, the place of Man and Woman in the web needs to be specified. In terms of the Matrix, Man is exclusive, Woman inclusive, and Mind-Memory inclusive. Within the web, the radials wandering out in separate paths seem appropriate to the exclusive, while the concentric bands linking together the radials are apt for the inclusive. The central intersection or nexus, represented by mountain peaks and crystals, is the inclusive.

Power in the Modern Basin

People living today often disparage their loss of the old ways, blaming a breakdown in an orderly transfer of knowledge across generations. They reproach themselves for a loss of memory and some have used this to suggest that the notion of power is essentially entropic. Thoughtful elders, however, point to themselves for the lack of manifest power at present, saying "We modern Indians have [b] gotten lazy." They hold that power is still there in an endlessly recursive flowing from source to summary and back again. The difficulty is that no one (or very few) will make the effort to train and discipline themselves to be attractive to power.

As more of the Basin is threatened or destroyed by massive building projects, more people have been motivated to seek out the old ways and revive them. In those families where power has always come unbidden, but has been turned away until recently, some natives are beginning to accept their responsibilities again.

Power remains diffused everywhere while also concentrated in web-like pathways, where it can still be encountered accidentally while traveling, provided that close attention is paid to surroundings. Locations of power concentrations can be predicted from the distribution of water and life forms, but it can only be contacted through dream, vision, fasting, meditation, trance, vigil. Only then can it be understood and controlled for the greatest good. Yet these necessary partnerships have not been forged during recent times, leaving power to flow untapped.

Sources for power are not only watering places, but also wherever life gathers for however long. Thus, some have taken the easier path of Christianity, with the source for its power in the mind of God and the memory of Jesus. Others adhere to the Native American Church, approaching power via peyote. None of these belief systems is antithetical in the native view because they all lead to the same center. Many people will belong to several religions and participate in Round Dances and fandangos, following the traditional teaching "the more religions you have the better for the welfare of self and family." This is not hypocracy, an Anglo notion anyway, but rather indicates good sense in appreciating the multiple sources that power can have within its universal pulsating web. [83]

Acknowledgements

This article supercedes an earlier one based largely on a literature review published in *Anthropos* (Miller 1980). For lielp and encouragement with both manuscripts. I sincerely thank Sven and Astrid Liljeblad, Don and Kay Fowler, Jackie Brady, Gary and Jean Palmer, Mike and Susie Ostanik, Claude Warren, Margaret Lyneis, Martlia Knack, and Fred Eggan. Warren d'Azevedo helped improve the earlier draft and provided Washoe examples. I thank advisors among six Southern Paiute and Western Shoshoni groups, particularly those at Moapa, Yomba, Duckwater, and Gosiute. For timely help with elusive references, I thank Dorothy House at the Museum of Northern Arizona Research Library and Laura Holt at the Museum of New Mexico Laboratory of Anthropology.

People, Berdache, and Left-Handed Bears:
Human Variation in Native America

Abstract
The Native cultures of North America recognize a bewilderingly large range of people, only some of whom are human. Focusing on four widely scattered tribes (Nootka, Keres, Kootenay, HoChunk ~ Winnebago) with examples from several others (Blackfeet, Pomo, Ojibwa, Tsimshian, Lenape Delaware), this paper examines the mediating role played by berdaches, bears, and others in these cultures. Consideration is also given to variations in the psychological, categorical, and symbolic aspects of gender and of the culture / nature continuum.

AN INTRIGUING FEATURE of Native American conversation is the frequent reference to "people" of various sorts, who are not usually human in European terms. Underlying these references, it seems to me, is a common view of the universe as anthropomorphic − if not in form then in emotions and personality − in keeping with what Mary Douglas (1970: 98, 104) has called a pre-Coperanican, or anthropocentric universe.

Over and over again, elders make reference to animal people, plant people, water people, spirit people, rock people, and many others, while at the same time recognizing the unique position of human people at the center of the overall plan of the cosmos. All of these cosmologies are based upon a pervasive belief in humanoid beings, suggesting that Amerind tribes use a flexible definition of what constitutes humanity in order to justify such a great range of people. As a preliminary attempt to grasp this definition, this paper will look at a few interrelated examples within particular tribes, which bear on the generalities involved.

Miller (1979) discussed several universal categories that are important for efficiently articulating the structural configuration (abbreviated as *struckon*) of a culture. In rank order from the most confined to the most extensive, these categories involve handedness, gender, and biota. In light of these categories, we will consider complex interactions involving the symbolic importance of left priority, the berdache ~ transexual, and bears, especially grizzlies. While information on these topics from each of the tribes is not always complete, such data do exist for the Nootka (West Coast People) of Vancouver Island, the Keres Pueblos of New Mexico, the Kootenay of British Columbia, and the Winnebago of Wisconsin. Because it has some bearing on the overall argument, we will also consider Delaware data relative to these categories, so as to suggest why the berdache role, so common elsewhere in Native America, was singularly lacking in the Northeast, among the Iroquois and the Coastal Algonkians.

From all of the available evidence, it appears that the Nootka, Keres, Kootenay, Winnebago, and Delaware use gender as the organizing, most pervasive tenet of their cultures. Complementarity of the sexes is, therefore, the dominant metaphor for expressing the tension that unifies and diversifies these cultures. Within the context of mythology, such a tension serving as the keystone of a culture has been variously called a paiduma by Leo Frobenius (Miller 1979) and an armature by Claude Levi-Strauss (1969). In practice, however, it is more like an echo reverberating throughout a culture, at all levels and times. [275]

These reverberations have different forms in different cultures, depending upon the way in which the components of the gender echo are defined in the format. Basically, the format has

26

three components, serially defined in terms of a notion of concentric degrees of confinement, or limitation. The echo itself consists of a dominant pair, one member of which is defined as exclusive (inside, closed, and positioned) within the other member, which is inclusive (outside, open). For example, in almost all human cultures, gender is defined such that Woman is the demarcated, exclusive category within the inclusive category of Man.

Further integrating these pairs is the notion of mediation, in which mediators are defined as inclosive, partaking of the attributes of each member of a pair as well as of qualities from a third dimension unique to mediators, making them inclosive of the entire system. Such inclosiveness is a constant in all cultures, although the hierarchical position of individual mediators will vary from culture to culture. For those with a Man / Woman tension, the most universal mediator is that of Mind (consciousness, thought, memory), variously represented as a high god, water, fire, or other sacred centers permeating the cosmos (Miller 1980a, 1980b) Mind itself shares with other mediators the quality of being a permeating nexus of channels, or webbing, for the reverberations of the cultural echo throughout the organization.

While the universal equation seems to be Man-(Mind)-Woman as inclusive / inclusive / exclusive, certain cultures have deliberately manipulated this analogy to establish their own distinctive configuration. Hence, while the Delaware follow this norm (as the Nootka and Winnebago also seem to), the Keres and Kootenay have reversed it so that Man is exclusive and Woman inclusive (Miller 1972). In fact enough comparative data already exists to propose that the pan-human norm is an equation of the inclusive with the dominant, the right side, Man, animals, and winter; or of the exclusive with the subordinate, the left side. Woman, plants, and summer. While exceptions do occur, they often appear to be intended to reinforce the tribal identity by emphasizing intercultural differences (Miller 1974). Other examples of this process appearing below are the left priority found in revitalization or nativistic movements such as the Delaware Big House Cult or the Great Lakes Midewiwin instituted by the mythic Bear. As right / left, Man / Woman, and animal / plant are obvious and rich polarities for coding the word and for relating to neighbors through similarity and reversals, so are some other natural phenomena appropriate for serving as mediators. In addition to the ones listed above, the following analysis will show that berdaches and bears also function as important mediators.

Throughout Native America, the bear is viewed as the great healer, patron of herbalists and shamans, because its large size, many human characteristics, and frequent grubbing for roots and plants encourages such links with medicines and supernatural power. Further, being omnivorous, bears are often in competition with humans for the same foods, and thus have been much in human awareness. It seems probable, therefore, that bears came to be regarded as left-handed, as a means of distinguishing them specifically from humans. As has been frequently noted, bears are often regarded as pseudohuman or humanoid, much as apes arc by many cultures; unlike apes, known to most Americans only from zoo cages, Native Americans correctly viewed bears as dangerous and unpredictable, sometimes equating them with the worst aspects of Nature. There is, moreover, the possibility that bears are [276] regarded as left-handed because their harvesting of plant foods links them with women. For example, out of great respect for the power of bears, most tribes never use the species name directly, but instead insist on the use of circumlocutions that often include a version of terms like "auntie" or "female affine" for addressing bears when they are encountered.

The justification for this seems to relate to a widespread belief in a special affinal relationship between hunter and prey in the Americas. Tales abound in references to the courtship and marriage between humans and other "people" who are often sources of food, with the right to kill and eat these species derived from a mythic charter setting up reciprocities as a result of the original marriage. Of note in this regard are the widely distributed stories about Star, Bear, Frog, Maize, Salmon, and other spouses. These marriages can be consummated and produce viable offspring because under the robe of each species the males and females are really humanoid. While this is implied for all species, it is most obvious in the case of the large mammals, most especially bears. In this way, bears have come to symbolize relations with the entire animal kingdom, making bears particularly suitable for spouses in myths chartering economic and ritual relations of reciprocity.

While this seems to be the context of generalized bear beliefs in America, specific tribes have developed their own versions within the framework of their own culture. In addition, bear beliefs can be compared with those associated with the berdache, since both of them seem to relate to the overall definition of humanness. Because they are regarded as intermediate between Man and Woman in some sense, berdaches also serve to mediate many aspects of culture. It is actually only the formal, institutionalized berdache role that has bearing here, not the effeminate characteristcs, relating more to personality than to social structure (Broch 1977).

The four cultures about to be considered represent four different languages and culture areas, suggesting that these relations are much more widespread in America than available evidence would indicate. The Nootka, now usually called West Coast People, comprised about a dozen political divisions along the western shore of Vancouver Island. With the Kwakiutl (*Kwakwala*), they make up the Wakashan stock and belong to the central province of the Northwest Coast, or North Pacific culture area. The Keres inhabit seven pueblos in central New Mexico, belong to the Southwest, or Oasis area, and speak a language classified as an isolate, although their participation in the Oshara archaeological continuum suggests an ultimate ancestry in the Hokan stock. The Kootenay also speak a language classed as an isolate, and are scattered in several bands along the river and lake of the same name, on either side of the British Columbia and Idaho-Montana border. While placed in the Plateau, or Intermontane culture area, the Upper (Eastern) Kootenay, along the river, were strongly influenced by the Plains area, while the Lower (Western) Kootenay, along the lake, were more of the Plateau type. Much Kootenay research remains unpublished, so the citations found below are all the more remarkable. Among the most recent revision^, to our understanding is the work of Lawrence Morgan (1980), rindicating that Kootenay and Proto-Salishan are collaterals of an earlier parent language. The Winnebago have largely remained in their homeland around Green Bay, Wisconsin, speak a Macro-Siouan language, and have been placed in the Great Lakes province of the East culture area. Yet for all these differences, each of these [177] four cultures shares beliefs about left-handed bears and berdache, within a general context of gender symbolism.

Nootka

like that of other Northwest Coast societies, Nootka social structure emphasizes rank and class within the ambilateral descent system common to the central province. In practice it happened that rank was a prerogative of the noble class, in contrast to commoners, the other freeborn class; both freeborn classes were distinct from that of slavery. Gender echoed through this society in terms of complementarity in economics, the inheritance of rank and privileges, marriage arrangements, and seating at feasts, potlatches, and shamanic dancing (Drucker 1951:

28

28ff, 36ff, 267). Fixed seating at public events was the prime expression of rank and class, so it is significant that at one potlatch chiefs sat at one end of the house, with men on the right and women on the left (Drucker 1951: 263). More importantly, during the initiation of new members into the Shamans' Dance, "the most important ceremonial of the Nootkan tribes" and key privilege of high rank (Drucker 1951: 439), seating ignored distinctions of rank and used only that of gender. Based on the elaborate rituals and patterns of female seclusion and the prohibition of women from ocean travel. Woman is the exclusive gender; the lack of any comparable retrictions suggest that Man is the inclusive one.

According to Drucker (1951: 331), both male and female transvestites were known among the Nootka, but they were few in number, generally characterized by a preference for the work of the opposite sex. Such women were famous warrior leaders who had been given supernatural sanction successfully to undertake such a career, while the men performed female tasks like berdaches elsewhere. As most tribes recognize only male berdaches, these females in male roles indicate the full complementarity of the sexes found elsewhere among the Nootka.

The Nootkans gave priority to the right, as indicated by the fact that eating with the left hand was considered a deliberate insult to everyone present. The only physical punishment Drucker (1951: 130) noted was striking a child's left hand with a warm stick, to encourage him or her to be right-handed. While in quest of a guardian spirit, children were told they could receive shamanistic power from a right hand sticking up from the ground and shaking a rattle, but to flee from a similar disembodied left hand, since it would confer only death (Drucker 1951: 153, 185).

Nonetheless, bears were considered to be left-handed by the Nootka. In his study of social dialects among the Nootka, Sapir (1915: 7) noted that in stories and jokes bears speak using left-handed speech forms. Northern Nootka bear hunters ate with the left hand so as to identify more closely with their quarry. Bears were killed to supply meat and grease, while the skin was used to make shirts for ritual bathers to warm themselves-Wafter a chilly ordeal.

Once killed, the bear was brought home from the trap and tied into an upright posture at the rear of the house, with four white mats holding dried salmon in front of it. A chief or other important person sprinkled eagle down on its head, such as was done for any ranking guest, and issued formal greetings. Later the bear was taken to another part of the house and butchered, while chiefs ate the dried salmon from the mats, since it was said to be a gift to them from the bear. Drucker (1951: 180) [278] was impressed by this ritual attention, but perplexed because bears were of such minor economic importance. The point of this ritual, however, is not economic but ideological; to borrow arguments from a characterization of totemism, bears are much better to think with than to eat (Levi-Strauss 1962), because of all the animal people they are the most similar to humans.

In a collection of tales written by a contemporary Nootka author and artist, we learn that "During the berry season Momma Bear would pick berries with her left hand. It is said that all bears are left handed. They do everything with their left hands" (Clutesi 1967: 65). According to another story, a famous bear trapper name?? Liaik once came upon a person with very white skin fasting, praying, scurbbing, and plunging at a remote pond in order to gain the power to defeat the two traps owned by Liaik. The trapper learned from his hidden observations and began to use the same procedures, vastly increasing his own hunting success because he had learned the techniques used by bears (Drucker 1951: 166). The point of the story is that bears without their skin robes are just like humans − able to speak, share the same ritual, and recognize a moral world. When women and others were frightened by bears in the berry patches, they shout to warn them away, calling bears by a title translated as "noble lady, wife of a chief, queen," regardless of the actual sex of the bear. The same title is also used for whales, which were courageously hunted by Nootkan nobles in the recent past. The implication is that by evoking these affinal relationships, eaters and eaten were reminded of their existing mutual respect and reciprocity. While the Nootka were fully aware that bear people have the same two genders as humans, their overall might and ambiguity made bears natural mediators between humans and other kinds of people, as will be more fully explored in the conclusion.

Keres

In the Southwest, the Keres Pueblos make much of the doctoring abilities of bears in keeping with the more widespread belief, but as with all other Pueblo cultures, they have formalized this belief into a number of institutionalized priesthoods working for the benefit of the whole community. Individual power is considered to be selfish and distrusted; only power channeled through a priesthood is ever acceptable. The remarkable aspect of this systemization, however, is that while each priesthood taps a particular power source, all of the priests as a group are known as bears, and accordingly use the left hand while curing. At the pueblo of Sia (White 1962), which in this regard is typical of all seven towns. Bear is the patron of all the curing priesthoods, the guardian of the west, sponsor of the Bear matriclan; a masked deity among the Katsina, and expressly left-handed. An individual who kills a bear must channel his success for the public good by joining a minor priesthood that constitutes a vestige of the warrior, or enemy-slayer cult. In this last regard, the killing of a bear is specifically equated with the killing of a human.

When a Keres medicine man, or priest, performs a cure, he wears a bear-claw necklace and bear-paw skins on the left or both hands (Lange 1968: 195). This use of the left is not limited to doctoring, however, since the Keres are one of the few cultures in the world who have a left priority (Miller 1972) as the general rule. In the theocracy governing each town, a leader is succeeded by his left-hand man, who [279] had previously served as assistant. The second assistant is the right-hand man, and he then moves up to become the heir and left-hand man. The most senior initiate then becomes the right-hand man. In all, then, men arc associated with left, priesthoods, animals, and death, because they are killers; women are associated with right, matriclans, plants, and birth. Moreover, Man is exclusive and Woman inclusive in the Keresan scheme of things, reversing the nearly universal pattern of gender and concentric attributes.

Male berdaches occur among the Keres, talking, dressing, and acting like women. White (1943: 325) provides a particularly detailed account of the way in which a boy was pressured and manipulated into becoming a berdache, indicating that the role represents a structural need in society. His data derive from an 1851 examination of an Acoma berdache by a surgeon, William Hammond. Female berdaches are not reported, although Curtis (1926:134) did learn of two women who became ill in 1910 and insisted on initiation into the Giant priesthood. After community uproar and sadness, they were initiated into this lesser priesthood on the stipulation that they act and dress like men during cures. From this account, it appears that the women did not become berdaches, intermediate between the sexes, but rather became men by a cultural fiction. This is much the same way in which the priest in charge of each town is said to become a woman after installation, even though he maintains a married, family life outside the office.

Similarly, in northern California, where most shamans were biologically women, they were known by a term meaning "real men," indicating that their long period of disciplined training had turned them culturally into men (Thomas Buckley, pc). These examples indicate the wide cultural range permissible to gender roles, including not only other physiological species, but also individuals with a physiological make-up more appropriate to one category, who through determination and training assume the other form. They transpose themselves between the genders, but do not blur these distinctions as does the berdache.

From this perspective, the berdache can be seen even more clearly as occupying a separate status, belonging to neither gender but standing somewhere between them. If individuals can choose or be made to switch their gender identity for reasons of personality, ritual, and ideology, the berdache must be regarded as having had a similar option to assume a third position mediating between the other two. This implies that there is not so much a continuum of human variation in Native America, as there is a set of cultural categories with which individuals can affiliate at will or via supernatural sanctions.

The Keres provide a telling case for the argument, since they have a left priority for humans and bears, male berdaches, and a highly structured society based on the tension between male cults and matriclans. After being killed, bears are welcomed into the household and community with the same regard as slain deer and other large mammals, much as honored guests are also greeted and feted. The affinal connection between humans and bear people seems to apply among the Keres as elsewhere, and bears and doctors are both considered nurturant and, thereby, Womanly in the Keres context.

The reasoning behind the left priority is based on the observation that the left hand is closer to the heart, the .locus of both thought and emotions. Among the [280] Keres, social class are based on access to knowledge of an esoteric sort, so that a closer association with the left and the heart for men serves to indicate that they are more knowledgeable. This reversal of the right / left polarity is, furthermore, in keeping with several other reversals in the association of the sexes and seasons that help to distinguish the Keres from close Pueblo neighbors such as the Tewa (Miller 1974).

Keres boys can become berdaches, but girls cannot, because the semantic categories already asser: thai men are only Manly, while women have the qualities of both genders because Woman is inclusive. A woman attempting to become a categorical Man would be losing much of her self-esteem, while a man becoming a woman-like berdache would be enhancing his own status to some extent, allowing for some personal opposition from friends or relatives who had their own plans for the individual. It is fitting that in the reported instance of women seeking male privileges they were attempting to become priests rather than ordinary men, although in consequence they had become like other men who had gone through a more natural initiation into the priesthood. As will be considered in the conclusion, these concentric attributes have much bearing on the handedness, genders, and biological solutions utilized in different cultures.

Kootenay

The Kootenay, like the Keres, use the concentric attributes of gender to link men with the inside and exclusive, women with the outside and inclusive. For example, when a man died the frame of the tipi was destroyed; for a woman, the floor and lodge coverings were destroyed. Unlike the Keres, however, the Kootenay associated men with right priority − the right side of the lodge was the honored section where men sat (Turney-High 1941: 60). The left side was associated with women and considered harmless.

Bear hunters identified with their prey by using the left hand, because "the grizzly bear is regarded as left-handed" (Schaeffer 1966: 50 #22). As myths make clear, animals are basically humans or humanoids wearing the cloak of their species. As Boas (1918: 93) noted, "the coat of Grizzly Bear is a skin. He put it on and became a grizzly bear." Both grizzly and black bears were hunted for their grease, meat, and hides, while the grizzly was also sought after as a very powerful, if dangerous, guardian spirit.

A special Grizzly Bear Rite was formerly held (before the tribe's conversion to Catholicism) in early March, when medicine bundles were unfolded and renewed while songs were sung on behalf of men and women bears. During the rite, everyone used the left hand. The culmination of the rite was an offering of pipestems buried in honor of the bears, who then judged the sincerity of the person making each gift and accordingly benefited, harmed, or killed the individual. From this we can judge that the supernatural power of bears was such that they could and did influence the life and death of humans. This is in keeping with their position as mediators between such vital categories as life / death, woman / man, human / supernatural, and so forth. Interestingly, the chartering myth for this rite involves a young boy who lived for two years with a bear mother and her cubs. After his return, he instituted the rite based on his observations of this bear woman. This association of bears with the [281] Womanly is also implied by the story of a man who angered the bears by saying that the grizzly was his wife and ordering her to come to him immediately. When she did so, the man was greatly frightened and asked forgiveness (Schaeffer 1966: 6, 45-47).

The Kootenay recognized with special terms both male and female berdaches, although the males were much more numerous. The females acted like amazons in that they became important war and diplomatic leaders. In the most famous instance, a Kootenay woman assumed a full range of male roles in marriage, military, political, and religious areas. She was widely known during the early historic period in the Northwest, until she was killed by the Blackfeet in 1837 for covering the escape, of some Flathead during diplomatic negotiations. Based on this and other cases provided by Schaeffer (1965), it appears that such women were physically large, tall, and robust to begin with and matched this size and strength with assertive personalities like those of the manly hearted women best known for the Blackfeet.

Once again, the Kootenay provide evidence of the co-occurance of male berdaches, left-handed bears, and the possibility for individuals to jump gender roles with sufficient provocation. The evidence of Man as the segregated and of Woman as the integrative categories, however, together with the mediation of the berdaches, make the Kootenay consistent with the same pattern among the Keres. A man gained additional dimensions by becoming a berdache, but a woman lost qualities by such a decision, whether personally or supernaturally sanctioned.

HoChunk ~ Winnebago

The HoChunk played upon this difference in psychological desires and categorical sanctions as revealed by their own ambiguous treatment of berdaches. This society was founded upon a thoroughgoing regard for the opposition between Sky and Earth, formalized in the two moietites of the same names. According to the origin myth, Earthmaker created four worlds, with the sky representing the last man created and the earth the last woman (Radin 1970: 329).

From this, we can deduce that Man is open and inclusive, while Woman, like the earth, is closed and exclusive. Mediation is represented by Earthmaker himself, a wise and mindful being with the appearance of a man and the creative abilities of a woman.

The patrimoieties consisted of twelve named sibs, with four named for birds belonging to the Sky moiety, but with four named for land mammals and another four named for water creatures, in the Earth moiety. Of these twelve, the Thunderbird sib led those of the Sky, as the Bear led those of the Earth. When the Bear sib held a feast, the members ate with the left hand, out of respect for their eponym (Sapir 1915: 7 #1; Radin 1970: 180, 274). In other situations, the right hand had priority – this use of the left was a peculiarity of bears. Bear clansmen acted as tribal soldiers and police, in addition to holding a special curing dance, given them by bears. Moreover, bears were hunted for food, quested after as guardian spirits, and generally respected by all. Those blessed by a grizzly guardian formed a secret organization, like that of others gifted by a particular spirit (Radin 1970: 63, 180, 299). As the Thunderbird sib represented the right, males, and the cosmos, so the Bear represented left, women, and the earth.

Data on HoChunk berdaches are sparse because Christian missionaries have taught them to be embarrassed by the subject, at least in public. Nonetheless, Lurie [282] (1953) learned that men who had received power from the moon, a female spirit, were obliged to become berdaches, performing tasks appropriate to women in addition to acquiring a special ability for prophecy. These berdaches were respected and highly honored, sometimes marrying a husband. In addition to this supernatural sanction, however, war captives and dishonored Winnebago men were sometimes humiliated by making them assume a female role in lieu of being killed. Women berdaches as such seem to have been unknown. The indications for the Winnebago, therefore, are that while some unfortunate men were forced to assume the female role, the only true berdaches were those who had a supernatural sanction to compensate for the loss of their integrative position as men and for assuming the mediating role of the berdache.

Other Examples

While other data have been sought to expand this comparison to other tribes, only tantalizing hints have been found. While it seems likely that left-handed bears and berdaches were much more common in aboriginal times, there are only the following scattered data to lend support to this.

Among Plains tribes, Schaeffer (1966: 50 #19) refers to Blackfeet myth where a man with bear power became a bear by having a companion scratch his left foot with a bear claw. Elsewhere, Schaeffer (1965: 221) also noted the presence of two male berdaches among the Southern Piegan division of the Blackfeet confederation, suggesting that the Blackfeet shared in the pattern found elsewhere with greater documentation.

In California, which was formerly populated by several species of grizzly bears now memorialized on the state flag, the Pomo had a class of ruthless shamans called Bear Doctors, widely distributed in other societies of western Native America. Among the Pomo, they would don full bearskin costumes, using the left hand (Barrett 1917: 458ff). [283] While female shamans are well known for the Pomo, there is only a vague reference to berdaches among them (Willoughby 1963: 59, Table 6), making this example dubious.

A particularly telling case that suggests that belief in left-handed bears was very widespread relates to the Midewiwin ~ Shamanic Academy, reformulated about 1700 by the

Ojibwa and diffused to other Great Lakes tribes. According to its origin myth, deities instructed Bear (or sometimes Otter, in other versions) to institute the cult among the Ojibwa by training a man named Cutfoot in the lore and ritual. While none of the sources specifies that Bear was left-handed, some of the birchbark mnemonic scrolls used in cult training and the memorizing of the details of myth, ritual, and song, indicate an importance to the left hand. Although many of the figures in the scrolls are armless, Dewdney (1975: 95) shows a master scroll from Ontario and a copy of it from Minnesota with twenty-four deities (*manito*), each holding a pouch insignia in the left hand; Landes (1968: 82) reproduces a scroll with many armless figures and four others holding rattles in the left hand. This use of the left is clearly related to the general respect shown to bears in America. One Mide (Midewiwin) master went so far as to say "the Bear is the strongest animal, so it came to represent God. A bear can do anything" (Dewdney 1975: 25). [283] Once initiated, the members, or Mide priests, were believed to become actual deities and to take on the qualities of Bear. The more selfish and dangerous ones were sometimes accused of wandering at night, dressed in bearskins, to harm people or get revenge (Landes 1968: 63).

This association of bears with the left and the Mide does not, however, mean that they had priority. In one origin myth, the Underwater Panther created Man in his right hand and Woman in his left, giving females an inferior, if more flexible position. The implication, by no means substantiated by the data, is that the right hand was associated with chiefs, while the left one was emphasized by Mide shamans. The link between left and Midewiwin was quite strong even when diffused, since among the Omaha, where the Mide was called the Shell (Cowry) Society and the white swan was a patron, "the down near the left wing should be worn on the head. The left wing of the bird would be a symbol of its power" (Fletcher and La Flesche 1972: 514).

Delaware: A Negative Example

Lastly we turn to a consideration of data from the Delaware of the Northeast, where the berdache role appears to have been singularly absent. Repeated questioning among modem Delaware has convinced me that there is no evidence for a formalized berdache role in this culture. The nearest equivalent is the term *malxkwe*, used to refer to a womanish, whiney man, but only in terms of personality characteristics, not social role. For the Delaware, Man was inclusive and Woman exclusive, with mediation supplied by a concept of mind-memory (Miller 1979). Priority shifted to the left, under much the same influences and reactions as those behind the Mide. Here the stimulus was a mid-1700 reformist movement called the Big House Cult, which codified traditional culture so that it could better withstand Christianity with its emphasis on the right hand of God. In addition, the Delaware had an elaborate Bear Rite and several other bear observances which indicate that bears held important roles in the cosmology (Wallace 1949; Tantaquidgeon 1972; Speck 1937). Unfortunately, there is no evidence as to which paw might have been given priority in this belief system.

From what data do exist, however, we can surmise that bears probably were considered left-handed, because the left hand was used in all rituals. Bears did serve as mediators, with their humanity, strength, herbal lore, and supernatural powers expressed in the Delaware practice of calling them "grandparent" or specifically addressing them as "grandfather" or "grandmother" if the sex were known. This kin term served to emphasize the attitude toward bears as old, wise, and respected.

34

The lack of berdaches among the Delaware, and by extension the culturally very similar Iroquois, seems to derive from two features of the culture. First, the definitions of concentricity made it unlikely that men would assume a womanlike, berdache role and lose their wider attributes of inclusivity. Second, both Delaware and Iroquois women had extremely high social status as compared to " women elsewhere in Native America, because their identification with the earth included extensive faining and reliable food surpluses. Unlike the Keres, where Woman is inclusive and the clans arc matrilineal, with both male and female members, the Delaware exclusive Woman suggests that their clans were matrilineal, [284] because blood (*humuk^w*) as a Womanly substance was closely circumscribed and the subject of special concern during the transmission of cultural continuity. Delaware women played important roles in the less public negotiations and in matters of home and kinship, while men managed the public and external aspects of the society and had considerable freedom to travel long and far. In this context of greater personal fulfillment, the lack of a berdache role or of any supernatural justification for it seems to be particularly revealing of the psychodynamics behind the berdache position.

Of the tribes cited above, only the Keres and Delaware practiced extensive farming, but among the Keres the men tilled the fields. The Nootka, Kootenay, and HoChunk had foraging economies with local specialities – whaling for the Nootka, bison for the Kootenay, and wild rice for the Winnebago. These economies were clearly expressed in the degree of complimentarity between the sexes and the categorical genders, but they by no means explain the gender definitions within these cultures. At best they are merely congruent with the conceptual logic and intertribal relations that provide the molding influences for a culture.

Conclusion

It remains for us to assess the overall significance of left-handed bears in the cultures of Native America. In his classic study of circumpolar bear cercmonialism, Hallowell (1926: 67, 73 #292, 77) specifically discounted from consideration the bear rites of the Delaware, Kootenay, and Ute, as radically different from the hunting observances that were the focus of his comparisons. In doing so he missed the most important feature of bear ceremonialism. In trying to explain why slain bears were welcomed into a home and given special treatment, he went through three possible theories. The economic one held that the propitiation was proportional to the usefulness of bears, but this proved inappropriate when it became clear that bears were economically important in an area larger than that where the ritual was observed. The psychological theory held that bears were so humanoid that their killing would cause some regret, if not guilt, and call for some ritual of propitiation. Here again, however, bears occur in a wider area than that of the ritual, so this supposed regret was not universal. Even within the area of the ritual, regard for bears varied greatly, from slight regard to serious reverence. Lastly, the historic-geographical theory held that the observances began in the Paleolithic, as seen by caches of cave bear skulls in Neanderthal sites, and has been gradually diffusing since that time throughout the northern hemisphere, from Scandanavia through arctic America. This theory accounts well for the facts, but only because it is post hoc.

Bear ceremonialism is part of a larger complex of hunting rituals emphasizing respect for animals so that their immortal souls will continue to be reborn and supply humans with protein. Often, the animal that is the focus of such rites is the staple in that habitat, either as the primary food and/or a dominant species. The First Salmon Ceremony of the Northwest, Deer Greeting of the Southwest, Bear Ceremonialism of the boreal forest, First Roots and Seeds of the Intermontane, and Acorn Rites of Native California are therefore all aspects of this same complex.

Ignored by Hallowell, the Bear Rites of the Delaware and Kootenay are really an intensification of this respect for animals, but involve bears because of the cultural role that bears play as mediators in many cultures. Bear spouses and child [285] adoptions that are the subjects of myth are another aspect of such intensification.

Bears are people in the same sense that other species are people. They are anthropomorphic under their species robes, exist in complimentary genders, and conduct themselves in a moral fashion through language, etiquette, and ritual. Yet bears are also left-handed in the cultures considered above, and probably in many others. While the Keres, Delaware, and Midewiwin members do have left priority, data strongly suggest a universal right priority for humans, except in cases of deliberate reversal, having to do with asserting a distinct identity, as among Big House adherents. This universal right priority has been linked to male dominance, so that left is associated with females (Needham 1973).

From the available evidence, therefore, it seems that bears are left-handed because they are in some sense like women, in addition to being strong and terrifying like men, and being mediators because they share in both of these attributes. To grasp the sense in which they are women, we must turn to the important article by Ortner (1974) where she follows Levi-Strauss in arguing for a cross-cultural recognition of the supreme importance of the opposition between culture and nature for all humans. In structuralist theory, culture is the predictable, humanly instituted, and exclusive; nature is unpredictable, awesome, beyond human, and inclusive. In other words, culture is part of nature because it is the biological adaptation of humans. The mediator between culture and nature is the concept of Mind, represented both by the physiological brain and by culturally appropriate thoughts.

Allowing for variation among individual cultures, as a general rule Man and right are closer to the pole of culture, especially in its public aspects, while Woman and left are closer to that of nature, since females menstruate with the lunar cycle and are more closely associated with such natural acts as birth, eating, and child socialization.

Left-handed bears would also be closer to the nature pole, allowing for their equally male attributes of ferocity. To understand their role as mediators, we need to recall the observation of Cassirer (1944: 82-83) that many cultures recognize in totemism and other beliefs about animals that there is a solidarity in the society of life, linking all living things together and centering them on the human model. It is in this sense, then, that all of these living species are recognized as various types of people, having ethical, tribal communities and genders like those of humans. Some of these species, however, provide particularly potent symbols for the interrelationships within the overall solidarity. Bears are but one example of such symbolic markers serving as halfway stations, or mediators, along the culture / nature continuum. The most widespread of these markers, based on mythology collections and my own Delaware, Salishan, and Tsimshian fieldwork, are dogs, mice, and bears. Dogs are nearer to culture, mediating between humans and other people as the only fully domesticated animal in North America. Mice are midway along the continuum, mediating between the inside and outside of the house and community, so that a mouse is often a polyglot in myths, translating for several groups involved in an activity. Bears are nearer to nature, mediating between the animal peoples.

It is extremely interesting that the Tsimshian have maintained prayers to an earlier deity called *gɔl* ("unknown, empty, void") only in rituals following the killing of a bear. Otherwise, they have become thoroughgoing Christians and have [286] rejected most of their older beliefs. Nature has sometimes been characterized as chaos, but this Tsimshian example suggests that there is only the void of space. The cosmos in such cases seems to be viewed as a bubble floating in the emptiness that is nature in its purest form. In tills context then, the Tsimshian appear to have preserved the use of the bear in a mediating role as a safeguard against the void, with Christianity serving to maintain the internal structure of the known world.

As with women, it may be the case that natural propensities in bears encourage this association with the left and mediation toward the pole of nature. Biologists have confirmed that polar bears really are left-paw dominant (May et al 1980: 25) and Fraser River Salish insist that when bears leave hibernation they hug the right side of the cave wall, leaving their left arm free for defense (Brent Galloway, pc). Yet these observations would only remain biological facts helpful to hunters were they not significant in a wider context, namely the span between nature and culture. As the most humanlike of the Animal People, bears are appropriate representatives for one extreme of mediation. They provide food and coverings to people, but are even better symbols for bridging the genders. As Tanner (1979) and Skinner (1914) make clear, after it was killed a bear was butchered and prepared so that the upper torso went to men and the lower body to women, all of which reinforces the argument that bears are inclosive mediators.

Similarly, berdaches are regarded by many Amerind cultures as part of the acceptable variation in the society of life. As some individuals are able to switch gender and reverse tasks or identity, so others can seek a compromise position that places them between genders and enables them to tap supernatural reserves of power or energy by virtue of this mediating status. Except where whites have made the subject taboo or embarrassing, berdaches had high status because they functioned like other markers along the culture / nature sequence. Hunting tribes were also astute enough observers during butchering activities to notice that other Animal People had hermaphroditic members, and often equated these with the berdaches, providing a larger status, ambiguous or not, in the society of life.

We began by inquiring into the curious references to "people" of many different species, of berdaches, and of left-handed bears. By now we have hopefully arrived at a recognition of all of these as within the culturally acceptable range of biological variation, differing in terms of their inclosive (mediating), inclusive, and exclusive concentric attributes, but, ultimately, all members in the fellowship of life. In terms of this larger context of mediation, bears and berdaches occupy positions at the extremes of the cuture / nature continuum, as can be expressed in this series:

CULTURE   berdache   dog   mouse   bear NATURE

These mediators provide a three-dimensional framework for the flatter relationships between the inclusive and the exclusive, usually represented by the metaphors of men : right :: women : left in the overall scheme of cultural life.

Indien Personhood
Commentary

In pulling together these pithy citations from respected Americanist works, sometimes now called Indienology, this commentary attempts a comprehensive overview of notions relating to the person, in both cosmic and personal senses, of Native North America. It uses the European solution for distinguishing those indigenous to India from those of America by the expedient of a single vowel: A or E. Moreover, to clinch the argument, comparable Inuit data are included. This treatment is intended to be balanced, indicating features that both helped and harmed individuals and communities, using citations from scholars who convey statements in a Native voice upholding the interconnectedness of customs, taboos, demeanors, and their likely outcomes.

Though reported as asides or seemingly obscure details for only a single tribe or instance, all these observations can be understood to have continent-wide distribution, providing a coherent worldview that was accepted, rejected, modified, or ignored depending on local conditions of terrain, history, customs, contacts, and inter-group hostilities. Local factors of population densities, social systems, and tending (foraging) or tilling (farming) lifeways are largely ignored here in the interest of tracing more generic patterns. Spatial orientations in worlds and homes are as significant as cultural rules since they provided the basic "staging area" for the active deployment of people and materials for larger tasks and activities. [122]

World

Every community seemingly had its own beliefs about their world. Not all were created in the same way or at the same time since fires, floods, and famines called for successive recreations before the emergence of the present world. For the North American continent, eight different creation epics have been located, though all agree that these universes are pervaded with a mindful flow of power-energy-force that is both diffused everywhere and channeled along rings and rays, like that of a web, with divinity at its center.[91] Over eons, articulations of space, time, and life took form through the applications of this deified power.[102] Earth often emerged from the primordial sea where it was held in suspension until realized by an "earth grasper" intent on global reform.[113]

Best described by the Southern Californian Luiseño, this *ayelkwi* ~ knowledge and power, provided the systematic means of relating all parts and events of existence through four means of access. Either it was commonly available to all, innate by birth within a particular family, residual as thrown around the landscape by their culture hero Wiyot , or formulated by prayers and rituals which enacted their history and laws conveyed in song. As elsewhere, it was engendered as diffuse for women, but particular and specific for men.[124] For the Navajo, the

---

[9] Anna Birgitta Rooth, The Creation Myths of the North American Indians 1957.

[10] Jay Miller, High-Minded High Gods in North America 1980.

[11] Daniel Brinton, The Myths of the New World 1969 [1876]: 209.

[12] Raymond White, Luiseno Social Organization, 1963: 137, 139, 140, 145; James Moriarity, Chinigchinx 1969.

world was transformed from knowledge, organized in manly thought, patterned in language, and realized in womanly speech and other symbolic activities.[135]

After initial thought and speech came lasting memory, since language itself consists of images projected and shared with others who pile up their own details and pictures as conversation goes on.[146]

The inevitable separation of land and water, earth and sky, moon and sun had long range consequences. For the Omaha, night and day became symbols of precision, while the bow came from the moon and the first arrow from a sun ray.[157]

"Primacy is universally revered,"[168] giving precedent to the first born, first kill, first picking, first fruits, first menstruation, and all founders because "all have special merit and powers of freshness" that come from the beginnings of a sequence. Land and sea remain inherently unsteady, except when anchored by mounds, giant snakes, or heavy landmarks.[179] Periodically, shamans, priests, and concerned members must renew, fix, and reinvigorate the universe, often using sexual metaphors and engendered ritual acts. General categories of center, inside, and outside were observed, but each community treated them in its own way. For example, Navajo sand paintings start at the center, but Pueblos ones at the edge.[1810]

All species are mutable. In season, beavers transform into geese, "Sturgeon change into bears when the berries ripen, whence the large number of bears at that season," and moose become whales.[19u] These changes derive from a belief that all beings are infra-human: they have human hands, faces, and bodies on the inside and an outer covering that can be put on and removed when going or coming home. Though shape-shifting, these immortals at base are shimmering, iridescent humans, sometimes described as rainbow-hued.

Among Inuit, an animal assuming its infra-human form raised its forelimb or wing to push its outer muzzle or beak up and back to reveal its inner [123] humanity.[2012] Ojibwa shamans wore bone and wood amulets carved into human faces to protect their souls.[2113]

Everywhere powerful local shamans met in caves or other holy homes with the giant immortal boss of a species in order to negotiate the exchange of human and animal souls to sustain the human community. Most often the souls of enemies were given up first, followed by those closer to home, with children and women going before strong hunters.

Overall, this universe is finite. Nothing can exist in or from a void. Everything came from something else. The Achumawi cosmos was made by World Heart, acting through his grandson, Annikadel, "whose underparts are blue and white so no one could see him moving through the sky." At the location of each town, he stuck in feathers that became the first humans,

---

[13] Gary Witherspoon, Language and Art in the Navajo Universe 1977: 34, 142.

[14] Keith Basso, Wisdom Sits in Places 1996: 84.

[15] Francis La Flesche, Omaha Bow and Arrow Makers 1926: 493.

[16] Irving Goldman, The Mouth of Heaven 1975: 49.

[17] Jay Miller, Instilling the Earth: Explaining Mounds .

[18] Ruth Underbill, Red Man's Religion 1965 232.

[19] Diamond Jenness, The Ojibwa Indians of Parry Island 1935: 80 #2; Frank Speck and John Witthoft, Some Notable Life-histories in Zoological Folklore 1947: 345-349.

[20] Jarich Gerlof Oosten, The Theoretical Structure of the Religion of the Netsilik and Iglulik 1976.

[21] Jenness, Ojibwa Indians: 68.

often a separate feather for the chief, for the woman chief, and for the poor.[22][14]

Settlements

Wherever people build their homes from local materials, the shape and layout of a house is usually the same as that of the cosmos, round with domed housing or square with apartments.

Inside, however, spatial arrangements vary by culture. For example, inside a tipi, Lakota men sat on the right half, and women on the left with their legs modestly drawn up alongside their bodies.[23][15] Throughout the Great Lakes region, encampments were ethnically obvious since Shawnee suspended a kettle from X-crossed beams, Ottawa from a straight suck, Wyandot between two trees, and Ojibwa from two sticks.[24][16]

Cleanliness was a concern of both hygienic and religious proportions. When a Mistassini Cree family left its hunting camp, everything was left clean with large bones from its kills decorating a single tree whose trunk was shorn of all but the top branches. This way, when the local spirit-partner of the hunt-leader flew over to make its inspection, it would approve and continue to send good luck.[25][17] Similarly, other foods were physically encouraged to re-propagate. The Ojibwa, for example, threw back into water a few grains of wild rice wrapped in clay.[26][18]

Habitat also played a role, with rivers providing the cohesive lifeline for communities linked by its flow. Such "natural" unity has been sadly overlooked by scholars who fail to see that those living upriver have an automatic obligation to those downstream. Dense population and aridity seem to affect this pattern, however, since Henry Dobyns found that rivers were borders among the Florida Timucua, while the Arizona Pai visualize a midstream-dividing backbone along the Colorado River.[27][19]

Womb

Engendering began in the womb, if not before, with parents making different contributions or infusions to the materials that "cooked" to become a fetus. Actual gender was determined by which parent reached orgasm first or had the stronger will. Oregon Tillamook believed a body template was sent from [124] a land where such beings lived awaiting birth. Patrilineal Kickapoo men reported that women were only a tray to hold the gestating new clansmember.[28][20] For Quechan (Yuma), successful conception required the conjoining of a father's dreams with a mother's desires. After this birth, a mother did not distinguish between the sex of her children, who all called her "mother," while a father did since his sons and daughters

---

22 Istet Woiche, *Annikadel*: The History of the Universe 1992: xxi, 87; cf. Malcolm Margolin, ed, *The Way We Lived* 1981.

23 Royal Hassrick, *The Sioux* 1964: 287.

24 CC Trowbridge, Shawnee Traditions 1939: 46.

25 Adrian Tanner, *Bringing Home Animals* 1979: 75, 171.

26 Jenness, Ojibwa Indians: 14.

27 Henry Dobyns, *Their Numbers Become Thinned* 1988: 166, 192 #81.

28 Felipe and Dolores Latorre, *The Mexican Kickapoo* 1976: 157.

called him by separate terms.[29][21]

During pregnancy a Delaware father determined the coming gender by hanging a toy bow or wooden mortar off his leggings to keep its spirit nearby. If a bow did not work, then a mortar would.[30][22] Similarly, when depositing the cord stump in hopes of an abundant future for the infant, Yuchi put a tiny bow and arrow with a son's umbilical, or a mortar and spoons with that of a daughter. Yuchi believed that twins and deformed children were sent to earth as special moral guides.[31][23] Throughout the Northwest, twins were equated with salmon, whose dual aspect was to go away and come back. Lakota make two effigies of a lizard or turtle, both difficult to kill and long-lived; one holds the umbilical cord and the other serves as a decoy.[32][24]

In a well-described example, a proper Cheyenne was conceived from three sources.[33][25] Two were the mother and father, who contributed blood and substance, but most critical was the Creator ~ *Ma'heo'o*, who provided two blessings. The first was a life soul, enabling a fetus to grow and move when it became bound into its body, diffused throughout, and indicated by the heart beat, pulse, breath, growth, blinking eyelids, and food digestion. Any loss of body parts, particularly amputations, diminished the effectiveness of this life soul. The second blessing came just after birth when the baby first inhaled *omotome,* or breath, air, speech, articulation, understanding, and power. For these people, a person was conscious of self, the moral order, kinship obligations, careful speech, understanding, virtues of immortal spirits, and a profound sense of being existentially alone, regardless of external appearance or species. Each human had body, breath, memory, and heart, allowing differing degrees of individuality, provided that everyone supported communal tribal identity and purpose.

Regardless of personal genitals, every Cheyenne balanced the genders because the inside of each body is female and the outside is male, with ribs as the divide. Yet because man was the generic, only boys could use sleds made with rib runners.[34][26] Among Navajos, body substance was considered an outer form (symbolic of woman) and spirit was an inner form (of man).[35][27]

Birth

Quebec Inuit held that an annoyed or stressed fetus could crack open to change sex at the moment of birth, a process called a *sipiniit.*[36][28] Biology is not destiny since in everything-is-possible epics men did give birth. Tohono O'Odham (Papago) tell of Handsomeman, who made all women pregnant in one night, then gave birth himself the next day. His baby cried so uncontrolably that the world flooded.

After a child is born, Ojibwa say it was "empty" of any characteristics and identity, so

---

[29] C Daryll Forde, Ethnography of the Yuma Indians 1931: 83-277, 148, 158.

[30] Jay Miller, Delaware Personhood 1991.

[31] Frank Speck, Ethnology of the Yuchi Indians 1909: 110.

[32] Hassrick, *The Sioux*: 270.

[33] Ann Terry Sawyier Strauss, Northern Cheyenne Ethnopsychology 1975; Being Human in the Cheyenne Way 1976: 141.

[34] Strauss, Being Human: 187.

[35] Witherspoon, *Language and Art*: 142.

[36] Bernard Saladin D'Anglure, From Foetus to Shaman 1994: 84.

spirits and parents had to fill him or her.[37][29] Delaware parents [125] bound a newborn to the earth by tying on wristlets and placing the afterbirth someplace where it would beneficially affect the child's career. For example, the afterbirth might be buried in a forest to produce a hunter. The Delaware also dressed newborns in adult clothes and moccasins with holes in them to discourage ghosts from luring them away. As a safeguard against illness, a pet was given to the child to attract any harm to itself.[38][30] Sauk made a cradle-board from a living tree to transfer its vitality to the child.[39][31]

Nicknames and formal names further assured a child's growth. Every Kickapoo baby was given two names, one used during life and the other after death.[40][32] Among closely related Sauk, the first-born joined the moiety opposite that of the father, while the second-born shared the father's.[41][33] If the father was light-color moiety, the oldest was dark, and the second was light. Sometimes, for her comfort and protection, a daughter joined the half of her elder brother.

Men occupied public offices, but Potawatomi women consciously filled in when men defaulted on their duties.[42][34] Women in the lower Great Lakes had their own strong leaders (see subsection entitled "Leaders" below).

Couvade

Unlike South America, where a new father commonly shared his wife's and baby's postpartum seclusion and taboos, this custom of couvade is rare to the north.

Engendering Childhood

The maturation of a child coincides with marked stages in his or her life. Various communities observed different milestones, such as the Cree "walking out" to cerebrate a baby's first steps, indicating special regard for feet among hunters.[43][35] After a Navajo infant's first laugh, salt and bread are given away;[44][36] an Oto's first haircut followed clan patterns to indicate larger memberships;[45][37] a Cheyenne mother's brother fed her child meadowlark meat and eggs to encourage fluency;[46][38] a Kootenay couple could resume coitus when their most recent child began to whistle; and Delaware, among many others, offered lost baby teeth with prayers for stronger new ones.

At six, Menominee boys were subjected to icy baths, long runs, and endurance tests.[47][39]

---

[37] Ruth Landes, *The Ojibwa Woman* 1971: 124.

[38] Miller, Delaware Personhood: 19. [137]

[39] Alanson Skinner, Observations on the Ethnology of the Sauk Indians 1925: 137.

[40] Robert Ritzenthaler and Frederick Peterson, The Mexican Kickapoo Indians 1956: 58.

[41] Alanson Skinner, Observations on the Ethnology of the Sauk Indians I 1923: 12.

[42] Ruth Landes, *The Prairie Potawatomi* 1970: 37.

[43] Tanner, *Bringing Home Animals*: 90.

[44] Witherspoon, *Language and Art*: 185.

[45] William Whitman, *The Oto* 1937: 69; cf. Alice C Fletcher and Francis La Flesche, *The Omaha Tribe* 1992 [1911].

[46] Strauss, Being Human: 207.

[47] Alanson Skinner, The Menomini Indians 1915 8: 41.

Time was spent in mediation and labor, building trenches, stone walls, or rock cairns. Ojibwa boys out on a quest remained in "nests" built as platforms in trees to be closer to hovering spirits,[48] though very young Potawatomi fasters slept at home for their parents' peace of mind.[49] In Ojibwa idiom, to "pity" another is to adopt him and care for him like a parent or grandparent. Thus the pitying immortal is bound to the protégé by the firmest loyalties in Ojibwa worldview. Discipline and attitude were hallmarks of those high born, though "Abstinence is considered a negative attitude of insulting indifference; whereas chastity is a positive attitude of desire held in leash."[50]

Being human for Cheyenne was a process of defining conscience on the basis of two antitheses – good or crazy, action or wisdom.[51] Good was anything orderly, controlled, careful, thoughtful, and proper, as taught by Sweet Medicine, the man [126] who learned Cheyenne culture from the spirits inside Bear Butte in South Dakota, and instituted the Council of Forty-Four Chiefs and the worship of the Four Sacred Arrows. Crazy was anything disordered, impulsive, or brutishly animal-like. Humans have both potentials, but should learn self-control to embrace the good and avoid the crazy. Both good and crazy were, in turn, bisected by the axis of action and wisdom. For example, men could choose between two role models, that of the active warrior or that of the sage chief or priest. In the circle of life, associations of these four principals are good ~ spirituality ~ white ~ east, crazy ~ sexuality ~ yellow ~ west, action ~ youth ~ red ~ south, and wisdom ~ elderly ~ black ~ north.

Ideally the young should be active but willing to listen, while the old should be wise and ready to instruct, so that these roles can easily succeed from one to the other. Greater latitude is tolerated in men more than in women, so young men might be crazy and active, but women should always remain good and wise to remain stable, tempered, quiet, and soothing. Some biological males, known as woman-hearted, became transgendered and strictly subscribed to the good of the female role, spending all their time among women (see "Transgenders" below).

The core of every person was the heart, which is why the Cheyenne call themselves "those like-hearted." Over a lifetime, the heart of a person filled with life history, spiritual growth, physical identity, and names; each tribal member did not develop as a distinct individual but as a part of the larger whole.

Associates of any person influence character. If these are crazy – liars, drunks, or thieves – s/he will turn out the same. For this reason, the Keeper of the Sacred Arrows for the Southern Oklahoma Cheyenne or of the Sutaio Sacred Hat for the Northern Cheyenne in Montana must be a superior person so that all Cheyenne will benefit. In ancient times, the Arrow Keeper indicated his willingness to suffer for his people by having four strips of flesh taken from along his arms, shoulders, back, and legs, along with a circle and crescent cut from his chest.

Though underreported, young men often lived by themselves, either roaming around the village to keep it safe by their unpredictable actions or in separate quarters, as was the case with the Gwich'in (Kutchin) boys dorms, which housed those males between the ages of fourteen and twenty-five.[52]

---

[48] A Irving Hallowell, The Ojibwa of Berens River 1992: 88.

[49] Landes, *The Prairie Potawatomi*: 186.

[50] Landes, *The Ojibwa Woman*: 6, 62.

[51] Ann Terry Sawyier Strauss, The Meaning of Death in Northern Cheyenne Culture 1978.

[52] Richard Slobodin, Kutchin, 1981: 524 Fig 7.

More rare still were Iroquois virgin dorms, *ieouinnon,* where girls were kept busy at minor tasks, helped by very young boys as servants.[53] More commonly, some Ioway and other women took up an amazon-Iike warrior role when they received a vision from Thunderers.[54]

Girls

rhe onset of menstruation was marked and celebrated throughout the Vmericas, largely because of the arrival of a woman's ability to confer life set ler apart from male activities concerned with killing, defending, and boasting.[55] For Kansas Potawatomi, menstrual blood endangered all medicine, youth, "tender" growths of any life form, and masculine life and appurtenances.[56] In one of the few accounts of its origin,lis said that the first [127] menstruation was a punishment upon young girls who mocked an old man with bleeding eyes. "If the girls had not made fun of the old man, men would menstruate [through the eyes] instead of women and would have to sleep outside alone for a certain length of time."[57]

For Dakota, "femaleness, as menstrual and lochial [birthing] bloods, was inimical to men, weapons, and horses. Despite this dogma, a few individual women in each village did drive buffalo on horseback, and did stalk, scalp, and mutilate enemy; often they were young women, of child-bearing age."[58] Formalized Dakota feasts were held as elaborate tests for chastity and provided outlets for honor and malice as a consequence of accepted or failed accusations of undue familiarity.

Among Ioway, fathers with high aspirations had to have their daughters formally tattooed before puberty, "or blood will flow from the wound in the forehead and spoil the mark," while loway boys were tattooed all life long in recognition of brave deeds.[59] Among related Siouian Oto, girls of high family were sometimes laced up into a buffalo hide at night,[60] similar to Lakota's use of string chastity belts.[61]

Among Tlingit and other Northwest nations, girls entered puberty with a feast to celebrate the insertion of a labret beneath the lower lip, reminding her to watch her mouth in terms of what she said, ate, and did.[62]

Marriage

All adults should wed. In considering partners, the Kickapoo looked for a wife who was

---

[53]   Joseph Francois Lafitau, *Customs of the American Indians* 1974 [1724]: 129; David Blanchard, "... To the Other Side of the Sky" 1982: 77-102.

[54] Alanson Skinner, Ethnology of the Ioway Indians 1926: 104, 106.

[55] Thomas Buckley{ "Buckley, Thomas" } and Alma Gottlieb, *Blood Magic* 1988; Mourning Dove 1990.

[56] Landes, *The Prairie Potawatomi*: 167.

[57] Thelma Adamson, *Folk-Tales of the Coast Salish* 1934: 95.

[58] Ruth Landes, *Mystic Lake Sioux* 1968: 40, 48.

[59] Skinner, Ioway Indians: 265, 269.

[60] Whitman, *The Oto*: 72.

[61] Hassrick, The Sioux: 124.

[62] Aldona Jonaitis, Women, Marriage, Mouths, Feasting ~ Tlingit Labrets 1988.

good-humored, honest, clean, fine-cooking, and hardworking, and a husband to be a sober hunter with integrity.[6355] New Yurok spouses exchanged the names of their hometowns to strengthen their co-identification.[6456] Anyone unwed among Tohono O'Odham was presumed to have a snake for a spouse whose potency left them uninterested in humans.[6557]

Among tribes from the Great Lakes, a *Manabus* robe, named for their Great Hare culture hero, was made of deerskin and adorned with tiny metal cones and a strategic hole. The robe was loaned or hired out from its owner to newlyweds to assure strong and healthy births.[6658]

Ojibwa and Plains nations might hold a divorce dance to display the fortitude and bravery of "discarding something that is dear."[6759] Plains husbands ritu-ally transferred spiritual power through access to younger wives,[6860] though shameless wives could and did arrange fatal "accidents" for demanding husbands.[6961]

Careers

Men and women had distinct, separate but equal,[7062] lives that mutually supported the good of die community and nation. For Delaware, man was container and woman contained. For Mescalero Apache, man is shield and protector; woman is center and protected.[7163] For Cheyenne, man is spiritual, woman is material.[7264] Since the fishing Sta:lo Salish regard dieir community as a salmon, men are its nose and women its backbone.[7365] [128]

Some activities were biologically determined, as when Coyote decreed for the Karuk that only women would pound acorns because a man's baby maker would get in the way; instead, a man hunted and fished for meat to eat with acorn soup.[7466] Pottery was a job for women working in seclusion since it involved a war between Thunderbirds and Watersnakes, as noted by the cracks that could appear to ruin a vessel. Like all else, this skill among Hidatsa derived from the proper ownership of sacred medicine bundles, with potters specifically owning this right through Big Bird, River, or Snake bundles belonging to matrilineal kin.[7567]

---

[63] Ritzenthaler and Peterson, The Mexican Kickapoo: 62.

[64] Lucy Thompson, *To the American Indian* 1991 [1916]: 190.

[65] Ruth Underhill, The Autobiography of a Papago Woman 1936: 27.

[66] Skinner, The Menomini Indians: 30; Observations on the Ethnology of the Sauk: 32.

[67] Landes, The Ojibwa Woman: 89.

[68] Alice Kehoe, The Function of Ceremonial Sexual Intercourse among the Northern Plains Indians 1970.

[69] George Bird Grinnell, *Blackfoot Lodge Tales* 1962 [1892]: 78.

[70] John Reed Swanton, Social Organization and Social Usages of the Indians of the Creek Confederacy 1928a: 385.

[71] Claire Farrer, *Living Life's Circle* 1991: 149.

[72] Strauss, Being Human: 396.

[73] Crisca Bierwert, Tracery in the Mistlines 1986: 340. Terms in nearby Salishan languages indicate that women are backbone, men are head, and chiefs are nose.

[74] John P Harrington, Tobacco among the Karuk Indians of California 1932: 99.

[75] Alfred W Bowers, Hidatsa Social and Ceremonial Organization 1965: 373-374.

Parry Island Ojibwa urge hunters not to concentrate entirely on their prey,[76][68] while Tsimshian[77][69] insist on total dedication to the game being sought. When planting, Jicarilla "men made holes with digging sticks. The women and children followed, dropping in the seeds and covering them up. It was believed that the crops would grow faster if the children, who were still growing, put the seeds in the ground." Children also kept birds and rodent pests off these fields, each bounded by a turkey feather set in its four corners.[78][70] Pawnee planted an even number of maize hills in their gardens since corn was a woman and breasts are paired.[79][71] Delaware kept the sanctity of their corn fields by preventing any misuse by humans or pollution by animals.

A proper Delaware adult displayed responsibility, respect, courtesy, self-discipline, generosity, and social graces. Their lives were a blend of "personal autonomy, respect for others, clan membership, selfless motivations, pleasant attitude, proper upbringing, and diligent training towards a productive adulthood as a man or woman" to produce children who were "empty" until becoming fulfilled by a "gifted" partnership with an immortal, or *manitu.* Delaware men worked constantly while women labored in spurts, exchanging the products of their separate labors. In old age, elders gained respect and attention for their wise advice, while extremely old women, after a life of dedication, finally had total freedom of expression.[80][72]

Men would fast, pray, and abstain from sexual relations before a hunt. Plateau women engage in ritual chastity before root digging.[81][73] These females were strictly forbidden to come within a half-mile of a salmon weir, yet one woman with Salmon power frequently swam around an Okanogan River trap without causing harm.[82][74]

Women generally had an especially constrained life, since they were under greater public scrutiny and pressure to conform to the roles of wife and mother. Exceptional visions allowed women to break from this mold, but only at the cost of great hardship. Flagrantly promiscuous, lewd, foreign, or adulterous women, particularly if without male protectors, were subject to gang rape,[83][75] euphemistically called "running through the meadow."[84][76] During heated arguments, women occasionally damaged or killed men by yanking out their organ.[85][77]

As a whole, the Plains culture area recognized at least six gender roles. Aside from "natural, normal" men and women, there were the *berdache,* contrary, or a super warrior who did everything backwards, amazon, and virgin. Among these famous women warriors were Apache Lozen (sister of Victorio), Kootenay Water Sitting Grizzly, Blackfeet Running Eagle, Ojibwa Chief Earth Woman, and Cheyennes Buffalo Calf Road Woman and Yellow-Haired Woman.[86][78]

---

[76] Jenness, Ojibwa Indians: 22.

[77] Jay Miller, *Tsimshian Culture* 1997.

[78] Veronica E Velarde Tiller, *The Jicarilla Apache Tribe* 1992: 27.

[79] Gene Weltfish, *The Lost Universe* 1971: 124.

[80] Jay Miller, The Delaware As Women 1974; Delaware Personhood 1991: 18, 23.

[81] Laura Klein and Lillian Ackerman, *Women and Power in Native North America* 1995: 95.

[82] Leslie Spier, The Sinkaietk or Southern Okanogan 1938: 160.

[83] James Adair, *History of the American Indians* 1930 [1775]: 149 # 55.

[84] John Reed Swanton, Source Material for the Social and Ceremonial Life of the Choctaw Indians Office 1931: 111.

[85] Morris Opler, Apache Odyssey 1969: 239; Colin Galloway, *Crown and Calumet* 1987: 171.

[86] Kimberly Buchanan, Apache Women Warriors 1986; Carolyn Foreman, Indian Women Chiefs 1954.

[129]

Lakota male virtues are bravery, fortitude, generosity, and wisdom; those of a female are bravery, generosity, truthfulness, and fecundity,[87] with patience and wisdom also mentioned.[88] Affinities with nature made elk the "Dakota symbol of masculine beauty, virility, virtue, and charm."[89] Overall for Lakota, "Man is a subset of woman, not only in the empiricality of childbirth but in linguistic terminology which identifies the stages of life."[90]

An Oto man was courageous, gentle, truthful, and generous; an Oto woman was ideally faithful, hardworking, and motherly.[91]

According to the Tohono O'Odham moral code, an adult should be industrious, enduring, skilled, and prepared for battle. In addition, a woman should seclude herself during menstruation, since this blood caused deer to avoid hunters, shaman's crystals to rot, and tobacco plants to shrivel,[92] Successful visionaries were called *meeters,* such as Hawk meeter. Coyote meeter, and so forth. Full time professional deer hunters remained in the mountains all year, except for two months, with male kin tending fields for him in return for venison.[93] "To many ... a good field, enough cattle to provide occasional meat and money, a few horses for prestige, and plenty of rain would make an ideal combination."[94]

Ultimately, however, final judgements about a person's life were and are made on the issues of their overall character, contributions, and determination to aid the greater good, along with occasional reports of their fate in the afterworld.

Transgenders

Because Natives lived within a totally engendered universe, special intermediaries functioned to keep it from halving or fragmenting. Often these were shamans, mediating among lonely mortals, sympathetic immortals, inter-species needs, and personal motivations. Certain animals, such as bears or frogs, also played this role across life-forms.[95]

Yet recent attention has focused only on transgendered humans,[96] often called *berdaches* as this term has been redefined and laundered by usage. At base, many may have had biologically androgynous bodies that encouraged them to take a special course in life. Others

[87] Hassrick, *The Sioux*: 32, 39.

[88] Marla Powers, *Oglala Women* 1986; William Powers, *Oglala Religion* 1977: 62.

[89] Powers, *Oglala Religion*: 77.

[90] Powers, *Oglala Religion*: 198.

[91] Whitman, *The Oto*: 63.

[92] Ruth Underhill, Social Organization of the Papago Indians 1939: 80, 163.

[93] Ruth Underhill, Papago Indian Religion 1946: 17, 86.

[94] Alice Josephy, Rosamond Spicer, and Jane Chesky, *The Desert People* 1949: 59.

[95] Jay Miller, People, Berdache, and Left-Handed Bears 1982.

[96] Claude Schaeffer, The Kutenai Female Berdache 1965; Charles Callender and Lee Kochems, The North American Berdache 1983; Charles Callender and Lee Kochems, Men and Not-Men: Male Gender-Mixing Statuses and Homosexuality 1986; Sandra Hollimon, The Third Gender in Native California: Two-Spirit Undertakers Among the Chumash and their Neighbors 1998; Sue-Ellen Jacobs, Wesley Thomas, and Sabine Lang, eds, *Two-Spirit People* 1997; and Will Roscoe, *Changing Ones* 1998.

may have had psychological or societal pressures to assume this role, which was not always as honored and esteemed as some recent authors have projected, though drunk whites were almost killed once by Creeks for undressing a woman suspected to be a hermaphrodite.[9789]

Hidatsa *berdaches* had strong religious sanction and hereditary ties to certain mystic bundles. S/He took up this career after a vision of Holy Woman Above, dressed as women but worked much harder, and was the brother or son of a man holding tribal rites in the bundles of Woman Above or Holy Woman. Though hemmed in by especially intricate taboos, they were very nurturing, often rearing orphans, taking center stage in ceremonies, and elaborating craftworks in skins and beads.[9890]

But Lakota *berdache,* whose "heart of a woman" was often held in high derision, lived at the edge of a camp with widows, orphans, and social misfits.[9991] Yet they also were regarded as *wakan,* or sacred, and gave special names [130] to children. In addition, it seems that warriors visited these Lakota for sexual release before battles and expeditions. In the Southwest, Quechan parents of transvestites were said to be ashamed.[10092]

Ruth Landes provided sensitive characterizations that above all indicate that a *berdache* was regarded as extraordinary, among both Potawatomi and Mystic Lake Sioux.[10193] Such a Dakota *berdache* was gently exiled from "his" natal village, as his interests became evident, "by adopting female forms of speech, female fears of water and of bodily exposure ... as always the lurer, the coquette, acting like cousin or sister-in-law of all the village men," commending "himself to women by his industry and helpfulness, and to men by his complete hospitality.... He was accepted by the strange group in a spirit of gingerly tolerance comparable to that covering a truce with enemy visitors; he was treated to the teasing, bitter, flirting conduct of cross-cousins and siblings-in-law.'[10294]

Leaders

As a general rule, officials on earth took their powers, positions, and authority from identical immortals in the heavens.[10395] Differences between leader and led were often imperceptible, yet very real, to the community. In an obvious example, every Ioway chief had two bodyguards who lived with him.[10496]

More typically, only the Chemehuevi "high chief could wear turquoise.[10597] In northwest California, only Karuk rich families had and have a wide, bare, and cleanly kept plot in front of the house where the wife and children live, apart from the abode of husband and sons in the

---

[97] Swanton, Creek Confederacy: 355.

[98] Bowers, Hidatsa Social and Ceremonial Organization: 167.

[99] Hassrick, *The Sioux*: 121.

[100] Daryll Forde, Ethnography of the Yuma Indians 1931: 157.

[101] Landes, *The Prairie Potawatomi*: 182, 195; Mystic Lake Sioux: 31.

[102] Landes, *Mystic Lake Sioux*: 112.

[103] Florence Hawley Ellis, Foreword, Architecture and Dendrochronology of Chetro Ketl 1983: xxiii-xxxviii.

[104] Skinner, Ioway Indians: 205.

[105] Carobeth Laird, *Encounter with an Angry God* 1976; *Chemehuevis* 1976; *Mirror and Pattern* 1984.

sweathouse.[10698] Nearby, ancient houses of the Yurok rich were guarded by rattlesnakes while members achieved luck and wealth through self-denial, prayer, fasting.[10799]

Among Western Apache, a woman chief was noted for her "industry, even temper, avoidance of gossip and trouble making or other quarrels, wise head, and strong body." The children of such leaders stood out as self confident, wise, unafraid, and unembarrassed. In contrast, other women were associated with a butterfly decoration because "women's minds are as flighty as butterflies and must be attracted by something beautiful, just as a butterfly is." At a Victory Dance, men were lewd, while a few loose women exposed themselves for pay.[108100]

In addition to the common joint authority of civil and military leaders for clans, towns, and nations, Ohio Valley tribes, including Shawnee and Miami, recognized similarly paired woman, whose duties of ritual, warfare, and community organization included the disposition of prisoners and the right to force an end to warfare and to community feuds.[109101] As mothers, sisters, and daughters of leading families, they cared for women's matters of planting, cooking, and feasting, when the peace woman cooked white corn and vegetables as the war woman did meats and coarser articles.[110102]

Healing

Health and well-being were topics of private and public concern. As a general rule, specific diseases were caused by an animal species in revenge for [131] human malfeasance, and cured using a particular plant intended to remedy it.[111103] Allowance was always made for individual expression, provided it was sanctioned by a proper vision and continued success. At its most elaborate, Lushootseed shamans cooperated to retrieve lost or stolen souls.[112104]

Though bundles must always be handled with care and respect, one Sauk warrior always smashed his bundle down onto the ground before a battle to make it so enraged that it would take the life of the bravest enemy warrior.[113105] Menominee who dreamed of Thunderers began to worship together, but soon their drum was struck by lightning so they quickly disbanded.[114106]

Among Mvskogi (Creeks), informal "brush schools" taught special cures so that a few youngsters would hire a fasting doctor to spend four days with them, teaching at noon and early sunset.[115107] They could return for advanced training over eight- then twelve-day sessions. Such

---

[106] Harrington, Tobacco among the Karuk: 263 #2.

[107] Thompson, *To the American Indian*: xxiv, 180,100.

[108] Grenville Goodwin, The Social Organization of the Western Apache 1969 [1942]: 167, 183, 306, 566.

[109] Erminie Wheeler-Voegelin, Mortuary Customs of the Shawnee 1944: 403.

[110] Trowbridge, Shawnee Traditions: 12.

[111] Raymond Fogelson, Change, Persistence, and Accommodation in Cherokee Medico-Religious Beliefs 1961: 216; James Howard, with Willie Lena, *Oklahoma Seminoles Medicines, Magic, and Religion* 1984.

[112] Jay Miller, *Shamanic Odyssey* 1988; *Lushootseed Culture and the Shamanic Odyssey* 1999.

[113] Alanson Skinner, Ethnology of the Sauk Indians: War Customs 1925: 84.

[114] Skinner, The Menomini Indians: 47.

[115] John Reed Swanton, Religious Beliefs and Medical Practices of the Creek Indians 1928 # 42: 473-672, 617, 618 1928.

a novice might be buried in a trench with only a cane mouth tube for breathing as a brushfire of leaves swept over his "grave," teaching the curer to cure by being cured.

More public expressions, in the Great Lakes region, ranged from the shaking tent occupied by a shaman with a host of spirits, to the Midewiwin, also known as Grand Lodge or Shaman's Academy, which was revitalized around 1700 by Ojibwa survivors of epidemics and dislocations. Both rites reversed "normal" time and space to make healing that much more sacred. Shaking tent polarities put the spiritual inside and the physical outside.[116][108] Inside, these spirits look like sparks or tiny people sitting upon its tier of hoops with Turtle on the bottom rung.[117][109]

Mide reversals are traced to its bear patron, who is left-handed.[118][110] Divided into earth and sky halves, each half included about four degrees represented by the pelt of an appropriate animal for earth or bird for sky. Wooden pegs with rounded tops were moved over a sand drawing of the lodge to show new members what to do.[119][111]

An initiate was sponsored by wealthy family members and "shot" by a cowry shell called a *megis* to "die" and be revived by senior adepts. Ioway shot an initiate four times in the right shoulder, left shoulder, right leg, and left leg.[120][112] Each Omaha member had two *megis,* believed to be a man and woman pair, to breed progeny of tiny shells that grew larger over time to increase their abilities and wealth.[121][113]

All Native doctors were expected to be wealthy, haughty, and demanding, both for themselves and their spirit partners. Indeed, "Because Jesus healed the sick without payment, he lost his power and perished."[122][114]

Masking

Throughout the Americas, people could enhance or expand their personae by adopting a mask. Matrilineal societies have a greater propensity to use masks, largely because the face is believed to come from the father.[123][115] The most complex expressions of masking are the Kachinas of the Pueblo Southwest, where Edmund Ladd, a Zuni and an anthropologist, reported that when Kokko, or Zuni Kachinas, first danced for humans, women became completely allured and followed them back to the lake of the underworld. Since [132] they were not dead, women could not enter the underworld, languishing there until humans were given the right to bring these masks to life as its actual spirit stood in front of the wearer, its movements distinct but visible in the masker. Every detail of dress and dance had significance, intent, and meaning such that, for example, painting was regarded as a "chromatic prayer."[124][116]

---

[116] Tanner, *Bringing Home Animals*: 218 #8.

[117] A Irving Hallowell, The Role of Conjuring in Saulteaux Society 1942: 51.

[118] Alanson Skinner, Medicine Ceremony of the Menomini, Iowa, and Wahpeton Dakota, With Notes on the Ceremony among the Ponca, Bungi Ojibwa, and Potawatomi 1920: 157.

[119] Vernon Kinietz, *Chippewa Village* 1947: 193; Indians of the Western Great 1940.

[120] Skinner, Medicine Ceremony: 165.

[121] Reo Fortune, *Omaha Secret Societies* 1932: 109.

[122] Jenness, Ojibwa Indians: 76.

[123] Miller, *Tsimshian Culture*: 102.

[124] Polly Schaafsma, *Kachinas in the Pueblo World* 1994: 18, 30, 171.

Sorcery

Greed, selfishness, envy, and revenge were causes for sorcery.[125,17] Most people were wise and cautious enough to take precautions, especially with body waste. All cut hair was burnt, for example, because there "is no way of countering sorcery that used human hairs."[126,118] In all, about one-tenth of the universe had hostile intent and needed to be restrained or avoided.

Death

Death was not the inevitable end of every short life. Shawnees were promised to live for "200 years," so deaths before that were someone's fault. Those dead who had been especially bad during life were reduced to ashes.[127,119] Just before and after death, stock was taken of a person's life. Often the heir to an office or position only received the final linchpin of vital knowledge as a last gasp to safeguard it for the holder as long as possible.[128,120] Effective transitions, therefore, required stable societies, adding another dimension to the destruction of Native lifeways that came from the epidemics rampant in the Americas before Europeans actually settled.

A Menominee soul on the way to the underworld was judged by a dog at a log bridge, either continuing on or plunging into the abyss if it had mistreated pets. The underworld chief had the arriving soul washed in a large wooden bowl, cured of all ailments, and purged of past memories so as to be endowed with heavenly lore to make them less intelligent but more supernatural than humans.[129,121]

Quileute components include an inner and an outer shade, along with a soul. A week before death, the outer shade went directly to the afterworld, joined a few days later by the inner shade after it had visited favorite places. The recombining of the shades forced the soul to become a ghost, causing death. Each ghost had an elongated human shape, moss covering, long nose, round yellow eyes, crooked gait, and shrill whistle. A spouse could not lie down to sleep for five days, so he or she slept huddled in a large basket. The whole family had to move very slowly and deliberately while mourning, carrying small black stones in their mouths and armpits to limit their speech and movements.[130,122]

Funeral

A Sauk grave was dug by women using "wooden bowls as spades," with the placement sometimes determined by clan. For example, people of the Turkey Clan were buried sitting up,

---

[125] Deward Walker, *Systems of North American Witchcraft and Sorcery* 1970.

[126] Landes, *The Prairie Potawatomi*: 167.

[127] Trowbridge, Shawnee Traditions: 3, 41.

[128] Fortune, *Omaha Secret Societies*: 40, where he likens this fatal transmission to a sort of parricide.

[129] Skinner, The Menomini Indians: 86.

[130] Leo Frachtenberg, Eschatology of the Quileute Indians 1920.

"in some isolated knoll under a tree suitable for a turkey roost."[131123] Females often dug graves because, "a woman has always [133] taken care of a man, all his life."[132124]

Navajo gravediggers prepared by removing all clothes, shutting their mouths, closing off the foreskin with a yucca thread tied in a special knot, heating fire and hot water for a bath afterward, using only gestures, and, later, brushing away all tracks to and from the grave.[133125]

Delawares had a friend speak to the deceased at the graveside to release its soul. Mourners are expected to linger around the grave, as it was considered disrespectful to rush away. For this reason, many of the grieving lamenters feasted there. Later, at home, all washed in cedar smoke to cleanse any harmful effect. For the next four nights a fire burned at the head of the grave to light the way for the soul along the Milky Way where a dog blocked the way of animal abusers. Unami Delawares hold a feast after these four days, while Munsi waited twelve days. Many families held and still hold annual memorials, where steam coming off fresh cooked food provides its essence to their deceased love ones before the living consumed the rest.[134126]

Most families took care to keep very powerful objects out of coffins or graves since these might be used, without deliberate malice, to harm the living. Throughout the Great Lakes region, Midewiwin members were buried with substitute emblems, particularly their cowry shell, ~ *megis*. Thus, instead of an actual gastropod, a stone or button was placed with the body out of concern that a *megis* could restore ~ revive the corpse, sometimes with harmful intent.[135127]

Remains were variously treated – some buried intact, while others dismembered tribespeople to dispose of the parts separately, with all or some of the parts cremated, as when the heart of an Achumawi chief or shaman was released into the sky to become a star.[136128]

Among the Subarctic Athapaskan, the Carrier, or porteur of French Canadians, were so named because a wife carried the cremated bones of her husband back to die summer salmon-fishing town if he died during the winter. This enabled his death to be noted and his title and consequent ownership rights to be passed on to his heir at a witnessed public feast.[137129]

Deading

The fate of the soul was largely the result of the life of the body and its treatment before final disposition. Often the body disassembled into its various components. Consciousness or life-essence was represented variously by breath, clear body fluids – like spit, tears, and sweat, blood, and flesh, in addition to bones, hair, or several intangible souls, shades, shadows, ghosts, or spirits. Cherokee recognized that each of these substances decomposes at different times and they accordingly treated each span as a further release of the life essence.[138130]

The loss of breath often began the countdown, followed by clear effluvia. Pawnee regarded a pipestem as "symbolic of the human windpipe and the breath was considered the

---

[131] Skinner, Observations on the Ethnology of the Sauk Indians: 37.

[132] Wheeler-Voegelin, Mortuary Customs of the Shawnee and Other Eastern Tribes: 383. [141]

[133] *Navajo Blessingway Singer*, Charlotte Frisbie and David McAllester, eds, 1978: 197.

[134] Miller, Delaware Personhood.

[135] Kinietz, *Chippewa Village*: 144, 208.

[136] Merriam, *Annikadel*: 49.

[137] Antonia Mills, *Eagle Down is Our Law* 1994: 40.

[138] Fogelson, Change, Persistence, and Accommodation.

essence of life itself."[139][131] The power of a Tohono O'Odham (Papago) shaman resided in quartz crystals primordially formed from the solidified spit of one of their creators.[140][132] Throughout the Americas, quartz crystals were the most usual insignia ofa shaman, suggesting that, regardless [134] of locale or language affiliations, this association of shamans, crystals, and clear fluids was an ancient one. A Kootenay hunter spit on his arrow to make it fly true, implying that his goodwill and respect for the game animal was given in return for its life.[141][133]

After death, among Jicarilla, if the dead had participated in sexual relations with outsiders their ghosts transmogrified into the animal form of that group, such as a Navajo Cougar, Ute Owl, Pueblo Prairie Dog, Mescalero Wolf, Mexican Burro, or American Mule.[142][134]

In the Northwest, a Makah ghost repeatedly returned to its corpse so as to remove all its flesh in order to reconstitute that body in the afterlife.[143][135]

After fleeing British depredations in the Carolinas for haven among Iroquois now in Canada, Tutelos, though long sociopolitically extinct, still hold a spiritual adoption within a year of death "to bring back the soul" for one night before it travels over the sun's rays on the next dawn to its "permanent celestial abode."[144][13]

Mexican Kickapoo held a memorial adoption ceremony within four years of a death or "the spirit turns into a moth and dies of hunger," blaming close relatives.[145][137] If a Shawnee was buried without rites, he or she was reborn a dwarf.[146][138]

Conclusions

These ethnographic bits, how-some-ever derived from memory, have the virtues of clear fact stated in proper context in Native voice. Strung together, they speak of integrity and coherence across the continent for notions of personhood as mixings, infusions, and layerings to combine spark, bone, flesh, soul, shadow, immortal partner, and ghost into a living whole that reverses the same series at death. They also speak of flux and flow in ways that many Americans would take for ambiguity and confusion, but this is the incomprehension of outsiders.

Throughout Native North America, an engendered person was and is the predominant outcome of genetics; anatomy; moods and attitudes; outside pressures from parents, peers, self, and role models; community or family needs; training; inheritances; namings; and outcome of vision quest, all accordingly expressed by appearance, gesture, ornament, clothing, and lifestyle.

Gender, for example, is open and fluid, shifting at the moment of birth, over a lifetime, or across generations if *there* is reincarnation.[147][139] One bewilderingly complex framework for modern sociological gender separates sex as biological, sexuality as erotic practice, sexual identity as type designations, gender identity as personal feelings of patterned subjectivity,

---

[139] Weltfish, *Lost Universe*: 475.

[140] Underhill, Papago Indian Religion: 271.

[141] Claude Schaeffer, Bear Ceremonialism of the Kutenai Indians 1966: 13, 48 #6.

[142] Morris Opier, Myth and Practice in Jicarilla Apache Eschatology 1947: 137.

[143] James Swan, The Indians of Cape Flattery 1870: 84.

[144] Frank Speck, The Tutelo Spirit Adoption Ceremony 1942: 10.

[145] Latorres, *The Mexican Kickapoos*: 283.

[146] Wheeler-Voegelin, Mortuary Customs: 406.

[147] Mills and Slobodin, *Amerindian Rebirth*.

gender role as prescriptive and culture-specific expectations of appropriateness, and gender-role identity as personal lived commitment to expected ideals.[148][140]

Yet "Chromosomes, hormones, sperm production, and egg production, all fail to differentiate all men from all women or to provide a common core within each sex." Instead, genitals and then body type provide primary and secondary attributes for assigning gender, though tertiary ones are usually more significant as culturally defined by posture, movement, dress, adornment, image, sexuality, intonation, speech, and job skills.

Additional influences are gender symbolism of perceived dichotomies, [135] gender structure dividing necessary social activities, and individual gender of socially construed personal identity, which is always "mediated by race, class, ethnicity, and sexual orientation" in lieu of "the numerous privileges of white, heterosexual, middle-class feminists who have the luxury of experiencing only one mode of oppression."

Even more extreme is one attempt to derive transgendered males, subcate-gorized as military, diplomatic, domestic, and religious *berdaches* with specialized functions, from rape and brutalization because "warfare was the incubator of civil institutions,"[149][141] in blatant disregard of the compelling Native motivations from personal psychology and sacred vision.

For Indiens, everything is connected in a web of energy and thought, uniting each and all together, via sharing across species and beings to hopefully benefit all. Indeed, denying charity can have unpleasant or fatal consequences.[150][142] The living tree used for a cradle-board has as much to do with raising a healthy child as parents and kin, food, clothing, and shelter.

Danger and harm came from "the devil's tenth," that part of participatory existence that was selfish, hurtful, and damaging. While theft, torture, and murder were practiced on enemies, they were sternly repressed at home. Thus, most intra-hostility had to be covert, producing criminals involved in sadism, sorcery, ill will, and abuse. Harm thereby worked by insinuation, though sometimes it became outright and deliberate. In vivid image, it was parasitic like a stylops, a blob that enters through a bee's skin, propagates through a vague brood canal, and, by absorption, transforms its host as colors brighten, behavior changes, and gender switches.[151][143]

In this heightening, a parasite is a perversion of the keen regard that should be given to the boundaries and passages making life possible, particularly the inter-species requirement to make up for whatever another "lacks." Thus Yup'ik turn driftwood to alleviate its boredom, give fresh water to slain seals, and provide sea oil to land mammals.[152][144] Thus, a good person constantly fills gaps to keep his, her, and their community whole.

American Indian Culture And Research Journal 24 (1): 121-141 2000

---

[148] Mary Hawkesworth, Confounding Gender, 1997 Signs 22 (3): 651, 653, 656, 661, 669.

[149] Richard Trexler, *Sex and Conquest* 1995: 64, 82, 102, 141.

[150] Basso, *Wisdom Sits in Places*: 24.

[151] Annie Dillard, *Pilgrim at Tinker Creek* 1974: 237, 239.

[152] Ann Fienup-Riordan, *The Real People and the Children of Thunde*r 1991; *Boundaries and Passages* 1994.

54

Indien Personhood II:
Baby in the Oven Sparks Being in the World
Commentary

The process, particularly as a series of sequential timings, of creating an Indien person, according to accepted ("traditional") beliefs, highlights the importance of fire, cooking, infusions, and, ultimately, dissolution.[153]1 The same pan-human use of fire, distinguishing them from animals, also accounts for the gestation of a baby, suggesting that ontology here recapitulates cosmology.[154]2 Indeed, the universal equation among the heart of a person, hearth of a house, beacon of a town, and sun of the sky underscores the importance of heat and light for all healthy, communal life.[155]3 In stark contrast, the "dark" includes disease, harm, danger, and death.

Though underreported, links between sparks, spirits, and life have been confirmed for the Ojibwa Shaking Tent, Delaware curings, Lakota Yuwipi, and, more universally, the flames, or tongues of fire, of Pentecost.[156]4 Moreover, esoteric beliefs among Pawnee, Delaware, and Lushootseed equate the kindling of fire by friction with coitus.[157]5

Each person is an especial instance of "mind" – that primordial vitality, force, movement, energy, and power deified by a high god or creator localized at the center of each tribal universe. According to southern California [156] Luiseño, "All things that manifest or are suspected to possess *ayelkwi* ~ knowledge-power are considered 'persons.'"[158]6

In the abstract, each person possesses four aspects that may be characterized as anatomy, attitudes, abilities, and associations.

Anatomy

In Plains Cheyenne belief, a proper person was conceived of blood from the mother, substance (flesh) from the father, and two blessings from the Creator – a life soul indicated by

---

[153] As in this article's antecedent Indien Personhood 2000, I use the European solution for distinguishing those indigenous to India from those of the United States by the expedient of a single vowel (A or E): Indian for the East Indies and Indien for the West Indies.

[154] Sometimes only mortal humans possess fire, as among Crow *Absoroka* who say their dead go to the Other Side Camp, inhabited by spirits, ghosts, and ancestors who are collectively called Without Fires according to the warrior Peter Nabokov, ed, *Two Leggings* 1967: 156.

[155] Jay Miller, The Matter of the (Thoughtful) Heart 1980; High-Minded High Gods in North America 1980.

[156] A Irving Hallowell, *The Role of Conjuring in Salteaux Society* 1942: 51; Jay Miller, Delaware Personhood 1991; Yuwipi information from Miller's field notes.

[157] James Murie, Ceremonies of the Pawnee 1981: 150; Delaware and Lushootseed statements are from Miller's field notes.

[158] Raymond White, Luiseño Social Organization 1963 48 (2): 143.

the heartbeat, pulse, blinking eyelids, food digestion, growth, and the like; a consciousness inhaled at birth indicated by breathing, speech, understanding, and access to cosmic power.[159]7

In greater detail, Alaskan Tlingit conceptualize the person as a container for holding the "mind" inside at the heart, surrounded by bones, flesh, and skin. As framework, the skeleton consisted of a spine and eight long bones, which hardened over a lifetime, located in the four limbs. Material, mortal components came from the father, while immaterial and immortal aspects derived from the mother, who represented her crest's matriline.[160]8

While each child represented a successful conjoining of kin dreams, desires, hopes, and prayers, its external gender was sometimes determined by which parent reached orgasm first or which possessed the stronger or more powerful will; at other times, a child's sex was left to greater cosmic forces. For example, among Quebec Inuit, couples yearning for a daughter set up their tent facing inland and far from shore; for a son, their tent faced the sea at the tideline, "the domain of the hunter and the large marine animals."[161]

In some sense, the pregnant woman provides an oven for the fetus, where water and blood in her womb provide the medium that receives semen from the father to ignite the cooking process of creation. Their heated conjunction congeals into infusions of ever increasing solidity, density, and growth that becomes the baby. In this manner, blood became flesh, semen became bone, and water became clear fluids, lymph, and fibers. The insertion of soul(s) produces a heartbeat, then a pulse, then a breath, most evident as condensed vapor. Similarly, delineation of a face leads to a permanent image that casts a shade ~ shadow which detaches at death and may continue on.

Full-bodied, a baby takes on peculiarities of appearance and attitude derived from its ancestry, both human and cosmic, and from experiences of the parents. Just as her blocking of a doorway will complicate delivery, so his staring at a rabbit will cause a harelip. Thus, both parents must constrain and modulate their actions and thoughts in the best interests of the birth to come. Serious sin or immorality of either parent results in a stillbirth, interfamily accusations of neglect, and, potentially, a divorce.

While life is often set off by a spark, the infant only receives this animating gift at birth, thereby sustaining the body heat its mother had provided until then. Indeed, this link between motherhood and ovens is confirmed by the widespread belief tabooing males away from both a birth and a pit oven while in use.[162]10 [157]

Attributes

Since Tlingit women provide the immortal and men the mortal aspects of life, a baby's face comes from its father. While each combination is unique, its personality traits derive from inherent links to relatives, as modified by social claims to adoptions, totems, crests, clans,

---

[159]   Anne Terry Sawyier Strauss, Northern Cheyenne Ethnopsychology 1975; Being Human in the Cheyenne Way 1976.

[160]   Sergei Kan, *Symbolic Immortality* 1989: 51, 52.

[161]   Bernard Saladin D'Anglure, Inuit of Quebec 1984: 496.

[162]   . For a summary of this pit oven taboo for men among the Salish of North America and Ge of South America See Claude Levi-Strauss, *The Naked Man* 1981: 612-613.

phratries, or moieties. Since many of these are named for animals, certain zoological traits were also expected to be displayed.

For example, in the Abenaki charter epic of the Maritimes, Giant Frog swallowed all the waters, causing a drought, and everyone began to die of thirst. People moaned that they were as dry as some animal – a turtle, beaver, wolf, trout, or haddock, to name a few. Their culture hero killed Frog, then toppled a birch tree onto its body to expel the water. Gushing down the trunk and branches, this flood formed river systems with a pond in place of the leaf at the end of each twig. As water reached the ancestors, some of them plunged in to drink, immediately changing into the animal whose thirst they claimed. Others remained human but took their named animal as the sign, insignia, badge, or totem to their ancestral lands, including camps and hunting territory, along a particular stretch of waterway.

Families were expected to inherit some physical attributes from their animal. For example, among Maine Penobscots, "The members of the Whale family (Stanislaus) are pointed out as large, portly, and dark persons, those of the Rabbit family (Newell) as small, timid, and weak, those of the Bear family (Mitchell 2) as orderly and dignified, and so on."[163]11

During a lifetime, moreover, character is strongly influenced by foods, friends, and other associates, both good or bad. Ideally, a person achieved final maturity and full respect as a grandparent, raising a second generation with less demands on earning a living, a parental task.

Styles of hair, clothing, and ornaments reinforce male or female identity. Sometimes, berdache wear clothing of both genders to emphasize their intermediate status, but babies with confusing genitalia were dressed as girls simply because boys went nude, as with the Nuu-chah-nulth founder of a famous whaling shrine until he forced the issue by raping two women.[164]12 Among Lushootseed, where few or loose clothing was worn, obvious anatomy provided primary identity since transgenders are always said to be "acting like" their adopted cross-gender role.[165]13

Abilities

Kinship also produced predisposition to particular careers, tasks, and specialties, as in Native California.[166] However, techniques were never enough for success, which relied first and foremost on access to or reserves of power provided by a guide, partner, or guardian met during a quest or vision. In the most dramatic, if extreme, example, an encounter with Thunder, especially as a lightning bolt (a flame writ across the sky), a Lakota visionary became a *heyoka*, a "contrary" warrior doing everything backwards. With the same intensity, for Skidi Pawnee, "Each step in the Creation was achieved through two thunderi storms, one to create the lifeless form, the other to revitalize it; [158] and, as the world was created in tempest, so every spring the

---

163 Frank Speck, Abenaki Clans – Never 1934 37: 528-530 1934; Malecite Tales 1917 30: 480-481 1917.

164 Arnold Pilling, Cross-Dressing and Shamanism 1997: 69-99; Aldona Jonaitis, The *Yuquot Whaler's Shrine* 1999: 145.

165 Jay Miller, *Lushootseed Culture and the Shamanic* 1999: 96.

166 William McKern, Functional Families of the Patwin 1922.

[thunder] storms revivified the dormant earth, signalling the beginning of the new year and the renewal of all things. . . . The male storm fertilized the female earth."[167]15

Yet no life runs entirely smoothly. In the event of serious dysfunction or misfortune, a person may default on hopes and expectations. Sometimes, inability to assume proper or expected male or female roles leads to cross-dressing and a transgender identity, sometimes as punishment for charges of cowardice and treachery.

Associations

Any and all of these serial infusions and additions is engendered as manly or womanly, so any person can and does combine both male and female attributes ranging from the mind, body, dress, and skills to strong spiritual influences. Overall preponderance of one gender over the other(s), however, determines personal identity, role, and activities. An equal balance between the two, however, seems to result in an honored transgender or berdache identity.

Disease, despair, disruption, or harm disable a person through the ill will of powerful others, contact with dangerous substances, puncture by a sharp object magically shot by a hired sorcerer, violation of taboos, or a general lack of self-care. Most can be cured or put right by shamans with powerful immortal allies, but some prove fatal.

Attacks of witchcraft were preconditioned by social anxiety about food, sex, health, success, honor, as well as intensifying frustrations dealing with kin, kith, and competing access to resources.[168]16

Dissolution

At death, or grave illness, the series that began life repeats in the same order to end it, starting with breath and ending with the skull, long bones, and valued possessions such as stone tools. At least one soul became a ghost or other postmortem residues. Another soul went to the afterworld, perhaps to reincarnate in the same family or another species.[169]17 Other souls in the joints, blood, or pulse points either dissolved or took on independent existences.

Generally, the timed diffusions within this series were marked by rituals, memorials, or post-funerals held by family members or the community for its deceased leaders. After the flesh was gone or removed, the bones could be bundled for secondary burial, sometimes in a communal ossuary, as among the Huron.[170]18 Skulls and stone tools were left at shrines, while in central California cremated remains were re-cremated at a rite called Lonewis a year later.[171]19 The advantage of these post-mortuary events was that they could be regularly scheduled because the timed series was generally known and guests could be invited with advance notice, unlike the death itself, which was rarely convenient. [159]

---

[167] Susan Golla, Skidi Pawnee Religion 1975: 43-44.

[168] Deward Walker, *Witchcraft and Sorcery of the American Native Peoples* 1989.

[169] Antonia Mills and Richard Slobodin, *Amerindian Rebirth* 1994.

[170] Bruce Trigger, The Huron 1969: 106-112.

[171] Robert Heizer, California # 8, 1978: 268, 297, 776.

Person II

Finale

Today, as science and medicine dominate knowledge of the person and the body, the series of infusions making up an individual involves a genetic code − of four nucleotides of DNA and RNA sequencing amino acids and proteins in chromosomes packaged as egg or sperm to produce a fertile zygote conditioned by intermittent hormones and chemicals, affected or not by radiation and other potent exposures − to produce a fetus that then gestates into a baby in timed trimesters until birth, when training begins to struggle with the tensions between nature and nurture.

Instead, for Native America, a timed series of about twenty infusions (counting by ten fingers and ten toes) combines specific genetic and community traits with cross-species bonds and cosmic forces to create one individual who is more a microcosm than a unique being, adding another spark to a world already aglow with complex, gleaming diversity. More than merely lighting one little candle, Indien personhood seeks to enhance multifaceted existences among all beings, throughout time and over space.

American Indian Culture and Research Journal 24 (3): 155-160 2000

Jay Miller holds degrees from the universities of New Mexico, Rutgers, and Princeton and conducts research throughout Native North America. He has taught at universities and tribal colleges in the United States and in western Canada.

Indien Personhood III: Water Burial
Commentary

In previous commentaries I discussed the generalized concept of personhood across Native North America.[172]1 I included funeral rituals in that discussion because of the widespread belief among Native Americans that how a person comes apart can instruct us on how he or she first came together. Well-known methods for disposing of the deceased's physical remains include burial in earthen graves, exposure on scaffolds, and cremation, but burial in the fourth element, water, is virtually ignored. Suggestions that this type of burial was practiced, however, do exist. Tulsa's Gilcrease Museum holds a huge painting that shows bead-and-feather-dressed Natives in Woodland canoes on the verge of sinking a bundled body. Docents are carefully instructed, however, to explain to visitors that the entire scene is the artist's imagining.[173]2

Yet the deliberate placement of human remains into water deserves careful consideration. Unfortunately, any review of the past literature usually begins and ends with reports that Alaska Natives unceremoniously threw their deceased slaves into the sea. For our own times the immediate image called to mind is the end result of a Mafia contract that has "Guido wearing cement shoes and sleeping with the fishes." Over and above all of these peculiarities, however, is the common knowledge that "water revives," although, as we will see, this is not always a good thing.

Water is both dangerous and powerful. Blessed as holy water it serves in many rituals and other acts of faith; raging as a tsunami, it destroys. Throughout the Americas, dangerous serpents live in water, perhaps most terrifyingly [122] embodied by mythic anacondas in the rivers of the Amazon Basin. Among the Tsimshian of the Northwest Coast, *spanaxnox*, the abodes of wondrous beings (*naxnox*) were ~ are avoided by all those lacking the spiritual strength to deal with them. Other water beings with great power include Tie Snakes of the Southeast, the serpentine Missouri River itself, the "drawer-unders" of the Delaware, and the Underwater Panther ~ *piasaw* of the Midwest.[174]3

Water also transforms, as shown by the amazing change of tadpoles into frogs. Folk beliefs go much beyond this, however, and report such wonders as barnacles becoming geese according to English and Scottish folklore. In the Americas, Pamunkey of Virginia said that frogs turned into birds (shy, webbed-footed sora rails [*Porzana carolina*] who add to the mystery because they migrate at night) after the frost and cold came. Northeastern tribes displaced to Ohio believed that geese changed into beavers to restock dams and that snakes became raccoons for the winter. Micmac of the Canadian Maritimes believed old moose stags went into the sea to

---

[172] See Jay Miller, Indien Personhood I II III.

[173] The Water Burial, by NC Wyeth (oil on canvas), Thomas Gilcrease Museum, Tulsa, OK, Thanks to Drs Jason Jackson and Dan Swan for drawing my attention to this source.

[174] See Robert Hall, *An Archaeology of the Soul* 1997; Ghosts, Water Barriers, Corn, and Sacred Enclosures in the Eastern Woodlands 1976; Jay Miller, *Earthmaker* 1992; *Tsimshian Culture*: A Light through the Ages 1997.

change into whales to revitalize their lives.[175]4 Chitimacha (Shitimushaw) of Louisiana said hailstones provided the spit that turned into clams on tidal beaches.[176]5

The most spectacular evidence for the importance of water burial is the archaeological site called Windover, on the central Florida coast.[177]6 Near the pad for the space launch is a small, dark pond filled with peat Between 7400 and 8500 BP hundreds of bodies were anchored into this shallow muck, held in place by stakes and heavy branches. Half of the pond has been excavated, yielding up 168 burials, evenly divided between males and females and between children (including adolescents) and adults. Of particular note, only females were buried with hollow bone tubes, often decorated with engraved geometric designs. Among the ethnographic Southeast tribes such tubes were symbols of life. In many ways this site points the way to the later development of mounds. Staking the bodies into the peat quagmire, even if it was to keep them submerged during postburial bloating, calls attention to the unstable and unsure world. Grave goods were highly varied, with fabrics especially so. Four types of close twining, one of open twining, one of mat twining, and one of plaiting stand in sharp contrast to the few types of later centuries. Clearly, these Early Archaic peoples had an ideal combination of leisure and skill. Though the bodies were bundled in fabrics and some hides, and some of the stakes stood above the water as (decorated?) markers, these mounded images were not played out on the ground for another millennium or more. Instead, stakes and jellied ooze secured ancestors in this uncertain land, unseen but not forgotten.

The cultural import of water burial best appears in two episodes in mythology. The better-known instance is in the *Popul Vuh*, the sacred text of the Quiche Maya. During their conflict with the Lords of the Underworld ~ *Shibalba*, the hero twins are coerced to jump into a bonfire. Later their bones are ground up and cast into a river, where they revive and reappear with their "same old faces" five days later.[178]7

Less well known is the life of *Ya'ukwckam*, who helped fashion the world of the Kootenay, a language isolate of the Plateau now living in Idaho, Montana, and Canada.[179]** After *Ya'ukwekam* provided the world with necessities for creating bows and arrows (wood, feathers, flint, sinews, tools), the people [3] became angry and resentful of him. They killed *Ya'ukwekam* and threw him into the river, where the fish tried to eat him. When he kicked away the fish, they explained that they were restoring him to life. Then he went ashore and followed his murderers, who had quickly broken camp as soon as they killed him. After careful consideration, he took revenge only on the chief and those who abused his own family.

What is unusual in this story is that there is sufficient biography on *Ya'ukwekam*'s life to explain why he revived. His mother was Young Doe, the granddaughter of Frog, who seems to be everyone's grandmother and is the steward of fresh water. Once, when Young Doe went to the river for a drink, a man named White Stone pulled her in and married her. *Ya'ukwekam* is their child, so he partakes of both land and water elements in his very being. Rejected and killed on land, his watery aspect saved him and, in fact, made him even more formidable because after

---

[175] Frank Speck and John Witthoft, Some Notable life-Histories 1947; Frank Speck, Chapters on the Ethnology of the Powhatan Tribes of Virginia 1928: 340.

[176] John Swanton, Indian Tribes of the Lower Mississippi 1911: 354.

[177] Glen Doran, *Windover* 2002: 11, 12, 18, 106.

[178] See Adrian Recinos, *Popul Vu*h 1950: 155; Dennis Tedlock, *Popul Vuh* 1985: 149.

[179] See Franz Boas, Kutenai Tales 1918: 89, 123.

he came back, people were "more afraid" of him. The irony in all this is that his name in Kootenay means "the one from down under," so his affinity with water would have been obvious to these Native speakers if not to those reading about him in translations.

Last, like the Mafia connection, there are indeed unsavory aspects of water, since the element that can revive can also drown. The best reference I know to such use in sorcery is buried in actual field notes, not in publications. In the early 1950s Skagit elder Charlie Anderson explained to graduate student Sally Snyder,[180]9 in more detail than seems prudent to repeat here, that a shaman could shoot a probe (*liatəd*) into a victim by holding a thin pebble under water in his or her hand until it enlivened and, directed by the shaman's will, shot off and into the other's body. Depending on where it struck, that person became ill or even died outright. In one instance with actual names, the pebble transformed into a bug that did the nasty deed. It was also possible to use a human hair, which was soaked in water and then squeezed until it bled profusely to kill its owner.

Since it was~is quite usual for sorcery to involve human bones, corpse flesh, and so-called ghost powder from human remains in order to kill victims, the availability or even the possibility of waterlogged burials anchored in shallow ponds begins to boggle the imagination. Surely, the regular visitation and continued use of a place like Windover was also, to a degree, a security measure to protect the living of the community.

Because a body is itself almost all water, it is remarkable that the watery grave evoked for sailors and others at sea was not much more common, at least in remote areas where such burials would not pollute a water source. Moreover, a fetus develops in amniotic fluid within the womb, water sustains all life, and after death liquidity is a major feature of decomposition.

Water burial is a way to return a body to its key primal element. It revives and transforms both the soul and the person. Sometimes water burial leads to a new life floating in a womb. Sometimes it disperses to provide a moist and nutrient-rich medium for a vast variety of other lives, making a contribution to the much larger whole.

Jay Miller, PhD, is the coordinator of American Indien Studies at The Ohio State University, where his research spans the breadth of the Americas and the enigma of earthen mounds. He has degrees from the Universities of New Mexico and New Jersey and has taught at colleges throughout the United States and western Canada to classes of all Native or mixed students. [2]

8/24/5 9:38:56 PM

---

[180] Sally Snyder, Skagit River field notes [1952-54], University of Washington Allen Library, Archives Division, Oct 21, 195?: 53.

Ashes Ethereal:
Cremation in the Americas

The ultimate inevitability for most Americans is death, but for the Native peoples of both these continents, death is not a single event but a prolonged process with stages between the living now and the deading after.

On December 12, 1997, I was standing in the chill of the Northwest, freezing from the toes up while waiting to help as needed with an annual "burning for the dead" in preparation for an evening candlelight service in the local smokehouse (Native church) at which everyone in attendance could light a candle in the name of a deceased relative, friend, or loved one. Regardless of religion – Catholic, Pentecostal, Indian Shaker, or traditional – participation was community-wide.

This sacrificial burning required a rectangle about five-by-fifteen feet composed of crushed papers, kindling, and logs. Upon this table, or pyre, plates of varied food were to be placed individually as the name of the person for whom it was intended was loudly called out. In addition to familiar groceries purchased from any store, plates also held Native foods and personal favorites. Inevitably, after an early afternoon of preparations spaced among long waits, the arrival of the officiating ritualists from Canada called for a renewed flurry of activity. All cedar logs had to be replaced with split alder brought from their home across the border. From the moment of their arrival, these ritualists took charge of the situation by organizing us into an effective work force to do their bidding.

Using special words (*dicta* ~ enchantments) inherited only in certain families, both ritualists prepared the blank table before it received thirty plates set in rows. Then more enchantments were recited to fix all the settings before [122] flames were lit. The paper plates burned smoothly and efficiently across the table, which was taken as a good omen. Near the end, certain people were called forward and quietly instructed by the ritualists about specific issues they felt had been expressed by the diners, and everyone was reminded that, via such burnings, those beyond are still with us and able to "discipline" now as they did in the past. Later that night at the candlelight, these female ritualists repeated the same message to the whole gathering.

As I helped pour drinks into cups to go with the plates, I keenly anticipated the fire that would soon be lit, knowing that its heat would come as a welcome relief from the chill of the day. If it had been raining, conditions would have been warmer, but instead it was clear and cold. In either instance, the fire would provide warmth and shelter.

That December day I was well prepared to muse on the meaning of fire, heat, and the dead, leading direcdy, of course, to a consideration of cremation.

Weeks before this burning, I finished teaching linguistics to Tsimshian speakers in northern Canada, and sporadically received commentary on my book-length study published that July.[181]1 In keeping with their nobility and dignity, my Tsimshian students, friends, and family have not yet found damning fault with the book, but rather quietly comment on what details were left out, clearly reminding me that they will always know more about their own culture, wherein light, as in fire, is a key metaphor.

Among my greatest oversights, we all agree, is a failure to emphasize that to this day,

---

[181] Jay Miller, *Tsimshian Culture* 1997.

after a funeral and burial, Tsimshian burn clothing and food on behalf of the deceased. Before the arrival of William Duncan as successful missionary for low church Anglicanism, moreover, Tsimshians cremated their high-ranking dead in a complicated process that might involve removing and burying the heart and filling the chest cavity with cedar bark to aid combustion.[182]2

Recently, prehistorians looking at the five-thousand-year continuum in Prince Rupert Harbor have been denying any archaeological evidence for cremation, regarding it as only an ethnographic tradition, probably introduced from Athabaskans. Unless the ashes were kept together or placed in some kind of urn, there is unlikely to be any permanent evidence, especially since historic cremations took place in a locale away from town. Sometimes ashes were redeposited inside cedar poles or boxes, themselves subject to decay in that damp climate. Indeed, the only lingering evidence for cremation might be stone monuments or memorials, though much less elaborate than the tombs built for cremated Hittite kings.[183]3

Instead, modern Tsimshian provide indirect evidence for the lingering importance of cremation because such incineration of offerings bridges the past and the present, calling for an examination of wider contexts. Was this burning a memento, a survival, a holdover from ancestral cremation? Probably. Yet, more importantly, we must ask, Why cremate in the first place? What are its correlations? What are some cultural explanations? As Richard Huntington and Peter Metcalf have documented, Robert Hertz expostulated that "the fate of the body is a model for the fate of the soul. As the corpse is formless and repulsive during the intermediary period, so the soul of the [123] dead person is homeless and the object of dread."[184]4 Unfortunately, only a few justifications of cremation have been published, phrased within tribal literature, particularly the epics of genesis, creation, reform, or finishing off, near the modern Arizona-California border among the Cahuilla and Maricopa, both considered in this article.

Certainly, cremation is ancient in the Americas, particularly in present Washington State, where, before Kennewick Man, there was Marmes Man from the Palus, a cover term for at least nine ancient humans, including five from a cremation pit in the range of 10,000 years old.[185]5 Further, about 7,000 years ago (8500-6000BP), an Eden-Scottsbluff cremation was left at the Renier Site in northeastern Wisconsin.[186]6 At the archaic mound site of Poverty Point, only cremation is suggested,[187]7 while it is well represented elsewhere during the Archaic Period and after.[188]8

---

[182] Miller, *Tsimshian Culture* 1997: 44.

[183] JG Macqueen, *The Hittites and Their Contemporaries* 1975: 136.

[184] Richard Huntington and Peter Metcalf, *Celebrations of Death* 1979: 14.

[185] Ruth Kirk, *The Oldest Man in America* 1970: 93.

[186] Ronald Mason and Carol Irwin, An Eden-Scottsbluff Burial in Northeastern Wisconsin 1960.

[187] James A Ford and Clarence Webb, *Poverty Point* 1956: 35.

[188] Jane Buikstra and Lynne Goldstein, The Perrins Ledge 1973; Dena Ferran Dincauze, Cremation Cemeteries in Eastern Massachusetts 1968; Richard Gould, Aboriginal California Burial and Cremation Practices 1968; Robert Neuman, *An Introduction to Louisiana Archaeology* 1984; John O'Shea, Social Configurations and the Archaeological Study of Mortuary Practices 1981: 39-52; Maurice Robbins, *Wapanucket* 1980; John Walthall, *Prehistoric Indians of the Southeast* 1980.

Cremation

In her survey of death customs, Effie Bendann[189]9 found eight "motives" linking fire and death and six involving cremation, which can be combined into eight examples to prevent the return of the dead, purify the pollution caused by death, protect the body from wild beasts, prevent sorcery, secure warmth and comfort in the future world, produce an ethereal body, hasten dissolution, and light the way to the afterworld.

In addition, my own review of the ethnography indicates that burning also provides a finality to tainted, dangerous, or explosive events, much as the local villagers assemble with torches to attack Frankenstein's castle in an all-too-familiar movie scene.

In a classic case, regarded by all as most bizarre because it was so totally out of character, fire closed an incident among the Western Apache. A married young man raped a divorced woman of his father's clan and killed her when she would not let go. As word spread, his mother announced that gifts would be collected to pay the mourning clan and the girl's family. Everyone, even boys, gave clothes, weapons, baskets, blankets, and horses. Lastly, his mother took off and added her own clothes to the pile, proclaiming that all these goods were to save all her other children and family members. The murderer, however, she gave up to his fate if anyone could find him. Then the girl's survivors set fire to this huge pile, taking away only the four horses. Shortly after, one of her relatives shot the murderer in the back of the head while he was eating in another camp.[190]10

In an interesting twist, Kashaya Pomo[191] cremated not only to protect the body from wild animals but also to prevent the body from becoming a wild animal itself because "if the dead are not burned they will become grizzly bears.... Hence cremation is an act of religion, of redemption, of salvation, which it were a heinous impiety to the dead to pretermit."[192]12

Today, in the Hispanic Southwest, Catholic mestizos recognize a certain appeal of cremation. For example, near the end of *Bless Me, Ultima*, the New Mexican classic, during a mock cremation exorcism, this ancient woman curer agrees that burning is a good way to return to the earth, avoiding the confines of a damp casket as "the spirit soars immediately into the wind of the llano and the ashes blend quickly into the earth."[193]13 [124]

Deading

Within the overall context of Native American death ceremonies, moreover, it is vital to recall that a series of intricate processes and rites marked the progressive stages of disassociation for the corpse and its physical and spiritual components.

---

[189] Effie Bendann, *Death Customs* 1969.

[190] Grenville Goodwin, Social Organization of the Western Apache 1969.

[191] The identification of Power's E-ri-o can be traced through Alfred Kroeber, Handbook of the Indians of California, Bureau of American Ethnology Bulletin 78: 234 1925, as the Pomo near Fort Ross, and Sally McLendon and Wendell Oswalt, in Robert Heizer, Smithsonian Handbook of North American Indians: California #8, Washington, DC: Smithsonian Institution Press 1978: 278, as Kashaya Pomo, derived from the Spanish *el rio*.

[192] Stephen Powers, *Tribes of California* 1976: 194.

[193] Rudolfo Anaya, *Bless Me, Ultima* 1994: 233.

Among the Delaware, rituals functioned as time-releasers to mark stages in the deconstruction of a body "into increasingly more resistant parts: starting with the loss of breath; proceeding to clear fluids, blood, flesh, hair, and nails; and finishing with the skeleton" from cartilage to the long bones and the skull.[194]14 Each stage also released spiritual components, such as a soul localized in the breath, blood, or bone. To ease messy biological realities, the body itself was equated with the chrysalis (cocoon), or more recently with a mere suitcase, from which a beautiful butterfly emerges.

The Tillamook of coastal Oregon believed in a Babyland on the other side. The template for each eventual human lived there in fetus form with others, including spouses, until he or she was reborn to human parents. In the womb, the other attributes and aspects of such a life were brought together and combined until the last of them, probably breath, was provided at birth.

In standard Native American belief, the mother provided the flesh and blood, the father the bone, and the creator the spark of life. In contrast, Northern Cheyenne say the father provides the blood, the mother the substance, and the creator the blessing spark of life-giving breath, which a newborn uses to inhale consciousness at birth, along with the potential to speak and a tragic self-awareness of personal loneliness.[195]15 Over the next twelve years, a child lost spirituality in favor of biology, learning to balance four internal tensions, two humane and good with two bestial and bad. Successful integration led to effective parenting and careers. Later, as a grandparent, life began to unravel, with spirituality increasing as an elder moved ever closer to the Milky Way, the path to the beautiful after-world of the Creator. At death, the fetal blessing from the Creator, previously diffused through the body, concentrated in the bones until these disintegrated and the vitality finally reunited with the Creator. At the death, however, any Cheyenne guilty of murder, suicide, incest, or promiscuity was cremated and its ghost sent along the short fork of the Milky Way also to vanish into oblivion.

In the Northeast, if a Huron drowned or froze to death, that body was taken to the town cemetery and placed between a fire and trench so it could be cut up. The flesh and entrails were cremated, but the bones were buried to appease angry spirits of the sky or water.[196]16 Here, cremation was a partial solution, also used for violent deaths and executed witches, to keep disruptive ghosts out of the common ossuary formed every decade at a Feast for the Dead called the Kettle.

Throughout the Southeast, tribes hastened the deconstruction process of disincarnation by dismemberment, with long-finger-nailed specialists called Buzzards picking the bones clean before they were reburied in specially made and measured baskets.[197]17 These procedures occurred along the length of the Mississippi River, although at Aztalan in Wisconsin such Mississippian mortuary processing was mistaken for cannibalism. [125]

---

[194] Jay Miller, Delaware Personhood 1991; *Shamanic Odyssey* 1988 32: 141.

[195] Anne Terry Straus, Northern Cheyenne Ethnopsychology 1975; The Meaning of Death in Northern Cheyenne Culture 1978. See also Miller, *Shamanic Odyssey* 1988: 131-132.

[196] Bruce Trigger, The Huron 1969: 104.

[197] John Swanton, Source Materials for the Social and Ceremonial Life of the Choctaw Indians 1931.

Maricopa

Among Yuman-speaking tribes of the Southwest, Maricopa[198]18 required cremation for all who entered their afterworld; otherwise he or she smelled bad.[199]19 Should a Maricopa happen to be buried, his or her ghost stayed only on the north side of a "deadline," wandering around carrying their coffin box on their head, sometimes putting it down to sit on. Twins and the deformed, who had a separate town, were reborn to visit the living for a time. An adult could be reborn up to four times, ending the last existence as a bit of charcoal lying in the desert.

Maricopa recognized that for each person four spiritual aspects transformed at death into a soul that goes to the afterworld, a ghost that becomes a whirlwind, a heart that becomes a horned owl, and a pulse that becomes a screech owl. The crucial importance of the heart is indicated by a belief that it is the last part of a body to burn.

The pyre was strongly made by first setting a big post into the ground until it stood a yard tall. Four logs were laid down to abut it to the west, with a smaller post set on the outside to hold these four in place. Logs were then piled up to a height of three feet, even with the top of the big post. Dry arrowweed was stuffed as kindling between the layers.

The corpse was removed from the house with four halts, the last resting on the ground beside the south side of the pyre. During each pause, a speaker orated. Finally, a man climbed onto the north side of the pyre, the corpse was handed up, and he briefly placed it prone with head to the east, before turning it onto its right side to face north. Its feet were unwrapped from the shroud and wedged between logs, left one to the north and right to the south, to anchor the body before it was covered by gifts of clothing and blankets. While the fire burned, an old man with a long pole kept the body hidden under burning wood. Everyone present fasted, hearing orations at the half way and end of the cremation. If a dead man had been a musician, his favorite songs were sung throughout his burning.

Afterward, four holes, two on the north and two on the south, were dug and the ashes divided among them. The fire tender first divided the remains from south to north, then west to east. While the ethnography is otherwise silent, these four deposits probably relate to the four souls.

The deceased's home and all possessions were burned or buried. After mourning for four days, family and officials returned to routine tasks. If the deceased were exceptional, a mourning ceremony (Cry) was held a few days later. Unlike neighboring tribes, it was not annual and did not involve effigies, only reenactments of great moments (battles, songs, orations) from that life.

California

The best regional overview of ethnographic cremation practices remains Alfred Kroeber's 1925 monumental Handbook of the Indians of California, still preferable to the quick-fix 1978 California Handbook,[200]20 though the California Handbook does provide the most current tribal

---

[198] Leslie Spier, Yuman Tribes 1933: 296, 299, 302, 308.

[199] To further offset this concern, the pyre used aromatic mesquite, extolled as "the ultimate in fragrant fuels" by Aldo Leopold, *A Sand County Almanac* 1978: 153.

[200] Heizer, California.

ethnonyms and its index [126] includes a useful entry for "recremation" under death practices of Lake Miwok and Pomo.[201]21

Throughout California, the usual reason for cremation or partial cremation was ease in transporting back home someone who had died at some distance that "All California Indians have strong sentiments on this point; old people will express satisfaction at the prospect of being buried adjacent to the house in which they were born."[202]22 Tohono O'Odham ~ Papago of southern Arizona add that cremating a body killed in battle also prevented its use in sorcery by enemies.[203]23

In northeastern California, Modoc cremated all their dead at spots associated with a patriline,[204]24 with everyone but shamans attending. Possessions and beads were placed on the pyre, but these goods, along with any slaves intended for immolation, could be appropriated by anyone present with due compensation.[205]25 Mourners and others sat during the burning, apparently to avoid interfering with the rising smoke. Later, the house was burned if the deceased was a child or a spouse to residents because of a "desire to eliminate any reminder of the dead person, and thus to ease mourning."[206]26

Pomo

In central California, "The Pomo were opposed to burial because they believed that the ghost of the dead person would continue to haunt the spot,"[207]27 so they cremated − along with beads, robes, and baskets − on a pyre set in a trench, with the body face down, head to the south, allowing the spirit to mo re easily lift itself to journey to the afterworld.[208]28 For Pomo, the essence of a person − variously called breath ~ sou, ~ knowledge − was contained in the heart (*kam*).[209]29 During the burning, mourners were so distraught in grief that family friends kept a tally of all gifts and offerings, such as beads, so these kin could later give proper thanks.[210]30 The close male relative who used a long pole to expose the body to maximum flames became polluted for a few years afterward and was forbidden meat, hunting, and gambling to emphasize this too-close association with human meat and the seriousness of the duty.[211]31 The next day, a father or other close male gathered up the remains, put them in a basket, buried it nearby, and then obliterated any further evidence of the pyre.[212]32 All possessions were burned so as not to attract the ghost with the potential of harming the living, even inadvertently.[213]33 Mourning

---

[201] Heizer, California: 268, 776, 297.

[202] Kroeber, Handbook: 499.

[203] Ruth Underhill, Social Organization of the Papago Indians 1939: 190.

[204] Verne Ray, Primitive Pragmatists 1963: 113.

[205] Ray, Primitive Pragmatists: 116.

[206] Ray, Primitive Pragmatists: 119.

[207] Edwin Loeb, Pomo Folkways 1926: 290.

[208] Loeb, Pomo Folkways: 287.

[209] Loeb, Pomo Folkways: 290, 296.

[210] Loeb, Pomo Folkways: 286.

[211] Loeb, Pomo Folkways: 292.

[212] Loeb, Pomo Folkways: 289.

[213] Loeb, Pomo Folkways: 291.

continued for a year, with women visiting the deceased's favorite haunts to sing and sprinkle acorn meal (*pinole*).

A year later at a rite called *Lonewis*, the remains were dug up and reburned along with donated gifts, a version of the famous Californian Cry shared with the Maidu.[214]34 Even after the Pomo began burying, they still burned offerings on the grave for the dead a year or so later.[215]35

Maidu

While other Maidu buried their dead, the hill (Konkow) and southern (Nisinan) provinces cremated. The Hill Maidu mourning anniversary was the [127] northernmost example of the Cry celebrated throughout the lower half of Native California in the fall to resupply the distinguished dead.[216]36

For each Cry, a round brush fence was set up on the community's burning ground, open to the west and sometimes also the east. A director led the whole rite, but the functional sponsors were bereaved families who had given payment to the director in return for a special necklace to mark their own mourning. The patterned sequence of beads, by colors and counts, in this loop was specific to that ground. After use in five Crys, a necklace was redeemed by return payment from the director, who then cremated it. Interestingly, a poor family could participate in this ceremony by receiving payment instead of giving it, highlighting the prestige that came from generosity across the Americas.

When a ground was ready for an observance, its director sent out to guests strings of knots, one untied each day so all visitors arrived on the same day. The first night, family mourners came to the old enclosure around sundown to keen and sprinkle acorn meal. The second day, the enclosure was repaired and poles up to twenty feet long prepared to hold offerings that had been amassed for a year or more.[217]37 A widow had probably spent the past year making many baskets to be burned. By evening, each mourning family had a dozen poles filled from top to bottom to set up as pairs across the fire at the north and south. Bulky items were placed around their bases.

For the noteworthy deceased, effigies were made of stuffed and decorated wildcat skins arranged to look like standing humans, staked near the entrance, and "fed" during the night. Each such effigy was literally called a "spirit within" because the ghost of that person actually resided in it during the Cry.

As an old man lit the central fire, bargaining began to rescue offerings in return for an exchange, barter, or purchase. Such rescue must be understood in the same way as the gifts given to guests at a memorial potlatch, where it is clear that, for hosts, others are both their guests and their dead, each substituting for the other but with the living bodies the more obvious.

When negotiations quieted, the director spoke about the intent, purpose, and procedure of the Cry, as Kroeber said,[218]38 "carefully instructing the people in what they perfectly well know

---

214 Loeb, Pomo Folkways: 288.

215 Loeb, Pomo Folkways: 294.

216 Kroeber, Handbook: 429-432, 859-861.

217 Heizer, California: 383, fig 10.

218 Kroeber, Handbook: 860.

how to do" in upholding high moral standards. For the rest of the night, in distinct groupings composed of mourning families, everyone wailed, keened, and sang. Their speakers periodically expressed pity and concern for these ancestral dead and placed 'bits of food into the fire to "feed" them.

At dawn, the tall poles were stripped and everything piled on the fire while the elders mournfully keened for their loved ones. Effigies were "walked" to the fire to enter the blaze. Mourners continuously exhaled forceful breaths, presumably to blow away harm. At first light, emotional intensity peaked and old women had to be retrained from throwing themselves onto the pyre. Everyone was totally exhausted with grief, prostrated from their lamentations.

In the morning, after the fire died down and everyone rested, the director urged all to eat, gamble, and have fun for a day or more to end their gathering on a happy note. Throughout Southern California, this Cry overlapped with the *toloache datura* cult, and in the Sierra Nevadas with Kuksu. [128]

Luiseño

Among the so-called Mission Indians, the Luiseño of San Juan Capistrano had hereditary officials in charge of all cremations. Like other Luiseños, the Juaneño shared a Polynesian-like epic of creation from the primordial union of sky and earth, culminating in the appearance of Wiyot, whose fearful powers led to his being poisoned and then cremated to protect his body from desecration. All this to no avail, however, since Coyote rushed into the flaming pyre, grabbed a bit of his flesh, and ate it.[219]39

To this day, the consumption of a bit of cooked flesh by a loved one remains an aspect of Southern California cremations,[220]40 recalling customs the breadth of the Americas − from South America, where cremated remains are turned into a drink because it is "better to be inside a warm friend than inside the cold earth," to the Northwest where the *Hamatsa* of the Kwakwaka'wakw and the *Xgyet* of the Tsimshian are metaphors for chiefly consumption of the possessions of their followers to enhance the prestige of their noble house by giving generously to others, both living and deading. Incidentally, the name of the patron of this consumption (consumer) cult among the Kwakiutlans has finally been carefully translated to indicate an increasing perfection into the human state because "you are what you eat."[221]41

Similarly, in Southern California, at a later time, in consequence to Coyote's cannibal act, Chungishnish, the founder of the *datura* jimsonweed *toloache* cult, appeared to finish the world by changing the first people into present species, spirits, or sacra before making modern humans from earth and giving them cultures, laws, and the ceremonial enclosure (*wankech*).

Kamia

Kamia of the Imperial Valley trace their culture to a hermaphrodite with two sons who moved south along the Colorado River into this valley, where most Kamia ancestors fled from them in terror because of their frightful appearance. One brave woman, however, stayed and

---

[219] Kroeber, Handbook: 637.
[220] Kroeber, Handbook: 740, plate 69.
[221] Susanne Hilton and John Rath, Objections to Franz Boas's 1983.

married one son, producing twins who provided corn and bean seeds, bows, arrows, war clubs passed out by patrilineages, and death ceremonies.[222]42

As death approached, a person's soul could be seen leaving his or her body, going south of Black Butte (*Wiespa*) in lower California, where it glided on the wind waiting to rejoin with a twin spirit, which arose from the body at the moment of death, but lingered nearby for four days, visiting everywhere that person lived.

As the body cremated, this spirit returned to gather the burnt clothes, rub charcoal on its eyes to enhance them, and go south, where it was escorted by deceased relatives and rejoined the soul to reconstitute that person, who lived, died, and was cremated four times. After each death the shape of the "body" changed until after the fourth death it became a black beetle or other insect that returned to the Kamia country. "If heart did not burn, it was buried in the pit with the ashes, to enliven and emerge as a young owl that later grew up."[223]43 [129]

Yokuts

In a declaration that resonates with Native understanding of this and all cremation, Yoimut, a woman who was the last of the Chunut Yokuts who lived on the northeastern shore of Lake Tulare remembered that her mother

> ... saved her money for a year and had bought a good suit of clothes at Mr Sweet's store in Visalia. She paid sixteen dollars for it. She had a good hat, shoes, socks, and underwear.
>
> Mother stuffed the clothes with tules and fastened them together so they looked like a man. She painted the face. Then she got out the fine baskets she had made to burn, and all father's things she had saved. Then she was ready for the *Lonewis*.
>
> By daylight everything was burned up and only a few people were singing and crying around their own fires. They kept that up all day.
>
> My mother worked hard to get the money to buy the clothes to burn in the fire for my father. She washed for the Blankenships and for Mrs "Fish" Rice. But you white people do the same thing. You save money and dress dead people in good clothes. You spend lots of money for coffin.
>
> Then you bury your father, mother, maybe your wife. You put everything in ground and all decay. We bum good clothes and they *do not* decay. They go to *Tih-pik-nits' Pahn* [great bird in charge in the hereafter + land] so our dead person always had good clothes to wear.[224]44

Łingits ~ Tlingits

Such insight and background now allows us to return to the Northwest, particularly the matrilineal north of the Tsimshian, Haida, and Łingit who once cremated virtually all their honored dead.

---

[222] Edward Gifford, The Kamia of Imperial Valley 1931: 79.

[223] Same: 71, 72.

[224] Frank E Latta, Handbook of Yakuts Indians 1977: 667, 675, 682.

Among Łingits, a person is believed to be composed of layers outward from a vitalizing "mind" located in the heart at the center of the body, then to bones, flesh, and outer skin, along with spirits or souls. The most ideal of persons was said to be dry, hard, and heavy − a humane and moral member of the nobility who dispensed cultural expertise in return for labor and help from others.

The great (if tragic) irony of a successful Łlingit life, however, was that a noble reached his or her apex just after death, particularly after cremation when they fully attained ideal attributes by being transmogrified into "heat, light, smoke, charcoal, and ashes"[225]45 as fire consumed one life in order to rekindle another.[226]46

When a Łlingit body reclined on the pyre, the soul spirit more easily arose to travel in stages from the cemetery,[227]47 into the forest, and up a mountainside where it entered the second land of the dead to take up residence in its ancestral house. According to an explicit statement, those who were cremated had the virtue of staying near the fire,[228]48 warmed and ready to receive offerings [130] sent by the living through mortal fires.[229]49 "In the house of the spirits the essences of the food, clothing, and other objects burned by the living descended through the smokehole upon the spirits sitting around this ancestral fireplace."[230]50 Indeed, the Łlingit root *gaan* gets compounded into words meaning burn, cremate, and shine.[231]51 "Located in the center of the house, which itself was the center of the human-occupied space, the fire was firmly associated with humanity and social life and was opposed to the peripheral domains of the rain-soaked forest and the sea."[232]52

The bodies of shamans and battle-slain warriors were not cremated. Shamans instead were encased and left on some lonely rocky point to become the object of questing for shamanic power, especially by a nephew (sister's son). Warriors killed in battle went into the sky to join the Northern Lights, where their life was spartan but well attended by slaves and slain enemies.[233]53

A year later, with the awkward body replaced by a monumental pole or other great artwork, a mortuary potlatch was held to install a successor to the name, persona, and position of the deceased, confirming the continuity of society and its eternal character as yet another person was given to a name so that, as Gitksan say, only the skin changes. Yet such transfer also involves an element of personal will since one Gitksan grandmother who felt neglected by her family threatened to be reincarnated outside of her matriline and, when really piqued, into some

---

[225] Sergei Kan, *Symbolic Immortality* 1989: 114.

[226] Miller, *Tsimshian Culture*: 44.

[227] Kan, Symbolic Immortality: 127.

[228] Kan, *Symbolic Immortality*: 112.

[229] This custom was reported in the first detailed, balanced, and coherent Americanist ethnography by Reverend Ivan Veniaminov, *Notes on the Islands of the Unalaska District* 1984: 398. This work was published in 1840 to describe and compare Aleuts and Indians (Kolosh), particularly Łingits.

[230] Kan, *Symbolic Immortality*: 113.

[231] Kan, *Symbolic Immortality*: 112.

[232] Kan, *Symbolic Immortality*: 112.

[233] Kan, *Symbolic Immortality*: 120-121.

72

undeserving Anglo baby.[234]54

Conclusions

All told, cremation cannot be understood apart from the reverence for fire throughout the Americas and the world. Whether or not a society cremates, all recognize fire as a portal between dimensions and existences. William Beynon, Tsimshian Wolf chief, collected a marvelous account of two friendly shamans, one on the coast and the other upriver, who sent each other gifts from a home fire through the other's smokehole. Thus, shellfish put in the fire on the coast fell from the interior smokehole, as chokecherries did in reverse.[235]55 As Mohave and Pomo noted, fire also improves smell, with cooking preferred to putrefation.

Via this fire portal, the dead are supplied with their possessions, houses, foods, and warmth at the time of the funeral and periodically thereafter. The late Wick Miller once told me how startled he was at a Gosiute funeral, which promised to be done the old way, when the deceased's house trailer suddenly burst into flames to mark his passing, presumably updating residence styles in their afterworld.

As Native California makes clear, cremation can be an expedient for transporting human remains back home when that is a priority, as Homer explained in the Iliad:

> after Achilles's stand-in (Patroclus) was killed by Hector, his shade came to Achilles in a dream to plead for cremation since hordes of battle dead kept him from crossing the river Styx into Hades. After explaining that burning would quickly send him through the Gates of [131] Hades, he predicted Achilles own death, asked that their ashes be buried together within the same gold urn, and then vanished in a wisp of smoke.[236]56

Thus, when deciding upon cremation, convenience is not as important a reason as protection of the body, relief of the bereaved, or quick release (clean break) of the innermost essence of a person. One explanation for Viking ship cremation is that the soul is a ray of the sun that must be returned at death to its source, with both fire and ships speeding the process.[237]57 Sometimes cremation has prestige, as among Tsimshian, Hittites, and ancient Germans, according to Tacitus, where famous men were cremated using special woods in the pyre.

Throughout northern Europe, burial followed a long period of cremation, as the sky god replaced the earth goddess.[238]58 "Cremation, appearing in the north as early as the Stone Age, two thousand years before Christ, becoming supreme in the Early Bronze Age and running through the Celtic Iron Age, is bound up with the belief that the soul is freed from the body with

---

[234] John Adams, *The Gitksan Potlatch* 1973: 32.

[235] Miller, *Tsimshian Culture*: 277 #44.

[236] Homer, *The Iliad* 1950: 414.

[237] Robert Hall, In Search of the Ideology of the Adena-Hopewell Climax 1979: 169, quoting Francis Huxley, The Way of the Sacred, New York: Dell 1976: 262; Robert Hall, *An Archaeology of the Soul* 1997.

[238] PV Glob, *The Bog People* 1969: 144-192.

the help of fire, and flies to a distant land of the dead, where it is re-born."[239]59 At one Danish mound, wings of jackdaws and crows were added to the pyre to assist this flight.

In addition to this predominant means of burial, Celtic religion made three modes of offerings to their trinity of Teutates by bloodletting, of Esus by hanging from trees, and of Taranis by burning.[240]60 Therefore, final disposal of a loved one must be distinguished from sacrifice to a deity.

Among California Mission tribes, burning the body protected it by removing a temptation to use it for bad intentions such as cannibalism or sorcery, although some violations of this taboo have led to compensations like the arrival of Chungishnish.

Among Pomo, removing the body, possessions, and house of the deceased served to take away reminders of this loss for the living, and, more importantly, keep any ghosts from being lured back to retrieve a favored item or person.

In a few cases, cremation was a way of making sure someone dangerous or repellant was really dead, but even that was not always certain. For example, in the 1840s Crees killed a Blackfoot warrior named Low Horn by driving an elk antler into his ear, since his powers turned away all bullets. Then, to be sure he was dead, they burned his body, but an ember exploded to produce a grizzly bear that attacked the Crees, who fled as lightning bolts killed several others. Low Horn later reincarnated into a boy who became a famous shaman who died in 1899.[241]"

Ultimately, however, cremation was a shortcut to transmogrification into another reality, freeing up intangibles like spirits, names, and honors to be reclaimed by heirs, as among the feingit and Tsimshian. This quick release explains the concern with easing the passage, with consideration given to the placement of the body, on the side for Maricopa, face down for Pomo, or reclining for feingit, so that souls can more easily arise and go forth. Such a quickening, the quick of the dead, also hastened their re-creation in the [132] beyond in some form.[242]62 In instances of a Babyland, the outer form seems to reconstitute as a fetal template, ready to recombine with other elements to become a newborn. The soul, shade, shadow, ghost resides in a land of the dead, sometimes a series of them, until, in the ultimate tragedy for Native peoples, it no longer has anyone among the living who remember it at all and thus it passes into oblivion or perhaps fuses with the Creator as a greater cosmic awareness. Throughout the Americas, memory is the ultimate binder holding together the past, present, future, and eternal.

As expressed in phrases like "flame of life" and "spark of intelligence," fire enlightens, binds, and renews. "Like the burning of fields in preparation for planting, or to encourage the return of game and other edible plants, burning corpses and their possessions emphasized the regenerative power of fire."[243]63

Crow of Montana explicitly say that the all pervasive power in the universe, which they call maxpe, appears as a white, wispy vapor, seen as clouds, smoke, cold breath, foggy mists, frosty earth, and more. Indeed, when set ablaze, tobacco, like a cremated corpse, changed into its essential soul-power form, as did words and prayers on chilly mornings.[244]64

---

[239] Glob, The Bog People: 145.

[240] Gerhard Herm, *The Celts* 1993: 157.

[241] Hugh Dempsey, The Blackfbot Indians 1995: 381-413, 396.

[242] Robert Hertz, *Death and the Right Hand* 1960.

[243] Kathleen Bragdon, *Native People of Southern New England* 1996: 235.

[244] Fred Voget and Mary Mee, *They Call Me Agnes* 1995: 6.

Thus death, funeral, burial, cremation, reburial, recremation, and timed memorials all serve to mark these passages in deading in the same way that namings, marriages, birthdays, and anniversaries mark such stages in living.

I want to end with some speculations about gaps in the ethnography, both distributional and emotional. First, since cremation shortcuts an elaborate series of ongoing deconstructions by cooking down the body, someone somewhere sometime should have a belief, probably esoteric, that the flames of the pyre provided the means to a higher existence, a new form of "enlightenment." Certainly among Pueblos, membership in various communal cults and priesthoods is still phrased in terms of metaphors of cooking so that non-initiates are "raw" while initiates are "cooked" and officials are "well done, ripe, ready, and finished." Throughout the Americas, standard belief held that spirits owned the land, the dead held it as permanent residents, and the living used it. Thus, graves and cremation pits served as deeds of claim.

Second, looking at distributions of mortuary practices shows them to be obviously discontinuous. In the prehistoric Southwest, for example, neighboring traditions used alternate procedures. Thus, Hohokam of southern Arizona cremated but the Anasazi to their north interred. Then the situation became more complicated when, after about 1200AD, Hohokam instead buried, suggesting to me that cremation traditions of present southern Arizona and California gave way to intercultural hostilities such that Yumans centered on the lower Colorado River kept cremation as they moved eastward, while Pimans dug in along the Gila and Sonoran desert by shifting to inhumation. Yet for the earlier Hohokam, Emil Haury astutely mused,

> Unexplained are the meanings of caches and the mass destruction of cultural goods, in both of which fire played an obvious part. These customs appear to be connected in some way to cremation as such. But I strongly suspect that the relationships of many activities derive from [133] fire as a revered and sacred agent, essential in death, in making sacrifices, and in ritual."[245]65

Similarly, throughout Native California, adjacent nations used alternate means with their dead. This patterning suggests that despite all its internal consistency as strong cultural beliefs, cremation or burial also provided a primary means of national identity. Therefore, any and all such practices need to be put into a regional context with the understanding that people will often adhere to something just because their neighbors do not.

Third, all sources imply that ashes have a unity of their own, with the integrity of each individual indicated by the separate treatment of his~her ashes, though the Mohave divided them fourfold. Yet the care that was taken to conceal these ashes suggests that there was a concern to protect them from use in sorcery against the family. This potential for divisive use seems to be the closest Native America came to the commodification of cremated remains so prevalent in modern America, where divorced parents divide up the ashes of their dead child, or, in Seattle, old Hoofers have packets of their ashes taken to many favorite scenic spots.

Cremation initially stuck me as both an anonymous and amorphous way of dealing with the dead, but my review has proven to me otherwise. By taking a loved one from flesh to ashes, mourners make the greatest manifestation of their regard. Natives who attend Anglo burials are often shocked when the family walks away from the grave with the coffin still resting above it.

---

[245] Emil Haury, *The Hohokam* 1976:166.

All Native funerals I have ever attended end with the family lowering the coffin and filling in the grave, often with separate lines of men or of women tossing handfuls into the grave to soften the later impact of loaded shovelfuls.

Cremation is definitive and quick. When a British Columbia trapper cut off his thumb axing through a tree knot, he saved both until he could invite friends to their combined burning as "Any bastardly chunk that can trick me out of a thumb has got a cremation coming to it."[246]66

With cremation, the passage from intact body to manageable ashes takes several hours of constant attention, but the results are both comparatively quick and lasting. Always, personal articulations by those involved stress not the convenient outcome but the ongoing careful concern with freshness evidenced by these mourners toward their lost relative.[247]67

In Japan, where cremation is the rule, friends assure me that their final act of picking out the remains of a parent at a crematorium was among the most intimate and psychologically satisfying releases in their entire grieving process. In contrast to the mechanized cremation of Japan, Hindu India continues a practice both ancient and full, integrated within a closed universe wherein "nothing new can be produced except by destroying, or transforming something else."[248]68 Benares has two *ghats* (cremation grounds) because this city is sacred to Shiva, who promised final liberating salvation to all who die there. The oldest *ghat* marks the place where Lord Vishnu sat for 50,000 years "performing the austerities (*tapas*) by which he created the world" and where the corpse of the cosmos itself will ignite at the end of time. "By entering the pyre here the deceased − as it were − refuels the fires of creation at the [134] very spot where creation began."[249]69 Death is counted not from the loss of breath, but from the moment a kinsman cracks the skull to allow its combustion within the pyre. Then the corpse rises as smoke from pyre turns into clouds, rain, and vegetables to be eaten and transformed into semen to repeat the process. Only small children, lepers, violent or sudden death casualties, and smallpox victims were not cremated, but instead immersed in the Ganges River, though an effigy of each was later burned. Only ascetics have no contacts with cremation at all. For Hindus, "Cremation is cosmogony; and an individual death is assimilated to the process of cosmic regeneration."[250]70

Thus, from situated local knowledge within Native America, we move globally toward the human condition, where anthropology still has the most to say in terms of cultural integrity, ethnic diversity, and cross-cultural understanding, especially when it gives full heed to the Native voice in its cultural context.

American Indian Culture and Research Journal 25:1 (2001) 121-137

---

[246] Roderick Haig-Brown, *Measure of the Year* 1990:183.

[247] Portability, however, remains a concern. Families that fled to America from the Baltic states quickly adopted cremation in the expressed hope that they would eventually be able to take remains of their loved ones back home, as many have indeed begun to do lately (Astida Blukis Onat, PhD, pc 31 October 2000).

[248] Jonathan Perry, Sacrificial Death and the Necrophagous Ascetic 1982: 72.

[249] Perry, Sacrificial Death: 77.

[250] Perry, Sacrificial Death: 76.

Weirs and Gear As Widowers:
Fishing Symbolism Across Native North America

Abstract

Weirs, as stationary fishing gear set across suitable waterways, are more than bits of wood and latticework. They were "persons" alive with intent to help or harm humans in need of food. Three widely-spaced cases over a span of three hundred years attest to the identification of fishing gear as a "person" who is a "widower", either a spirit or transformed primordial human, in greater need of food than someone with a wife to cook and sustain the family. This symbolism underscores the balanced and engendered roles associated with fishing during time-constrained migratory runs.

Aligned fish weir stakes were revealed at deep levels on Greys Harbor during recent testing for a new WSDOT graving basin, to make and float the multi-chambered cement pontoons needed to repair floating bridges in western Washington (Friederich 2010). This discovery led to a literature review which has bolstered claims by local elders that a weir has a spirit and is a living 'person' (in some sense). Three cases from America's ortheast, California, and Northwest, moreover, suggest that such catchment gear is further personified as a 'widower'.

Weirs were constructed of stakes pounded into a shoreline and braced with latticework panels or brush to guide upriver-bound fish into impounds, net pens, basket traps, or other containments (Steward 1977: 98-123). Once completed, rituals blessed and consecrated the new weir as a fully-formed person. Trapped fish were extracted with gaff hooks or nets and distributed communally for drying or smoking for winter use. Archaeologists have a general sense that these contraptions have "consciousness, social sense, and agency" consistent with belief in animism (Losey 2010); linguistic sources describe construction details as well as the mortal dangers of attack from upriver communities, especially their shamans, to downriver builders who block off entire fish runs (Andrade 1931: 7-8, 152-155).

When not actively engaged in fish harvesting, panels from weirs were removed to deactivate its personhood and consciousness, as well as to allow fish easy passage upriver rather than suffer the moral harm of dying unused in a neglected weir. During the early 1800s, at the mouth of the Nooksack River, locals were paid by in-migrating Lummi to rebuild and spiritually prepare weirs until subsequent intermarriage enabled descendants to inherit the rights and rituals to consecrate these weirs for their own successful use (Miller 1999: 17-18).

Weirs have a world-wide distribution (Connaway 2007), but this paper focuses on three cases from Native North America.

Huron

The earliest report comes from the Jesuit Relations of the late 1630s, written by Fr Paul Le Juene in Huronia (modern Quebec), and concerns an empty seine or fishing net. Le Juene gained fame when he overwintered with a Huron family, learning the language and survival skills at first hand. Readily available references in standard ethnographic summaries are presented before the actual, more detailed texts. These summaries specify an explanation in a dream, while the texts emphasize shared interspecies intelligence as the basis for such communications.

Ceremony of the Marriage of
Two Virgins to the Seine

Only one calendric ceremony, to insure successful fishing, is mentioned by the Jesuits. In the spring, two young, virgin girls (in at least one case these were about 6 or 7 years old in order to insure they were virgins) were married to the Seine. At this feast, the Seine was placed between the two girls and told to catch many fish. In consideration for their marriage with the Seine, the families of the girls were given part of the catch. This [80] ceremony was introduced into Huronia by some neighboring Algonquin, the latter having gone to fish some years before and having caught nothing. Surprised and astonished at this unusual event, they did not know what to think. Then the *oki* (spirit) of the Seine appeared to them as a tall, well-formed man, who said, "I have lost my wife, and I cannot find one who has not known other men before me; that is the reason why you do not succeed, and you never will succeed until I have been given satisfaction in this respect." The Algonquin then held a council and decided that to appease the Seine they should present him with girls so young he would have no reason to complain and that they should give him two for one. This done, the fishing succeeded. The Huron, their neighbors, having heard about this, took up the custom and repeated it every year (Tooker 1964: 79-80).

> A ceremony in which two girls who had not yet reached the age of puberty were married to the spirit of a fishing net. This ceremony, which was said to insure good fishing, was reported to have begun among the Algonkians when the spirit of the net appeared to a man in a dream asking for a bride to replace the wife he had lost. The ceremony then spread to the Huron. In return for consenting to the marriage, the girls' families were given a special share of the season's catch. The marriage apparently lasted only for a year (Trigger 1969: 33).

While these texts specify a net, the intent seems to include any impounding fishing gear, from net to trap to weir. As the most complex apparatus, moreover, a weir includes other types of gear such as baskets, nets, and impounds. Huron seines were deployed both in open water and at gaps in weirs.

The actual translation of Fr. Paul Le Juene's French includes more details, including the month when fish runs arrived, particularly of herring. Later in the year, whitefish were taken. The motivation for Jesuit inquiry is made clear because a girl convert was to be involved, her family was to benefit ("profit") from the catch, but, in the end, no rite was held that year. The spirit personification appeared in human guise, though probably of a more shimmering appearance. In 1636, he wrote:

> Let us come to other mysteries. [p197]
> In the middle of the month of March, the season having arrived for fishing with the Seine, they talked of marrying it, according to the custom of the country, to two young girls, or rather to two children, who had never had intercourse with men, – and then [p199] of celebrating the nuptials or feast, at which, according to the

formality, the Seine would be in the middle, and the two young girls beside it. On this occasion, then, the Seine is vigorously exhorted to be of good courage, and so to act that the fishing be successful, as has been more amply told in preceding Relations.

They had in mind, among others, one of our little Christian girls, four or five years old, to be one of the two brides. We are informed of this, and immediately begin to investigate the matter, in order to understand what we ought to say about it. We have ascertained, then, that some years ago the Algonquians, – who are neighboring people, very intelligent, and excelling in all kinds of fishery, – having gone at this season to fish with the Seine, at first took nothing. Surprised and astonished at a result which was for them so unusual, they knew not what to think. Thereupon, the Soul, the Genie, or the Oki of the Seine, for our Savages [sic] call it by all these names, appeared to them in the form of a tall, well-formed man, greatly dissatisfied and in a passion, who said to them, "I have lost my wife, and I cannot find one who has not known other men before me; that is the reason why you do not succeed, and you never will succeed until I have been given satisfaction in this respect."

The Algonquians, thereupon, hold a council and decide, that to appease and give satisfaction to the Seine, they must present him Girls so young that he would no longer have reason to complain, – and that, for his greater satisfaction, they must present him two for one. They do this, then, in the manner that I have related above, at a feast; and immediately their fishing succeeds wonderfully. [p201]

The Hurons, their neighbors, no sooner got wind of this, than lo, there was a feast, and a solemnity was instituted, that has ever since continued, and is celebrated every year at this same season. This being so, I leave it to be imagined what we said and counseled to the parents of this Girl, and lo, there ensued a grievance. For, as the whole family profit considerably from such a marriage, – part of the fish caught reverting to them in the year when it takes place, and being then due and appropriated to them, in consideration of such an alliance, – to refuse their consent to such a marriage is to deprive and defraud an entire family of the greatest pleasure and the best opportunity that can be found in the country.

I do not know whether God were pleased to intervene especially in this affair, and break it up altogether or not; at all events, the ceremony did not take place, in any form.

In 1639, the Jesuit added observations about the incompatibility of the dead with vitalities concerned with the feeding and care of mortals. Such taboos also kept women away from actual fishing sites. Instead, they butchered and processed fish away from the water, doing heavy, sustained work that lasted the fish run.

They hold that fish are possessed of reason, as also the Deer and Moose; and that is why they do not throw to the Dogs either the bones of the latter when they are hunting, or the refuse of the former when fishing; if they did, and the others should get wind of it, they would hide themselves, and not let themselves be taken. Every year they marry their nets or Seines to two little girls, who must be only from six to seven years of age, for fear they may have lost their virginity, which is a very rare quality among them. The ceremony of these espousals takes place at a fine feast, where the Seine is placed between the two virgins; this is to render them fortunate in catching fish. Still, I am very glad that virginity receives among them this kind of honor; it will help us some day to make them understand the value of it. Fish, they say, do not like the dead; and hence they abstain from going fishing when one of their friends is dead. But lately, when they took up from the cemetery the bodies of their relatives and carried them into their Cabins, on the [168] occasion of the feast of the dead [Kettle], some brought into our Cabin their nets alleging as a pretext the fear they had of fire, – for it is usually in this season that fire often ruins entire Villages; that in our Cabin we were almost always moving about, and slept very little; that we were at some distance from the Village, and consequently were in less danger in that respect. But all this was talk; the true reason was, as we learned afterwards, that they were afraid their nets would be profaned by the proximity of these dead bodies. That is something, to be sure; but here is the foundation of a greater part of their superstition.

Saanich

In the Northwest, the nearest parallel appears in unedited, unpublished fieldnotes from the Saanich of Vancouver Island, speakers of Straits Salish and users of specialized reef nets made from willow bark (sgwala, updated as sx^walu').
for the sockeye and humpbacked species they [Saanich] used a larger purse-net called sgwala. The top and bottom ropes of this net were generally made from twisted cedar boughs, and the meshes from willow, gathered in May or June, peeled, and split into thin strands that were then twisted together to form a long rope; but the Westholme natives fashioned their purse-net from a flax-like plant that grows on the mainland. Stone made convenient sinkers, and blocks of light cedar served as floats (Jenness 1935: 14).

In the origin story by 90-year-old David Latess accounting for this gear, a young man provides the model to his inlaws. Of note, his bride has singed hair, a sign of mourning that is being observed by the women in that settlement, strongly suggesting that they were mourning another woman. The youth may also be more serious than his mates because he is still mourning for his first wife. While the link to her widower is not specified, this mourning context is clear. A diagram of a deployed reef net appears in Stewart (1982: 93-94).

Origin of the Willow Fishnet
(Jenness 1935: 14)

A Saanitch [sic] couple and their marriageable daughter joined some relatives on a fishing excursion to Blaine, in the state of Washington. There the girl used to wander outside the rush wigwam and sit by herself at night while her parents were sleeping. One night someone approached her, and, before leaving, arranged to meet her again the next night. Thereafter they met night after night.

Shortly afterwards some strange youths began to join the girl's brothers and cousins as they played around the camp, and she wondered whether one of them might not be her nightly visitor. Towards evening, therefore, she smeared red ochre on her hands, and when her suitor joined her, playfully rubbed them on the back of his clothing. The next day she noticed in the crowd of players a youth who seemed more serious than the others, and when he turned his back to her it was red.

When night came her suitor urged her to go away with him, but she refused unless he first spoke to her parents. He was afraid that if he spoke to them they might be angry and send him away, and suggested that it would safer if she herself told them. She did so, and her father consented to their marriage if they remained for a time with her family. So she married the youth, who thereafter ceased to play with the other young men and occupied himself with serious matters about the camp.

Soon afterwards fish became very scarce, and the community was threatened with famine. The youth then said to his young wife, "Tell your father and his people to bring me a lot of sgwale." No one knew what he meant by sgwale; all the names, indeed, that he gave to the various plants and land animals were strange. They brought him bundles of one plant after another, but he rejected them all until they brought him bunches of willow. From its bark he made a net sgwale, showed them how to use it, and taught them the expressions that should accompany its handling. Then they were able to catch plenty of fish again."

Now that they were prosperous once more, he proposed to his wife that they go to his home. With the consent of her parents, the two of them embarked in a canoe, taking with them a large number of mats. Instead of heading, however, for some point or island in the distance where one might expect a village, he steered the canoe toward a very deep place in the sea not far from shore, where it vanished from view. Not many days later the girl reappeared above the surface of the water, showed herself to her people, and vanished again. They knew who it was from her singed hair, for along with other women of the camp, she had been mourning the death of a relative. But she never returned to them, because she married the fish-spirit sgwala.

The implications are that this young man was a spirit fish living deep in saltwater but with an affinity to willows, which thrive in freshwater.

Klamath River Yurok

The association of fishing gear, especially a weir, with a widower is most detailed for the famous Kepel Fish Dam on the Klamath River of northern California. Within a broader ritualized context, Salish tribes of the Upper Columbia River provide details about the recognition of weir construction stages. "Prior rites of thanksgiving were held for the trees cut to make the weir, for the dried poles carried to the stream banks, and for the completed weir. The salmon tyee [priest] spent five nights at the [p266] trap praying and singing to consecrate its use" (Miller 1998: 265-266).

On the Klamath, at Kepel, a priest called _Lo'_ directs the activities, with one or more assistants. Men live separately from women during this time. The fish weir is built over a ten day period, used for ten days of the salmon run, and then allowed to come apart, so salmon can go upstream to spawn and be caught locally by tribes farther up.

On the first day, everyone stays indoors while _Lo'_ travels around the area to prepare the land. _Lo'_ cuts three ten-foot stakes that will mark the ends and the middle of the trap. Then he enters the sweatlodge for four days. He cannot look at women or the fire for the duration of the rite. His wife cooks one meal a day that he eats after dark.

Meanwhile, everyone is gathering materials, which they bring to the location on the fifth day. *Lo'* builds a sandpile topped by a flat rock in a secluded location. This pile becomes his seat where he can see the work but not be seen by the workers. A boy who has never before helped build the weir crouches low as he carries the center stake to *Lo'*, who splits it. Everyone yells and begins to split all the stakes they have brought to the site. Visitors cannot look at the weir while it is under construction, presumably because they are not assuredly "of one mind" with the builders.

Every morning the materials to be added to the weir are prepared, and then installed in the afternoon. They bring to the site only what they will use that day, as apportioned by *Lo'*. They build from the ends towards the middle. Ten gaps or "gates" are left, each one opening into a trap built by a team of men who jointly divide and share its catch.

On the ninth day, men go to gather redwood boughs to plug the bottom of the weir. They encounter a <u>widower</u>, who receives a new "wife" and tokens in return for allowing the cutting of the boughs. On their return, men have a canoe race, with the winner taking any rejected stakes across the river to be burned. The boughs are passed through the smoke, and the fire's charcoal residue is turned into face paint worn on the final day. [emphasis added]

On the last day, the boughs are packed along the bottom of the weir, the women dance before rejoining the men in daily interaction, and the *Lo'* is capsized in a canoe. Though TT Waterman wrote he did not understand this event, it clearly evokes the familiar story of salmon leaving their homes beyond the horizon in the form of humans paddling canoes, which tip over to transform them into salmon.

Songs, dances, and joking occur at all stages of these preparations, adding to its sanctity and communal empowerment. Once the builders have amassed winter stores of dried salmon, the weir is abandoned for another year and salmon freely reach the upper waters of the Klamath River.

In all, the symbolism connected with this weir is extremely complex. On the ninth day, when the redwood boughs are gathered, compensation is offered to a man acting the part of a widower. He seems to be a stand-in for the redwoods themselves, who are transformed humans: "they are redwood trees, they were persons" (Waterman and Kroeber 1938: 69).

Construction materials are gathered by upriver or downriver teams. Three variant accounts describe these efforts and their association with widowerhood. Everyone from downriver of the trap gathered up flat stones, representing valuable obsidian blades, and took them into a certain stand of redwoods. Of note, such compensation is doubled at successive offers (2 for 1). A rock represents the hoped for permanence of the new wife.

> At the redwoods the party builds a fire. Next a man is chosen "to lose his wife". He sits down and begins to cry, accompanied in chorus by the whole group. In the fashion of a regular mourning party, they plaster his hair with mucus. Then they get ready to take the redwood boughs for which they came, but the mourner objects on the grounds that it interferes with his "sad" feelings. They proceed to offer compensation for the injury, tendering a payment of two "obsidians." He refuses, and they offer four. The mourner says he will agree if they will give him a woman plus two additional flints, plus a fishing place called *oterä'u*, together with a spring,

tere'qsūr, which is to be found near it. The fishing place is a very good [60] one …
The bereaved man is finally offered all that he demands. The woman named in the
bargain is invariably some well-known character; for example, some lazy woman, or
a famous woman at Blue Creek who has no nose. When the bargain is struck,
someone suggests that they have a Deerskin Dance (Waterman and Kroeber 1938:
59-60).

When they [downrivers] are at Kepel-ito flat, they designate one who [is to pretend
he] has lost a wife. He sits apart from the rest, who are congregating, and begins to
cry. They say, "Let us pay him, so that we can dance." They send a man to him.
The messenger takes mucus from his nose, rubs it on the mourner's hair, and says,
"It is too bad you lost your wife." "Yes." Then he comes back. Another goes to
him. Many go to talk to him. Sometimes one takes four [imitation] obsidians [of
ordinary stone] to him. But the mourner says, "I won't accept them, I want a
woman." The messenger agrees. There is an old woman at *oyoL* who has no nose;
they say they will give her to him. He answers that he will accept her if they also
give him the spring on Kepel bar [where all the women bathe when the dance is
over], because when the women wash there he wants to peep at them from behind.
When they agree, he himself begins to dance because now he has a new wife and the
spring too – then they go a distance up Kepel creek, make camp, and sleep there
(Waterman and Kroeber 1938: 66).

Then some of the dam workers start to go uphill while some stay at the redwoods
for which they have paid. Those on the hill cut sticks, small firs and pines, for the
dam. As they come down again, they hear crying and stop.

The old men say, "Well, I think someone has died here; I hear crying." Then they
send a man to where the crying is. He comes back and says, "The man lost his wife;
he is a redwood, and he wants pay, before we dance again." They agree and send
him obsidians. The messenger comes back to say, "He wants one more obsidian and
a woman." The old men are prepared with obsidians, knowing how many will be
needed. They also pick up a fair-sized rock, which they call a woman. This is taken
to the tree, which says, "Good, I'll take her." Then everything is settled; they have
been paid twice, just like head men owning the dam at Turep. Then they dance again
on the flat on the hillside opposite Kepel (Waterman and Kroeber 1938: 69).

The tree that lost his wife cries and says, "My wife is dead." The old men have
picked out several who stayed at the trees when the rest went uphill after sticks, and
have told them how to cry. One cries for his wife, another acts as his brother, and
others as his relatives. As they cry, they take the mucus from their noses and rub it
on the head of the one who acts the widower until it is covered, so that it looks as if
he were really in mourning.

When they all start back to the dam, they bring the brush cut on top of the hill
(Waterman and Kroeber 1938: 69).

For other areas of the Americas, clear body fluids such as tears and mucus are associated with fragile qualities of life and vitality and so are emphasized in mourning rituals (Miller 1988, 141, the progression is breath, clear fluids, blood, flesh, hair, nails, bones). The generative power of mucus is attested by the story cycle involving Mucus~Snot Boy of the Klallams, who is named for his source substance ejected by a grieving mother (Gunther 1925: 125-31). Mourners do not dance in ceremonies nor participate in fun activities for a year after a death, as a sign of their grief. Others intent on enjoying themselves will gift mourners for that loss while acknowledging their own freedom to enjoy fun.

Summary

Fishing is a cross-gender activity, especially during the brief time of an intense fish run, as when salmon or herring are available in abundance. The hard work of weir construction and use is the responsibility of men, while the sustained effort of preserving fish is the work of women. Children help as age and size allow. Fish themselves are often equated with children, as English does with "schools" of fish. While the "blanket" of fish flesh is removed to feed humans, with proper treatment and handling, the spirit or soul of a fish returns to its home, reborn from its skeleton for another season.

Bodies and outer forms can change, while the soul remains the same. For Hurons, a seine spirit assumed its ultrahuman form to appear in a dream. For Saanich, a fish willow spirit took human form to court and re-marry. For Yurok, humanoid spirits assumed the shape of redwoods, and a rock was identified as a woman intended as a wife. The emotional ties are such, moreover, that the widower grieves and observes the rules and taboos associated with mourning for mortals, such as no dancing, fun, or frolics for a year. To assure continued reincarnations, a series of rituals are held as equipment is readied at various stages, as well as to welcome the fish leader at the first catch.

Spirits are engendered, but paired on the basis of mutual attraction and aid, not for sexual union. Sexuality is an attribute of mortals, not of immortals. By marrying a seine to underage girls, who will still be underage when their year of marriage is over, mutual obligations are met without the threat of sexuality. Gender is the basis of labor such that men generally provide valued food and women prepare it. Children need food from a mother, so a widower represents a particular plea for pity. He can harvest fish, but he can not prepare it for storage, and he may not be able to prepare it for meals, either, given certain taboos that apply during a run as well as the mourning period.

Fishing gear, especially weirs, therefore substitute for human fishers, and add to their efficiency during times of need and scarcity by appealing to humans in need of female mates who are industrious, loyal, and dedicated.[251]

---

[251] An interesting aspect of the role of weirs in cosmology appears in Native California where a Hill Patwin woman reported that Lame Bill, their prophet during the 1870 Ghost Dance, preached that a flood would destroy the world but the Indians would be saved by a big fish trap as everyone else was washed away (Du Bois, *The 1870 Ghost Dance* 2007: 151).

Kinship, Family Kindreds, and Community

Native peoples have always lived in mutually supportive communities whose members included diverse ranks and species. Communal ties exist at many different levels – immediate and extended families, "fictive" kin relations that make community members into family members, "made" kin relations with strangers, and a broad understanding of the relatedness of animals, plants, and landscapes (see Irwin, Kidwell, this volume). The nature of these relations has changed during the last 500 years, but kinship itself, with its des, obligations, and sanctions, has continued to structure most – if not all – native societies. Likewise, as a critical part of social analysis, kinship has long been the focus of ethnographic study. Indeed, in many ways kinship studies have denned scholarship just as surely as kinship itself helps define Indian worlds.

Based on a cultural interpretation of biology rather than straight genetics, any kinship system is largely taken for granted by its members, who regard it as somehow innate. Europeans, for example, often imposed a naturalized Protestant notion of the "feeble family" – a married pair with children – on the native "full family." A grouping of all who ate, slept, worked, and lived together, whether by birth, adoption, marriage, or proximity, the "full family" seemed to many Indian people equally innate and natural. Scholars have sought to put analytical order, not only on "full" and "feeble" families, but on an even greater diversity of kin relations. Families (as an abstracted analytical unit) mesh into larger kinship networks that scholars have defined using three well-known types – unilateral, bilateral, and ambilateral.

Unilateral (one-sided) kinship occurred in more complicated and populous societies where it was traced only through the father, only through the mother, or through each parent for different purposes. In these cases, family households were submerged within lineages, transgenerational linkages through fathers and sons or through mothers and daughters within larger institutions. But patrilineages and matrilineages were not mirror images of each other because men always took the public community positions of leadership in both. In other words, while men were [140] both leaders and kinsmen because of who their fathers were in a patrilineage, for a matrilineage-based community, kinship depended on mothers but leadership passed from brothers to nephews through the common link of a woman who was sister to the office holder and mother to the inheritor, as described for the Iroquois and Hopi since the 1600s.

Lineages are, in turn, components of larger groupings such as clans, phratries, and, sometimes, moieties. While lineages rarely have a name apart from the oldest living grandparent, all of these larger clanship units are named formally. Whether a patrician or a matriclan, real or metaphorical kinship was traced among all clan members, so they could not marry each other. And when, for example, a member of the Turtle clan traveled, he or she would receive a warm welcome and open hospitality in any Turtle clan household, even of another tribe. The virtues of this mystical bond of clanship, therefore, are readily apparent because of the wide range of kin, mutual caring, and supportive protection which are automatically assumed among clans-people. If a member is hurt, injured, or killed, men of the same clan as the victim are obligated to take revenge or otherwise seek justice.

Clans, in turn, gather into phratries, often on the basis of some logical parallel that forbids intermarriage. Thus, clans called Crane, Frog, Sand, and Willow might belong to a Water phratry. Among the Hopi, phratries protect rituals owned by clans from extinction. A ritual's last official will teach its rite to a man in another clan within that same phratry so it can then take over hosting that rite.

Moieties, whether composed of phratries or only of basic households, divide a community into two halves, bisecting the universe into sky or earth, land or water, right or left, and any other likely opposition. In the south, moieties called Red and White, symbolic of War and Peace, characterized the sophisticated Mississippian farmers, the ancestors of tribes who later emerged in the Southeast such as Creeks, Cherokees, Choctaws, and Catawbas. Along the upper Mississippi and Missouri River, various Siouan peoples had Earth or Sky moieties, each composed of a number of clans aligned into land, water, and air phratries. Among the Pueblos of the Southwest, Summer / Winter, also known as Squash / Turquoise, defined the characteristic halves.

Bilateral (both-sided) systems included only about three generations. They focus around a set of individuals who form a kindred, a unit also found in modern American society. Members of a kindred can be traced through both the mother and the father as far as acceptable memory allows. Among tribes, therefore, kindreds were huge. In practice, however, kindreds functioned in terms of significant individuals who guided and directed the membership. Most commonly, a nodal kindred formed around the node of a married couple, and, after their deaths, around a cluster of iheir children, siblings (brothers and sisters) with their spouses and children. A typical example is the *tiospaye* of the Lakota, larger than a married couple for protection but smaller than a tribe to be easily fed. In cases where an office or fetish was inherited, successors formed the descent line of a stem kindred, as with the transmission of certain sacred bundles among towns of the Skidi Pawnee confederacy.

Ambilateral (chosen sides) descent can be traced through both parents, with the resulting discrete units called septs, though actual residence determines which of the possible septs someone belongs to at that moment. Where primogeniture or primacy [141] is vital, high ranks trace membership in a ramage composed only of privileged links such as that from first-born son to first-born son, who in turn marry only first-born daughters, important in the proper inheritance of high or chiefly rank, as among Wakashans of central British Columbia.

Thus, kinship was and is not everywhere the same. Settling among the farming towns of the Northeast, Frenchmen came face to face with elaborate "mother right" matrilineal systems. Again and again, across North America, curious observers would discover yet another tribe or nation with what came to be technically called matrilineal descent, because it challenged or contrasted so strongly to their own naturalized "father right" of kinship traced through men.

Inland in central New York, the Hodenosaunee, renamed Iroquois, gave a strong political cast to their matrilineality by assigning each of the fifty name-tides of the *royaner* ~ federal chiefs of their league to a particular matriline of mothers-daughters within a matriclan named for an animal, plant, or other species-like natural entity. These clans formed phratries and moieties, all traced through women composing the original league of Five Nations (Mohawk, Oneida, Onondaga, Cayuga, and Seneca).

This array of descriptive kinship terms has its own history. While features of Iroquois and related Huron matrilineality were mentioned in Jesuit Relations, perhaps the earliest analytical treatment of native kinship came from Joseph-Francois Lafitau (1685-1740) in his two-volume comparison of the Iroquois with ancient Hebrews, Egyptians, Greeks, and Romans (1724). Indeed, for over a century training in the classics proved vital in establishing frameworks for the interpretation of Indian kinship diversity. Unfortunately, this framework –

86

set in a racist, colonial, Eurocentric context – was avowedly evolutionary, with England or France set unabashedly at its apex.

The most influential of these interpretations was articulated in the massive research and publications of Lewis Henry Morgan (1818-81), the "inventor [father!] of kinship studies." Life experiences in central New York did much to precondition Morgan's interest in kinship. He came from a large wealthy family of half-siblings, married his own cousin, and suffered the loss of his children while away conducting kinship research among tribes in the West.

Trained as a lawyer, Morgan became involved in a men's literary club that modeled itself loosely on the Iroquois Confederacy. He became interested in land frauds that threatened to dispossess remaining Iroquois, and he befriended Ely S Parker ~ *Hasanoanda*, a sixteen-year-old Seneca interpreter and lobbyist who went on to become a civil engineer, Civil War aide to Ulysses Grant, and first native Commissioner of Indian Affairs.

In return for his help in the struggle for their homeland, the Parker family assisted Morgan in his research on Iroquois society, thus pointing the way toward his scholarly career. Relying on his knowledge of Latin and law, Morgan adopted classical terms in order to generalize his findings, though not all have remained in use. Nor was his terminology consistent, using, for example, both tribe and gens for what is now called clan, as in his *League of the Ho-de-no-sau-nee, or Iroquois* (1851). Still, Morgan's treatment is remarkably sophisticated, covering recent history, geography, leadership, councils, beliefs, rituals, reforms by the prophet Handsome Lake, dances, [142] games, settlements, clothing, grammar, trails, place-names, and failures of United States Indian policy.

Having worked out Seneca kinship terminology with the Parkers in 1846, Morgan was delighted to discover a similar pattern in 1858 among the Ojibwa near Marquette, Michigan, where he was pursuing the legal work for railroads that, in rime, made him wealthy. Financial security allowed him to pursue his consuming, detailed, intellectual interest in kinship terminology and systcmatics. Following established procedure, Morgan made a list of 286 possible terms for degrees of kin relationship by descent or marriage. During the early summers of 1859-62, he visited many tribes in the West, filling out these schedules carefully and consistently. Supported by Lewis Cass, Secretary of State and himself a scholar of Great Lakes Indians, Morgan sent copies of this schedule to Indian agents and, seeking global comparisons, to foreign diplomats.

With meticulous care, Morgan assembled and analyzed these lists in his monumental *Systems of Consanguinity and Affinity of the Human Family*, finished in 1866, accepted by the *Smithsonian as Contributions to Knowledge* 17 in 1868, but not published until 1870. Using known linguistic classifications, he arranged the schedules into so-called families (Darnell, this volume). Seeing the "families" in terms of social evolution, he named each after a useful invention thought to characterize a particular stage. Adopting Aryan from "plowing" and Turanian from "horsemanship," he coined for native North Americans the Ganowanian family (from Seneca *gano* "arrow" + *wa-a-no* "bow") and gave lists for 80 tribal examples, divided by language stock into branches according to topographical region, geographical subregions, male or female line, and "rovers" or villagers.

In contrast to American political divisions – town, county, and state – he regarded Ganowanians as organized by tribe, nation, and confederacy, "founded respectively upon consanguinity, dialect, and stock-language" (Morgan 1870: 141). For all of humanity, he argued, kin-term systems were either descriptive or classificatory, depending on whether primary terms were modified to apply to each relative separately and distinctly (e.g. mother's brother) or to generalized clusterings (e.g. uncle) of like relationship (Morgan 1870: 12).

Pursuing larger implications of these data in terms of social evolutionary tenets, Morgan outlined a model of "human progress" in his *Ancient Society ~ Researches in the Lines of Human Progress from Savagery through Barbarism to Civilization* (1877). In the book, he distinguished the social development of the community (*Societas*) from the political development of the state (*Civitas*). Though now embarrassing and discredited, what makes Ancient Society constantly useful is the raw data it marshals and its unhesitating willingness to compare societies cross-culturally. Rome and Greece are treated the same way as Australians, Iroquois, and other American nations. Morgan's terminology here is modern and consistent, using gens for clan, phratry for clan clusters, along with tribe, nation, and confederacy for land based polities. Still missing, however, were terms for lineage and moiety.

Despite its Anglocentrism, Morgan's work truly laid the foundation for much subsequent Americanist research. Later American and British scholarship did not invent a whole new focus (Reining, 1972; Fortes, 1972), but instead returned to data [143] in *Systems of Consanguinity and Affinity of the Human Family*. In Morgan's own lifetime, Scottish writers used his forms to refute some of his own arguments. His spellings have been updated and his lists filled out, but Morgan's data remain fundamental to all subsequent work in kinship. He forever changed the way in which all human societies were studied.

The American West and Northwest presented the next great challenges for this developing model of ancient American (and world) kinship. John Wesley Powell of the Bureau of American Ethnology gathered substantive data on the Numic speakers of the Great Basin, noting polyandry (a woman with several husbands at the same time) and resource territories. Powell proved unable to grasp nodal kindreds as the bases of these small and scattered communities, and he too let himself be misguided by a social evolutionary schema.

Columbia University's Franz Boas, a founder of academic anthropology, researched extensively in the Pacific Northwest and trained several native people to record tribal ethnographies in their native languages. His closest collaborator was George Hunt, son of a Tlingit mother and Scottish trader father raised at Fort Rupert where the dominant tribe was the Kwakiuti (now included among *Kwakwaka'wakw*, "those who speak *Kwakwala*").

The entire Northwest Coast is filled with exceptions to many cherished rules, and it particularly calls into question crude linkages between language, subsistence, and social organization. Though fishers and gatherers, Northwest Coast nations organized themselves as confederacies or chiefdoms similar to the most intensive farmers. Along the modern Alaska-Canada border, matrilineal peoples symbolically based themselves in "houses," variously expressed as cedar plank longhouses, inherited crests and treasures, and corporate holders of fisheries, lands, names, and ranks assumed to be immortal.

Along the mid-coast, among Wakashans like the *Kwakwaka'wakw*, people talked about their membership in *numaym*, a stem kindred that baffled Boas. Understanding of these non-unilineal groupings came in the 1960s among scholars who had worked in the Pacific among islanders with similar systems (Davenport 1959). To existing understandings of unilineality and bilaterality was now added ambilaterality, with "ambi-" indicating that members had a choice in tracing their affiliations. Thus, almost a century after Boas first grappled with the *numaym*, further comparative work in the Pacific (Firth 1957) revealed the importance of choice and claims to prestige for many patterns of descent.

Final clarification of the issue came from a Toquaht chief on the west coast of Vancouver Island, who reminded a Welsh anthropologist (Kenyon 1980: 86), confused about local kinship, that the Nootkan system was much like her own with nobles concerned about both existing kinship and pedigreed descent traced through genealogies of first-borns, while commoners had only kinship to trace relationships to people living in the here and now.

Of Boas's students, Robert Lowie had the greatest concern with kinship (Graburn 1971), but it was Alfred Kroeber (1909), seeking to avoid Morgan's classificatory / descriptive dichotomy, who first codified eight basic kinship principles. These are:

differences between persons of the same or of separate generations, between lineal and [144] collateral relationship, of relative age within one generation, of sex of relative, of sex speaker, of sex of person through whom relationship exists, of "blood" relatives or by marriage, and of life condition of the linking persons through whom relationship exists.

Forty years later, George Peter Murdock (1949: 101) condensed these as the criteria of

generation, sex, affinity, collaterality, bifurcation,
polarity, relative age, speaker's sex, and decedence

Though not common, decedence, a change in kin terms after the death of a linking relative, occurs along the Pacific coast (Miller 1999: 122-9). In all societies, of course, death calls for circumlocutions and polite forms, rather than the use of separate kin terms. Often, these consisted of adding tags, lexicals phrased as "the late," or actual *necronyms* (death names) for defining classes of people who re mourning specific types of relatives (cf. Buchler and Selby 1968: 170).

Among Coast Salish, decedence was such a prominent and wide-ranging feature that it was applied to both affinals (in-laws) and collaterals ("blood" kin on the sides). While expected remarriages explain the affinal shifts, new kin terms for collaterals appear problematic because they involved surviving siblings (aunts and uncles) and their niblings (nieces and nephews), the children of the deceased, who then came under their care for the sake of "family" honor and prestige (Miller 1999).

In all societies, marriage is an alliance between larger families, expanding a network of kin to care for children, both natural and adopted. Rank has always been a factor in these arrangements, because every society has a range of proper and disorderly members. Stable, supportive marriages, with betrothal before birth, often marked high status, while casual liaisons did not. Members of leading families had stable unions so that their homes could provide havens for those orphaned and displaced within the community.

In many native societies, a wedding began as a series of visits and exchanges that sted as long as the alliance. The mother of the groom or her representative brought eat and "male foods" to the bride's family, returning with small gifts. Then the bride's mother came to the groom's family with plant and other "female foods" to show that her daughter knew how to take care of a family. Extreme respect shown after marriage to in-laws, as among Apaches and others, forbid any speech with a mother-in-law, though they shared the same home. In contrast, same-age in-laws, tended for remarriage at the death of a spouse, engaged in ribald joking to prepare them emotionally and socially.

All kindred or clan institutions influenced marriage choices in Native America, and e reflected in six standard kinship types, based on how "cousins" (using the Anerican English term) are classified. Each type, named for the culture in which it is first identified, is found throughout the Americas (Edmonson 1958), and suggests a scale of increasing complexity. The Hawaiian ~ Generational type does not cognize any distinctions except that of siblings, "brother" and "sister," so everyone your generation is either one or the other. Similarly, everyone in the older generatiosns is "father" or "mother," and "grandfather" or "grandmother." Eskimoan, shared with modern America, has separate terms for siblings and for cousins, as well for parents and for uncles and aunts. Iroquoian makes the fine distinction between siblings and cross cousins, the children of your parents' opposite-gender siblings [145] (father's sisters and mother's brothers). Children of your parents' same-gender siblings were parallel cousins (children of father's brothers and mother's sisters). Since your male parent and his brothers are all called "father" and your female parent and her sisters are all called "mother," Iroquoians called parallel cousins "brothers" and "sisters," reserving their "cousin" term for cross cousins. The Sudanese type 'carefully distinguishes siblings, from cross, from parallel cousins.

Most complex are the Crow and Omaha types, which involve clans, matrilineal for Crow and patrilineal for Omaha. Sometimes, to allow for affiliation with the father's clan among Crow or mother's clan among Omaha, a child will be described as born of the proper clan and for the clan of the other parent. In addition to sibling and cousin terms, a special transgenerational term sorts out the linkage and clan of the other or "for" parent. Among Crow, this term applies to father's sisters and all the women who transmit his clan and matrilineage. For Omaha, the term is "mother's brothers," who do the same for her clan and patrilineage. Often, among leading families, marriages occur at least once between the same two clans in each generation to perpetuate a position of power and influence to children.

During Boas's last decade (he retired in 1939 and died in 1941), University of Chicago anthropologist AR Radcliffe-Brown helped shift Americanist research toward a functional mode. Among his lasting contributions was to insist, after a century, that scholars return to Morgan's argument that kin terms and social institutions were mutually interdependent. Scottish writers had long argued that such terms were only "salutations" of little theoretical or institutional import.

In particular, Radcliffe-Brown directed Fred Eggan (1906-91), the premier authority on Americanist kinship for fifty years, to probe Morgan's 1870 schedules yet again. Eggan's long career provides numerous milestones in the technical study of Americanist kinship systems, from the publication of a classic collection in honor of Radcliffe-Brown (Eggan 1937, 1955) to a recent tribute by his students (DeMallie and Ortiz 1994). Eggan and students such as Alexander Spoehr studied tile way in which native kinship systems – as terms, relationships, categories, and behaviors – underwent changes due to pressures toward American bilateral, patri- , centric, kindreds based on "feeble families." Indeed, the major change in native societies has been the growing importance of the so-called nuclear family, a couple and their children, insisted upon by missionaries, government agents, and law courts. Yet these studies show that the "nuclear family" but was not only imposed upon Indian people, but was also used by them as one strategy for living in a hostile world.

"The individual family," observed Alexander Goldenweiser in 1915, "does not often appear as a specific social, ceremonial, economic, or political unit," since the sole contribution by a married couple is "education" in etiquette, life skills, and lore (Goldenweiser 1915: 365). Since a native "full family" could include several wives, and rarely several husbands, it was more of a kindred. Chief Moses of the Colvilles, when repeatedly told to give up all of his many wives but one, responded that he would never "break up his family." White male scholars early concluded that since the father-headed household and family was the culmination of human development, matrilineality was lower in scale (although above chaotic promiscuity). The shift from mother- to father-right, therefore, was regarded as an important step in human social evolution. [b]

A century later, it is clear that societies can and do shift from matrilineal to patrilineal patterns and vice versa, depending on the needs of either gender to cooperate in life skills and tasks. While a shift to patrilineality seems to be unencumbered, the reverse requires an intermediate stage of double descent, where fathers or mothers confer different inheritances on their children, as among the Keresan Pueblos of New Mexico. Classic examples include farming tribes who enthusiastically adopted horses in the 1700s and moved out onto the Plains as bison hunters, abandoning matrilineality for either weak patri- or bi-lineality.

At mid-century, several significant volumes dealing with kinship appeared, including Robert Lowie's masterly summary *Social Organization* (1948), George Peter Murdock's sociological and statistical *Social Structure* (1949), Claude Levi-Strauss's innovative *Elementary Structures of Kinship* (1949, English translation 1969), which presented exchange and alliance theory on a global scale, and Eggan's own *Social Organization of the Western Pueblos* (1950).

Looking at the Hopi, Eggan (1950) developed an all-purpose Pueblo model based in the "abstract" matrilineage and expanding into clans, phratries, moieties, and towns. He then argued that differing structures among Zuni, Keresan, and Tanoan Pueblos were variations produced by ecology and by history – increased proximity to Spanish and then American authority and towns. As an intellectual ideal, Eggan's model has been much discussed. Additional fieldwork among these Pueblos, including efforts by Edward Dozier and Alfonso Ortiz, both Tewas with PhDs in anthropology, suggest that modern Pueblos, speaking languages of four very different families with very different origins, are similar in name only.

In particular, Keresan Pueblos, whose language is an isolate, share a culture distinctively their own, though Eggan tried to divide them into western and eastern segments in order to bridge the matri-Hopi and the bilateral Tewa. Instead, based on fieldwork at Cochiti in the Rio Grande, far to the east of Hopi, Robin Fox (1967a, 1967b) found a double descent system based in matri-clans and patri-kivas (religious chambers). Jay Miller (1972) further explored a model based on gender, with woman a subset of man and left having priority over right, to explain variations among seven modern Keresan towns as logical permutations and to predict a missing eighth town destroyed about 1700. The regional significance of esoteric Keresan priesthoods among other Pueblos, moreover, added a prehistoric dimension that implicates the Keresans as builders of Chaco Canyon.

Ortiz's (1969) research in his home Pueblo of San Juan explicated the importance of Summer / Winter moieties, patrilines, and priesthoods of "made people" for understanding Tewa society. A similar breakthrough in understanding moieties came when fieldworkers visited Tsimshian towns that had not moved to trading posts or missions in the period 1830-60. Boas and his student Viola Garfield had consistently reported four phratries called Orca, Raven, Eagle, and Wolf (Halpin and Seguin 1990). Yet these in-place towns had moieties, like neighboring Haida and Tlingit (Miller 1981, 1997). It then became apparent that moieties had long been the north coast pattern, though relocation of the downriver Tsimshian towns gave an impression of phratries. John Dunn (1984), by analogy with Australian kinship, called these four groupings semi-moieties and found mythological and social evidence linking Orca with Wolf [147] and Raven with Eagle. Moreover, comparing regional kinship terms, he traced a macro-Crow system across three very different languages, whose high-ranking families; frequently intermarried now as in the past.

New theoretical strategies were introduced in 1964 when, after years of toil, Floyd Lounsbury, a brilliant Iroquoian linguist, published a mathematically formal description of kinship semantics (1964a), using Morgan's terms from Seneca though his own E work centered on the Oneida. He also presented a formal account of Crow-Omaha systems (1964b), with stated rules to derive major variants that had been virtually ignored.

During the 1970s, attention shifted from such formalism to the pragmatic uses of kin terms. Scholars began studying how terms are applied in real-world situations ' according to personal intentions among actual or would-be kinspeople. Indeed, in small communities where everyone can be related in multiple ways, someone can be addressed as an "aunt" in the morning when everyone is visiting happily, a "cousin" in the afternoon when money is being asked, and "damn you" at night during a fight. Sometimes relationships are briefly if playfully denied so that teams can be formed for a gambling game, since a firm rule usually prevents kin from betting against each other. Rather than give up gambling, it is easier to give up the relationship for a short time.

This observation, of course, was not new but merely became a focus for systematic inquiry. In his *Omaha Sociology* (1884), James Owen Dorsey inserted a frequent disclaimer about some fixed rule of kinship: "Two Crows denies it." In 1911, *The Omaha Tribe* by Alice Fletcher and Francis La Flesche presented a magisterial overview of this Siouan community, gifted with the insights of La Flesche, himself the fluent Omaha son of Joseph La Flesche (Iron Eye), one of the moiety tribal chiefs. Seeking to reconcile differences with the Fletcher ~ La Flesche monograph, Dorsey made further inquiries among Omaha leaders, sometimes resulting in vague answers. Much later, RH Barnes (1984) suggested that the many overburdening Omaha " rules for and against marriages with various members of other clans were expediently bypassed by maintaining short genealogical memories, deliberate amnesia in the service of alliances. Of greater note, Barnes (1990: 222) discovered a touch point in the "potential for embarrassment between Two Crows and Joseph La Flesche" caused by the marriage of Sioux Solomon, Two Crows' brother, to New Moon Returning, Alice Cline La Flesche Solomon, the second wife of the widowed Francis La Flesche, who married her in 1879, had a child, but became estranged by 1881 and divorced her for adultery in 1883.

Francis La Flesche spent his adult life as an anthropologist dedicated to revealing the complexities of native philosophies. Among his more controversial acts was the purchase and removal to Harvard's Peabody Museum of Omaha sacred objects. In 1989, Omahas of Nebraska repatriated the Sacred Pole known as *Umon'hon'ti* = "Real Omaha" that was the axis and beacon of their universe (Ridington and Hastings 1997). In 1991, its female twin, the White Buffalo Hide known as *Tethon'ha*, came back to stay, after being stolen for a century. With the return of these male and female sacra, Omaha people anticipate a renewal of their community, both

92

materially and spiritually, on their own terms. The importance of such objects points to the larger: dimensions of kinship organization – that of the community as a whole. [148]

While kinship has long been at the defining core of anthropology, community studies have been interdisciplinary across the humanities and social sciences. Though most intense in the 1930s, interest in community studies dates back to the nineteenth century efforts of Swiss-born Albert Gallatan – diplomat, Jefferson's Secretary of the Treasury, and comparative linguist. Indeed, in the Americas, interest in local community scholarship was long stimulated by Swiss and Scottish thinkers, countries known for their intense regionalism.

At the same time that Morgan was collating kinship schedules, the United States was moving into the Southwest. Early military reconnaissance reports drew scholarly attention to the Pueblos as communal, farming, ritually complex, apartment builders; Indeed, the richness, diversity, and complexity, along with intense suspicion and insularity, of all Southwestern nadve peoples – including Pueblos, Pimans, Utes, Navajos, Apaches, and Quechans – encouraged research that proceeded from community to community. Swiss-born Adolph Bandolier was perhaps the first to study communities. Under Boas and Leslie White, however, such separatism became a formal research strategy.

Similarly inspired, Frank Speck studied East Coast Indian people on a community by community basis, as have his students. A Irving Hallowell (1992), for example, expanded the concept of community and culture for all of anthropology when Ojibwa people called his attention to the many "persons" of their universe who were other-than-human. These immortal beings of awesome meaning and purpose help define any native sense of community, though they have largely been ignored or avoided by academics (Galloway 1995; White 1991).

Kinship terms, learned within the household, might be applied throughout the universe. Terms such as "mother" and "father" applied to a broad range of individuals, only some of them human, who were equally persons in native belief. Thus, the Earth and other sustaining forces might be addressed as "mother" in prayers, while "father" indicated the Sun and various supernatural beings who instructed, protected, and sometimes threatened a child.

To be viable, communities existed within a system of checks and balances whose tensions crossed species and extended beyond the eco-system to the co-spiritual. From a native perspective, local communities were defined on the basis of sound. All those living within hearing of the distinctive village call, drumbeat, waterfall, and distinguishing dialect could be regarded as belonging to that community. At least once a year this membership was given public expression at one or more major unifying rituals.

Positioned between place and planet, any community and its constituents required the sponsorship of immortals that were the real "owners" of that territory. The most powerful of all served as patrons, virtual totems, of the community through generations of linkages with its hereditary leaders. This array of place, people, patron, and purpose can be seen, for example, in the mystical totemic (from Ojibwa "emblem, friend, mate") expressions among the Maritime Abenaki. Vital links between kindreds and lands took the form of an animal crest, explained in an epic concerning a Giant Frog who swallowed all the water. As thirst became unbearable, "people" moaned they were as dry as a particular animal – a turtle, beaver, wolf, trout, haddock. [149] Frog was killed, then crushed under a birch tree to force out the water, which ran down the trunk and branches, to form rivers and lakes. During this flood, people became their various animal species, emblems for unifying humans, animals, and their : ancestral lands and waterway (Speck 1915a, 1915b, 1917, 1935; Strong 1929).

Along the Klamath River of northern California, after the beginning of the Karuk world, various immortals sank into the earth in special places. They are visited each year during a world renewal ceremony called the Fixing. During the course of ten days, a priest goes to each spot to light fires, pray, make offerings, sweep away refuse, and set aright stones and other landmarks. Keeping his right hand empty, and his legs crooked, he seeks to attract "luck," the coveted ability to bring wealth and well-being (Kroeber and Gifford 1949). His entourage includes men and boys who shoot arrows to fix the earth in place, and two women who reshape a sand mound and provide firewood so that the priest can stand through the final night looking up at the Karuk sacred mountain. The next day, the White Deerskin or another Dance is performed to display heirloom treasures. The Fixing prevents famine, disease, and cataclysm. By recognizing local immortals, by showing respect for the landscape, and, by setting landmarks on firm footings like the focal mountain, the Karuk world is remade, steady and reliable as a community of relationships.

In the frozen north, Yup'ik of southwest Alaska believe in a primordial, undifferentiated universe whose shifting and permeable boundaries depend on human attention to rules, especially for sharing food, providing gifts, and making up for what others lack. Kinship and community define the nature of human and non-human behavior. A proper person was ever concerned to restrict his or her breath, sight, thought, speech, and body movement; carefully wearing a belt and hood to limit their actions, deter unclean influences, and hold in their life force. Weapons, tools, and containers were carefully made and decorated both to please that artifact itself and to attract game animals.

Before going after seals, hunters prepared beautiful weapons, kayaks, and gear that would appeal to the animals. Women sewed new clothing for the men, who also fumigated their bodies and tools (sitting mat, pack basket, food supplies, and kayak) so as to smell like the land, which attracted seals. Immediately after a seal was killed, it was anointed with fresh water on its mouth and four flippers. Similar regard was shown to land animals, except the five-point anointing used seal oil, because these "persons" yearned for the sea. Yup'ik people demonstrated their active awareness of human duties toward the greater moral universe, where they connected as community members (not as isolated or alienated individuals) by supplying what other "persons" lacked − fresh water to seals, light and heat to belukha whales, and dry land to fish. A good hunter focused on making a passage, a clear way, between himself and the animals he hunted, constantly thinking about and working hard to attract their attention. Clearing snow away from any openings provided a clear view of a man's face so animals could decide to offer him their own flesh. After proper treatment of their outer remains, the spirits of these animals were reborn. Indeed, for Yup'ik, existence was an endless cycle of birth and rebirth, with the same "persons" (both human and non-human) interacting over eons within self-perpetuating communities. Today, as in the past, Yup'ik out on the tundra "feed the land" by burying food and offerings to [150] show their regard for this larger mindfulness. Everything has to be done with slow, careful deliberation to avoid offense. Berries are picked with individual regard, and a good person always turns driftwood to give it a new outlook.

Communities and kinship relations have been transformed repeatedly by various kinds of historical change. According to the careful work of Francis La Flesche with Osage native priests, after uniting on the earth as Sky and Earth moieties, they reorganized their community three times, each phrased as a "move to a new country". First came an internal reordering begun by Water people of the Earth division, with the Isolated Earth priests responsible for a symbolic "house" where all Osage children were named, the Land (particularly Bear and Puma) priests given charge of the "house" where war ceremonies were held, and war or hunt leadership assigned to the Bear, Water, Sky, and Isolated Earth.

Prompt action, however, was impossible because of this excessive ceremonial, so a second reordering improved military tactics, though each expedition was still led by a priest. This "move" allowed various clans, as needed, to organize three types of war parties – composed of men from all the clans, a few clans within one moiety, or a single clan. The third move, by two chiefs from the Ponka clan of the Earth and the Sky clan of the Sky, instituted the civil government. Such leaders held vigil until a spirit patron revealed to each the contents of a great bundle, either medicines (symbolized by cormorant and a root shaped like man and woman) or long life (symbolized by pelican and tattooing).

The goal of this complex religion was a community composed of kin, unbroken lines of descendants stretching far into the future. Today, having deliberately "unloaded" older religious strictures, many Osage people have reordered once again through the Big Moon peyote rituals of the Native American Church, an institution that provides a larger sense of community across the tribes, languages, and races who share its songs, rituals, and tipi churches.

Because natural disasters, from flooding and volcanic eruption to enemy attacks, were ongoing, native communities constantly broke up and reformed, always around the special relationship between local totem and leading lineage, either by inheritance or by revelation. Intermarriage outside of kinship degrees also added to the mix of communities, though the extent of remixing after European devastation was particularly intense. Still, the consistent use of language and kinship reckoning from those former spiritually based communities set the standard for all newcomers.

Today, after 500 years, native kinship has proved remarkably resilient; matrilineality, which has been particularly attacked, survives in the Northeast and Northwest because chiefships and rituals are still derived from mothers. Matrilines can now live far apart, in separate homes instead of a shared longhouse, because phone, van, fax, and e-mail keep everyone in touch. No matri-family is too poor that someone will not have access to this equipment, perhaps at work or the tribal headquarters. Young people lured away from reserves and reservations to earn a decent living and raise a family nonetheless return for the annual powwow or ceremonial, and they too phone home. Later, when they retire on a pension, they return home to live and, often, to help with the costs of ceremonies if they do not take up religious duties themselves. [151]

Even now, members of the First Nations of the Americas uphold the axiom that everything comes down not to a matter of money but to a matter of kinship. Who is connected to whom, from mortals to immortals, defines these tribal universes as much today as it has always done in the past.

Culture, Language, Religion, and Land

It is now generally accepted by the scholarly community that the development of culture and of language coincided with the unique development of the human species. In other words, both culture and language have a single origin and a common underlying system. As human beings have diversified, so too have cultures and languages, but each of these remains translateable into the others because of their shared origin.

That said, however, there remains the fascinating if perplexing problem of accounting for the range of variation among the cultural expressions of different human societies. Thus far, the best explanation is the interaction between a particular set of cultural preconceptions and a specific environment. It is in the intermeshing of people and land that different cultures develop and maintain themselves.

This is an interaction that takes place on a very human level because throughout the world among indigenous populations the land is alive. Land is not property or object; it is a both a being in its own right − with stones for bones and vegetation for hair − and populated by a vaste assortment of being having claim to particular localities − glens, valleys, streams, mountains, and so forth. It is a tradition very much part of the lives of European peasants to this day, yet in the lands colonized by their forefathers, the analogous native beliefs have been disregarded or condemned so that land as property could be usurped. These beliefs have persisted, nevertheless, among the local populations because they have continued to live in intimate [2] association with their homelands.

The relations between humans and ancestral land, therefore, are phrased in terms of access to the spirits or beings who are the immortal residents of an area. In the native view, every aspect of prosperity and everyhuman endowment is somehow traced to the bounty of these spirits.

In fairness to these religious systems, it must be pointed out that, by and large, these references to numerous spirits cloak a fundamental belief in a single deity who is the source for the power apportioned among the various immortals. In short, these many spiritual beings, under close examination, turn out to be merely aspects of a unifying belief in a first cause or High God.

Generally, the complexity of all these relations between humans (as groups and as individuals) to the land base are represented in the mythology of that community. In these sagas, told with increasing detail among the more elite families, are specified the ways and means in which the world has come to be as it is and the proper manner in which immortal inhabitants are to be approached and petitioned. In this way, the religious system is instituted in terms of rituals, sacred places, and objects of power such as medicine bundles or personal tokens.

Often, their Genesis ~ Origin Saga specifies that when the human population was created and scattered, the particular group giving the account will state that the Creator reserved the best gift of all for them, including the original language. Hence, a bond between a culture, a language, a [3] land, and a deity was forged. This belief is sufficiently common to be found in the Bible, where a special relations is specified between God, the Jews, the Holy Land, and Hebrew. Even among the early Christians, Hebrew was believed to be the language of God.

Other cultures held analogous beliefs, Two recent anthropological studies provide case examples with particular relevance to Canadians.

96

Among the Navaho, Dene people of Arizona whose ancestors moved from western Canada a few centuries ago, some of their immortals moved south with them and others became familiar to the people after arrival. In his definitive study of the interrelations between culture, language, and art among the Navaho, Witherspoon (1977: 5) asserts

"all cultures are constructed from and based on a single metaphysical premise which is axiomatic, unexplainable, and unproveable ... A single premise can serve as the starting point for more than one conceptual scheme or ideological system. From this single premise a conceptual scheme developes by the positing of an opposition to it, from which it is them expanded into a more complex structure utilizing analogy, opposition, and synthesis as its tools of construction."

For Navaho culture, this axiom is motion / pause or active / static mediated by air, expressed as Holy Wind (same: 48, 53). Similarly, Navaho and other Athapaskan languages place great grammatical emphasis on these same categories, suggesting that the axiom of the culture applies equally to the component social institutions such as language.

By extension, motion is feminine and pause is masculine, which are also respectively outside and inside. "The symbolic [4] action of ritual is the process by which the Holy People [Immortals] are controlled and compelled. The goal of the earth surface people [humans] is to die of old age after a long life of beauty, harmony, and happiness ... The inner forms of the various natural phenomena are humanoid. They can hear the speech of ritual and can see the movements and prestations involved in the symbolic action of ritual. These inner forms (in-lying ones) of natural phenomena also have inner forms (in-standing wind souls). Just as with the earth surface people, it is the nature or class of the in-standing wind soul that determines whether the particular Holy Person is benevolent, malevolent, or a combination of these" (same: 35-36).

For the Navaho, "This world was transformed from knowledge, organized in thought, patterned in language, and realized in speech (symbolic action). The symbol was not created as a means of representing reality; on the contrary, reality was created or transformed as a manifestation of symbolic form. In the Navaho view of the world, language is not a mirror of reality; reality is a mirror of language" (same: 34, emphasis deleted).

Witherspoon has provided the most sophisticated treatment of another philosophical system currently available for Native North America. He makes clear that the Navaho believe that the world was thought into being by immortals gathered together in a sweat lodge, creating through pulsating rhythm a series of inner and outer forms nested together to create and populate the universe. These immortals provided language and land for the people, who keep in touch with them via religious rituals. In all, a [5] seamless web was created, woven tightly together, of humans, immortals, language, and land.

Among the Mistassini Cree, the long academic controversy over the character of family hunting territories has been resolved by Tanner (1979) in terms of a mystical bond between a senior hunter and the resident spirits of the game animals, particularly the "boss" (or spirit ancestor) of the area. "A central attitude in the conduct of hunting is that game animals are persons and that they must be respected" (same: 130).

"While membership in the hunting group may change from year to year there is continuity of leadership, and the leader is identified with the area used by the group in such a way that we may speak of the leader having overriding title. However, in order to have this title generally recognized the leader must have a history of residence in the area, and a prestige built up on his demonstrated relationship with the animals, in the religious sense..." (same: 186).

"when the group abandons a campsite they must spend some time cleaning up, in order to avoid offence to the spirits, but this mainly involves seeing that the bones of game animals are properly disposed of. If the campsite is not left in a proper condition it is thought that the animals will not return to the area. A Rupert House man explained the same idea to me in a different way. He said that a short time after a group leaves a place where they have camped the 'spirit' of the hunting group leader flies over the site. If he finds everything left as it should be he is pleased, and gives the group good luck in their future hunting. The hunting group leader's spirit cares about [6] between spirit, language, and locale.

I know of two cases of this. A boy from Puget Sound visiting in the Okanagan inadvertantly acquired power and a song using Okanagan words from Rattlesnake. A white woman living around Ellensburg, Washington would sing in Wenatchi Salish about her guardian spirit, although she was otherwise ignorant of this language. I was also told of an Interior Salish man who gain power in Nez Perce territory and sang in that language, but I was never able to confirm the details.

It has taken tens of thousands of years for natives to adapt to the continent of North flmerica and develop many distinctive ways of relating to this landscape. Since the arrival and settlement of Europeans, many aspects of their bond with the land have been shattered and gutted. Nevertheless, its outlines persist in general native beliefs.

To help explain such persistence, the distinction between culture and society needs to be introduced at this time. Culture, as we have seen, is the conceptual framework providing order and meaning to a distinctive lifeway as selectively derived from the canons of universal Human Culture. Society is its behavioral expression, heavily based on the biology of the species. Society consists of closely intermeshed institutions related as a system, such that a change in one produces changes in the others. Yet of them all, science is best able to plot the changes from the most tangible institutions like economy to the least tangible, such as ideology. Two institutions seem to crosscut the others, involving all of them. These are language and technology. Language intrudes on the [8] others because it supplies the order and the terminology for articulating them. Similarly, technology provides the means and representations of them, from the dibble of the farmer to the idol of the deity. Changes in the economy are most likely to have far reaching consequences for the other institutions, particularly language and technology. These are obvious, tangible changes, but they may be more apparent than real since they do not seem to influence the axiom of the culture itself.

Schematically, the meshing of society and its institutions can be represented as follows:

t	Economy	
e		l
c	Polity	a
h		n
n	Kinship	g
o		u
l	Ritual	a
o		g
g	Ideology	e
y		

Accordingly, changes in the economy effect the organization of the group and its leadership, often modifying the kinship system by changing the pattern of residence, fill of these, of course, alter relations with the supernaturals, requiring new or modified rituals and explanations. The vocabulary and grammar of the language are changed or even replaced by another, often after a period when speakers are bilingual to some extent. Yet, as we are only now beginning to realize, the replacement of one language by another does not mean that fundamental relations are broken or changed. In Australia where English has replaced some aboriginal [9] languages, linguists are now aware that speakers are not using standard English, for they have turned English into an aboriginal language in terms of etiquette, intent, and meaning. The same can be said of the English that has replaced many native languages in the Americas.

The difficulty with all this change, of course, is that the society is never balanced or content. The system remains disharmonic while struggling for a new synthesis, vulnerable to outside and hostile pressure in ways that result in reactions that are more intense and severe than previously. Throughout this period while stability is sought, the rudder is provided by the on-going relations with the land and its innate inhabitants, who have provided the wisdom and council from ancient times. It is this sacred and eternal link of human to land that provides the surest hope and opportunity for continued existence and intelligent use of the planet.

Followership

Ray Fogelson, during off moments, often suggests that, instead of discussing the "problem of leadership," academics should instead look at "followership." Evoking its difficulties, using one of his frequent antediluvian references, he seeks to encourage such efforts by offering the Sammy Kaye Award for northern Athapaskan leadership. As part of his act, Kaye, known as the "master of swing and sway," would select someone from the audience for a contest he called "So You Want to Lead a Band," hand over his baton, and watch as everyone convulsed as this "leader" failed miserably to get anything tuneful from the trained musicians. Clearly, if you can not lead, no one can follow. Positions have to be both reciprocal and mutually supportive.

During the 1960s, when young native leaders were coming to the fore, uniformed in crew cuts and pen festooned pocket inserts, Ray actively wondered about the basis for their followerships, particularly in terms of Weberian notions of authority. He expressed concern with how and why people listen to a leader, on the basis of both institutional contexts and interpersonal skills.

> Continental social history, as mentioned previously, de-emphasizes the role of the individual in history. In partial contrast, American scholars – anthropologists as well as historians – have tended to single out individual Native Americans as leaders, heroes, and subjects for life histories, even though the idea of biography or autobiography is foreign to most non-Western cultures. Americans seem almost obsessed with a cult of leadership and tend to ignore what Max Weber recognized long ago: that systems of authority, be they traditional, charismatic, or bureaucratic, must be conceived as <u>social</u> relationships. I look forward to the time when we will see institutes, training programs, and Newberry conferences devoted to the topic of followership (Fogelson 1985 : 82-83).

Throughout the Americas, communities commonly divide between civil and military leaders, between what Fogelson calls peacefare and warfare and others call chiefs and captains. Yet both leaders, most especially as representatives of their large families, remain so central, Fogelson suggests, by analyzing them in terms of the ventrality or dorsality of variable human social structures and, in particular, defining those pivotal junctures where these ends meet.

For far too long have academics merely assumed that followers are automatically "there," ignoring the needful processes whereby they, like leaders themselves, must be socialized to learn the tricks of their deferential trade, telling someone how great s/he is in hopes doing no more than is necessary, supporting someone else as chair to avoid sitting in it themselves, and, generally, staying in the shadows to be spared any searing heat during moments of intense crisis.

While the lesser restraints and greater freedoms of a follower receive some appreciation, the more common attitude among the jaded mainstream is that unless you are the lead sled dog, the view from behind is the same. Unfortunately, such a quip is unfair to the multitudes and varieties of those who saunter along behind, setting their own pace by the beat of a personal drum.

Indeed, more than anything else, followership is about pacing, staying and keeping together with a shared assurance and identity. Understanding this characterizing motion becomes easier if notions inherent in English emphasizing nominals, stasis, and product are put aside in favor of native notions extolling verbal, dynamic, process, and flow. Thus, in native America, everyone is already moving, so the trick was and is to forge together in the same direction. Such a shared motivation toward cohesion involved any and all of the special interest groups (*sigs*) that made up all native communities. Generally, while effected by season and locale, these sigs fit into the four domains led by a chief, a captain, a shaman, and a matron, respectively concerned with welfare, protection, wellness, and production.

These sigs each have a focal adept (a *siger*, Miller 1997) to provide coordination among all the members. As such, sigs are fundamental to all other social forms, whether egalitarian or stratified, variously expressed as societies which were more flat or those which were apical, prone or peaked, level or layered.

As the archaeological record shows, particularly for Mississippian centers of the Southeast, local communities remained much the same after the collapse of a chiefdom, continuing the same routines before, during, and after the hegemony of a regional polity such as Moundville (Galloway 1995: 63).

Thus, any attempt at a distinction between Durkheimian conceptions of mechanical or organic solidarity must regard these as sequentially overlapping rather than absolutely either/or because all prior community organizations expressed by sigs survive within an apical form, though they become more tightly or extensively integrated within the whole. With the collapse of that chiefdom, however, this tightening dissolves and older patterns reassert their own greater autonomy.

Within seemingly level societies, such as those in the Great Basin, authority rests with various "experts" often called task leaders in the professional literature, although "sigers" is used herein to indicate that each such adept contributes to the multiple facets of sigs, ranging much more widely than strictly economic concerns. In all instances, a spiritual sanction from an immortal patron provided the basis for any authority and instilled the necessary confidence for someone to stand out in front to take the lead. Indeed, while such communities are typically treated as egalitarian, they are pervaded with inequalities based on the ownership and transfer of such valued knowledge and expertise.

More than anything else, the native Americas defined themselves in terms of such information systems, the control of knowledge, often esoteric, about the very profound dimensions attached to the most seemingly ordinary and prosaic things, such as gender and the food chain. Such knowledge, carefully and selflessly used, conferred access to immortal power and assured long life to the holder and his or her kin and sigs. Total knowledge, however, was diffused among all these sigers for the benefit of all, since concentrated power was suspect since it was regarded as especially likely to be used or abused selfishly.

By widening the definition of both leadership and followership to include interest groups, narrow limitations concerned only with tasks of subsistence or kinship are overcome and all collective activities or intentions from schooling to aesthetics and entertainments are included. By analogy, any member of a sig might be designated a "sigee," if necessary, to detail the full network of relations involved in any process. Thus, sigee/siger provide the basis for any socio-political unit, enabling the transfer of accurate knowledge of benefit to larger organizations needing expertise, coordination, and goal-oriented success.

For example, in the Subarctic,

> In the traditional system of the Chipewyan, leaders were able to attract adherents because they were men who so understood the bush that they were able to make skilled decisions about locations that led them to food. As their skill was displayed over time, less skilled judges of the environment ... followed their lead (Sharp 1988: 90).

In this way, all benefitted from the skilled knowledge of a siger, regarding his "luck" as divinely inspired so as to be of benefit to all in his overall care. Assured success bolstered the confidence of all those involved, strengthening their shared sense of identity.

Within each settlement, the chiefly family assumed the role of being a siger of sigers, of serving as executive coordinating all sigs and sigers into an effective and productive system by acting as the nexus of information flow so as to make the best overall management decisions. Channels of communication had to remain open, so he had to judge dispute settlements, as among the Tahltan Subarctic Athapaskans, where each chief listened carefully to his own followers before going outside to announce their consensual position loudly into the air. All those in hearing then understood the differences and sought their resolution. Thus, without direct confrontation, each chief worked toward a compromise in a society where

> "The chieftainship even of old was more a position of honor than of power. In time of peace a chief represented the family, within which he arbitrated all disputes, and took precedence on all occasions of ceremony. He was accorded the place of honor at feasts, and received proportionately the greater number of presents. Generally of larger means than his fellows, his following was thereby increased, and he was the recipient of service and presents from his household, but he hunted and worked as did others. His obligations to the poor and dependent members of the family were recognized. In case of war his counsel was sought and, age permitting, he was the logical leader. Each family was a distinct organization, controlling its internal affairs, recognizing only the authority of its own chief [siger], and meeting the other families on common ground" (Emmons 1911: 28).

While a singular form often identifies someone as "the chief," such responsibilities were actually split between two genders bridged by a married pair in which the wife was siger for women's sigs and the husband led both men's sigs and those of the entire community. Members, of course, recognized themselves as segregated into female or male activities, sharing information across this division within the marriage bed. Children and the aged had the advantage of greater flexibility in that they could fill in where and when as needed.

The Western Apache (Goodwin 1969: 131) provide the best discussion of these women sigers.

> "Industry, even temper, avoidance of gossip and trouble-making or other quarrels, a wise head, and a strong body were the main characteristics of a woman chief. In this she was the example par excellence of what a woman should be. She was never idle but continually engaged in household tasks, care of children, basketry, preparation of

buckskins, farm work, or gathering and preparing wild foods. She differed from her husband in that no work was below her dignity, and through her hard work and diligence she became wealthy – another prerequisite of women chiefs. Social patterns decreed that those who were wealthy must also be generous, and so the woman chief was continually giving away food to poorer people who came, knowing that they were not likely to be refused. Such a woman's wealthy was augmented by her husband's success, as was her husband's wealthy by her industry" (Goodwin 1969: 167).

Western Apache women chiefs harangued at war dances and sometimes spoke in councils, but

"Their principal function, after setting a good example by their behavior, was to organize other women into wild-food-gathering parties and harangue them on the necessity of having plentiful food supplies for the winter. During large feasts women chiefs encouraged other women to help prepare and cook the food. When a war party was out, she would tell the other women to prepare plenty of food and *tulibai* for the men's return. She spoke to other women concerning family matters such as care of children, respect for husbands, and avoidance of quarrels. Her efforts gave her prestige not only in her own family cluster but with women in other units of her local group, and because of her social position, she was treated with respect" (Goodwin 1969: 168).

Within regional systems, such as those articulated by a waterway, valley, or other passage way, a chiefly family in the most central location, such as the river mouth, had precedence or centrality in the overall flow of information, using hospitality and generosity to attract and disperse such knowledge to their advantage. By virtue of their convenient location on the landscape, such a chiefly family also had a large resident population of supporters.

Moreover, as shown by the archaeological record of the Southwest and Northwest, when defense was needed against a human or other foe, military leaders arose within closed spaces to become sigers at a third or fourth higher degree with supporters now producing for their own needs, as well as for taxes, tribute, and surplus to support that nation.

Followership was organized by existing routines in each society, called into play when signaled by internal conditions and external restraints. While the more inclusive notion of sigs is used here, a classic statement, appropriately Cherokee, involves the "structural poses" defined by Gearing (1962) leading to the development of modern Cherokee government from that of the local towns. These four and more poses, unfortunately limited only to the domain of men in each autonomous town, served to structure roles, statuses, ranks, and intent when signals appeared to indicate the activity of councils and rituals; aggressive acts like warfare, ballplaying, and diplomacy; clan matters such as marriage and revenge; hunting and householding; or, perhaps, male contributions to farming through ritual observances and brief labor (Gearing 1962: 12, 29). For women, two likely poses involved provisioning and childcare, which provided the "cadence" for the local community (Gearing 1962: 2). Fogelson (1971: 329) noted that these poses neatly split between White concerns with peace and womenly affairs or Red conflicts mobilizing men.   Passage between these poses, sigs, and roles was regulated by ritual transformations, supervised by elderly priests on behalf of the community.

Authority was vested in the elders, known as "beloved men," which also formally included "beloved women" (*gagi*), of whom Nancy Ward was probably the most famous for her charity to the British.   Because deference was automatically given to the aged (Gearing 1962: 59), Cherokee upholding their all-pervasive Harmony Ethos made the explicit equation that old = good = honor (Gearing 1962: 60), with the understanding that good = artfully circumspect (Gearing 1962: 61).   A lifetime devoted to these ideals gave an elder a valued reputation for moral virtuosity.

Leaders, setting themselves slightly apart from all others, were expected to exhibit assurance, inner strength, modesty, self-awareness, self-control, and decisiveness that was always morally appropriate but never overbearing.   While captains could compel during hostilities, chiefs could not command, instead only being able to persuade by good natured, clear, and colorful reasoning.

For Cherokee, men "must exercise foresight so as not to intrude," being quiet, cautious, inoffensive, and circumspect, but, most especially, avoiding direct confrontation, overt hostility, competition, or self-assertion at all costs (Gearing 1962: 31-32).   Instead, Cherokees nudged action from others by eloquence in public and compelling magic in private, though this combination was discretely overlooked when John Howard Payne, the journalist ethnographer, was told that "chiefs bind the hearts of their subjects [by] native politeness alone" (in Gearing 1962: 11, 39).

Career advancement was determined by age and ability, along with ongoing attrition of other obligations,

> when a Cherokee man reached his late forties or early fifties, subtle changes occurred in his life style.   As his prowess as a hunter and warrior began to decline, he started to "settle down" and achieve a greater degree of parity in the domestic household.   Cherokee often mark this juncture in the life cycle as taking place when a man's hair starts to turn gray.   Gray hair connotes accumulated wisdom, knowledge, and power.   The active, assertive, and impulsive strength of the warrior is transmuted into the passive, self-constrained, measured moral force of the tribal elder.   Generally his position within the family becomes increasingly solidified, particularly with the departure of this wife's brothers upon their own marriages, with the death or decline of the wife's father, the departure of a man's own sons after their marriages, and the respect and support accorded him by his daughter husbands.   In other situations where this process of progressive integration is impeded, a man might separate from his wife and return to his natal village to reside with members of his own matrilineage, where he might enjoy the status of a "beloved old man."   In sum, this critical juncture along the life cycle, involving the structural transition from the status of young man to old man, can be conceptualized as a non-repetitive transformation from Red to White (Fogelson 1971: 329-330).

In most cases, the aim of any life was, for good and all, to perform an adequate job with the means and resources at hand, making any (over-)achieving adepts all the more attractive because they were so few and far between. Most people wanted to get along with a bit of hedge against hardship. Their lives were made that much more satisfying if someone else took responsibility to guarantee this insouciance would be possible.

Several strategies helped to attract supporters and followers to a siger, allowing for different degrees of complexity. Common to all of these was the assumption that humans are social primates, expecting to live and die as members of some collectivity where give, take, and motion were inherent to existence. Yet, like amoeba pseudopodia, certain attractions or thrusts toward specific directions tended to carry along the rest of the organism by shear momentum. Like amoeba, most such movements are based on the needs of provisioning, the primary role of every community siger (and a noteworthy Fogelson propensity).

For example, among the Subarctic Wet'suwet'en (Bulkley Carrier), multiple wives and slaves assured a chief of providing largesse

> A stingy chief who sought only his own profit soon lost his influence....Only a chief could lead a war expedition, because no one else possessed the means to gather the stores of food necessary to feed the warriors from different places who assembled to take part in it; but if it succeeded, he was given all the captives, who there forward became his slaves.... If the Indians demanded from their chiefs liberality, protection, and leadership, they in turn could demand that voluntary submission to their rulings without which the phratries and clans would have lost their coherence and the chiefs their prestige (Jenness 1943: 518).

As always, some strategies are universal, occurring at all levels of societal integration, while others are obviously confined to the apical. Among the most general are the obvious fact of willing participation, based on consensus that was a reflection of good breeding by the family, kin, and community. People worked together for the common good because they knew and understood the many advantages of a shared identity. Paramount for this good was general immediate satisfaction, making long range planning that much more difficult even though deliberations, as Iroquois say, should involve any lasting effects over "seven generations."

Followers might have any or all of several motivations for taking their cues from a siger. First and foremost is their shared (self-) interest, which might be expressed as loyalty, kickbacks, or doling out. Everyone is already in motion, so the concern becomes to orient members toward the same direction. Sometimes, the motivation comes from outside, as when a perceived or real threat forces people to band together for mutual protection. More than safety in numbers, such decisions are strongly influenced by "blood is thickest" arguments about the requirements for family solidarity in which the eldest kinsman sets the pace for all others.

Followership has been expressed by at least four metaphors, viewing their common identity – as family, as team, as body, as clock, or a chorus.

Foremost among the expressions for shared roles with clear and ready advantages was that of members of a <u>family</u>, a kinship unit traced through both or either parents from the past into the future. Often the entire community regarded itself as a family at more inclusive levels, with the chief siger called the "father", or, among the Keres Pueblos and Haida, the "mother" of the town.

With more integrative purpose, supporters viewed themselves as members of a <u>team</u>, with their siger acting as a coach to help them achieve some common goal. Indeed, during times of particular stress, such a team model was invoked to restore social harmony, as among the Tewa

Pueblos where Summer / Winter moiety tensions were overcome by forming Married / Unmarried teams crosscutting the entire town (Ortiz 1969, 1965: 393).

Sometimes, followers viewed themselves as a <u>body</u>, as among Lushootseed (Puget Sound) Coast Salishans, where a chief is called "the nose" because he went out in front as others came after at their own pace. In this manner, the siger had more of a directional than a determining effect, although someone with too slow a pace could be left behind or temporarily abandoned by the group. A Suquamish who chose to finish a canoe rather than join the other villagers move to a fishing camp found himself ostracized until he apologized and proved his recommitment to the communal ethic (Miller and Snyder 1999).

Often, building on body imagery, a group has the attributes of a <u>clock</u>, a union of place and time. Yup'ik Eskimos of coastal Alaska nicely capture this temporal and spatial unity in their language with words like *ciuliaq* = "ancestor, leader" from *ciu-* meaning the forepart of a body, front area, or time before; in contrast to *kingu-* meaning rear end, back area, or time after (Fienup-Riordan 1990: 202, 212).

The most elaborate example of this fusion occurred among the Maya, who once derived a regional siger as a consequence of "seating the cycle" of their calendars. For example, in Yucatan, the Mayan Itza and the Toltec Xiu, though they remained dogmatically 4 <u>katuns</u> apart,

> agreed that the right to seat the cycle conferred upon the city that did it dynastic and religious primacy over the whole country for 260 <u>tuns</u> [a <u>may</u> ?? of 13 <u>katuns</u>, or about 256 years]. At the end of that time the primate city and its road and idols were ritually destroyed, and a new cycle seat was established.... The seat of the cycle enjoyed an overall preeminence, but the actual rule of the country was vested in the lord of the <u>katun</u>, the Jaguar (<u>Balam</u>) and his Spokesman (<u>Chilam</u>), and was supposed to rotate among the subsidiary cities. Commonly more than one city claimed the honor, which conferred tribute rights, control of land titles, and appointments of public office (Edmundson 1982: xvi-xvii).

Sometimes, supporters regarded themselves as something like a <u>chorus</u>, with a leader indicating their same rhythm or harmony. Of interest, this model has survived centuries of repression in that, today, at least two Tsimshian hereditary matriclan chiefs are church organists, setting the musical pace for their own congregations despite leadership by ministers from the dubious or hostile "outside" (Miller 1998).

Apical sigers were more coercive than coordinating, relying on force – physical, spiritual, psychological, magical, or vaguely implied – to achieve an enlightened self-interest. Often, such "high chiefs," whether men or women, had bodyguards, the right of life or death over subjects, and retreats at some remove from the general populace. As the rich everywhere, they had larger houses and more of them in strategic locations. In the Andes, the sheer rock wall verticality continually reinforces intertwined metaphors among mountain peak, anatomical head, and political leader, along with mountain mass, human body, resident followers ( ). The imagery comes from the landscape, but its expression was very much political among the Inka.

Thus far, only straightforward, <u>quid pro quo</u> communities have been treated, but there are others, such as those halved by moieties where followers must cross or crisscross their own identities to provide needed services for "the other side." Of course, they have already done so at births, marriages, and deaths if exogamy was the rule, so they were already "half convinced" to do their duty. The rest of the push came from the universal ethic throughout Native America of "selflessness," of what I have called "oblique responsibility" in which all persons are more obligated to others for his or her own welfare rather than only to themselves. Such persons blend aspects of geology, climate, biology, and the spiritual such that each relies on the others for the welfare of all. Thus, everyone of note needed a guardian spirit or immortal patron because native societies recognized and valued the needs of others, in all places, dimensions, and senses of being.

In this way, the <u>duels</u> built into society between the civil and military also became expressed in the <u>duals</u> of moieties where it was expected that your "other" side would welcome you at birth, gift you at marriage, build your house, and bury you at death in return for feasts, enjoyments, and other compensations from your "own" side.

Such recognition given to "sides" within an overall unity harkens back to the gender division of husband and wife in the self-same role usually designated "the" chief. In addition to its complementary expression by married couples in all societies, as sigers of male and female domains, it also had an asexual aspect in that the members and sigers of matrilineal clans expressed such engendered pairings as siblings, where the brothers were the public sigers of the clan while the sisters were the corporate but more private providers of both future supporters and nephew heirs.

In sum, the relation of supporter/siger relies on the basic flow of information to assure a satisfying life, not a maximized one. Instead of excess, the goal of this balanced relationship was shared identification and assurance as members of the same unit. In much the same way, the laird of a Scottish clann became The McGregor to all the others of that name, as their metonym.

The intensity and comfort of such an identity, faceted by gender and age, is lost on most academics, as Edward Said (1978: 27) has charged Orietalists and John Demos (1994: xii) has self-confessed for Americanist historians. Yet such identification is all consuming, a kind of rooting in time and in place.

While the sources of followership include shared primate biology of sociability, personal autonomy modulated by oblique responsibility, and spiritual imprimatur, such rooting − a profound telluric sense of place and time, an overall identification with an earth bound landscape. In the same way that sigers constitute the basis of/for expert authority within any society, so are all of its aspects localized in time and space. Native languages routinely fuse these time-space dimensions as the "deictic," but a more useful term for ethnographically understanding such symbolism is the word "tysic" contracted from the phrase "time-space center." Most often, a culture expands on its *tysics* as a series from the heart of a person to that of a siger, through the hearth of a house, sacred fire of the town, sacred bundle of the community, landmark of the region, sun in the heaven, and mind of the creator (Miller 1980a, 1980b). In this regard, sigers serve as magnets within the overall national territory as fixed by local geology, climate, settlement, and season.

To follow, for all of the Americas, therefore, required knowing your own place and time (such as the Chicago of Raymond Fogelson) and a willingness to share and help with others, who thereby provided you with their own support, encouragement, and bounty to lead an adequate but not extravagant life of benefit to everyone, everywhere, and everywhen. Since all of these facets are already thoroughly interconnected, any and all purposes were best served when all agreed to the same syncopation.

Changing Moons:
A History of Caddo Religion

Abstract

From their homeland around the intersection of modern Arkansas, Texas, Oklahoma, and Louisiana, Caddos had a great impact throughout the heartland of Native North America. This impact, developed over a thousand years as the westernmost Mississippians, can best be considered from a broad comparative perspective, extending over space − from the Southwest to the Plains and Southeast − and over time − from the fires of temple mounds to the fireplaces in tipis during peyote meetings of the Native American Church, spread along the Caddo diplomatic network. As with famous examples from the Northwest Coast, Caddos once had complex class rankings. The history of Caddo religion, from ancient priests to the recent prophets known as *yoko*, recapitulates the collapse and rebirth of the great nations of North America, except that Caddos have had the sure guidance of Moon (*neesh*) and his changing representations. Keywords: Caddo; religion; leadership; origin myths; temple mounds

those of Christ, and while the aged priest in charge of the perpetual fire atop temple mounds has faded from the historic record as Catholic priests became entrenched, the more flexible role of the *yoko* long survived to engage in prophesy and to rekindle yearly a sacred fire.

Overview

Caddos, belying their decimated numbers in recent centuries, have had great influence in native North America as traders, prophets, and politicians.[252]1 Their theocracy − composed of towns with complex ranks headed by a priest called *shinesi* (*tsah neeshi* ~ "Mr Moon") empowered by the Creator (*a'a caddi ayo* ~ Father Above Chief) and the culture hero (neesh ~ Moon) − involved elaborate ceremonialism, confederacies headed by a high priest (*gran tsah neeshi*), and international networks, including postharvest fairs, that extended their authority through the Plains and Southwest. Caddo also shared features of ranking and ritual with the Southeast, the Circum-Caribbean, Mexico, and even the North Pacific Coast.

Over time, Caddo religion has used "moon" to refer to rings of posts, circles of fresh-cut reeds, a vision-inspired "foundation," and most recently the crescent altar at peyote meetings. Similarly, the miracles of *Neesh* (Moon) have been blended with [b] Caddo ancestral homelands, historically occupied by about 30 "tribes," were located away from bayous, along upriver

---

[252] The Caddo interviews that sparked this paper were a dividend of my ongoing interest in the Delaware. To better understand the Delaware background of Anadarko elders, however, I had to ask for information about their own family traditions. Since the Hoag sisters spoke Lenape (Delaware) and Caddo, and were superb sources for both, my Caddo data grew appreciably, although it took a decade to analyze its significance. Moreover, having done fieldwork throughout North America, particularly in the Southwest, Southeast, and North-west, I quickly sensed among "high class" Caddos a similar regard for status, privilege, and ranking. The full extent of Caddo impact, however, only became apparent when I was able to track the profound and extensive effects of their regard for Moon.

sections of the Neches, Red, Ouachita, and Arkansas within the oak, hickory, and pine woodland of the Trans-Mississippi South (Gregory 1986; Newcomb 1984). Caddo culture developed after AD 800 (Hughes 1968; Perttula 1992), as indicated by maize farming, mound towns known as civic ceremonial centers, and the continuous manufacture, use, and trade of salt, bows, bear grease, fine pottery, and soft, black, velvety hides.[253]2 As in the Great Basin, each tribe along a home river was often named for a local food, such as pawpaws (Natchitoches), blackberries (Nebedache), or honey bee (Anadarko).

Before epidemics, estimated to have killed as high as 94% of the population between 1690 and 1890 (Perttula 1992), the peak Caddo population may have been 250,000, as suggested by the shadowy complexity of their religious, political, and social institutions. Survivors of many dispersed hamlets amalgamated at mound centers, fostering three confederacies: Cadohadacho at the great bend of the Red River in the southwestern comer of Arkansas, Natchitoches on the Red River in Louisiana near Shreveport, and Hasinai along the Neches drainages of East Texas.[254]

The predominant language family on the pre-horse Plains, the Caddoan linguistic family (Holder 1970; Parks 1977; Wedel 1979)[255]4 consisted of Caddo proper. Pawnee to the north (including the three South Bands, Skidi, and Arikara) (Dorsey 1904a; Parks 1991), Wichita

---

[253] The process of producing the soft black luster of vegetable-dyed skins was apparently known only to the Hasinai (Griffith, *Hasinai Indians of East Texas* 1954: 97).

[254] Memberships in these confederacies shifted overtime, ultimately consolidating into the modem Caddo Nation of Oklahoma under the guidance of Jose Maria, By the 1600s, the Cadohadacho ("real Caddo " at the great bend of the Red River near Battle Mound (cf 117 #270) included Upper Nasoni, Upper Natchitoches, and Nantsoho (Neuman 1974).

The Natchitoches included the Doustioni, Ouachita, and, later, the Lower Yatasi. From about 1702 to 1713, after a flood and crop failure, many Natchitoches lived with the Acolapissa on Lake Ponchartrain (above later New Orleans, founded in 1718 as the Spanish were settling San Antonio). Andre (Penigauh) Penicaut (1953), a master carpenter who served as their escort, reported their Choctawan Acolapissa neighbors massacred 17 Natchitoches and captured 50 women. Such attacks were frequent in the region since another Choctawan group, the Mugulasha ("other siders"), had been wiped out in 1700. Motivations included the opportunity offered by an unguarded moment, taking women to swell tribal ranks, or a growing fear that the migrants were taking away some sacred talisman.

The Hasinai (specifically the Haynay ~ Hainai) of East Texas led the Nacogdoche, Nadako ~ Anadarko, Lower Nasoni, Nacao, Nacachau, Neche, Nabedache, Nacono, and Nechaui. Before they split up and were eventually absorbed by the Anadarko, the Nasoni probably lived along the upper Sulfur River. Unconfederated neighbors were the Eyeish ~ Aish and Adai ~ Adaes).

On the frontier nearest Osage enemies, the 1687 Cahinnio Caddo of the upper Ouachita River delayed the inevitable by concentrating at a single town of 100 cabins (near Camden, Arkansas), before they dispersed among the Cadohadacho, Minto Wichita, and Quapaw.

[255] The Caddoan language family was defined in 1891 by Major John Wesley Powell of the Bureau of American Ethnology.

(including historic dialects of Wichita[256] ~ Tawakani-Wako ~ Iscani), and Kichai, whose few survivors mostly joined the Wichita.[257]6 More remotely, the Caddoan proto-language seems to have been related to Iroquoian and Siouian linguistic stocks.

Caddo (South Caddoan) included related dialects of the Texan Hasinai, described in Spanish sources (mostly the writings of Catholic priests),[258]7 as well as more diverse dialects, particularly Cadohadacho or Natchitoches, found along the Red River, as reported by French officials and traders.[259]8

The Caddo language itself provides fascinating glimpses of past greatness. For example, polite forms indicating status include the title of *sah*, translated as Ms ~ Mrs, and *tsah*, translated as Mr.[260]9 Parsons (1941: 26) translated it "sir," although "lord" or "lady" might also be appropriate. Throughout the languages of the world, the use of such honorifics indicates the importance of social classes with graded ranks. That Caddo has preserved these terms suggests past societal complexity. Also indicative of ranking were diplomatic protocols (a variety of "courtesies" paid to visitors), including formalized weeping as a greeting, extending the right arm in salute, and being carried into town, sometimes on utters. Moreover, the gesture of reverence with outstretched arms, known to the Florida Apalachee as the "gua (Hann 1988: 339), was addressed to Caddo high leaders.

Wallace Chafe (1976, 1979, 1983: 245), a linguist who studied both Caddoan and Iroquoian, noted that Caddo shares with Muskogean languages meaningful particles indicative of ritual elaboration, such as *-kid-*, indicating "something done on a raised surface like an altar," or -*haat*; meaning "something done in water," as when worshipers at a Creek Busk Green Corn Ceremony "go to water." Today, the present Caddo word for church (*'iniku'*) also means hill,

---

[256] Wichita proper included Wichita, Towahesh, Minto, Ita, Kirikiris, Akwiis, Isiis, and others.

[257] The name Kichai was translated by Kai Kai, the last known speaker, as "going in wet sand," while Pawnees render it "water turtle." About 1774, Kichai split into two groups, associated with either Wichitas or Caddos. Today, their mixed descendants still maintain two distinct cemeteries near Anadarko. Such diverse alliances, even while their numbers dwindled, suggests that their most likely homeland was a Caddoan archaeological complex in the well-connected Arkansas Valley of eastern Oklahoma (Rohrbaugh 1982: 55). Their multiple alliances, continued as separate cemeteries, suggest that they once occupied the ceremonial and trading gateway at [257] Spiro Mound, where the lumpy exterior of Craig mound (over the great mortuary chamber) implies larger ramifications. Given the continent-wide symbolism of the turtle, a possible association of Kichai, Craig Mound, and the world turtle should be investigated.

[258] Spanish Recollect Franciscan missions rebounded in 1690, 1716, and 1721.

[259] In their warm homelands, Caddos wore few clothes until missionaries imposed a sense of modesty and forced migrations northward encouraged them to adopt features of tribal costume from Delawares, Kickapoo, and Shawnees. Men wore many shell ornaments, pulled a topknot of hair through a silver tube and, dangling from the nasal septum over the mouth, wore a medallion or animal, which provided the Caddo's designation in the gestures of Plains sign language as "pierced nose."

[260] While the Spanish *don* ~ *doña* seem near translations, linguists interested in sound symbolism related to gender, in this case ts/t/s, should note that Lushootseed Puget Salish uses *ti* to indicate "the (man)" and *tsi* "the (woman)."

mound, and prayer (Parsons 1941: 26) because, some say, one has to go up to pray to God. More likely, the word means "building, build up, arise," whether referring to an artificial earthen pile, wooden frame, or heart-felt words.

The Caddoans began the 1600s spread of the calumet (pipestem) ceremonial fostering intertribal diplomacy, strategic alliances, and formal adoptions. After the 1700s, the Cadohadacho had quantities of French trade goods, like guns, while the Hasinai had ample Spanish horses. Caddo leaders maintained their political and religious importance[261] by visiting and trading with the people who had been their guests at previous rituals and trade fairs (Schambach and Rackerby 1982: 92).[262]11

Caddoans dominated the Spanish Borderlands West until about 1800, when other tribes, pressured by US expansion, were forced across the Mississippi into Louisiana (Kniffen and others 1987) and Spanish Texas. Combined epidemics, depopulation, migrations, overhunting, and Osage depredations led to relocation of the historic Caddo centers to the Cypress Creek basin (east Texas, draining to Caddo Lake) and to the Little, Ouachita, and Red Rivers (Perttula 1992: 83).

Extensive contacts between the Caddos and Pueblos under the auspices of the Jumano, probable Plains Tiwan speakers (Hickerson 1994), enabled Juan Sabeata (Swanton 1942:41) to carry word of the failed 1687 French colony into Mexico, where the Spanish reacted quickly. Thereafter, international interests kept recrossing.

Such interweaving is illustrated by an Upper Nasoni community, identified as the Hatchel Mound (AD 1400-1700), located at a Red River ford near Barkman, Texas (Wedel 1978). In 1691, Governor Domingo Teran de los Rios drafted a famous map of its scattered neighborhood compounds, complete with a temple mound. In 1718, [244] at the same locale, Benard de la Harpe, a French trader assigned land among the Cadohadacho, founded the vital Nassonite (St Louis) trading post, which lasted until 1788 (Carter 1995: 214). Born at this fort was Francois Grappe (called Tulin, Touline), metis son of Alexis Grappe and Louise Marguerite Guedon, a Caddo (or Chitimacha) woman. For over 30 years, Grappe worked as an interpreter and trader, supplying important information to the first US Indian agent. Dr John Sibley,[263]12 who described the Cadohadacho as like the Knights of Malta, holy warriors with an international reputation.

In 1835, after immigrant tribes overhunted local game, Caddos signed a treaty with the U.S. ceding their Louisiana lands, just before their value soared (Lange 1974: 86) as Henry

---

[261] It bears frequent repeating that throughout the Americas trading was both an economic and a religious activity (Hamell 1983).

[262] Curious and intriguing is a suggestion that Caddo technology (material culture), particularly ceramics, did not disintegrate with the rest of Caddo society.' 'If anything, Caddo pottery making reached a peak during the period [V], in types like Nalchitoches Engraved and Keno Trailed, which include some of the most beautiful and technically excellent vessels the Caddo ever made" (Schambach and Rackerby 1982: 92). Given the great population decline of this period, the heartfelt mortuary use of these objects seems to have enhanced their artistic quality.

[263] Sibley, born in Massachusetts in 1757, became physician and US Indian agent at Natchitoches, exchanging letters with Louisiana Governor William Claiborne, US President Thomas Jefferson, and Secretary of War Henry Dearborn.

Shreve's steamboat removed (from 1833 to 1838) the Red River Raft, three huge logjams (Carter 1995: 262). These Caddos joined the Hasinai in the Mexican territory of Texas until forced in 1859 to the Wichita Agency at Anadarko, escorted by the martyred Robert Simpson Neighbors. Today, about 4000 Caddo have their tribal headquarters there.

Among the few elders still speaking Caddo in the 1980s, the daughters of Chief Enoch Hoag, Lillie Hoag Whitehorn and Esther Hoag Homovich, were particularly helpful in providing continuity with the Caddo past, as quoted below. Other members of their family had contributed to the published record. During the winter of 1921/22 in New York City, Elsie Clews Parsons (1941) interviewed Mike Martin, a Hoag first cousin (father's brother's son). Together, Martin and the Hoags corroborate traditions about leaders such as Jose Maria and Moonhead, who were their close relatives.

In 1859, Caddos were led north by the famous Anadarko chief, Jose Maria, whose mother nicknamed him Eyeish (Aish, Iyesh), after that back-country tribe. Since Jose Maria's mother was the sister of the Hoags' great grandmother, they called him grandfather. As Lillie Whitehom recalled,

> Texans got pretty rough on us. We had to be guarded by soldiers at Fort Belknap near Mineral Springs.... They got rough on us, and moved us (pc, 9 December 1986).

> When Caddos make their gardens, plant things, just when everything was getting good, here they [Texans] come along. They [Caddos] have to leave it or take everything away with them (pc, 16 December 1986).

> The Wichitas they always wanted to be the leaders, they wanted to be the nation, which they were not Come to the showdown, it was Caddos who were the nation. They decided to settle on the north side of the [Washtta] river through Anadarko (pc, 9 December 1986).

After Jose Maria in 1862, Caddo high chiefship passed to *Tinah, Walupi* (Guadeloupe, *Nahahsanah*), Caddo Jake, Whitebread, and eventually Enoch Hoag, who was bom near Waco, carried north as a baby, and named in school for the St. Louis Indian Agent. After Hoag died in 1929, Fritz Hendrix, a nephew, succeeded, although Newkumet and Meredith (1988: 56) reported that the chiefly position went to the Edge family.[264] 13

In Oklahoma, Caddos in the forefront of important native religious movements included Moonhead John Wilson, a Hoag in-law active in the Ghost Dance, Catholicism, and the Big Moon Peyote Church which spread along the Caddo international network. Later, a less elaborate version of these rituals was advanced by Quannah Parker and other Comanches and Kiowas, but the continuing designation of a peyote altar as a "moon" strongly resonates throughout past and present Caddo culture.

Enoch Hoag and others also sponsored Ghost Dances north of Binger. Lillie Hoag Whitehom cautioned,

---

[264] Parsons(1941: 10 garbled the Edge family name into Age.

Government said they [Ghost Dancers] danced for spite, because they whipped Custer and all that But that was not the meaning at all. They had prayer songs to ask God to have pity on them. We learned an Arapaho song that prayed "Thank you Lord for letting me roam around this earth, on this Mother Earth. Thank you. Pity me" (personal communication, 5 January 1987).

Origins

The complexity of Caddo epics bespeaks a large, dispersed population distinguished by ranks in social classes, yet all acknowledging the primacy of *Neesh* (Moon) for instituting their world. Cecile Carter(1995: 73) is probably correct in noting that this title, written as xinesi by the Spanish (also chenesi ~ shenisi), was a mishearing of the [245] Caddo title Mr Moon (tsah neeshi) for the high priest of the fire temple mound. He was Moon's representative in each community, with Mr ~ Lord Full Moon serving as the *gran tsah neeshi* of a confederacy.

Fray Juan Augustin de Morfi[265] reported Caddo origin myths without adding, as did George Dorsey (below), that water [rain?] was the tears of the Moon.

Of little consequence in their traditions, they give assurance that the fire produced them. And at other times they say that the first men who populated the earth came forth from the sea. Recognizing both fire and water as their creators, they call both by the name Niacadi [first chiefs?], but in spite of their belief, when in need they always appeal to the fire, without heeding water. They also say on some occasions that some of them are descended from bears, others from dogs, beavers, coyotes, etc. Their forefathers seeing the danger caused them by the Devil, to deceive his malice, transformed themselves into those brutes, without losing their minds, and retaining the faculty of restoring themselves to their primitive being when convenient to them (Morfi, in Swanton 1942: 215).

In 1716, Fray Isidro Felix de Espinosa[266] gave another, fuller version of the creation, though wrongly attributing it to the Caddo Creator instead of, correctly, to Moon, also known to both Caddo and Wichita as "unknown man."

From the very beginning, the earth had plants, animals, monsters, and a woman with her two daughters, one a virgin and one pregnant. One day, while the chaste

---

[265] Born in Spanish Austria, Father Morfi moved to Mexico about 1756 as Professor of Theology at the College of Santa Cruz de Tlaltelolco, and became a Franciscan in 1761. As chaplain to the commandant of the Internal Provinces (Don Theodore de Croix), he kept up a summary of other reports to produce Memorias para las Hisloria de Texas, current to his 1783 death, and Historia de la Provincia de Texas, 1673-1779, which remained in manuscript until it was published in 1935 (Swanton 1942: 73).

[266] Father Espinosa (1769-1755) became a Franciscan in 1696 at the College de Santa Cruz de Queretaro, served as priest at San Juan Bautista de Rio Grande in 1709, became president of Queretaro mission in 1715, left the Hasinai during a 1717/18 drought, returned in 1721, wrote his cronica in 1722, then ended his career as guardian of his college.

sister was grooming the head of the pregnant one resting in her lap, a horned monster attacked, shredded, and devoured the mother-to-be. The other woman fled into a tree [an oak, to explain the acorn cup, below], which the demon downed by gnawing, clawing, biting, and gouging, while the girl jumped into a lake and escaped. The mother and daughter went to the site of the murder and found an acorn cap holding a drop of the slain daughter's blood. They covered it with another cap, and put the blood away in a comer jar. The first night, the grandmother heard a gnawing noise from the comer and peeked inside the jar to see a tiny boy. The second night, the noise indicated that he had grown into a large man, who emerged and was given a bow and arrows. When he asked for his mother, the women told him about the monster so he tracked it down and hurled it far away from [b] the tip of his bow.

The probable religious intent of all this "gnawing" is suggested by a bizarre reference in Penicaut (1953: 64) to three tribes who "do not have a temple, but a hut in which they go and claw. In their language clawing is a kind of invocation of their Great Spirit."

Just after the turn of this century, as part of his comparative study of Caddoan religion, George Dorsey (1904a, b, 1905a, 1906), with the help of James Murie, a Skidi Pawnee, published a Caddo account of origins, as told by Chief Whitebread (Dorsey 1905a: 7-13), in which an "unknown man" appeared suddenly in the darkness and the world sprang to life. After working in haste, this "man" was identified by Coyote as "Moon," the first chief (*caddi*) because "he was wiser and abler than any other man." Neesh then selected his own assistant, organized people into groups − giving a drum to each leader − and led the Caddo out from the underworld. Judging the earth too small, however, he sent half the people back before urging westward those already outside. He threw up dirt to create mountains (probably also mounds), and watched from the top as people scattered over the land, developing their own dialects of Caddo. He named the directions by reference to Sun's movements, after Coyote slowed its pace, and decreed that the dead would become stars if six days of mourning and a noon feast were strictly observed; otherwise, the dead might return to haunt as ghosts.

Caddos once observed these strictures throughout life and death. After birth, a bright fire warmed and protected the infant during a 10 day seclusion. Then, as the child grew up, elders instructed him or her in proper behavior by recounting moral tales and anecdotes. Children were carefully warned about the six bad obstacles on the way to spiritual fulfillment in the afterworld. Youngsters were expected to conduct their lives so as to overcome these after death.

The first was the place of dogs, where the dog chief awaited anyone who mistreated dogs, insisting that the deceased groom him for fleas. As the "ghost" bit down to crack the shell of an insect to kill it, he or she turned into a dog, at the lowest and most abused rung in the pack. Each burial, therefore, included a bead on a little finger. By biting it [247] instead, the dog chief was fooled. At the second obstacle, a voice called out and all gossips waited there forever, forgetting to go on. Third was two boulders pounding together across the path. If the person had a good memory, he passed safely between the rocks, but if the person was forgetful, he was crushed "to death" (again). Fourth was a raging river looking deceptively like a creek. If the person had been quick and efficient in life, he or she arrived when the banks were close together and walked across, but if the person had been a laggard, the banks were so far apart and the water so swift that he or she fell in and became a fish. Next were persimmon trees, where those who had been greedy and demanding stayed as raccoons. The sixth obstacle was a man who asked the "ghost" for help. If the person had always left things undone, he or she was detained forever, working hard while wasting away to skin and bones, dying and being reborn to the same debilitating labor again and again (Dorsey 1905b).

Lillie Whitehorn also shed light on why, after death, souls go to a house to wait for others before going on (Swanton 1942: 204). She explained that the funeral feast is held at noon because at that moment "the Gates of Heaven are open" (pc, 5 January 1987). Thus, when the sun is at its highest in the sky, the way to heaven is open for dead souls.

In ancient times, finally, Moon (*Neesh*) taught men about using a bow and arrows, before calling everyone together at the town called Tall Timber Atop A Hill where he predicted the arrival of a wondrous baby, who would name himself Medicine Screech Owl on his first birthday.

Game became scarce because a Buzzard couple hoarded the prey. For survival, some humans became animals, able to revive ten times from their own spilled blood, just as Morfi reported. Later, during a flood, some people became water animals like alligators. To find the lost herds. Coyote pretended to be a dog, followed the Buzzards, and released bison from a cave. Before this, bison had been man-eaters so Coyote took away their teeth and made them eat grass. In punishment, buzzards have since lived on carrion.

Meanwhile, Moon had committed incest with his sister, a widespread theme throughout the Americas, and was banished to the sky. Medicine [b] Screech Owl became chief, telling everyone that [rain?] water was tears shed by remorseful Moon.

Coyote eventually caused difficulties, until ostracized by the chief. Gossip and discoid were started by a berdache, a man dressed as a woman, in revenge for being called a coward. After several attempts, he was finally killed when an arrow pierced his heart hidden in the little finger of his left hand. Guilds or cults of shaman doctors were also instituted, apparently each responsible for one of six special medicines.

In Espinosa's version of the epic, characters were treated as humans although they must have been immortal women, with a few men, associated with elements of the cosmos. To this day, Caddos address Thunder as grandmother, and the Earth as mother, using a kin term borrowed from the Osage to mean my own mother". The chaste aunt, also considered as a woman, may have been Water, since she escaped through a lake. This trinity of women was matched by a male one consisting of the Creator and his twin sons, perhaps the same as Thunder and Lightning. In all, these women and men were probably once addressed by kin terms indicating they all belonged to the same family.[267]

When the world was new, many adventures had lasting consequences, particularly those of two [twin] brothers. Thunder and Lightning, probably related to the *kokonikis* ("little ones"), the twin sons of the Sun seanced by the shinesi, so like the Pueblo war gods. Most likely, this was a polite title for the boy pair named Thunder and Lightning, both with long hair and the latter with a long sharp nose – reminiscent of archaeological "long nose face" shell ear pendants (Williams and Goggin 1956) and masks with two-foot noses reported hanging in a Calusa temple near the tip of Florida (Hann 1991: 195). Since spirits are said to be like birds everywhere in the

---

[267] Overall, this epic is reminiscent of the Northern Plains version of the hero twins, ripped out from their mother's womb [b] by a monster and thrown separately to the edge of the lodge or into a spring. These brothers rid the world of monsters until Spring Boy became the Missouri River (Miller 1992: 147-151, for Hidatsa).

Americas, such a beak indicated sacredness, along with the "piercing" power of a lightning bolt.[268]17

While any recent inquiry about such twins has always resulted in a negative response, one hint of continuity survives. As Enoch Hoag began the near-death vision which established his "foundation" (a clay altar used in peyote ceremonial),[269]18 he saw a man sitting on Moonhead's round peyote moon. According to Lillie Whitehorn, [248]

> He said he seen a man, a Caddo man not of this world, of the next world. That man was a little bitty man, a little bitty person. He had on a buckskin suit He had his hair parted down the middle.... There were two brothers of those men. They were grown men. They had wives (pc, 18 December 1986).

In ancient times, women married various beings, such as Turtle, Star, or others, to forge relations with other aspects of the universe. After various heros had killed many of the early monsters, Coyote called a council that decided to incinerate the world and start over. People went into the sky, while Snakes burned all the land. Bat made sure no monsters escaped by chewing through the rope into the sky and by tickling the nose of a huge carcass where many had taken refuge. Sneezed out, these last monsters completely burned up. When the embers cooled. Bat announced the earth was safe and people returned from the sky.

At a later time, in the Caddo Flood epic, a handsome man came to warn an old woman to seek safety on a hill because a deluge was about to destroy the Caddo for wasting fish by catching them and leaving them to rot As the woman and her family took flight, it started to mist, then drizzle, then rain, then pour. Led by a drumming *yoko* (prophet, discussed below), they danced around his fire atop a mound until a bird showed a green leaf exposed by retreating waters.

Today, the most common account of origins involves Caddo Lake or, more specifically, "Crying Place," a cave in a hill beside a lake on the south bank near the mouth of the Red River. There, an old man came out holding a pipe and fire in one hand, a drum in the other. His wife came out with the seeds of corn and pumpkins. People, both humans and animals, emerged until Wolf closed the passage, leaving kin behind in the underworld, symbolized by the hollow inside an earth mound under each temple. Indeed, the use of this name for the prairie around Battle Mound (Arkansas) suggests the existence of tribe-specific openings.[270]19

The repeated emphasis on the drum probably had to do with its function for defining town membership. As in rural Japan, a community included all those living within the sound of

---

[268] The famous Big Boy stone pipe from Spiro wears a long-nosed face on each ear lobe.

[269] The Hoag family uses the term "foundation" for this vision-sanctified clay altar covered with geometric designs filling most of the floor inside a peyote tipi. Enoch's foundation has now been cast in concrete (cf Hale 1987: 183, 203).

[270] Battle Mound, named for a land owner not a conflict, was the largest of all, located along the great bend of the Red River on Long and *Chicaninna* (Crying Place?) Prairies, variously measured as 205 m long, 98 m wide, and 10.4 m high (Perttula 1992: 24, 118), or 592-672 feet long, 157-320 feet wide, and 33-34 feet high (Carter 1995: 363 #7). Clarence Moore (1912: 566) described three tiers on the south side and two on the north. A ramp led up the east side.

a big drum kept in the local temple. Particular rhythms announced specific activities or gave warning. [b]

Mike Martin (Parsons 1941: 67) said he was familiar with a Caddo phrase meaning "six humans came out" when the world was new, but he had no context for it beyond the repetitive use of the pattern number six.[271] Most likely, it had to do with a faint memory of the founding of the six special medicine guilds.

Based on comparative mythology, an origin in the underworld explained where the general human population came from, but the founder of each chiefly family was somehow "elevated," either by coming down from the heavens or appearing at the top of the center's temple mound. For example, on the Hatchel Mound among the Cadohadacho (here called Caddoques), Grappe told Dr Sibley,

> By the side of this lake [oxbow] the Caddoques have lived from time immemorial. About a mile from the lake is the hill on which, they say, the Great Spirit placed one Caddo family, who were saved when, by a general deluge, all the world was drowned; from which family all the Indians have originated. To this little, natural eminence, all the Indian tribes, as well as the Caddoques, for a great distance, pay a devout and sacred homage. Here the French, for many years before Louisiana was ceded to Spain, had erected a small fort (Grappe, in Gregory 1986: 7 29).

If the chiefship was not (re)founded by a family, as after a Flood, it was begun by a woman, called *Sah Caddo*, "Lady Caddo," whose children grew into positions of leadership. In some sense, this woman. Moon's kinswomen, and the Pleiades (called Women) were all interrelated kinswomen.

Involving all the temples, shrines, and officials, the yearly cycle mirrored the crop sequence, since all Caddoans were intensive farmers, planting two maize crops a year. Little, corn-like short popcorn grew from April to May, then flour corn was planted for harvest in late July. Fields were planted communally by rank, with those of the *gran shinesi* going in first Communal work parties also planted the fields of Pueblo priests, while the Apalachee (Hann 1988) planted for chiefs, ball players, shamans, and, later, their resident Catholic priest, school, and church.

Caddos also hunted bison, deer, and bear with specially trained dogs. To protect the crops before harvest, each dog had a front paw tied to its muzzle to keep it from eating cobs. Their "surprising large [249] use made of fish" (Swanton 1942: 135, 138), which instigated the Flood (see above), contrasted with the custom of the Wichitas, who, like the Pueblos and Sioux, avoided fish entirely. For Pueblos, fish are taboo because they include some of their own transformed ancestors (recall the human > fish transformations at the fourth obstacle taught to Caddo children).

Yearly rites marked the progress of the farming cycle. In February, shamans brewed casina ~ Black Drink that was taken by elderly men to forecast the coming year. In the spring, women held a pre-planting ceremony. An old woman was in charge, providing cane strips that were woven into mats, probably the three left as offerings in a fire temple alcove. Throughout

---

[271] Six is for Caddos what three is for Judeo-Christians – the number used for satisfying repetitions.

summer, a bit of each maturing food resource, especially from the bison hunt and tobacco harvest, was offered in thanksgiving. Fat from a bison heart was regularly burned in a temple.

The Green Corn Rite before the harvest gave thanks, blessed the crop, and prevented snakes from biting those who were overly hasty to gather maize. Each town had its own version of this maize ceremony, to judge from the varying Spanish and French accounts (Swanton 1942: 226-232; Griffith 1954: 112). In some, women harvested enough corn for a feast, which was eaten only by the young. In other settlements, the priests and elders ate the first crop, consecrating it for everyone else. Such rites probably also varied according to local conditions. Elders were more likely to take charge of the rite during a time of hardship when their wise maturity was in demand. When everything was going well, the young and inexperienced could participate without causing inadvertent harm.

The major rite occurred in September, after the harvest, when the Mvskogees Creeks once held their masked dances. Six days before their assembly, hunters were blessed and sent from the temple mound to hunt game for the feasting. In the evening, priests, doctors, and officials gathered in the temple for prayers, smoke offerings, and a narcotic drink (reportedly made from wild olive or laurel, but identified by Berlandier [1969: 144] as mescal). Around midnight, women, marching by threes to the temple, left bread and offerings on behalf of their families. All these foods were [b] divided up among the officials to take home and serve to guests.

Meanwhile, an official watched for the exact moment when "the women" (Pleiades constellation) stood directly over the temple so the *shinesi* could come out to circle a ring of standing fresh green reeds [a moon?] around a bonfire in the plaza. Women filed into the area to seat themselves according to age and rank, each holding another food offering. From an aroor in the east, warmed by a small fire, three festive old men marched toward the central fire, pausing at intervals while the priest and women sang, accompanied by gourd rattles. When these men reached the middle, the oldest exhorted on the good and helpful life. Young men acting as ushers went among the women to carry their offerings to a stack outside the ring. If there were many people, the procession, speech, and collection was repeated.

Everyone remained in the plaza all night, alternatively singing and resting until dawn, when they greeted the sun with loud thanks. As the sun rose, all ran in a foot race along a marked course, much like runways still used for Pueblo foot races to encourage the Sun.

After praising the fastest runners, everyone danced in place, forming an inward facing circle made up of male and female pairs. Music came from 20 singers, assisted by eight men beating a log drum and others with rattles. They danced in thanksgiving until noon, when the sun was at his peak. A huge international trade and harvest fair was held during this autumn rite, drawing guests from a wide area to the temple mound (Swanton 1942: 193).

Cultural Background

Prehistorically, Caddoan settlements along the many waterways were graded from family farmsteads, hamlets, villages, and towns to a tribal capital marked by an earth mound with, on top, a temple sheltering a sacred fire. In that very mound, the temple priest (*tsah neeshi*) was buried, after an elaborate and labor-intensive funeral, accompanied by many grave goods at the bottom of a ten foot deep shaft (Perttula 1992: 123). Important early status markers were wooden stools, earplugs such as those that marked the Inca nobility. Galt bifaces, and copper insignia, such as the wooden [250] parrot with copper sheath found by Mark Harrington (1920: 221).

Other mounds marked the burial places of members of the governing elite or the home of the high priest (Perttula 1992: 13). Members of ordinary families were buried in community cemeteries, while infants were buried under house floors (Perttula 1992: 55), which was a general Native American practice to assure the rebirth of a baby's soul into a family member.

Throughout the Americas, though best known for Pueblos, the leadership of a human community derived from positions held by immortal beings in the heavens. Thus the Sun, Moon, Stars, and Planets were held to be powerful spirits whose conduct affected all the world, including human societies such as that of the Caddo (Sabo 1987). Everything was suffused with a religious sense so that the theocracy reflected the celestial order, because, as Florence Hawley Ellis (1983: xxxvi) noted, "Each officer was the personal representative of a parallel member of the hierarchy of [immortal] beings. A man took his responsibility and the power which implemented it directly from his supernatural counterpart."

For comparison, in every Pueblo town in the Southwest, a pair of leaders was associated respectively with the sky as Father Sun or with the land as Mother Earth. Each community was led by an "inside" chief who was the highest member of a curing priesthood associated with the earth and maize, sometimes also belonging to a clan of that name. This high priest, usually called a cacique,[272] was the nexus of all relations, charged with praying, fasting, and conducting rituals for the good of all. His counterpart was the "outside" chief, associated with the Sun and warfare to protect the town borders, with the help of two assistants who embodied the twin war gods, sons of the Sun and a virgin girl. These brothers were small, stocky, tough, and feisty heroes who rid the world of cannibal monsters before instituting important manly rituals. The locus of these priestly rituals was called a kiva, a round room, often set into the ground although some were also built into upper towers or rooms to honor spirits of the air.[273]22

Caddos had a similar system. Atop the mound, the temple dome[274]23 symbolized the sky, with the inside fire linked to the sun and, by [b] extension, each household hearth and every heart (Miller 1980a) was graced by heat and light from the high god of the universe (Miller 1980b). Associations with the earth and the underworld were represented by the mound itself, which, throughout the Southeast, was believed to be hollow inside (Knight 1989) and the home of certain spirits.[275] 24

---

[272] The title of *cacique* was taken into Spanish from a Caribbean native term.

[273] Scholars have been slow to recognize prior pan-Pueblo confederacies. Each modem Pueblo has its own cacique and captain, mirroring the ancient pan-American distinction between civil and war leaders. Massive archaeological complexes, such as Chaco Canyon, as well as records from major events, like the 1680 Pueblo Revolt, indicate that some town leaders also served as the heads of greater linguistic and political unions.

[274] From the outside, Caddo temples and houses looked like haystacks because they were thatched with bundles of grass. While only Caddos had such temples, grass-covered houses were once used by all Caddoans (Wedel 1979: 194). Along the Red River bend, however, Cadohadacho built connected wattle and daub houses like those of the Creeks (Swanton 1942: 153).

[275] A European equivalent is the Sheed, the hollow hills of pre-Christian Ireland inhabited by the immortal spirits known as the Shee, of whom the best known is the Banshee who comes to

Inside the Hasinai temple was an altar holding a reed mat, as well as benches with a pipe, tobacco, and pottery dishes for burning offerings and incense. At the back, other gifts were placed on a low bench, like a *duho* stool, signifying leadership and authority throughout the Caribbean (Swanton 1942: 155, 236). "The high seats resembled small tables and were reserved for use at special ceremonies. Only a *caddi* and the *chenesi* had the privilege of sitting so high above everyone else that their feet were placed on a bench" (Carter 1995: 77). Fray Francisco Casañas de Jesus Maria[276] noted that "whatever this official says or does is carefully heeded, just as the Catholics obey the Holy Gospels. If he issues a command it is more strictly obeyed by these Indians than the ten commandments are observed by Christians" (Carter 1995: 77). Strangely, the priest did not compare this practice to a bishop speaking ex cathedra, "from his chair."

In a side alcove of the temple, like the "bed nooks" found in every house, were one large and two small mats, presumably for the Creator and his twin sons. The sacred fire had four logs forming a cross, exactly like those at modem Creek towns.

The pipe in each temple was probably a calumet, with its long stem decorated with bird skins and feathers. Indeed, the calumet ceremony (also known as the Pawnee Hako; Fletcher 1904) was spread by Caddoans via international alliances and intertribal adoptions throughout the Plains and East The decorated pipestem provided safe conduct, an advantage used by Marquette and Joliet on their 1673 journey down the Mississippi. Far to the northeast, the Iroquois, who refer to the calumet as the Eagle Dance, joined this network only a century ago.

The Hasinai *gran tsah neeshi*, a dignified old man, lived near the center of the confederacy along the Angelina River. Though the position was hereditary, only old men held this office, probably aged by a long and involved apprenticeship. [251] Witnessing the elaborate ten-day funeral of such a high priest. Fray Casañas described dances around "moons" made of a ring of poles near a grass ball, called the earth, hanging from a staff near the deceased *gran tsah neeshi*'s doorway. By contrast, funerals for a *gran caddi* lasted eight days.

Near the main temple was a single or double building identified as the abode of twin boys, the sons of the Creator, called the *kokonikis ~ koninisi ~* "little ones". Inside were a central fire and two small trunks. Devoid of all clothes, the *gran tsah neeshi* entered this shrine accompanied by caddis and other officials, darkened the room, and consulted these twins about the outcome of future events, much like the Lakota *Yuwipi* and Colville seances (Miller 1990: 130-135). While other town *tsah neeshi* had temple mounds, only the *gran tsah neeshi* had this twins' shrine, which was destroyed with the Hasinai fire temple in a 1714 Yojaunes Tonkawa attack (Smith 1995: 42). Neither the fire nor the priestly office ever recovered.

---

[276] warn of a death in the family.

While Alonso de Leon was seeking La Salle's French outpost, Father Damian Massanet founded 1690 Hasinai missions. Father Casañas, born to a French noblewoman in Barcelona 35 years before, stayed at the Neches mission of Santisimo Nombre de Maria, where he composed an ethnography. Nearby was the intriguing Father Francisco Hidalgo (Swanton 1942: 52), who moved onto the Rio Grande missions, suggesting the ease of Caddo and Pueblo links. Returning to the Hasinai in 1709, Hidalgo sparked new French efforts that culminated in the remarkable career and family of Louis Jucherau de St Denis, a French Canadian married into the Ramon family of Spanish officials.

A variety of shamans, or native doctors ~ *kunah*, some organized as guilds, cults, or priesthoods, cured the sick and looked after community welfare. These doctors treated illnesses with herbs, charms, sweating, ritualized techniques, and some surgery. Each disease was attributed to a barb shot by spirits into the patient. Among spirits, owls served as doctors (as they did among the Coast Salish and other tribes). A cure involved healing songs accompanied with a rattle, wooden rasp, flute, and feather fan. Medicines were made more effective by blowing into the liquid to make a foam, as is done by Creek medicine makers and Pueblo rain priests. A doctor who lost patients, however, was often killed by next of kin for dangerously misusing power.

In historic times, at least, each Caddo town of scattered homesteads was a separate linguistic and kinship unit led by a *tsah neeshi*, and a chief called the *caddi*. Other town officials included one or more *canaha ~ canha* ~ elders ~ subchiefs ~ deputies), *chayas* ~ messengers, and a *tammah ~ tanma* ~ herald ~ town crier). War leaders, usually called captains, were drawn from the ranks of *amayxoya* ~ war heroes.

Moreover, in the ethnography, the special legal status of *caddi* was indicated by the death sentence imposed for wounding or killing [b] members of his family (Swanton 1942: 183). The high-born women of this rank were distinguished by the title *akwidaw* (written as *aquidau* in Spanish), particularly the wife of a *gran tsah neeshi ~ gran caddi*, the religious and civil heads of a confederacy based at the capital temple mound.

Epidemics, devastation, and enemy attacks long plagued the Caddos, yet they remained resilient Their huge population had encouraged a complex theocracy of hereditary leaders with powers and legitimacy drawn from beings of the primordial age. Yet, diversity among the component towns of each confederacy provided Caddo salvation. When the eternal fires were extinguished, the temple mounds abandoned, and the eternal priesthoods extinct, lesser officials concerned with annual renewal took over until Christianity supplanted much of the ancient establishment. Foremost among these offices was the *yoko*, who was somewhere between a priest and a shaman, responsible for the annual rekindling of the sacred fire of the town and predicting the fate of his charges. Based on information provided by the Hoag family, we have only glimpses of him at the start and end of a 400 year period that marked this transfer of the sacred fire from a mound closer to the heavens to a room set upon the earth. The various offices of Caddo leadership are diagrammed in Figure 1.

Yoko

Supplemented by Anadarko fieldwork in 1927 with James Inkanish and Grayson Pardon (Ninnid), the Parsons (1941) monograph was contrasted with earlier historical records by John Swanton (1942: 3), who observed,

As might have been anticipated, the ancient tribal cult connected with the temples has disappeared along with those collective functions such as are assumed by our Departments of State and War. The Ghost Dance and Peyote cults have acted powerfully to affect the former and immersion in white institutions the latter. What has survived are the minor social relations between individuals and families, much of the kinship terminology, customs connected with naming and marriage, with the relations brought about by marriage, some of the burial customs, and customs connected with medical practices and witchcraft.

Suggesting a course for these changes, [252] Swanton (1942: 121) looked from the sacred fires in the temple mounds to the Franciscans to the central fires of the peyote moon altars inside the tipis used for meetings of the Native American Church, set up according to the teachings of the prophet *Nishkantu* (John Wilson), literally "Moonhead" in Caddo. His father was a Delaware and his mother a Caddo of the Anadarko tribe.

It is interesting to remember that peyote was used by medicine men among the Hasinai at the beginning of the eighteenth century, and, recalling the elaborate ritualism of the Caddo, as well as their various contacts with Christian missionaries, including the presence among them of established missions for about three decades, one wonders whether such a background does not constitute part of the explanation of John Wilson. It may put the ancient fire cult of the Natchez and Caddo, Franciscan teachings, the Ghost dance religion, the peyote cult, and the North American churches founded on the last mentioned in one line of descent (Swanton 1942: 121).

Caddo Leadership

		Ranks		Foci
Cosmos		Creator ~ Father Above Chief		sun
		Moon (*neesh*)		moon
Confederacy		*gran tsah neeshi*		
		Yoko		twins
				annual fire
Tribal Town				
	caddi = akwidaw		*tsah neeshi*	temple mounds
	canaha	*tammah*	*kunah*	medicines
		chayas		
	warriors	men = women	animal lodges	prowess
				hearts

Figure 1. Caddo leadership. Civil (left) and religious (right) ranks were bridged by intermediaries (central column, top to bottom) concerned with prophecy (*yoko*), news (*tamah*), errands (*chayas*), and supplies (town residents). Social class (elite, ordinary, captive) and gender (=) were other components of the system.

Even more specifically, this transition from temple fire to peyote moon involved the priestly *yoko* ~ *yuko*. While Parsons (1941: 34, 61) recorded information about this office, she did not [b] grasp its full significance. Inkanish (Parsons 1941: 34) said the Caddo had three kinds of doctors or shamans, with the strongest one called Beaver (*t'ao*), the next strongest called *yuko*, and the last called *daitino* ~ Mescal Bean doctor. Once, while two brothers were raiding a camp, one was riddled with bullets. To survive he jumped over flames because "it meant that he never left the fire." His brother, who was a *yoko*, found him, removed the bullets, and restored him to normal life. From this account. Parsons inferred that a *yuko* "treated wounds." But he was much more than just a physician, he was an oracle of the sacred fire.

According to Pardon, *yuku ~ yoko* were doctors who could tell what was going to happen, and could find lost things, they could bring back a stray horse. Yuku could find out a man's supernatural "partner" or p'itauni-wan'ha (to have power from). Pardon's grandfather, known as Mike Pardon, was a yuku. He could foretell the coming of an epidemic or of anything else four days in advance (Parsons 1941: 34).

To confirm such clairvoyance. Pardon told the story of an old man who was a powerful witch (naiiti) who could not be killed until "The chief [253] got yuku [medicine men] to tell about him. Yuku said the witch had his power in a little basket with a little bow and arrows under his right armpit." They shot and "This time he stayed dead" (Parsons 1941: 61).
According to the Hoag sisters,

Every Caddo band had a *yoko* who was higher than those other leaders, of course. Those are like prophets, sacred, kind of strict with everything. They were the ones who could predict things. You could not get over [overcome] them. You could not fool them. They were special. They warned of floods before they came (personal communication, 9 December 1986).

Yoko means, like, for instance, you would say, something like in the Bible where it talks about Isaiah, the prophet That is what it means, the prophet (personal communication, 5 December 1986).

The Caddos, the strict Caddos [Cadohadacho] lived in different villages, and some had temples. They had some way of starting a fire with a rock, a flint rock. I don't know just how they did it. They got grass, some wood to catch the sparks. They start the fire that way. Anyway, a power was given by the Almighty to the Caddos that they could do things. But some way, all what they learned was lost in history. Lost They must have done wrong somewhere. That was taken away from them.

This fire, they say, comes from the Sun. The Sun is hot. God created it My father used to say, too, whitemen could get close to everything else, but when they tried it, they could not get to that Sun. It is so hot It was created that way. That is why the Indian, especially the Caddo that I know of, that I see, [respect it]. When the Sun comes up, they were not worshipping that Sun. That did not mean that It means that God, some Supreme Being, put that Sun there to throw light to the world. And throw heat to everything. They raise their hands toward it to bless themselves, to be thankful that God gave them this light They go by the Sun in everything. When they go somewheres, then they go by this fire.

Well, this fire, my father used to say, they had certain ways to get the fire, the heat, down from the Sun. They had certain ways to do that They must have went wrong somewhere so that was taken away from them. They could not do it no more.

When they did bring it down, they used to have a man [for it]. They call him *yoko*. Those that could do those things like that. There is certain ones that could do that When they do get that, they have a certain place [probably it] must be a temple. I heard my aunt [father's sister, wife of Caddo Jake, [b] Natchitoches leader] talk about it one time. She was telling it to her son Fritz Hendrix, and someone else. I was a small girl at the time.

They had a special room and they got the fire down and set it there. The leaders, those with say-so, of every band came inside. All those leaders were under one head in those days. One head one. At the time they made treaties it was a man named Wolf (*tasha*) [indeed, the lead Caddo signatory in 1835]. He was the head of all them others.

Anyway, when they bring this fire down, they let it burn for a certain time. Let it bum. All the leaders are told to come get some of that fire. They come, and get ft, and take it to their own village. They start a fire in each camp or whatever [dwelling]. That is the way they did it.

And then at certain times, when it was time (they knew when the time came) to do away with that old fire, when it was time to start a new one, the people did that to the fire. They [let ft go out, cleaned up the ashes,] go to the east, and bury them away from the houses. They bury it toward the east, they bury that fire there. They start a new one here [in the room]. They do that a certain time of the year.

You do not dare to pour cold water on that fire, nor spit on ft, nor punch it with a sharp stick. Everything there, they had to be careful with. Only certain ones came near it Usually, it was always a man to start that fire. That is the way that they did. They have to be careful. They teach their children to call that fire Grandfather. Grandpa. Because he takes care of you. You warm up there. You got your heat there when you are cold. You did your cooking. You come to the fire. All that had something to do with it. That is the way they say.

That foundation, that altar, later that Peyote Moon, also had ways, too. Each tribe had its own ways, but only some knew the real meaning of ft. Others just copied ft without knowing why. Moonhead had only a round Moon, he had no foundation. Moonhead was married to an aunt of my father, Enoch Hoag (pc, 5 December 1986).

Echoing the story of the two brothers, one a *yoko* and the other riddled with bullets, Lillie Whitehorn said,

They told us to respect that fire, to call it Grandpa. It is taking care of you, fixes your food. When you are cold, ft warms you up. These young boys, when ft is war time and enemies chase you, do not run from ft. If you are going to die, you go right behind that fire. It will protect you. You will die there. If you run, ft is no good (pc, [254] 5 January 1987).

For Lillie Whitehorn, the universe changed with the arrival of Christ, who replaced the time of miracles with the true church. Today, many Caddos equate Christ with their culture hero Moon. Indeed, Lillie Whitehorn said that it was a *yoko* who told people who Christ was before he gave special customs and foods to each tribe. Caddos say their prayers are like a Catholic litany, starting with God and then mentioning everything by name down to the lowest

People over there in Europe, the whole continent, they ought to be far smarter, far ahead of this country here, cause Christ came there first and he taught everybody. If Indians were wild, surely they were wild, too (pc, 6 November 1986).

Things could happen in ancient times, in the time of Christ and before. Things happened that you would not believe. They used to say that even the animals could talk. They see you and they turn into a person, a human, and another time it came as something else. They used to talk that way. That was way back, maybe before Christ When He came, everything changed. It had to be changed because the Devil was controlling the world before that. That is what we hear. I don't know [for sure].... God felt sorry for us and put us here (pc, 18 December 1986).

Lillie's sister Esther added,

In their time, Caddos were very religious people. They kept up the fire, day and night. Then they had a certain man to carry the bowl of coals. Each year, they put out the fires, and they lit a new one. Everybody goes to the temple to get that fire (pc, 9 December 1986).

In more recent times, the fire was kindled in a room with a door to the east The men involved fasted for three or four nights before the *yoko* lit the new fire and everyone had a big feast as the Mescal Bean doctors danced upon hot coals.

Esther agreed that Caddos must have committed sacrilege to lose their religious rites. She recalled,

The last all-Caddo doing was held at the foot of the hill where Indian City is now. Down at the bottom. The last time Caddos had something of their own. It was Mescal doings with fox hides. During the Beaver lodge, they used a Bear in there. He took part in the ceremony. For the Mescal, they brewed a tea and wore other beans on string (Esther Homovich, pc, 9 December 1986).

Continuity of this office of *yoko* and the shamanic animal lodges suggests another solution to the scholarly debate about clans among the Caddo (Bolton 1987: 72-74). What have been called "clans" were probably animal lodges like those of the Pawnee. Since the Hoag children belonged to the Delaware Turtle clan through their mother, their denial of any similar unit for the Caddos is significant. While no members of the Caddoan language family definitely had clans in late historic times, most of them had and have cult lodges sponsored by an animal spirit doctor, with those of the Pawnee best known. Over time, however, newer Ankara and Pawnee rituals derived from the Caddo rites, since people in the northern Plains looked to the south for religious innovations, which, ultimately, had some Mexican inspiration.

Morfi and others reported that Caddo acknowledged animal spirit ancestors, and Caddo Jack identified, for both James Mooney and John Swanton (1942: 163-165), ten named units called Bear, Wolf, Buffalo (or Alligator, because both have a roaring bellow). Beaver, Eagle, Raccoon, Crow, Thunder, Panther, and Sun. Because Caddo Jack was Natchitoches, Swanton suggested that these names were those of clans diffused from the Southeast, where they still occur among Creeks and others. That they were somehow ancestral is shown by a taboo on killing the family namesake.

Writing from Natchitoches on 17 November 1763, commandant Cavallero Macarti noted "They are divided into four tribes or families, known by the names of Beaver, Otter, Wolf, and Panther (Lion)." In 1910, White Bread, whose family came directly from Louisiana to the Kiamichi valley of southeastern Oklahoma (Carter 1995: 342), gave Swanton a ranked list that included Buffalo (*ta'naha*), Bear (*nawo'tsi*), Panther (*ki'shi*), Wolf (*ta'sha*), and Beaver (*ta'o*). While Caddo once ranked classes of elites, commoners, or war captives, this scaling implies species-apportioned powers like the Caddoan animal lodge cults.

Indeed, these 1763 names are duplicated among the Pawnee, where Murie (1914: 604-608) [255] described the four animal lodge cults of Bear, whose members wore bearskins draped lengthwise along the shoulders, Buffalo, Deer, whose members took a tea made from mescal beans and cured snake bites, and Blood, also known as Otter, whose members vomited blood and cured hemorrhaging. There were also the Irushka, whose members treated bums and controlled the life of fire.

These cults changed over time. Deer came north from the Wichita about 1842, although deer ceremonialism itself, with piled antlers like Pueblo hunt shrines, was an ancient feature of a Great Bend mound center (Crenshaw site) during AD 1000-1100 (Schambach and Rackeroy 1982: 122).

At a reconstructed Big Doctoring Grand Opera of the 1867 Skidi, the south side of the lodge held guilds named for Deer, Black-tail Deer, Buffalo, and Bison. Northern booths were Eagle, Osprey, Coyote (Wolf), and Bear (Weltfish 1977: 274).

Therefore, except for Panther, direct equations among these lodges can be made since Caddos linked Beaver and Bear, while Pawnees matched Otter and Blood, along with Fire and *Irushka*. Moreover, panther (cougar) can be matched by comparison with the Apalachee , where, at the first ballgame. Sun Woman's son battled Banked Fire, whose helpers were "panthers, wolves, and bears, all the daric and strong animals" (Hann 1988: 334).

These animal cults reflect a three-way division, pervading all of Pawnee society, into offices of the priest (*kurahus*, literally 'old man") whose powers came from the sky, the chief (rarrsaaru) who amassed a variety of powers, and the shaman doctor (kuraa'u) whose powers came from the earth.

Indeed, Susan Golla (1975) analyzed such recurrent three-way relationships for every Pawnee institution, each distinguishing an elderly owner, a mature executive, and youthful supporters. For example, every sacred bundle had a wealthy owner, a priest to conduct its rituals, and faithful kin.

Among the Pawnee, Ankara, and Wichita, the universe was structured in terms of these all-important sacred bundles, a hide covering around significant items dictated by an immortal ally. These bundles – graded to sanctify personal, [b] guild, tribal, or confederacy activities – were the basis for every successful use of power by a public official.

Yet the Pawnee also recognized as sacred peculiar geomorphic buttes and hills believed to be the "holy homes" of the spirit patrons of an animal lodge. In addition to these separate cults, a Medicine Lodge of leading tribal doctors met in the spring and the summer to sing and dance, followed by a major rite ("grand opera") for a month in the fall to perform amazing cures.

Each member of one of these lodges of earth-empowered doctors, complementing the sky-based system of priests and bundles (Chamberlain 1982), received a vision of one of the "holy home grounds" (*rahurahwaarvkstii'u*), 14 animal lodges identified by name (Parks and Wedel 1985). The most famous of these places, also revered by other Plains tribes, was Waconda Spring Mound, Kansas.[277] 26

Pervading the entire Pawnee universe, as well as every other nation of the Americas, and embracing all of these three-way divisions was the basic pairing of Man and Woman. Indeed, the Pawnee pattern duplicated Caddos in tracing kinship through women and public offices among men, creating dual lines for descent or succession within the elite families. Moreover, bridging all of these differences, kindling a fire was universally equated with the "heat" of sexual union and was thus, in and of itself, a mediation of the genders (for Pawnee, cf Murie 1981: 40, 150).

Therefore, it is entirely possible that so-called Caddo "clans" were never corporate unilineal units, but instead were animal lodges, such as found among other Caddoans, associated with geomorphic irregularities (Parks and Wedel 1985) in their aboriginal tribal homelands.[278]27

The antiquity of the *yoko*, whose more flexible office survived longer, as opposed to the *tsah neeshi*, whose role as high priest faded when the perpetual fires of the temple mounds were extinguished, is glimpsed in the Spanish records.

One time Father Espinosa, asking them why all the tribes of the Ainais [Haynay, foremost tribe of the Hasinai] and Neches did not go out together on buffalo hunts, as did the Nasonis and Nacogdoches, a [native] priest replied, that it was a prudent caution, so that the sacred fire would not go out on account of the absence of those who cared for it; [256] that the Nacogdoches and the Nasonis had a different fire, which they lighted by rubbing two little sticks and, leaving these in the temple, were sure of finding their fire when returning to their houses, and this was why they did not perish, but that the Ainais and Neches kept their fire burning without interruption, from the time they received it from their forefathers, a tradition which they

---

[277] Located in north central Kansas, this low mound with an artesian spring, about 1884, became a health spa for local whites, who bottled and sold its water.

[278] Such a solution makes the Caddo comparable with other Caddoans, none of whom had clans or any kind of quasi-unilineal units. By contrast, among Keresan Pueblos, where four of seven towns link membership in particular matriclans to the leadership of specific priesthoods, named like animal lodges, these clans and guilds have distinctly separate designations. No such dual naming has been reported among Caddos, indicating the singularity of these animal lodges.

hold with the greatest tenacity (Morfi, in Swanton 1942: 225-226; see p. 222 for Espinosa original).

While the Hasinai took their home and tribal temple fires from that of the confederacy fire temple of the Haynay, which was eternal, some tribes kindled their fire annually, or, as Lillie Whitehom said, "brought the heat down from the Sun" every year. Drawing down this flame and keeping it was the main obligation of the *yoko* as tribal priest. In all likelihood, distinctive features of his office can be traced to the Anadarko tribe (which absorbed the Nasoni and Hasinai), and provided leaders such as Jose Maria, Moonhead, and the Hoags.

Conclusion

Along with their grasp of Caddo culture, memories of the *yoko* prophet and of shamanic animal lodges (probably mistaken for clans) was retained by members of the Hoag chiefly family. By their very lives, serving in world wars and using oil money to finance pilgrimages to Robert Neighbors' grave in Texas as well as to the Vatican in Rome, they exemplify the ongoing international stature expected of Caddo leaders.

For hundreds of years, therefore, Caddo intertribal influence has relied on their special national relationship to the Moon, as variously expressed through sacred fires kept by priests (either Lord Moon or *yoko* prophets), diplomatic bonds forged with calumet pipestems, and, most recently, pan-native regard for the peyote moon (a crescent altar near the central fire, itself associated with the sun). These expressions have spread along ancient Caddo networks dedicated to international worship, trading, and diplomacy.

Thanks

Lillian and Esther Hoag were introduced to me through the combined efforts of Nora Dean, Jim Rementer, Lucy Blalock, Linda Poolaw, Duane Hale, Henry Inkanish Chisholm, Evelyn Kionute, John and Luceen Dunn, Carol Hampton, Howard Meredith, and Blue Clark. Over the years, advice came from Helen Tanner, George Sabo, and Raymond Fogelson. Editorial help came from LeRoy Johnson, Ann Schuh, Donna Steinburn, Julian Baumel, and Marilyn Richen.

Enoch Hoag's Vision For A Peyote Moon Altar
As Told by Lillie Hoag Whitehorn
Anadarko, Oklahoma 6 November 1986

Background: The Big Moon version of the Native American Church was Sounded by John Wilson, whose Caddo name was Nishkantu, which translates into English as Moonhead. His father was Delaware, and mother was Caddo. Enoch Hoag, named for the Superintendent of the Bureau of Indian Affairs based in Saint Louis, was the Caddo Chief. His wives were Delawares, and that was the language of their household. Jay Miller's annotations are in angle brackets < >, while Lillie's asides are in square brackets [ ]. Lillie explains her father's experience with early the peyote religion, a vision he had at a meeting, and then a subsequent mortal illness, recovery, and rights to found a special "moon" altar of his own.

My father was Enoch Hoag, a well known Caddo chief. His first wife was Caddo. She died when she was young. They had a little baby boy, but it died too. Then he stayed single for a long time. Then he met Clarence's mother, but that was before. It was before even Clarence's mother when he met Moonhead Wilson. See, Caddos are all related. Friendship relations. They know one another and the whole tribe. I want you to understand there were lots of Caddos when we were down in Louisiana. Lots of different bands, maybe about 26 or 29 bands. Each one had a different pronunciation, but yet they understand one another. That is the way they were when they were down there.

So, anyway, talking about Moonhead now. Moonhead's father was Delaware and his mother was Caddo. I can't tell you their names way back. I'm not that old. Moonhead's father was Delaware because he used to go up that way <to Dewey, Oklahoma where the Delaware majority settled>. His mother was Caddo -Nadako band. [I'm not sure how they related around. I get mixed up.] Moonhead was born here and then he'd go up to Dewey to see his father [known in English only as Old Man Wilson]. That's where he met them Osages. That's how that went.

He used to have these Peyote meetings between Binger and Lookeba. There's a creek that comes into that Sugar Creek. They say he used to live around there. These creeks flow into Sugar creek, which comes on down into the washita River. That's where they used to live. They say Moonhead, he was a man that could predict things. [2]

And he used to be dancing with them Cheyennes and Arapahos. A man name of Sitting Bull had this Ghost Dance. That's where Moonhead used to keep the dance up. Dance of the Caddos. And one time a bunch of Caddos went to Washington, DC. It was time for them to come home.

And while he was dancing [and they say he used to have visions when they dance, you know] and one time, when he got like that, and he come to, he told those people: "Some of you hitch up a team and go meet those people over there. They're coming in." And some of them wouldn't do it. They didn't believe him. You know how people are. But this man, he said, "If nobody don't go, I'll go." So he got up. He got his team ready, and he went to meet them. And sure enough, he brought them in. There was four of those men that come back. That was number one [first time] that he find out things.

My daddy was a young man at that time. He was a young man and he was living back in a canyon from the Binger Y [road intersection]. We used to live back in there. My grandmother did, my aunts and all his people, his cousins. They all lived around there. Pretty much two miles from Binger Y. But anyway, they were living there.

One time, he and his uncle went. His mother's brother, the other one. There were three of those men [who] were his uncles. This one, the oldest one, he didn't use no peyote, but the [4] second one did. I've seen this one, a young guy. I got to see him. But these other two, I didn't know them. So, when he goes to meeting with Moonhead, he goes with his uncle. They ride horse.

("Now you listen good. Now you may not believe me, but if you don't it's all right. It's up to you. ")

So, they go over there. Course, he's been having them meetings off and on. Before then, my dad used to go in a wagon and on horseback. He'd go to Comanche meetings. Like William Sofidy, oh, different ones, Neverclear and Mawacoby, them oldtimers. He used to eat Peyote with them. He knew them. They used to invite him. Sometimes, he go by himself. Sometimes, he carry somebody with him. That's my dad when he was young.

And he said, them days, they were kind of wealthy, them Comanches. They butcher their own beef. They work <hard>. [You'd] See women cooking around and getting ready for the meeting. They run theirs differently at that time. So dad, he comes back <from the Comanches>. Then he goes over there. He hear about Moonhead. Sometimes, they invite him. He goes over there. When he got there, everybody was busy working. The women were cooking and, of course, they had everything, getting ready for the night. And he goes in the meeting with them.

He's been there before, but this time when he went, he [5] said, when they got in there, they never had no drum. They didn't have a drum. They had a tin can. They used that for drum. They used that. And they had an old gourd. It wasn't no fancy gourd. No kind of beadwork. Just one of these gourds you plant in February. Those seeds in it, you clean them out.

[Moonhead] was running it. He was conducting the meeting. There was nothing. Just that moon [altar] there. Just the [crescent] shape of the moon, made of dirt piled up. Everybody was sitting there. And then, of course. Moonhead, he started talking, telling them what it's about. What's going to take place, you know. Of course, it was in his [own] way, the way he believes. He smokes and he tells them, you know, all about what's going to go on. He rolled a cigarette and then he prays, you know.

Very first of all, he told them: "You see this cigarette ("Of course, he said it plainly. I can't say it all. "), this cigarette, now, I got in my hand. I want you all to understand this. I don't want anyone to do that, to imitate me, just to be doing it, or to imitate someone else. Just for the fun of it. " He said, "This is no plaything. What we're going to do. God created us. He made us here. And whatever we do, whatever we say, we've got to be honest about it. If you get up and make that cigarette. He'll talk to you. You know what your doing. Whenever you belong to God or what. " So, he [dad] said, he goes [6] up there, and then blows smoke up in the air, blowed it east, and west, and north, directed crosswise. Then they started singing.

He had ways. He had rules in there. Nobody comes in during the night. You got to be ready during the evening and you don't be running out for nothing. Unless you really have to. He tells them everything in there. My dad said that was when he was a young man. He said,

130

they kept passing that peyote around, eating that herb, you know. He said, certain time of the night, he said, I used that herb in there, like they told. He said, I found myself.

There's fire right here. They build that fire. He said, "You keep your mind on that peyote. And you keep your mind on that fire. Now, this fire here is no plaything," he says. "God made this fire. He put it here, for certain reasons." The Caddos always worshipped it before they ever came this way. They call it Grandpa, Fire Grandpa. He says, keep your mind on there. You all sing. Don't be talking and laughing. You sing. You help whosever got the drum. You sing. He said, that's the way they did.

He said, during that night, past midnight, I couldn't sit still ("I'll just tell you certain part, you know, the main thing".) I couldn't sit still. My legs and knees just quiver, all over, my flesh. I couldn't hold still". He says, "I look [7] over there where that peyote was sitting He [Moonhead] had three of them. There was a small one, and a large one in the middle, and then another one on this side. And, that middle one, he said, I seen a man sitting there. He was a very small man, real tiny. He was facing this way. He had on a buckskin suit. It was buckskin. It had fringes right here [on the sleeves] and on the leggings. He had three marks right here [behind/beside each eye], and his hair was parted, hanging down, kind of wavy. He was sitting down, had his legs crossed, like that" <intersecting fingers>. He said, "I seen him. He's tiny, real small. I knew that person. I knew that man [and his brother when they were alive]. He's not of this world. He's gone. " He said, "When that happened, it made me worse."

Moonhead had already said not for us to be making this cigarette. So, I called for a cigarette. He heard it. Then, he called for them fire chiefs [men who tend the fire]. He told them, you all heard it, what he said. Come over here and get them [tobacco and wrappings]. ("They didn't use [corn] shucks them days. They used to use dried leaves of red bud trees. In April, they have pink buds. They must be about the first ones to bloom. It blooms early. Leaves are brown. ") They used them kind of leaves. He come and got that. They had some of that. He rolled that. They gave him that and he rolled a cigarette. They told them, make it for him. They got that tobak. And when [8] he rolled it, they told him, bring it over here. So, he had that in his hand. Moonhead, he took that cigarette already rolled. He told the people, "You see this, look at it. This is what I'm talking about. This thing here. This is what I mean. I don't want any of you to be imitating, doing it just to be doing it. If you do, you'll know what you're into. " He <dad> said he took that, he told him, put <touch> it on top of his head, and put it in his mouth. He said before he did that, when he got through talking, he had that in his mouth, and they lit it for him. <A special cigarette was rolled by the firemen and blessed by Moonhead before it was given to Enoch to smoke. > He smoked and he throwed that smoke way up in the air, like that, and he whooped.

He made a noise, a loud noise. He throwed [blew] it [smoke] east, and north, and south, and west. Then he started smoking. He told them <firemen>, "Take him back over there, take him back to his seat" . They had to catch hold of him, both sides. He was just quivering. He said he just couldn't sit still. His legs had a little quiver, like that, and his hands. He was praying. He talked a long time till that cigarette was kind of short. Then, when he got through, he took that cigarette, and he got up. Moonhead got up. He went over there. He started where the water was. He come right straight on down to that fire, where that fire was. Then he came on around. [9]

When he come on around, he went all over where they had those feathers. Somebody had feathers there, along with things they use in the meeting. He came down [carrying] that arrow, that staff <roadman's insignia>. He put it on top, up there, and worked his hand on down, clear down. He looked like he was looking for something. He went and put it where that tin can was, what they use for drum, you know. He couldn't find it. It looked like he was searching around for something.

Then he come to that peyote, that first one. He didn't find nothing. He skipped the middle one, and come down to this one. The one that was on the north side. Same thing happened. Then he come back. He put <touched> it right on top of that peyote, like this. Then he come on down on the side there. He stuck it right there <in the ground>. He put that cigarette, like this. He worked it down. [He set the cigarette perpendicular to the peyote button.] He [dad] said, he pointed his finger at me. [He pointed his finger at my dad.] He told him, "This is where you seen that man. Right here, right here.

That's where you seen it. But that means for YOU, not for anybody else. It means YOU. He pities YOU. He come. He seen YOU. He seen about you. It means for you, no one else. Now, he says, he told him, that's what I'm talking about. " That's what he told the people. "That's what I'm talking about. I don't want any of you to be doing it for nothing. Just to be, [10] you know, imitating or showing off. That's up to the Almighty. He's going to show you something." That's the way it happened.

Then he told them to bring my father over there. And they brought him over there. Moonhead used to call my father [by the term for] son. He prayed for him. He said, "You'll be OK. " Dad said he could hardly walk. [He] just quivered all over. It was early in the spring, getting green. Dad sat there. It was getting light. Everything was green. He saw a tree with green leaves. Everything was good. He heard birds singing. Those birds, when they sing, flying around, they're not chirping. They're praising God. Each bird is praising God when you hear them. Dad said he prayed to them and he understood their language. He had to start singing. Everything was easy, those songs.

While he was doing that there was a man in the meeting. He was kind of old. He wasn't in his right mind. He come and sit by dad, right next to him. [Dad said,] "He was kind of leaning on me. He kind of bothered me. He kept leaning on me [so I got up and went outside]".

The man followed and said, "It's good. It sure is good in there, but when you're [my dad's] gone, everything just crawls up on me. I see all kinds of snakes and centipedes. Everything just come around. But as long as you're in there, everything's good. But when you go out, they crowd around me. When you go [11] back in there, I want to go with you. Can I go with you?" Dad said yeah. Finally, he said, get up and let's go back in there.

They went back in there. He was all right then cause dad was with him. Then he said, it wasn't too long when dinner was ready. Those women had everything out. They told them that dinner was ready. They washed and drank <water>. Lot of people were out there, sitting on canvas. All the food was spread on the ground, covered over. Everyone was sitting around. They had their dishes ready.

Moonhead got up and made a talk. The menfolks got up and got water for everyone. Then they started serving the food. Moonhead got up. He had a cup and bowl. He went and he got some hominy, real fine hominy, and brought it to my dad. He said, "Here, son, you eat this hominy. It's good for you. You shouldn't feel that way." [Dad said,] "I couldn't hold still. I took it. I wasn't hungry, but I ate cause he told me to." Of course, they were all eating, visiting. They talked a while. Somebody went and seen about their horses.

132

Somebody [Moonhead] told him, "Well, you better go home now. When you go home, heat some water. Tell them to heat up some water, warm water, and put some of that red clay in there. Get some of that tobacco and put that in there. You'll be all right. I'll come around. I'll come to see you. " They said, all right. [12]

So, they helped him get on that horse. They went alright, so far. When they got about half way home, [They were near Lookeba, northwest of their home, where Moonhead lived, going over those hills.] I guess he passed out. He didn't know any more. His uncle and him, they had to ride double. Lead that other horse. They had a long ways to go. When they got over there, they just barely made it. They run in and told grandma about it. They rushed out. Made a pallet. They undressed him. Loosen up them clothes. He didn't know anything. He was sick for a long time. Moonhead come to see him just one time. He never come back any more.

They gave him hominy, some kind of soup, to keep him alive. My dad, he just turned all black. His skin was all black, dark. He was sick for several months. He got more and more thin and weak. I guess he died. Grandma and them knew he died. They got a cloth and put it over his face. They got water and got ready to put him away. They got water to wash him.

Grandma sat there a long time watching him. All of a sudden, he made sort of a cough. Grandma, [who] sat there a long time and watched him, heard it. She pulled off the cloth. One of his uncles said, "Take that cloth off." Grandma was crying right here, right close, while he lay there. She heard what he said.

When he got well, he told afterwards that he heard a [13] woman's voice a long way off. Each time he heard it, it was kind of getting bright toward day like. Here it was her, all the time. Grandma was still crying when he came to. He couldn't talk. She grabbed hold of him and said, "Son, did you get all right. You feel better?" He looked around when he came to. One of his uncles said, "You all give him a bath, wash him off. " The womenfolk went out then. [They washed his clothes.] They had to feed him soup and fine cornmeal. They kept him up. That's the way it happened.

He was just like a little baby, could barely move. Finally, he got stronger. He could sit up, then stand up. Could walk a bit. He got a little better each time, and could walk. He could sit outdoors. When he got strong, when he got plumb well, he told them what happened. "Mother, I'm going to fix a place." [He's talking about that foundation now.]

< His illness and death vision empowered him to build an egg-shaped peyote moon altar, which became the center of a tip! when it was put up for meetings. The crescent moon was at the larger end of the space. Eventually it was cast in concrete and survives on his rural homestead, see illustration in Petrullo (1934, Plate 58). Eventually the nearby graves of he and his wife were moved into the Anadarko town cemetery. > [14]

He said, "I'm going to fix a place. I'm going to see it. It's like this. I have to have white clay. I see the marks. There's a mark there, it goes right straight east. At this moon [Curved like this cane here, rounded off and spread out.], with points far apart, the headman sits on the center here. This mark here. And right on that hill ridge, there's three roads on each side. That one that goes right down where that arrow is pointing in. There's a star there and a heart there. You're going over that crescent ridge hill toward that fire. There's a fire, a heart there, the shape of a heart. And there's another line, that cross there. Then there's a diamond there, a small diamond, and three rows so far apart [making 4 concentric diamonds]. The next one and next one goes on. There's a heart there, then it goes on down to where that water is.

"Now I'm traveling. I was coming down to that fire. When I got close to that fire, they stopped me right there. It was in the spirit world. They called my name and said "We're going to stop you right here. This is as far as you go. When your time comes, we'll let you come on. It's not time for you now. When your time comes, this fire's going to split up. This is a spiritual fire. [At that spot, I saw many footprints.] Lot of people, men and women, old and young, even to little babies. I seen those tracks. They went through the fire. When you go [15] past that fire, you're gone for good. You don't come back no more. " Now they told him, "You take care of yourself. Take care of your life. Don't throw it way. This is the place [altar]. That fire is spiritual fire. It is very hard to see. You can't go by it any way. That's where you loose your life, when you don't live right in this world. You have to take care of yourself. There are rules."

That is the way it happened.

Precious Gifts

Before federal laws, firm assertions of tribal sovereignty, and possessive lawyering up; cultural information, especially sensitive religious thoughts and activities, was saved and recorded by the dedicated pairing of informed elder and trained academic. Their agreed-upon concern was the greater good of a lasting memory of pan-human diversity and comparative understanding. Indeed, they saw themselves as fellow intellectuals of noble purpose denying nay-sayers by sharing privileged esoteric data which would be selectively available through secure archives and academic outlets: journals, monographs, and memoirs held in specialized, often research oriented, libraries. Such credentialed scholarly involvement further validated native knowledge, keeping it privileged but not public until the era of the indiscriminate internet.

Today, a more open democratic process – assured by public, moral, and legal safeguards, involving possessive officials – often closes off further connoisseurship unless such scholarship deliberately challenges governmental regulations. Today, this personal bravery usually involves a last speaker of a tribal language intent on preserving a lasting record despite tribal governmental insistence on control of access to that speaker and necessary approval of research permits. Sometimes their own counter-motivation is a tribal language program run by political choices rather than fluency or training, frustrating their final concerns though it assures an income for a native family with political connections.

Nay-saying continues, charging these elders with selling out, money need ~ greed, presumptuousness, knowing nothing, and being lured by alcohol. Rather it is their far seeing selflessness to safeguard what they know, learned, and were entitled to by experience that sets them above the commons.

Indeed, any "ordinary" American is also most unlikely to support academic research, apart from medical tests that might clearly benefit their health and wellbeing. Yet in societies where wisdom and knowledge advances with age, elders ~ elderlies are scholarly and practical reservoirs whose depths are only occasionally committed to written and printed pages. Instead of disparaging those who made the extra effort with an educated scribe, their singular contribution to human knowledge deserves praise and honor. Today, the apt phrase is "The death of an elder is the loss of a whole library of information."

Because of special circumstances, often a handicap, early isolation, or family trauma, they develop a wider bifocal view of the world, and find a place in it to contribute endangered instances of diverse creativity which are pieces in the understanding the larger human puzzle.

Dzoga Tsmsyaan a ̱kala ksyan ada 'na gyiyaaks. Gaba da hoon dił helda wil liks gyigyeda wüünaya. ̱K'piil di gupl wil büs baasxga gatsiiptsap. A 'na'na ganoonakit. Saigat txaalpxa. p'teex wil ksi wit 'waat ga gyet Gispwudwada, G̱anhada, Laxsgiik, Laxgibuu. 'Na smhawksa da Naxnox ada halaayt. Nago̱ga dmt dit wilaays ga smoogit ga laxaga'a. Dat ama doo wila waalm smoogyit, smgyigyet, liikagyigyet ada łałuungyit. Gyaawin ła dzoo̱ga Tsmsyaan a'na gwa'a dił 'naka boson.

The Tsimshian live along the Skeena River and sea coast, eating salmon and many other foods. They are divided into a dozen tribes ~ tows. Through their mothers, people belong to four p'teex named Gispwudwada, Ganhada, Laxsgiik, Laxgibuu. They believe in *Naxnox* and *Halaayt* before they became Christians. They are organized into chiefs, councilors, ordinaries, and slaves. Now Tsimshians live in Canada and Alaska.

Dzo̱ga Tsmsyaan a ̱kala ksyan ada 'na gyiyaaks.

  The Tsimshian live along the Skeena river and sea coast,

Gaba da hoon dił helda wil liks gyigyeda wüünaya.

  eating salmon and many other foods.

̱K'piil di gupl wil büs baasxga gatsiiptsap.

  They are divided into a dozen tribes~towns.

A 'na'na ganoonakit. Saigat txaalpxa. p'teex wil ksi wit 'waat ga gyet Gispwudwada, G̱anhada, Laxsgiik, Laxgibuu.

  Through their mothers, people belong to four p'teex named gispwudwada, ganhada, laxsgiik, laxgibuu.

'Na smhawksa da Naxnox ada halaayt.

  They believe in naxnox and halaayt

Nago̱ga dmt dit wilaays ga smoogit ga laxaga'a.

  before they became Christians.

Dat ama doo wila waalm smoogyit, smgyigyet, liikagyigyet ada łałuungyit.

  They are organized into chiefs, councilors, ordinaries, and slaves.

Gyaawin ła dzoo̱ga Tsmsyaan a'na gwa'a dił 'naka boson.

  Now Tsimshians live in Canada and Alaska.

An Overview of Northwest Coast Mythology[279]

Abstract

Past and present research on oral literature, particularly mythology, of the Pacific Northwest ~ Northwest Coast is reviewed for significant features of style, content, and social context, along with series of protagonists such as tricksters like Raven and the various transformations, ending with a bibliographic essay on sources.

Native peoples of the Northwest Coast (NWC) have a rich and varied oral literature, as suggested by separate words for 'myths' as distinct from 'stories' in these languages (Boas 1916:565; Ballard 1929:142; de Laguna 1972:839).[1] Boas (1916: 565) noted that a myth pertained "to a period when the world was different from what it is now," and purported to detail how an already-existing world was modified during the Myth Age. There was little if any interest in how this world was itself created. The Myth Age has been described as prehistoric (Boas 1929: 407) and as chaotic and precultural (Jacobs 1959a). However, Myth Age Worlds are better described as ichoate, exaggerated, and undifferentiated into modern categories ~ forms.

Spatially the world of myth and the world of the present are the same because events mentioned in the myths permanently altered the terrain in ways that account for existing features. For the northern tribes and some Oregon Athapascans, the primordeal world was in twilight or darkness until daylight was found, stolen, or simply dawned. Among the more northerly tribes the protagonist called Raven arranged to steal and scatter the luminaries and other existing features. Further south, other protagonists, generally called Transformers or Changers, modified the Myth Age world. For example, along the Washington coast, Transformers found people walking upside-down and set them upright. As Boas (1929: 409-410) noted, Raven as a character altered the world in his selfishness and greediness, benefiting people only inadvertently, incidentally, or accidentally. The Transformers, however, recognized the existence of people and often accomplished their feats in order to spite or thwart people.

Another feature of the undifferentiated Myth Age was the lack of any clear distinctions between humans, animals, and supernaturals. All of these intermarried and had basically shimmering human forms, although some wear animal or bird skins over these. While the myths involve beings called Beaver, Raven, Ice, Southwind, and so forth; these should be viewed as anthropomorphized characters having animal or climatic names and attributes. Animals as such did not exist until the Myth Age was transformed into the contemporary era. This transformation might be gradual, as in the Raven series, or instantaneous, as among the Twana Salish who described the world as 'capsizing' (by analogy to a canoe, Elmendorf 1960:536), sometime after the Transformer had turned the anthropomorphized prototypes into representations of modem animal species. We will consider these myth series or cycles in more detail below, after we treat some of the more important aspects of the style and content of NWC mythology.

Style

Any discussion of NWC mythology must keep in mind that our myth collections are richer and fuller for the northern, matrilineal Tlingit, Haida, and Tsimshlan; less so for the

---

[279] This article was published in *Northwest Anthropological Research Notes* 23 (2): 125-141.

central Wakashan (Nootka and Kwakiutl) and Salish an tribes; and meager for the southern Penutian and Athapascan Oregon tribes. There is a slight possibility that the entire published record represents an unintentionally selective range for a tribe, kin unit, or ethnic group.

While the myths were presented as separate or discrete events or episodes, it is important to remember that they were drawn from a common fund retained by the members, or more especially the elite, of a society. The characters, events, and places in different myths actually represent only pieces of an integrated mythic fabric. For example, Boas (1916a) was able to present an overview of traditional Tsimshian world view by analyzing a large collection of myths recorded by Henry Tate, a Tsimshian. While Marius Barbeau (1917) criticized the collection because Tate's status as a commoner (and thereby not entitled to the sacred histories *[adaawx]* of noble houses) meant that these myths had to be unjustly vague as to ownership and social context, and Maud (1989) argues that the texts were recorded first in English; the data on world view nevertheless speak for themselves.

Accordingly, the earth is a flat disk supported on a pole resting on the chest of *Am'ala'* ('smokehole'), who replaced a previous supernatural. In the Myth Age, all of the future people and animals lived together at Prairie Town on the upper Skeena River. After a flood, everyone left Prairie Town and settled in separate towns or houses on the earth. The animals retained their human forms in their own settlements. When a male bear had his fishing line break or a female bear had her tumpline snap, it meant that they had been killed by a human hunter; only to return to Bear Town a few days later provided that they had been treated with proper ritual by the hunter and his kill. On the edge of the earth, Pestilence Chief, his daughter, and maimed people lived together. The ocean surrounded the earth and in it lived fish and sea mammals. The killer-whales divided into the same four semi-moieties (phratries) as the Tsimshian themselves and displayed their crest membership by the form of their dorsal fins. Across the ocean are different worlds inhabited by anthropomorphic beings such as dwarfs, ghosts, and salmon. In the Salmon Country, each species has its own town, with the Spring Salmon furthest away and the Silver, Steelhead, Humpback, Coho, and Trout successively closer to the ocean and the earth. Over-arching this terrestrial realm is the Sky World, from which various supernaturals, generally called 'shining youths,' have descended to the accompaniment of four flashes of lightning and four claps of thunder in order to help or to marry a mortal.

The populations of all of these Tsimshian worlds mirrored NWC concerns with rank in that distinctions between nobles, commoners, and slaves were either specified or implied. The various details or descriptions of these characters, places, attributes, and events were embodied in different myths; yet it was only in the context of the entire mythology that these pieces made sense. The mythic totality was more than the sum of its parts because it could constantly generate new variants of the mythology. The separate myths were especially important, however, for providing stylistic, content, and social information.

Stylistic features of NWC mythology included conventional beginnings and endings, pattern numbers, performance styles, and metaphorical usages and themes. In the instances where researchers have thought to ask, conventionalizations have been recorded. Jacobs (1972) was an especially important source for stylistics in native Washington and Oregon. Not every myth necessarily included them, however, they were generally understood by implication. A common beginning immediately introduced the protagonist of a myth and/or other participants. Endings usually conveyed a sense of finality unless it was a long myth occupying several evening recitations, in which case only a halt was indicated each evening before the last one.

Our best examples are Clackamas Chinook (Jacobs 1949:221) for whom the usual beginning specified that an individual or group lived together in a house or village and the common ending was the reduplication story, story or the indication "the people are coming soon."

Four was the pattern number for the reoccurrence of events or individuals among the northern tribes and five was the pattern number among the southern ones. The Tillamook, however, used four repetitions for female characters and five for males, while three was sometimes used in northwestern Washington (Jacobs 1972).

Performance styles were seldom recorded. One Yakutat Tlingit told Raven myths with "the most energetic sound effects: tappings, slurps, belches, explosive pows, and dramatic dialogue" (de Laguna 1972: 841). The animal character called Raven by the Lushootseed of Puget Sound speaks with an intense nasal quality when mimicked by narrators. Recitations were punctuated by a distinctive sound or response which indicated the continued interest of the audience. Some myths include brief songs which belonged to specific characters. Robert Miller (1952) for the Makah and McClellan (1970) for the Tlingit and others have discussed the affect which the life circumstances of a narrator can have on the order and the performance of stories.

Metaphors were not frequent but were exemplified by the ravenous gluttony of Raven for the northern tribes and by the equation of long hair with beauty and of baldness or pendulous breasts with ugliness among southern tribes. One Coquille Athapascan speaker used metaphors such as the deer ran like thunder (Jacobs 1972).

An important literary device was reversal (Miller 1988). The seasonal and diurnal cycles were reversed for the land of the living and that of the dead. Animals appeared as humans in their own villages, but as animals around people. In the example of the Salmon Country given above reversal was important. The Spring Salmon sent scouts up the Skeena River to see if what they called their salmon were spawning. At an affirmative report, the Springs started out announcing the good news in the other Salmon towns as they passed them. The Silvers, Humpbacks, and Dogs said they would follow shortly; the Cohos that they would wait until fall; the Trout asked to accompany the Springs; and these two together continue on to meet the Steelhead who were already returning from the Skeena. What the Salmon called their salmon, humans called cottonwood leaves which have fallen into the river (Boas 1916: 454).

Content

The content of these myths expressed vital NWC social and environmental concerns. Among the former were rank and wealth, and among the latter were the sea the forest, and the weather.

Slaves and commoners, if they appeared at all, were superficial in the mythology. The very performance of various exploits served to indicate that someone was wiser, stronger, and wealthier than other stock characters. A protagonist might appear poor, orphaned, and dirty; but he, or rarely she, was eventually revealed as wise and/or wealthy: a member of the elite and as such the worthy recipient of supernatural aid, gifts, and power. Only the Chinook character called Bluejay constantly showed presumption by trying to outdo people of higher status. Under-pinning the elite status was the concept of wealth as it was reiterated m material terms. Copper, dentalia, and abalone had great value along the entire coast. Among northern tribes were found such wealth-conferring supernaturals as a Beaver with copper eyes, claws, ears, and teeth. The power of such metaphors was indicated by the fact the Tlingitized Tagish attributed the famous Klondike Gold Rush of 1898 to an Indian's encounter with Wealth Woman, who had gold fingernails and wore martin skins, dentalia, and copper (McClellan 1963).

The great concern of all coastal peoples with the sea included visits to the Undersea World to acquire supernatural aid or a spouse. In the process, the shore terrain was described and listeners were assured that the beings below the sea recognized the same social ranks and economic values as do humans. Among the noble spouses of humans were Sea Otter, Frog, Seal, Salmon, and so forth. The human married to them generally arranged for her or his kin to receive sea products, such as fish and whales, in fulfillment of expected marital exchanges.

The dangers of the sea and also of the impenetrable forest bramble were represented by various monsters forming an interlinked series from the Land Otter People of the north to the Sasquatch or Wild Man of the central area. For the Tlingit, Haida, and Tsimshian , Land Otter Men captured drowned humans and metamorphized them into Land Otters with human fingernails. Land Otters were especially feared because of their ability to mimic the appearance of someone that a human alone in the woods happened to think about or long for. The Kwakiutl recognized a Wild Man called *Bukwus*, who captured people by offering them food and who was associated with a crew of Land Otters who appeared as the victim's relatives, minks who appeared as paddles, and a skate who appeared as the canoe itself (Boas 1935: 146). The Fraser River Salish have a similar being called Sasquatch, who stole women and food.

Concern with the weather, sometimes life threatening on the coast, evoked personifications as Fog Woman, Four Winds, and Thunderbirds. Some myths also imply that native life-styles became sustained or successful once fair weather began during the Myth Age.

Many of the motif distributions on the North Pacific Coast have been worked out by Thompson (1966) in conjunction with his more general concern with North American folklore. The NWC shared with the rest of North America such motifs as the origin of death (Thompson 1966: 284 # 151), the deluge (286 #51), misplaced genitalia (288 #57), bungling host (301 #103), *vagina dentata* (309 #115), star husband (330 # 193), Orpheus (337 #215), and the rolling head (342 #238). Particular motifs of more limited distribution which the NWC shared with other culture areas included a person swallowed by a monster becoming bald-shared with Siberia (322 #166a); a woman stolen by killerwhales − shared with the Plateau (342 #235); dog husband-shared with the Arctic, Subarctic, Plateau, and Plains (347 #247); and the princess who rejected her cousin − shared with the Plains and Southwest (349 #256). Motifs or motif versions specifically localized in the NWC included the variants of the heat test motif of a burning food test for the Haida and of the swallowing of red-hot rocks for the Haida and Comox (312 #120a, b); miraculous creation motif variants of birth from tears along the northern coast or from body secretions among the Haida and Kwakiutl (323 #166a, b); the motif of the marooned hunter on the northern coast (326 #175); and the motif of the death of Pitch by exposure to the sun, specifically localized on the north and central coast (356 #285). Randall (1949) has also compared the Cinderella theme as it occurred on the NWC and in central Europe. The distinctive NWC series dealing with Raven, Mink, and Bluejay will be treated separately below.

Social Context

Much of the vitality of these myths can also be attributed to their social context. A full command of the myth traditions of a town, social group, household, or tribe was the mark of a properly educated member of the elite. Boys destined to be chiefs, social leaders, or advisors were carefully instructed in the myths associated with their group. These were generally conveyed at what Jacobs (1972) called "predawn pedagogic sessions." For a native perspective on the instructive value of legends and stones, Hilbert's (1985) Preface is superb.

While myths could be casually discussed at any time, their telling was closely circumscribed. Winter was the proper season, the elderly the proper raconteurs, and during the evening when the people were weather bound, the proper time. Among the Tlingit, myths were not recited during social events such as potlatches. The educated already knew them, asserting their shared nobility through oratorical allusions, songs, dramatic dances, art works, witty remarks, moral admonitions, and apt proverbs derived from the myths (de Laguna 1972: 839). Myths, or rather particular myth versions, were considered social property, at least in the north. Garfield (1953) noted that the story of the man called *Kats*, the hunter who married a Bear woman, belonged to the Tlingit *Teqeodi* clan and to certain Nishka Tsimshian and Haida lineages who claimed Kats as an ancestor. An exemplary collection of Tlingit house stories [*at.oow* − sacred histories], presented in poetic format, comprise the first volume of Tlingit oral literature published by the Dauenhauers (1987).

It is now appropriate to return to the great mythic series so closely associated with the NWC, although they are not exclusive to this region. These were generally called the Raven series and the Transformer series, with the Trickster series either forming a part of the Raven series in the north or a separate series involving Mink or Bluejay in the central area.

Raven Series

The wide appeal of the protagonist called Raven was bound up with the complexity of his character, allowing an audience the possibility of both identity and catharsis with Raven. Some of his important characteristics were superhuman powers and abilities, social license, and entertaining incongruities. Raven accomplished the gross distinctions of the modern world by skill, cunning, and incredible feats. Humans could identify with his omnipotence and craftiness. In this guise, Raven was a Transformer. However, Raven was also a Trickster when he was a bumbling host, an amorous interloper, and a devious glutton. Then Raven had complete license, as did the raconteur, to say the unsayable, plot the unthinkable, exalt the lowly, and defame the mighty. This was the cathartic ability of Raven. Further, Raven myths included some delightful paradoxes, as when be convinced Bear that a stone had insulted it, or when Raven was swallowed by a whale and lived inside it by stripping off meat and cooking it. In a rather full discussion of the Raven series, Boas (1916: #84) indicated that "Raven was really an umbrella term for many different names associated with a protagonist shared on both shores of the North Pacific."

There was some disagreement as to the proper sequence of episodes in the Raven series. They did not seem to be free-floating. Boas (1916:562) believed that a sequence could be established by a comparative study of the relative frequency, and thus popularity, of the episodes as found in published collections. Louis Shotridge, a Tlingit, said that the serious or Transformer episodes should occur in a logical order, while the humorous or Trickster myths could occur anywhere that a narrator felt his audience would appreciate them (Boas 1916: 582 #1). Garfield (1953) made the point that Raven's own life cycle established a chronology for the series. An additional complication was that, while the outline of the entire series may have been generally known, the particular details and episodes were the property of particular social groups, who distinguished their privilege by varying the incidents.

Raven was born in the sky of an incestuous or an unfaithful mother. He descended to earth as a Shining Youth, but became humanized both by a ritual adoption as well as by eating scabs. The overall effect of this was to make him voracious, which set the tenor and motivation for his subsequent adventures. Oblivious of humans, his greed led him to differentiate the world by tricking various owners into releasing the Sun, Moon, and Stars; Fresh Water, Candlefish, the Tides, Fair Weather, Fire, Death, Salmon, and Land. He gave many animals their present attributes, painting colors on birds and cutting out the tongue of Cormorant. In still other episodes, Raven was humiliated, teased, and maligned. Always, he sought food. Finally, Raven moved out to sea, invited the sea monsters to the first potlatch, feasted and entertained them, and either received their promise not to harm humans or turned them and himself into stone.

Transformer Series

As the Raven series presented the gross differentiations of the world, so the Transformer series presented a concern with details and particulars. While Raven usually worked alone, there were usually multiple Transformers, whom Melville Jacobs (1959: 196, 232–236) preferred to call Announcers, although only one was named and the others were ancillary twins or brothers (Boas 1916: 586).

The Transformers might simply appear on earth, descend from the sky, or be the offspring of marriages between animals and humans. Transformer myths ranged from the Straits of Georgia to the Oregon coast. Throughout this area, the Trickster myths formed a distinct series featuring Mink toward the north and Bluejay toward the south. The Trickster series concentrated on the amorous adventures and improprieties of these protagonists.

In contrast, the Transformer traveled around meeting the ancestors of humans and animals, interacting with them, tricking them, and leaving them permanently changed in preparation for the advent of the present world. The Transformers created features of the contemporary landscape, legitimized the ancestry of names and privileges, invented useful tools, and gave animals their present forms and attributes. For example, the Transformers met people sharpening weapons, intent on killing those who were changing the world, and used the same weapons to transform the people into animals. The rectal insertion of a spear created mink or otter, while that of a knife or paddle created beaver.

Finally, the Transformers left, replacement teams of Transformers no longer arrived, or, according to the Quinault and Quileute, the Transformers turned to stone near the mouth of the Columbia River.

Conclusions

In addition to the major myth series, NWC mythology abounds in various incidents of the Myth Age which testify to the importance of interpersonal behaviors and processes, such as marriage, sex, aggression, altruism, and exchange. In general, the mythology as a whole can be said to reinforce traditional concern with wealth, rank, and prestige; to codify the knowledge of the world and the larger cosmology; to suggest alternative solutions, whether negatively or positively valued, to cultural concerns and paradoxes; to educate youngsters of the elite in the proper names, crests, privileges, and etiquette of their station; to entertain people when they were weather bound; and to permit an emotional outlet for both narrators and audience. As de Laguna (1972:838) remarked:

> Narrative, rather than exposition or abstract explanation, was the form in which the conceptual schema and the values of the social and moral order were verbally expressed.

Essay on Sources

The interpretation of Northwest Coast literature displays the heavy stamp of four scholars: Franz Boas, Melville Jacobs, Claude Levi-Strauss, and Dell Hymes.

Relying on Native folklore collectors like Henry Tate and William Beynon for the Tsimshian and George Hunt for the Kwagiulth, Boas amassed a great store of myths and stories. Around the turn of this century, mythology became a central concern of the Boas research strategy because it was distinctive of different cultural backgrounds, readily acquired in linguistic transcription and English translation, and provided a strongly empirical means for tracing the historical movements of traits and motifs. Boas held the opinion that Culture was "reflected" in mythology both in terms of detailed ethnographic information encapsulated within the content of myths and in terms of the secondary explanations which the myths themselves provided to integrate traits from disparate historical sources into the coherent patterns of a culture (Spier 1931). In his classic account of Tsimshian mythology, Boas was able to draw from the myths valid ethnographic information on house construction and occupation, social structure, kinship, prestige system, rituals, religion, supernaturals and cosmology, while at the same time suggesting an interior origin for the Tsimshian which more recent research has discounted. Most recently, the careful ethnopoetic translations of stories by John Dunn (1988) has revitalized Tsimshian research, which has been further encouraged by the publication of Marius Barbeau and William Beynon materials (Cove 1985; MacDonald and Cove 1987).

In the mid-twentieth century, Melville Jacobs used the fine linguistic texts he had previous collected to probe deeply into the psychological dimensions of mythology. Using myths and, most particularly, myth characters, he drew inferences about the anxiety-provoking conflicts inherent in Clackamas Chinook and other cultures. He strongly argued for the equation of mythology not with poetry or narrative but with drama − laconic characterizations rich in aesthetic and emotional complexity. Jacobs was a student of Boas and provided the finest evaluation of Boas' work in folklore (Jacobs 1959c). Moreover, he wrote, late in life, two articles for a popular audience which are must reading for anyone seeking an overview of Native mythologies from Washington state and Oregon (Jacobs 1967: 1972).

By the late 1960s, Levi-Strauss had refined and focused his methods of structural analysis to produce four massive volumes (mythologiques, mytho-logics) devoted to myths from Native South and North America, beginning with an Amazonian myth about a marooned egg-gatherer and ending with a volume (Levi-Strauss 1971: 1981) considering myths from the Northwest coast. Throughout, he showed that mythologies represent rational attempts to consider alternative cultural strategies, to intellectually solve paradoxes inherent between real and ideal behaviors, and to work out elaborate affirmations that the world is logical. He attributed to this "mytho-logic" the full canonical power that is reserved for "science" by the industrial nations.

The current leading figure is Dell Hymes (1965, 1968, 1975a, 1975b, 1976, 1981), who has concentrated his attention on Chinookan mythology to provide reinterpretations and insights into performance and ethnopoetic measures overlooked by earlier researchers.

Building upon his insights have been the work of Dale Kinkade (1983) for Salish texts and John Dunn (1988) for Tsimshian ones. Publications by the Dauenhauers (1987), the husband is a poet and the wife a native speaker of Tlingit, set a new standard. Further, the book by Hilbert (1987) combines careful translations, some in measured verse, with the insights of a cultural insider.

The majority of Northwest Coast oral literature collections have been published in periodical series founded by Franz Boas and his students. Thus, *Columbia University Publications in Anthropology* include important text collections by Frachtenberg from Coos (1913) and Lower Umpqua (1914), by Andrade on Quileute (1931), and by Boas from Kwakiutl (1910, 1935a, 1935b, 1943) and Bella Bella (1928) and on Kwakiutl religion (1930). This series is notable for close-translations of native language texts on the same or adjoining pages, but the texts lack abstracts and performance annotations.

Bureau of American Ethnology, Bulletins include folklore from the Chinook and Kathlamet Chinook (Boas 1894, 1901), Tsimshian (Boas, 1902), Skidegate Haida (Swanton 1905), Tlingit at Sitka and Wrangel (Swanton 1909), Alsea (Frachtenberg 1920), and some Nootkan and Quileute material (Densmore 1939). The series is characterized by generally close English translations from native texts which are usually provided together with short abstracts. There are no details on performance. Among *Annual Reports of the Bureau of American Ethnology,* the 31st is the Boas (1916) study of Tsimshian and comparative NWC mythology.

The University of Washington Publications in Anthropology contain fairly close English translations by Ballard (1927, 1929) for Puget Sound Salish myths, by Gunther (1927) for Klallam, by Jacobs for Coos (1940), Kalapuya (1949), and Clackamas Chinook (1960), and by Spier and Sapir (1930) for Wishram and Wasco. These volumes generally include some performance and life history material on the narrators.

The Anthropological Papers of the American Museum of Natural History published mythology compiled by Boas from the Bella Coola (1898b) and by Boas and George Hunt (1905, 1906) for the Kwakiulth. The Swanton (1905c) summary of Haida ethnography includes abstracts of his Skidegate, Masset, and Kaigani Haida texts.

The Memoirs of the American Folklore Society include an uneven volume on Coast Salish myths (Adamson 1934), one on the Bella Coola (Boas 1932), and the final statement on the Kwakiutl by Boas (1935): *Kwakiutl Culture as Reflected in Mythology.* These memoirs are limited to English translations of varying quality, which depends on the abilities of the collector; abstracts are often included.

Journal of American Folklore is the best source for short collections of myths published in English. After 1950, authors have included more psychological, performance, stylistic, theoretical, and cultural information (Miller 1952; Hymes 1985).

Important other treatments are the work of Melville Jacobs (1959c) analyzing the content, style, and psychological tensions in Clackamas mythology as dramas, the Nehalem Tillamook collection by Elizabeth Jacobs (1959), and the careful discussions by Viola Garfield (1953, 1961, 1966) tracing the cultural import of mythology among the matrilineal tribes. Readers should be especially warned, however, that the popular collections by Clark (1953) and by Reagan and Walters (1933) were expurgated and/or cast in European molds so they do not reflect true Pacific Northwest literature.

Some terms for "myth" as distinct from "story" are:

Bella Coola	*smaiusta*	(McIlwraith 1948: 293)
Tlingit	*tłagu*	(de Laguna 1972: 839)
Tsimshian	*ada'ox*	(Boas 1916: 565)
Kwakiutl	*nu'yam*	(Boas 1916: 565)
Chinook	*ik!anam*	(Boas 1916: 565)
Puget	*sx̱wiya'b*	(Ballard 1929: 142)

According to Boas (1916: 584) the designations for Raven include:

Tlingit	*yeł*	
Haida	*nAnkilsłas*	'He Whose Voice Is Obeyed'
Tsimshian	*txamsən*	'Giant' ~ 'Raven'
Bella Bella	*he'mask.as*	'Real Chief'
Nootka	*qo'icinimit'*	

With regard to the Transformers, Boas (1916: 586ff) reported that among the Kwakiutl (?), Nootka, Quinault, and Chinook, they were twins. Some names for the Transformers are:

Comox	*Kumsno'oc*	(Boas 1916: 586)
Nitinath	*alis*	(Boas 1916: 586)
Nootka	*Mucus Bay*	(Boas 1916: 586)
Puget	*Dokweboł*	'Moon' (Ballard 1929: 69ff)
Katzie	*Swaneset, Khaals*	(Jenness 1955: 10ff)

North Pacific Ethnoastronomy:
Tsimshian and Others

Jay Miller, editor and associate director of the D'Arcy McNickle Center for the History of the American Indian at Chicago's Newberry Library, has published over four dozen articles and six sole-authored or edited books on various Native American peoples. We required an almost impossible task from him: summarize Northwest Coast ethnoastronomy. Although these several societies are both well-studied and well-known, there is very little known about their indigenous astronomical systems. Truly this is salvage work, for the systems are no longer intact.

Overcast skies and steady rain may not seem conducive to astronomy, but along the North Pacific coast, observations made from fixed locations ("seats") played a vital role in these maritime societies. Families ranged widely between routine camps and towns at strategic locations on the landscape, using resource locations which were owned and inherited by members of a House, a feudal − like corporate group identified by heraldic emblems. The heads of households led the kin groups and towns, assisted by specialists like artists, environmentalists, and advisors. Foremost among these specialists were elders knowledgeable about the skies in terms of stars and planets, along with winds, tides, and other shifting indicators of time. Skylore had both practical application for the extensive navigation typical of the coast and cultural import for the ranks within society. In this region, members of the elite were and are believed to have a special rapport with nature. Their lives reflected the divine favor of Heaven, as indicated by peculiar combinations of social and environmental events. Thus, the summer birth of an elite baby might be accompanied by a brief snowfall, or the [194] death of an old chief by a sudden squall. To predict and monitor such convergences, specialists watched the skies and seas to advise the leader of changes in nature that were both expected and spectacular.

Indeed, the American-Canadian Northwest remains justly famous for the complexity of its societies and the richness of its environment. Here, too, the sky is reflected on the earth, with varying degrees of intensity. More provocative than comprehensive, available data indicate the importance of the sky for understanding how and why things function on the earth. While early travelers, missionaries, explorers, and traders were quick to note a belief in a sky or heavenly God, they were not generally concerned with details of astronomical lore. Thus, our first reliable information was collected by some of the most famous early anthropologists as part of their general interest in recording ethnographic derails. This paper briefly summarizes what is generally known of Native Northwest Coast astronomy before considering the Tsimshian in greater detail.

Quinault

The most succinct statement on skylore for the region comes from the Quinault of the coast of Washington State, as summarized by Olson (1936: 176-77):

In a region where the winter season is one of almost continuous rain and storm one scarcely expects to encounter the reckoning of the winter solstice, yet the Quinault kept definite track of both solstices. At several villages there were "seats" (a stump or stone) where the old men watched both sunrise and sunset. Usually they sighted from the seat to a pole placed in the ground, or to a designated tree. [Note 70 adds that the sighting was done by marking on a stick placed horizontally the spot where the shadow of a certain tree fell at the moment of sunrise. One such mark indicated fifteen days until the solstice.) If the sun traveled farther north than in ordinary years(!) it was considered a sign that a good year with a heavy run of salmon would follow. If the solstice occurred during a waning moon it moved but little each day, indicating that it was heavily loaded (with food) for the year to follow. But after a solstice which occurred during a waxing moon the sun traveled far each day and indicated a lean year to follow, with sickness and famine certain to come. The winter solstice was called *xa'ttaanm* (comes back, the sun). There was no name for the summer solstice but it was observed in the same fashion. It was believed that at the summer solstice the sun set four or five times at exactly the same place. [195]

As indicated, observations of the sky were to mark both seasonal and nightly events. Thus, winter solstice was also the time for exceptionally high tides, when Quinault whalers made contact with their supernatural patron (same: 177), drawing spirits, humans, and whales into a complex network of preparatory ritual and energetic sea hunts. Only a few star and constellation names were recorded. Bob Pope, a Quinault said to have been born in the 1830s, was able to identify the Evening and Morning Stars (regarded as chiefs), Pleiades, Orion(?), North Star, and Great Dipper. If someone were able to count all nine of the Pleiades, that person would become rich and a chief, presumably because such attention to detail and knowledge of the sky could be put to use for the greater good of the community.

Living on the outer coast and looking toward the western horizon, which other Salishan speakers called "the edge of the world," the sky filled the Quinault universe. Knowledge about it was pooled among the elders of the present (or the nobles of the past), who checked it against the periodic observations made from fixed locations. The movements of the sun played a major role in these systems, probably because it so dominated the day, when people were actively pursuing economic and social pursuits. For longdistance voyagers hugging the coast, some skylore also had navigational significance.

Kwakiutl

For the Kwakiutl, living along the Inside Passage of British Columbia, the universe had four realms: the sky of immortals, the earth of mortals, the underworld of ghosts, and the undersea of wealthy immortals, which included the land of the salmon people on its rim (Boas 1935: 125-40).

Of these realms, the sky had priority. A world like that of earth − except that its inhabitants, houses, and resources were all vastly more significant − the heavens were the home of the sun, moon, stars, Thunder-bird, and ancestors who came to earth to found many of the tribal houses. The sky chief, associated with abalone and the sun, governed this realm. In some town histories, the sun is called his son and the clouds his daughters. In others, the chief, whose tribe is the stars, is called Post of Heaven, and he went down to earth along a copper pole to establish hereditary treasures and trails of benefit for human communities. In other instances, the ancestors of many of the Kwakiutl tribes were believed to have lived in the sky as birds, [196] generally the Thunderbird and his younger brothers, who flew down to earth and assumed human form to become the founding ancestors of important Kwakiutl social units, called *numaym* in this native language.

Even now, some mortals can still go to the sky and stars during dreams in order to receive important revelations. Coming to various people at different times, such dreams are individual events, separate from the sacred histories which validate the claims of corporate houses to hereditary crests: inherited, heraldic art forms involving song, dance, design, and drama. Crests have two contexts for expressions, with winter ceremonials – dramatizing the rituals of ancestors holding sacred names – and potlatches when families give away food and wealth in honor of other, more historical names. Ancestors believed to come from the sky were described or impersonated during both of these events. Taken together, such dreams, winter ceremonials, and potlatches served to emphasize the importance of the sky for individuals, families, and towns.

Nuxalk ~ Bella Coola

According to Nuxalks, the sky is the location of *Nusmatta*, the gigantic house of the Creator (*Ałquntam*), who was and is the first cause (McIlwraith 1948). It is from the sky that everything came and it is to the sky, specifically *Nusmatta*, that all return. The Creator sent the ancestors of various kindred families to specific locales on the earth, often wearing the skins of specific bird species when alighting on particular peaks. There, they removed the skin cloak, which went back to heaven and assumed human form. Ever since, the route between earth and sky via such a peak has been followed by the souls of members of the same family as each is born and dies. Named immortals made these passages and constituted the actors of the sacred history, which is transmitted through the families and households of their descendants, enabling each generation to perpetuate these immortal names.

At the beginning, the Creator set up a tally post in *Nusmatta* for every Bella Coola who would ever live. Since mythic names were and are hereditary, it seems likely that these posts represented ancestral names, rather than specific individuals, since each post is emblazoned with a crest (species cloak) of the first ancestor. When the person linked with the post becomes ill, the post leans. Shamans will sometimes go above to straighten it up, if possible, or to estimate the duration of that life by the precariousness of its angle. [197]

Also in the beginning, the Creator set up an enormous wash basin with many little compartments holding water. Each one holds the water of life for a designated individual (or name), and shamans also may have gone to inspect these in ancient times. Even now, the washing of patients during shamanic cures seems to be related to the symbolism of this basin.

At death, a person divided into corpse, shadow, and ghost. The spirit becomes a ghost and travels back through its generations of ancestors until it reaches the spot where the first of them was sent to earth by the Creator, dons the cloak of the species it used to float to the mountain top, and ascends to heaven to live in *Nusmatta*. Existence above is like that on earth, but all personal skills and abilities are enhanced.

When a member of a secret society died, a drama was enacted to make it appear that the body itself was carried away through the smokehole by the ancestral crest, graphically representing the journey of the dead along its ancestral route back to the sky.

After the funeral, memorials were held, of which the most significant was the Bella Coola version of the potlatch, whose hallmark, setting it apart from that of their neighbors, is the central importance given to the dramatic enactment of the return of a deceased relative in the guise of a crest (Mcllwraith 1948: 45 8). Equally unlike similar ceremonies by other tribes, there was singing but no dancing (Mcllwraith 1948: 470). As described for the Bella Coola with unusual clarity during such rituals, the priority of the sky is expressed through the association of life, death, and immortality with Nusmatta and the Creator.

In contrast to the cognatic ~ ambilateral societies of Salishans and Kwakiutlans along the southern coast, those of the northern coast are matrilineal. Here the crests, lore, and offices belonging to a household are passed from mother's brother to sister's son.

Tlingit

Among the northernmost of these nations is the Tlingit, where astronomical knowledge was also important, although we know little about it. In a fine collection of narratives, arranged as poetic verses, Dauenhauer and Dauenhauer (1987: 95, cf. 330) include within a sacred history of a clan house:

> People who were elders
> routinely
> sat outside. [198]
> We used to call it "*a.an.*"
> Here they checked
> the stars
> Venus
> And
> the Milky Way.
> They would check where they were now,
> and where the moon was rising from
> and where the sun was setting from.
> They would check.
> People used this as a map.
> They used it also to work by
> That's what he would look at toward evening.

Thus, from opposite ends of the coast, we have accounts of elders at fixed seats checking the sky and stars. Presumably, they were watching the weather, the seasons, the winds, and the availability of resources which are influenced by these.

Probably all peoples in the Northwest shared these beliefs, but they have not been well reported in print. To suggest some of the richness of such knowledge in the past, I now consider the better known Tsimshian peoples of the Skeena and Nass Rivers, in addition to offshore islands, of northern British Columbia.

Tsimshian

Among the Tsimshian, areas of knowledge were controlled by specialists acting as advisors to the royalty, the most elite members of the heraldic houses of their communities. Alas, the last of the traditionally trained sky watchers for the Tsimshian town where I have been most involved died two weeks before I made my first visit there. My information has been drawn, therefore, from conversations with his heirs and from the available literature.

The Tsimshian have had a complex development. Over ten thousand years ago, there were people living along the North Pacific Coast near the mouths of the Skeena River and trading for obsidian from the interior. Trails in this territory were part of an established trade network by five thousand years ago and have been in continuous use since then, now as [199] paved roads. By three thousand years ago, prestige goods were traded within a ranked society like that of historic times. Graves indicate warfare as well as trade, with a trophy head cult that echoed the Old Bering Sea Complex of Alaska and Siberia and of Shang (1600BC) China. Sites in Rupert Harbor show cedar-plank houses and towns gradually increasing in size and layout. By two thousand years ago, Tsimshian society stabilized, with resource areas claimed and utilized by uncontested owners. Members of Tsimshian Coastal towns wintered near Metlakatla in Rupert Harbor, went to the Nass River for spring runs of candlefish, and utilized tributary streams of the Skeena during the summer. These aboriginal patterns continued until Russian traders began modifying them about 1750.

While the complexities of Tsimshian culture and society have been difficult to grasp, the new generation ofTsimshianisrs has made significant contributions by building on the turn of this century work by native collectors like Henry Tait and, particularly, William Beynon, and by working together with scholars such as Franz Boas, Marius Barbeau, Viola Garfield, Wilson Duff, and others. My own work has been both community-specific and comparative so as to present a holistic model of the Tsimshian.

As now understood, Tsimshian society was consistently structured in terms of a series of fourfold divisions. Politically, there were the Coastal / Southern and the Nishka / Gitksan tribal − drainage − linguistic polities. Socially, there were four classes of royals, nobles, commoners, and slaves, with the freeborn classes having membership in the semimoieties of Blackfish-Wolf / of Raven-Eagle.

The most common associations of these fourfold divisions had to do with habitat zones associated with various immortals. The sources of greatest power are at the bottom of the sea or the height of heaven, with the life zones grading from sea to beach, to forest, to peak, to air, and to sky.

The basic unit of the overall system was the House, a feudal corporation localized in a cedar-plank building with interior space arranged by class, rank, and sanctity. Slaves stayed nearest the door, the most vulnerable location, and the ranking family lived at the rear beside the carved and painted screen that set off the compartment where the treasures (crests and wonders) were stored.

The House had four aspects: (1) an architectural building, decorated with heraldic art; (2) a corporation whose membership descended through females, a matrilineal descent group of householders from lineages, clans, semimoiety, and moiety half; (3) a repository for corporate treasures, inherited artforms such as songs, dances, designs, and outfits based upon [200] sacred histories detailing the adventures of the primordial holders of the immortal names; and (4) real estate, the named sites of the House, seasonal camps, resource-gathering areas, and fishing places.

Families moved with the seasons to these hereditary resource areas, gathering together in fall camps for games and festivities before settling into the large plank houses, along sheltered bays and banks for the winter ceremonial period.

Tsimshian chiefs, those holding the immortal "great name" of a House – and with it a ranked position (a "seat") within the hierarchy of clan, community, and tribal houses – held two roles during a year. In summer, the season devoted to economic pursuits, the chiefs were known as "real people," who celebrated the successful harvesting of their resources at potlatches when House members hosted guests from other houses at feasts sharing their bounty while displaying and validating their crests in public. The most important crest of a House was usually a special hat, worn by the chief during the potlatch. During winter, the sacred or religious time, chiefs "put away" their crest name(s) and "put on" their wonder (*naxnox*) name(s), each associated with a mask.

All of Tsimshian society responded to these summer / winter, economic / religious, crest / wonder dualisms that subsumed the foursomes also permeating the society. Within each town, moieties were distinguished as Owner or as Other. The Owner moiety was descended from the immortal name who founded a House and used that place and territory. The House of the greatest name of the Owner moiety occupied the center of the town, with cadet houses on either side of it and the houses of the Other moiety farther along the row of buildings facing the beach or river.

This pattern was jumbled by Eurocanadian contacts and the movement of Tsimshians to the vicinity of trading posts and mission stations. It was in the newly settled neighborhoods at Port Simpson, Prince Rupert, and both Metlakatlas that most fieldwork before the 1970s was conducted. Members of all four of the semimoieties, various towns, and the full array of ranks and classes shared space there, complicating the data. Within this novel context, Tsimshian leaders sorted themselves out by staging elaborate events, called rivalry potlatches, whereby chiefs strove to outdo each other and assume a position in an overall ranking of town chiefs. These rivalry potlatches caught the attention and ire of government officials and missionaries, who managed to convince the Canadian government to ban potlatches and wonder displays in amendments to the Indian Act in effect between 1890 and 1950, when these were decriminalized. [201]

The Wonder System was abandoned by the Tsimshian when they became Christians through the efforts of William Duncan, an Anglican lay missionary who devoted his life to their conversion and to the development of successful economic cooperatives in the model town of Metlakatla in British Columbia. After an argument with his bishop about dispensing communion, Duncan led his converts to an island near Kerchikan, Alaska, where the community continues in American jurisdiction.

The modern Tsimshian now celebrate potlatch – like feasts during the Christmas holidays when most family members are able to return home. Crests are still made and displayed, but Christian humility has somewhat muted prideful one-upmanship. Other vestiges of the ancient society also remain, and among these is a keen interest in the environment.

While the society has changed, its cultural underpinnings have been maintained. Tsimshian culture is based on an axiomatic tension of related oppositions (between open and closed, lenses and lids, wonders and crests) expressing the fundamental importance of Light as the source for existence.

In the beginning, the universe was in twilight and its apex was a deity called Heaven, who was very sensitive. If angry, pleased, or touched by humans, he sent radiant messengers ("shining youths") to earth, each accompanied by four flashes of lightning and four crashes of thunder. Several fathered human children and started royal lines. One such father, wearing a bright garment decorated with a rainbow with stars above and the sun or moon on either side, brought his sons back to earth (Barbeau and Beynon 1987: 268-69). Alas, the design is only verbally described, so we have no idea whether the stars related to a specific constellation or the general symbolism of the sky.

One shining youth became contaminated by humans and grew ever more greedy and lustful, becoming Raven, the Tsimshian culture hero who eventually stole Light (sun, moon, and stars) from its primordial owner and released it over the earth while greedy for candlefish (eulachon). Ever since, light and dark have alternated. At that moment, Tsimshian learned to regard the sky, the movement of the luminaries, and the will of Heaven (Dunn 1978: 57, #1102: LAXA; noun: heaven, sky, storm) as basic to their universe.

Though proverbs are rare among Native Americans, the Tsimshian have a saying:

Heaven looks down on him; said of a poor man who is suddenly favored by good fortune. Heaven is considered the Deity, and the man upon whom he [202] casts his eyes is successful in all his undertakings. Therefore it is a common prayer of the Tsimshian : O Heaven, look down upon us, your children! (Morison 1889: 285, #5).

As Heaven had his retainers and messengers, so too did every Tsimshian chief.[280] Although the same chief changed from summer crests to winter wonders by wearing different outer garments, his (rarely, her) staff was divided into seasonal specialties based on participation in the Crest or Wonder dichotomy. For example, there were separate artists for heraldic crests or for religious wonders. The first was concerned with natural phenomena and the second with Heaven in his majesty. A few members of the staff with general skills served year around, particularly the astronomers who advised the House and its members about the proper time for scheduling events involving resource harvesting or predicting the fate of various activities. Thus, during an expedition to counter witchcraft, disguised as a war party, the leader, after reversing the sorcery, called off the warriors.

That night, Mediks who was a seer and astrologer, read in the stars and said, "I see a very bad omen for us. It is well we shall return and delay our attack on the Kitselas (Barbeau and Beynon 1987: 154).

Although sometimes called an astrologer because of this ability to prophesy, the Tsimshian term is more precise.

---

[280] While Tsimshians are now avowedly Christian, Heaven reflects ancient Native American beliefs in a high god (Miller 1980).

GYEMGAT. noun. astronomer (specifically, a moon reader, a person who can predict the food seasons) (Dunn 1978: 31, #575).

The term means someone who is literally "moon-struck" (fixated, or obsessed), derived from GYEMK (verb intransitive: hot, warm; noun: heat, month, moon, sun (Dunn 1978: 31, #576) and GYEMGMAATK (noun: moon (same: 31, #577]). As elsewhere, each astronomer used a fixed location from which to make observations. Some, often an old man, sat on a stump that was chopped out like a chair with seat and backrest (cf Quinault and Tlingit). He visited his seat every day at the same time, usually just before sunset to observe where the sun went down. The horizon line of the Northwest is quite rugged so it is easy to trace the course of the sun as it moves north and south with the seasons to mark the yearly calendar.

While the sun was watched daily, and particularly at the solstices, it was the moon that defined the months, when particular resources and festivals were celebrated. Based on such observations, the astronomer advised the chief on the proper time for undertakings by house and community. [203]

A comparison (Dunn nd) of seven versions of Tsimshian calendars indicates nine food moons divided into three seasons, along with winter, which had three recognized winds in the first of two stages. During the winter season of overcast skies, the astronomer relied on the winds, which were both obvious and seasonally specific: "Winds drive the cycle of the seasons" (Dunn nd: 4). By name, these three seasonal heralds were Leaf Scabber, a strong North wind bringing the first killing frost of the year; Mould Flusher, an ESE wind coming immediately after Leaf Scrubber to purge the streams of the fungus that grew on the bodies of spawned-out salmon; and Blizzard, a NNW wind with powder snow that marks the start of Famine Winter, the second, dreaded stage of that season.

In sacred history, everything has a human form under the cloak of its kind, with immortals being much more powerful than other species. Thus, Stars, Sun, Moon, and four Winds are all humanoid immortals living in plank houses in the sky. Sometimes vengeful, they used their powers to punish a boy who mocked the Stars by taking him into the sky and tying him outside their smokehole so sparks would fall on him (Barbeau and Beynon 1987: 306-8). In stories, the four Winds are variously treated as men or as women. Confirming the calendars. North Wind was opposed by South Wind, whose allies were East and West Winds. The daughter of South Wind married the son of North Wind and nearly froze to death until rescued by her youngest brother. Together, South, East, and West Winds forced North Wind to confine himself to four months of the year (Barbeau and Beynon 1987: 47-49).

Other famous sky dwellers, born to the son of the Sun and a woman who survived the massacre of her town, were the Heavenly Children sent down to earth with crests on their house fronts.

On the house of the oldest was Sun; on the next were Stars; on the next Rainbow; the next, Sky-Above; and on the youngest's house. Mirage. They were all on the front of the houses, and were painted in bright colours. The paintings were as if they were alive and supernatural (Barbeau and Beynon 1987: 263).

Ever since, their Tsimshian descendants have had the right to portray such designs on their own housefronts to represent their relationship to the original Heavenly Children.

In another legend, Heaven became angry at noisy children and sent down a pretty feather, which carried all of them into the air and dropped them to their deaths. A secluded girl survived and from her mucus were [204] created wondrous children who restored the dead.[281]2 Her sons went on to marry the daughters of the women who controlled the Winds. North Wind's daughter was Northern Lights, Souths was Cloud, East's was Ripener, and West's was Sunset (Barbeau and Beynon 1987: 54-55). In general, each Wind had an associated season: North and Winter, South and Summer, East and warmth, and West and ripening.

In the same way that the chiefs of each house and town joined together every winter as members of exclusive secret societies or orders, their specialists also held periodic meetings upon an elevated peak far up the Skeena River, an interior promontory – remote from most Coast, Southern, and Nass communities – and ideal for their observational purposes because surrounded by mountain ranges on all sides.

Pierce (1933: 152-55), the author of the following quote, was the son of a Tsimshian mother and an English father. Though a missionary noted for his strictness to Victorian ideals, his cultural and linguistic education as a Tsimshian obviously taught him the importance of such traditions, as he relates:

> Andancaul is situated on the right bank of the Skeena River, almost five miles below Kitzeguela village. It was formerly a large fishing camp belonging to the Kit-wun-gah tribe. Behind this camp is a very high hill – the highest on the Skeena.
>
> The name of this hill is Andimaul, meaning the "Seat of Native Astronomers." The top of this hill was a specially selected place for the astronomers belonging to the different tribes to gather on an evening watching the sun sinking away on the mountains. By watching the sun in the spring of the year, and again in the fall, they claimed to be capable of discerning just what the coming season would bring forth.
>
> In the spring, they could tell whether berries were going to be plentiful or scarce, and whether there would be a good run of salmon or otherwise. Also whether the summer would be hot or cold, wet or dry. In the fall, they knew what kind of winter to expect; whether severe or mild and whether a light or heavy fall of snow, also whether any epidemics would be prevalent.
>
> One branch of the "Grease Trail," extending from the Nass [River], led right past this seat on the hill, and along this route travellers were continually passing and repassing.
>
> Today any traveller passing by may see several little spots, here and there, which is claimed to have been worn away from constant use as seats by these astronomers in the olden days.
>
> When sitting there in consultation and each one agreed, then a messenger was sent to all the different tribes warning the people and telling them [205] what they might expect to happen. At the present time astronomy at Andimaul is a thing of the past. This place is now a fishing camp only for a few families from Kitzegeula who have

---

[281] According to one Tsimshian, this story took place on Digby Island where the Prince Rupert airport is now located. As an outer island of the harbor, it has unusually good sight lines for air traffic which might have also been beneficial to earlier sky watchers.

made it their home, and as they joined the Salvation Army this is now a small Salvation Army settlement with an officer in charge.

It is fitting that the Tsimshian, one of the most complexly organized societies on the North Pacific coast, would also, as shown in the quote above, have one of the most sophisticated systems for coordinating astronomical observations. As each town had its "seats" at fixed locations for checking observations, so the nations had Andancaul, a hill still revered for its memorable links with the past.

All of the peoples of the North Pacific were mariners of a high order. As such, they had practical reasons for knowing and using the stars and sky, although their routes were within sight of shore rather than pelagic. Little of this practical knowledge has survived, although what did is sufficient to indicate that celestial observation involved several overlapping systems involving the sun, stars, winds, tides, salmon migrations, and seasonal harvests. Modern Canadian place names and landform charts now dominate marine travel, so the lore of crest displays and former wonders has now become the primary conveyor of traditional knowledge. In the past, such lore would have been subjected to complex interpretations passed on during the training of apprentices by family experts in various fields. What survives of this lore reiterates Heaven as high god and skyforms as beings, immortals having humanoid essences, living much like traditional humans. Throughout, the metaphor of the House pervades all; even the universe itself was considered one enormous dwelling.

But most important of all is the metaphor of "seats." The immortal names are treated as though they occupied fixed positions within a building. The present holders of these names, similarly, occupy fixed "seats" at potlatches and other public events. In a universe believed to be in constant flux, with concurrent movements in the sky, sea, and earth, it stands to reason that those with fixed points for observation would have a better view of the panorama of life, whether it was displayed in the sky or on the earth.

Spirits, Songs, and Spaces:
Degrees of Knowledge in Native North America

In recent decades, the study of the Northwest Coast has become estranged from the rest of the Americanist tradition. Thwarting this search for commonalities has been the rise of regional specialities, each more concerned with North American local differences than with similarities. Indeed, the very mention of words like "potlatch" and "crest" are themselves regarded askance by other Americanists, even though these are just Northwest Coastal variants of feasting and clanship.

Such regional distinctions are no where more apparent than in the study of the most important native institution of all, namely religion. While native religions have undergone profound changes since Christianity arrived in the New World, native perspectives have nevertheless asserted themselves after conversion, particularly when Christian forms have been rendered into native languages, as Shaul (1982) illustrated in his back translation of the Hail Mary from Piman. By tracing the origins and distributions of such native words, the ebb and flow of both native and European influences become all the more apparent and the tendency to simplify or homogenize distinct native traditions can be avoided or, at least, counterbalanced.

By playing off data from the Northwest and the rest of North America, however, an understanding can be reached for four types of degrees in religious systems, exemplified by Coast Tsimshian , which were the native equivalent of "higher education" for their elites. By drawing comparisons between each of these Tsimshian systems and similar patterns in native North America, some age-area speculations can be made, based on the theory that the more widely distributed a pattern, the more ancient it is likely to be. Parks (1941) used this theory to trace successive overlays in Great Basin rituals in the festschrift for Edward Sapir, who Americanized this method.

Here, however, particular note will be paid to border overlap in the distributions of these four systems. Supporting data will be drawn from Americanist publications and from personal research with Tsimshian in the north coast and with Salishans to the south, along with other nations throughout North America.

These four systems are called Natural, Tribal, Regional, and Noble. Arranged in this way, they range from most universal (the natural) to most specialized (the noble). Each is discussed in turn.

1. Natural

The natural system is based on the all pervasive belief throughout the Americas that everything has a spirit, whether or not it is known to humans. Each spirit has the potential of contacting one or more humans and teaching him or her a particular skill or ability that will enable him or her to be successful. Ruth Benedict's doctoral dissertation dealt with this system, which she called the guardian spirit complex (1923).

According to this belief, each spirit has the shape of a human when living in its "holy home" at a particular place, such as inside a hill, waterfall, rapids, cave, or spring. Humans who visit such locales see only humans living in a house much like their own. When these spirits leave home, however, they put on the cloak or covering of their species. Famous examples of this among the Tsimshian are the Salmon towns beyond the horizon and the Bear town where a princess married, thinking she was among fellow humans until Mouse Woman told her otherwise.

As the spirit (in human form) departed from the first encounter with its human partner, it briefly shimmered as the shape of its animal counterpart, allowing that human to know its species. During this transformation, the spirit sang a song to become fixed in the mind of the visionary and, ever after, used to summon the spirit whenever that human was in need.

In some cases, different humans, non-kin, met the same spirit and accordingly sang the same tune with different words. In the East, people who shared the same spirit often formed an "fraternal" association that met together to honor their spirit patron. For example, Winnebagos with a Bear spirit feasted together every year, and, like the bear, ate using their left hand. Other spirits had similar injunctions (taboos) that had to be followed for the partnership to continue, often to prevent over-identification with the spirit that might flare into a dangerous vortex of power. Thus, those linked with Spider could not play or hear a stringed instrument because these were too much like webbing.

In keeping with tribal beliefs about the inter-connectedness of all things, each spirit has a differential amount of power to transmit. The source and summary of all this energy flow was and is a creator being at the center of a pulsing weblike network where power was concentrated. While most of these creators were male, Ocean Woman brought the Great Basin into being and the Shawnee acknowledge Grandmother as their highest deity.

While Tsimshian have such a high god, Heaven ~ *Laxha* "on high", the actual transformer of this power was Raven, who came to earth as a *naxnox* (a shining youth called Txamsen) but, through the ill will of a slave, became the glutton Wigyet.

Tsimshian now use the term *naxnox* for a kind of dangerous spirit, but available evidence suggests that Tsimshian religion shared with the rest of the Americas a system of guardian spirits they called *naxnox* and represented by a elaborate series of masks. Elsewhere in the Americas, paint and gestures served to represent the spirit each human bonded with, but the availability of red cedar and a tradition of carving encouraged these masked portrayals in the Northwest.

The only other two regions, both of them matrilineal, where masking was elaborated were the Northeast, among Iroquois, and the Southwest, among Pueblos. Of interest, both Iroquois and Pueblos say their masks portray only one group of spirits, those who farmed, rather than being a sample of all of the spirits available in the landscape.

Another ramification of this natural system, exemplified among the Lushootseed Salish of Puget Sound, has to do with the duration and accessibility of this spirit and power. Throughout North America, summer was the time of economic pursuits and winter was the time of religious ones. Thus, while someone could only be a success with one or more spirits to help and advise, innate ability considered to be insufficient by itself, human and spirit were directly linked only during the depth of winter when full time could be devoted to expressing the bond. Thus, throughout the Americas there were Winter Dances when people sang their power songs and impersonated their spirit guardian.

Yet, another kind of human, vital to the wellbeing of each community, maintained a constant link with his or her spirits. This was the native doctor or shaman, whose spirit was constantly nearby and ready to help cure human maladies. Among the Salish, where shamans still cure, no one should walk behind a doctor because his or her spirit hovers above and behind him or her and might injure an unprotected human who ventured behind a shaman at any time. Thus, among the Salish, the world is populated by two different kinds of spirits, ordinary ones – who enhance a career, and special ones – who benefit only curing by shamans. Shamans, moreover, have not only more direct links to their spirit, but many more of these spirits than other humans. Each encounter with a different kind of spirit conferred another song and the ability to cure or deal with another kind of malady.

As much of the *naxnox* system has faded from modern Tsimshian belief, so too has native shamanism, although several terms for different kinds of shamans have been recorded. More important, however, than the traditional system of shamanism, called *halaayt* by Tsimshian, was the influence such beliefs had on the development of the other religious systems that spread along the Pacific coast.

2. Tribal

Though evidence is unclear for a tribal system among the Tsimshian towns, its wide distribution along the coast suggests that it may once have been a part of their religion. Based in a special reverence for place, the tribal system is predicated on the belief that a group, either based on kinship or residence, descended from a legendary ancestor who lived at that place until permanently consigned to human shape by a transformer. In this way, along the Fraser River or the outer coast of Vancouver Island, a being – simultaneously shimmering or shape-shifting as a human, species, spirit, or space – became permanently fixed in the form of a human ancestor. Many of the Nuchahnuulth (misknown as Nootkans) came from Spirit Wolves, still reverenced during mid-winter Wolf Rituals. Sometimes this transformation was more complicated, as when the first ancestor of the Katzie changed his daughter into the first Sturgeon and sent her to live in Pitt Lake (Jenness 1955: 10). The most famous example of this, of course, is the Bella Coola belief that the creator sent ancestors, often as pairs, to particular mountain peaks in their territory. After sending back to heaven the bird or animal skin they wore in their descent, these beings took human form and founded particular Bella Coola towns. During winter ceremonials, some of these ancestors were represented by masks worn by human descendants.

Also, along the central coast, the earliest Kwakwaka'wakw (misknown as Kwakiutl) ancestors "had no Cannibal ceremonies in their winter ceremonial ... they merely inherited the "crests" or "privileges" of the animal from which they descended" (Boas 1966: 258).

Tsimshian has a perfect context for such a transformation, but there is no evidence now it was ever so developed. After Raven stole the light in a box from the head of the Nass, he tried to exchange it with people fishing for some candlefish (eulachons) but was refused. At the blinding moment when time and space began for the Tsimshian, when Raven opened the box, all of the spirits who had been living in twilight took on their present shapes. Only frogs, who were close to shamans, retained much of their primordial shape. By associating specific spirit fishers with locales, the Tsimshian might have attributed each ancestor to a place or town, but this remains speculation.

Among the Salish of Puget Sound were such evidence for a tribal ancestor is slim, there is artifactual evidence in the standard outline shape of the spirit planks used during Snoqualmi Soul Redeeming Ceremonies (Miller 1988). Each board was cut to represent the shape of a porpoise-like animal which was changed into the first ancestor of a downriver village according to legend.

158

By linking the spirit of a place with a group of humans, social units are formed, ranging from corporate clans to the "game totems" of the Maritime Algonkians in the far Northeast, often known as Abenaki, Wabanaki, or Dawnlanders. There, rivers, lands, and families were bound together by a special relationship with a ancestral patron animal spirit that was created at a moment of transformation when the earth's waters were released. These Abenaki (Pennacook, Saco, Androscoggin, Kennebec, Wawenock, Penobscot, Passamaquoddy, Maliseet) were organized on the basis of who did and did not share this bond among spirits, animals, humans, and lands.

According to this charter epic, Giant Frog swallowed all the waters and everyone began to die of thirst. People bemoaned they were as dry as a particular animal − a turtle, beaver, wolf, trout, haddock. Gluskap, the culture hero, killed the Frog, then toppled a birch tree onto the body to force out the water. It ran down the trunk and branches to form a specific river system with a lake in place of the leaf at the end of each twig. As the water reached families, some of them plunged in to drink, immediately changing into the very animal whose thirst they claimed. Other family members remained human, but, in memory, took that animal as the sign or badge of their lands, including camps and hunting territory, along a particular stretch of waterway (Speck 1917a).

Penobscot call this section, *nziibum* "my river," while Timagami Ojibwa call it ndakiim, "my land." Its boundaries were marked by emblems depicting the family animal itself. This patron totem was called by Penobscot either *baohiigan*, "empowerer" or ntuutem, "my parent-in-law" or alien partner, although the formal relationship could be based variously on descent, marriage, or adoption. From the coast inland, Penobscot patrons (with some of the equivalent English family names in parentheses) were Lobster (Mitchell), Crab (Susup), Sculpin, Eel (Neptune), Bear (Mitchell 2), Toad, Insect, Fisher, Whale (Stanislaus), Beaver, Sturgeon (Sockalexis), Wolf (Polis, Susup), Frog, Squirrel (Attean), Raccoon, Wolverine (Lewis), Mermaid, Otter (Saul, Nicola), Lynx (Fransway, Penus), Rabbit (Newell), Yellow Perch (Penewit), and Raven. The highest ranks were Bear and Squirrel, who provided band leaders for land totems, or Frog and Sturgeon, who provided water totem band leaders (Speck 1915).

Families were expected to inherit some physical attributes from their animal. For example, among Penobscots, "The members of the Whale family (Stanislaus) are pointed out as large, portly, and dark persons, those of the Rabbit family (Newell) as small, timid, and weak, those of the Bear family (Mitchell) as orderly and dignified, and so on" (Speck 1935: 530).

Aside from certain South American origin sagas about the human inhabitants of a river being delivered by a gigantic anaconda canoe or North American traditions of Stars founding communities,282 the Maritimes is also only other area where totemic ancestors for a whole tribe are mentioned, each tribe using the picture of a certain kind of animal or fish as a means of national identity.

Among the Wabanaki (Abenaki confederates), tribal game animal emblems were portrayed as out in front of two humans in a canoe, representing the collectivity. The Passamaquoddy two men held paddles and followed a pollock fish, the Maliseet held poles behind a muskrat, the Micmac on either side of a peaked middle gunwale held paddles behind a deer, and Penobscot held a pole and a paddle with an otter in front (Speck 1917: 13). These

---

282 In the Greek world, a similar role was played by crewmembers of the Argonauts, each of whom left Jason to found particular towns, as claimed by their versions of the myth.

tribal emblems were also scaled in terms of the intensity of the self-identification with them, with the Passamaquoddy most explicit since their tribal name literally translates as "those who pursue the pollock," a fish.

3. Regional

Often regarded as distinctive of the Northwest Coast are the system of sects, cults, or degrees that were spreading during recent centuries from the Bella Bella to the north and to the south. Tsimshian call these grades wi*halaayt* (great *halaayt*), and each degree represented greater knowledge of esoteric lore, and greater access to power and prestige, much like a "mystery religion" of the ancient Near East. What is fascinating about this system is that it effectively blends personal and social features into an overall system that involved the freeborn members of a town and of the larger society.

The most elaborate series was at Bella Bella where survivors of 6 Heiltsuk towns resettled together. Like other Wakashans, Bella Bella had a double series of degrees, either inspired or frenzied (Harkin 1988, Olson 1955). The inspired series (*dlu'elaxa*) was unmarked in that chiefs appeared in their usual guise with a variety of insignia. For example, a member of an inspired degree often wore a frontlet or masks painted in a variety of colors, particularly red. The spirit-possession frenzied series (*tseqa*) was marked in that insignia were highly specific and included masks painted black, along with violent shamanic states of ecstacy. Now, when button blankets are worn, the red side decorated with crest emblems is worn for the inspired series, but, for the frenzied displays, the blanket is worn inside out with the black side showing.

In all, about 16 degrees (here called dancing societies) existed and everyone was expected to be initiated into at least one. The lower grades, from levels 16 to 6, were open to those of good family, while those from 5 to 1 were open only to the elite. The dance and song of the lowest group was the most gentle and placid, but that of the highest was the most violent and feared. Each group owned insignia, particular cedar bark rings of appropriate color and design, and names, that is, winter holy names as distinct from summer secular names. Whistles, the breath of the spirits, were special emblems most carefully concealed from the sight of non-members. Members were expected to move up through the degrees to achieve the highest rank possible, very much like the cargo system that still motivates political authority in Spanish America.

A child of an Heitsuk important family began his or her progression through the series at ten months with a first naming potlatch. Since human gestation was believed to take ten months, this naming marked the social birth of the child. Only those eligible for the position of high or town chief (*galaxa* = first off) went through the full series so that six spent four years in the first rank called tanis, before passing it from mother's brother to eldest sister's eldest son. Initiation depended not on gender but on family rank, as a member of a chiefly family from one of the six original towns, so some women became tanis, although most were men.

While Boas and others introduced the translation of tanis as "cannibal," a better translation is "consumer" since careful linguistic work by Susanne Hilton and John Rath (1983) revealed that because "you are what you eat" the dramatic consumption of flesh symbolized the increasing perfection of the human state. It was this highest degree of consumer that spread furthest along the coast as the personal privilege of the most prominent chiefs, creating a ritual network among the same elite that was most likely to intermarry.

160

Tsimshian call the Heiltsuk the Wdsda ("enchanters) and recognized their superior reserves of power. Indeed, some texts by William Beynon, the native Tsimshian ethnographer, make it clear that the greatest of Tsimshian shamans went to Bella Bella to be "finished."

Tsimshian had 5 degrees of wi*halaayt*, two social and three personal. The two groups, with large memberships, were the dancers (*Miła*, which means "to miss" in Heiltsuk, as in a missing person) and the dog-eaters (*Nułm*), while the personal privileges, limited to special individuals, were those of fire thrower, destroyer, and consumer (*xgyet*). Each degree was distinguished by particular whistles, songs, gear, and gestures.

In comparison with their neighbors to the south, these Tsimshian coastal degrees show the influence of both the Bella Bella and the Owikeno, for whom only Fire Throwers made up the council that supervised the annual frenzied series; while the Destroyers ranked highest in the inspired series and indicated readiness to become a consumer, with a winter name that made reference to the Sky or Heaven ~ *laxha* the most remote and powerful of Tsimshian beings, along with evoking remote associations with similar Asian high gods.

Membership was not just a matter of initiation, however. So important were these degrees that there were at least four ways to acquire this status: gift, bribe, trickery, or murder. The greatest chiefs, who were also skillful traders, gave membership as a gift to each other. Others with great wealth could purchase the goodwill that "insured" initiation. In certain circumstances, the insignia, particularly whistles, were captured, thereby forcing membership. In a famous example, a Kitimat chief had an affair with the wife of a Bella Bella chief so he could steal a whistle and force his own initiation. Sometimes, members of other tribes were killed and their membership taken along with other possessions.

While only the southern Tlingit chief at Wrangel was a member (Emmons 1991, Kan 1989), if Europeans had not come, other Tlingit chiefs to the north would have been initiated.

The Haida (Swanton 1905), whose degrees came from both the Tsimshian and the Bella Bella, may have had as many as a dozen degrees, with members described as "inspired" or "insured," but, there too, the consumers ranked first.

At the southern end of the distribution along the coast of Washington, some interesting overlaps can be noted. Dog-eaters, under the guise of Wolves or Warriors, occurred under their Nootkan name (*Łokwaali*) among the Quileute, a language isolate. As the largest membership, its foreign origin contributed to its prestige. In fact, four of the five Quileute degrees originated elsewhere. The Fishers (*tsa.yiq*) recall the Wakashan name for the frenzied winter dance grouping. The Whalers ("oily voiced") came from the Makah, and the Weather Workers ("south voiced") from the Quinault. Only the Hunters were indigenous, and appropriately conferred the power to hunt elk upriver in the Olympic Mountains. In each case, membership could either be inherited through rank or purchased through wealth and bearing.

Among the Coast Salish, only some of them (the Straits) had a single degree (*xədxədəb*) called the Growlers and involving death and rebirth symbolism like other shamanic systems. Hosted at one town, teenagers, both boys and girls, from several tribes were initiated to provide them with a power source before they began more serious questing for spirits. By virtue of this initiation, these children shared the same spirit, a giant bloody baby who migrated with ducks.

The nearest parallel to this system of graded and diverse memberships occurs in the Great Lakes and Southwest. Growing out of older shamanic groupings of related powers, about 1700 at Chequamegon on a Lake Superior peninsula in Wisconsin, amalgamated Ojibwa shamans forged the Midewiwin ~ shamans academy. In full form, it has 9 degrees, four of the earth, four of the sky, and another for ghost members. Each grade has an animal skin pouch appropriate to that level, such as a ground dweller for lower grades and a bird for higher ones.

In the Southwest, for over one thousand years as indicated by the building of kiva chambers, specialized priesthoods have evolved from shamanic concerns. Among the Keresan pueblos, whose priesthoods had precedence over those of other Pueblos, a complex hierarchy distinguished man or woman diseases, caused respectively by angry animals or witches, cured by appropriate priests, all male – although aided by male or female spirit doctors. Each priesthood was divided into the grades of novice, adept, and high priest – distinguished by their degree of knowledge and ability. In turn, the priesthoods were ranked with those treating minor complaints regarded as less powerful than those charged with curing major diseases and, yearly, exorcising the entire town. The leader of the most powerful priesthood, as part of his responsibilities, was also initiated into all of the other orders and, possessing complete esoteric knowledge, served as the priestly leader of his town. In this capacity, however, he was equated with the Keres creator, Thought Woman, and, as such, was ceremonially regarded as a woman, though he was a husband and father in ordinary life.

4. Noble

Privilege was the basis for the fourth system among the Tsimshian and other coastal nations (Miller 1997). Membership was limited to leading families in various communities, with initiation signaling their confirmed elite status. Since only members of the highest class could belong, this system, called *smhalaayt* (real *halaayt*) by the Tsimshian, was truly international in scope. Its insignia were the frontlet (*amhalaayt*), woven robe and apron, and raven rattle. Tradition says this outfit originated among the Nisga'a and spread to chiefs of other First Nations. Indeed, for over a century Tlingit chiefs have lain in state wearing not the hat of their crest, as previously, but instead the *shakee.at* frontlet that indicated their elite status to everyone along the coast.

While uncertain, a likely context for the creation and spread of these chiefly insignia was the 1700s displacement of the Tongass Tlingit from the lower Nass River by Nisga'a moving downstream to control the lucrative eulachon fishery. The name of the Nass derives from the Tlingit word (*naas(i)*) for "intestines" because it was the "food belly" of the north coast in the spring (Emmons 1991: 8). The Tsimshian term for the Nass River is, instead, *klusms*.

To find a similar elite system in the Americas, however, we must look into the archaeological record of the Mississippians, who led the North American heartland for a thousand years before the Spanish arrived. There, among the trappings of the Southern Cult, were copper and other emblems that signaled membership in a set of interlaced chiefdoms much like those of the historic Northwest.

Perhaps influenced by these Mississippian chiefdoms, the League of the Iroquois has a parallel to the frontlet in the *gastowe* ~ chief's cap of the *royaner*. In ancient times, from both the archaeological and linguistic record, such chiefs wore deer antlers as a badge of office, but after the 50 chiefly names of the original five nations were entitled by Deganawidah at the founding of the League, the five tribal versions of the feathered cap were worn.

Another possible parallel was the eagle feather headdress with full length tail, symbolizing a comet among its Pawnee originators, as a badge of high chiefship among Plains peoples.

162

The clearest example of a Mississippian priesthood was provided by research among the Osage by Francis La Flesche (Bailey 1995), himself an Omaha and a native speaker of this related Siouian language. Largely spared devastations from epidemics until the 1880s, when their population was almost 4000, Osage preserved much of the system that must have characterized mound centers like nearby Cahokia, the ancient city near modern St Louis.

Concentrating on initiation rituals, which both prayed for blessings from the Creator (Wakonda) and explained the universe in stages, he totaled 170 such rites.[283] Clan priest initiations generally lasted four days, most of the time spent alerting all the universe for the finale. After pledging to be inducted and undergoing the penalty verses, a candidate had seven years to gather the necessary gifts and food. A tribal priesthood induction occurred much more rapidly, lasting only one day, because the unseen power of the universe hung in the balance.

In addition to two tribal priest initiations confirming the ownership of the sacred great bundles concerned with the invisible world, the rest (168) were initiations, concerned with the visible world, into a clan priesthood, where each of the 24 clans had 7 degrees culminating in the Sayings of the Ancients.

For Osage, rituals were equated with books since they preserved and transmitted knowledge through a complex interaction of words, actions, and objects, intended to puzzle the serious, intrigue the curious, and impress the literal minded. Each ritual combined songs (*wathon*), actions (*we'gaxe*), and recitations (*wi'gie*), which repeated many of the same poetic verses, except that the main image, often symbolic animals, varied according to that specific clan and degree. A vital identifying phrase specified "I am a person who has made of a X his body" to indicate the clan's life symbol through which they approach the Creator. Examples vary from the immensities of the Sun, Water, and Stars to animals, plants, objects, weather conditions, colors, and abstractions.

The embodiment of each clan and priesthood was a sacred bundle. That of a clan, called a "hawk," held a hawk skin, woven mat bag, deerskin bag, buffalo hair bag, buffalo hid rope, eagle leg, scalp, and buffalo hide hanging strap.

Each initiation involved a set of officials who served formal or functional roles (Bailey 1995: 76). Typically, these were the candidate and his wife, a sponsor, an assisting sponsor, priests of all 24 clans sitting at fixed positions, a sacred warrior holding all 13 honors, a messenger, widows of former priests, and singers. The candidate and sponsor had formal claims to a clan and degree, while the assisting sponsor was the one who thoroughly knew the involved ritual in all of its intricacy and precision. The songs were particularly important to bring the universe "to life," with special verses acknowledging their human ancestors's ability to think, to search with the mind and thereby learn (termed wathi'gethon) "to bring things to pass." Songs and recitations were context sensitive, describing a body from head to feet to indicate birth and new beginnings, or from feet to head for growth and maturity.

As all of life, the original Osage came from the sky (called father) to the earth (called mother), where they met one clan who had always been there and so became known as the Isolated Earth. Between the sky and the underworld was and is the "snare of life," linked with a sacred spider (Bailey 1995: 241, line 13), along the surface of the earth, holding everything

---

283. A third tribal priesthood devoted to pipes of peace had no induction rite (Bailey 1995: 56).

together between birth and death. On this snare, the clans were organized between Sky and Earth moieties, also called halves, sides, or divisions. Earth further included Land and Water.

Symbolic oppositions between these moieties included Sky with left, six, morning star, male, father; or Earth with right, seven, evening star, female, mother. Other associations include East with sun, birth, life, red, male, or West with moon, death, destruction, black, and female. For example, sleeping, those of the Land held the head to the right side; if Sky, head to the left.

Each clan had a sacred bundle whose contents provided various means for identifying it. All of the sacred objects ("life symbols") of the clans were called *waxo'be*. Moreover, the two clans referred to as Men of Mystery and Buffalo Bull were the symbolic keepers of all the clan bundles, while the great bundles keeper was the Gentle Ponka and that of the great medicine bundles was Gentle Sky. The Elder Water clan was the symbolic keeper of the peace pipes symbolizing unity, with their own great bundle priests (the *wawathon*). Among secondary sacra were war standards, rattles, war clubs, sacred bows and arrows, charcoal, and other things. In addition, known only to the adept, were unconsecrated symbols, called "those carried to excite enthusiasm" (*wazhawa athinbikshe*) and therefore not real (Bailey 1995: 47).

After uniting on earth, Osage priests reorganized their society thrice, each phrased as a "move to a new country." First came an internal reordering began by Water people of the Earth division, with the Isolated Earth priests responsible for a symbolic "house" where all Osage children were named, the Land (particularly Bear and Puma) priests given charge of the "house" where war ceremonies were held, and war or hunt leadership assigned to the Bear, Water, Sky, and Isolated Earth.

Prompt action, however, was impossible because of excessive ceremonial, so another reordering improved military tactics, although each expedition was still led by a priest. This "move to a new country" allowed various clans, as needed, to organize three types of war parties – composed of men from all the clans, a few clans from one moiety, or a single clan.

The third move instituted the civil government by two chiefs, titled *gahi'ge*, from the Ponka clan of the Earth and the Sky clan of the Sky. To distinguish these as the source of chiefs, they added "gentle" to their name because that was a defining characteristic of such leaders, who held vigil until a spirit revealed to each the contents of a great bundle, for either medicines (symbolized by the cormorant, a man and woman root) or long life (symbolized by the pelican, and tattoos). The other great bundle priests had the pipes, particularly one with a human face carved into the black pipebowl and, hanging down, 7 shell beads for the Earth and 6 copper beads for the Sky. Such emphasis on shell and copper is distinctly Mississippian.

While clan houses were arranged in order around the edges of the town, the two houses of these chiefs were across the central east to west path of the sun. While each house had a door facing north or south across this plaza, these chief homes had a door on both east and west ends.

The goal of all this complex religion was an unbroken line of descendants stretching far into the future since the greatest belief of all was that nothing in the universe ever moved backwards. Today, having deliberately "unloaded" these arduous religious strictures, Osage seek the same intent through the peyote rituals of the Native American Church.

Such complex elaboration was probably once typical of the pre-epidemic Americas, where proper inheritance of kin and rank was confirmed by progress through graded rituals that ennobled the leaders of the community and confirmed their successors.

5. Summary

Motivations for joining these four systems were both personal, familial, and communal, but all were concerned with politically and religiously acquiring prestige and power to safeguard one's self, family, kin, rank, and community. Different experiences formed the basis for particular bonds between humans and spirits. In cases were more than one human shared the same spirit, this association was celebrated by common attributes, injunctions (taboos), and feastings. In more elaborate instances, these nonkin groupings acted as priesthoods devoted to particular cures or concerns.

With this general American pattern as backdrop, other distinctions were developed into the tribal, regional, and noble degrees. The common tribal totem provided a means for ritual unity lacking in the political realm, while the regional system of graded groupings functioned much like clan memberships to distinguish internal divisions but relate them to those elsewhere. Only the noble system seems to be more distinctive of the Northwest, although so many chiefdoms of the East and South were devastated by European epidemics that the Bella Bella dance series may also provide a glimpse into Mississippian or other archeological network of international elites.

In each case, the system was based on a type of knowledge that could be partitioned, taught by degrees and examples, through one or more initiations. In this way, as with all groupings, the distinction was made between those who were "out" and those who were "in," along with the factor of "in-tensity." It was not enough in these systems to just be "in," one also had to progress deeper into the knowledge to add power and prestige, paying superiors for the privilege by an act of simony.

In the process of sustaining a vision, with or without degrees, a general equation was enhanced such that knowledge = power = long life. But the ultimate source of this knowledge was not other humans, but the spirits, themselves other-than-human persons, the immortal owners dwelling at favored sites in the landscape. Yet, while human and spirit were bonded for a lifetime, the spirit, except in the case of a shaman, was not continuously present. Therefore, some kind of a key was needed to reopen this bond every time it is needed and that key is the song provided by the spirit at the initial vision that created that partnership. Singing it make it verbal, giving it the power of "word" to impact on reality.

In all, therefore, though expressed in at least four modalities of degrees among the Tsimshian and other First Nations, American native religions nevertheless express a belief in an underlying equation such that, as expressed in Tsimshianic:

Knowledge ~ *wilaay* = Power ~ *goypax* = Life ~ *diduuls*
Spirits (*naxnox*) activated by Song (*limi*)

Tsimshian Ethno-Ethnohistory:
A "Real" Indigenous Chronology

Abstract

Tsimshian of the North Pacific Coast of Canada and Alaska insist that *adawx*, the term for one of their densely cultural epics, be translated as "history." Each saga is firmly based in their matrilineal social structure (of houses, clusters, towns, and matriclans) and intensely both private and personal within these kinship networks. Despite massive depopulation and crushing outside pressures, Tsimshians have long committed themselves to perpetuating these "histories" because of their guarantees of renewing immortality, providing a sequence of at least *səm-* "real" fifteen episodic overlays across ten thousand years.

In the beginning was the word, and the word became a name, and the name became a story linking together places, people, and events into a culture.

Thus, from their own perspective, might begin a contemporary version of genesis and subsequent history for any number of Native American tribes. Unfortunately, popularly and dubiously regarded as "myths," these epics have often been slandered by the insensitive and slighted by scholars seeking to impose their own sense of detail and linear chronology on much more complex narratives.

Yet any truly Native (ethno) history must focus on the tribes' own profound sense of these events as both spiritually and temporally informed. While episodes of Euro-American history are sometimes abbreviated into the name of a significant individual involved, such as Washington, Pontiac, Lincoln, Sitting Bull, the events themselves – the American Revolution, French Defeat, Civil War, End of the Frontier – are understood to have been much more complex and complicated, sometimes even allowing for "the hand of God" in the outcome. These personal names, however, provide mere tags to events regarded by Euro-Americans as solitary and unique, [659] rather than, according to Native Americans, exemplary and worthy of repeated emulation, as these names are passed on in native families in subsequent generations.

Within Native North American, the Maritime North Pacific ranks as one of its most complex culture areas. Yet at all times and places, relations with local lands and waters dominated all other sources for providing basic cultural understandings, as is well illustrated by recent insights among members of the Tsimshianic language family, speakers of an isolate composed in the interior of Nishga (Nisga'a) on the middle Nass River and of Gitksans (*Gitxsan*) on the upper Skeena River, and, near the ocean, of Coast and Southern Tsimshians. Neighbors to the north were the Tlingit, to the west were the Haida, to the south the Wakashan speakers, and to the east various Athapaskans, called *Ts'ets'awt* by Tsimshianic speakers. For thousands of years, these nations interacted through trade, warfare, ceremonial exchanges, and royal intermarriages, effectively overarching differences of town, tribe, or parent language.

With the publication of my holistic study of Tsimshian culture based in institutions metaphorically dealing with refracted light (Miller 1997), I return herein to the wealth of native sources to find an alternative way to represent the same information.[284] In my initial eagerness to

---

[284] For years, Raymond Fogelson has been calling for such an ethno-ethnohistory, relying on

assure an overview of the complexities of traditional Tsimshian religion, replaced by an enthusiastic Christianity for over a century, I avoided probing deeply into the *adaawx*,[285]2 the revered if "messy" histories fixed in time and space to be passed down with precision through the heads of noble houses (Boas 1916; Spier 1931). Indeed, the *adaawx*, along with clans (*p'teex*) and heraldic crests (Garfield 1966), survive quite well among modern Tsimshian, while the *naxnox* (masked wonders) and *halaayt* (elite privileges in four [260]

Figure 1. Coast Tsimshian Homeland.

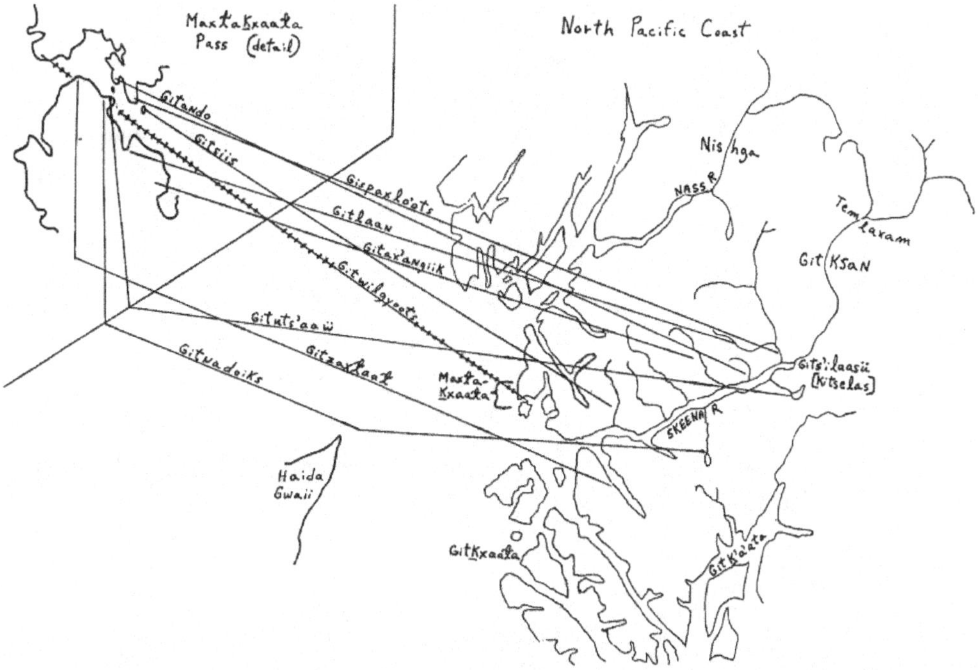

For several thousand years, after Coast Tsimshian congregated at *Spaksuut* ("fall place," renamed Port Essington) for brief festivities, they spent the winter at neighboring towns on either side of the channel called *Maxlakxaala* ("calm passage," renamed Venn Passage) near the harbor of Prince Rupert, British Columbia. These movements, indicated by straight lines, are traced from summer economic homelands along tributaries of the Skeena River to ceremonial towns along the

---

native sources and interpretations of their own sense of history, more than just the blending of written and oral sources of the same events during colonialism. Simultaneously, Helen Tanner has reminded one and all that native history is ipso facto personal and family history. Moreover, this labor is dedicated to the memory of Alfonso Ortiz, who now gets his revenge for my avoiding Pueblo epics of clan migrations while he was mentoring my writing of a dissertation on the Keresans, southern neighbors of the Tewa. In parallel fashion, such migration epics of the Tsimshian and Pueblos lay out a vast but relative chronology from earliest times to the present which pays little if any attention to later European interlopers. For Tsimshian, moreover, reality is clearly specified by the presence of the word sm, as in smgigyet, the word for "chiefs" literally meaning "real people."

[285] In Tlingit, the term *at.oow* is equivalent to the Tsimshianic *adaawx*.

saltwater passage, which appears both at the center of the map and as the inset detail. The *Gitwilgyoots* (formerly with the extinct *Gitwilksaba*) shared their homeland, the southern end of the Tsimshian Peninsula, with other tribes from the northern side of the Skeena. Southside tribes wintered on Digby Island, now the site of the Prince Rupert Airport. Fort Simpson, built by the Hudson's Bay Company at the northern tip of the Tsimshian Peninsula, became and remains a similar Coast Tsimshian gathering place. To get away from its frontier character, William Duncan and his Anglican converts returned to the ancient wintering place to found the cooperative community of Metlakatla, until most of them moved to Alaska. [660]

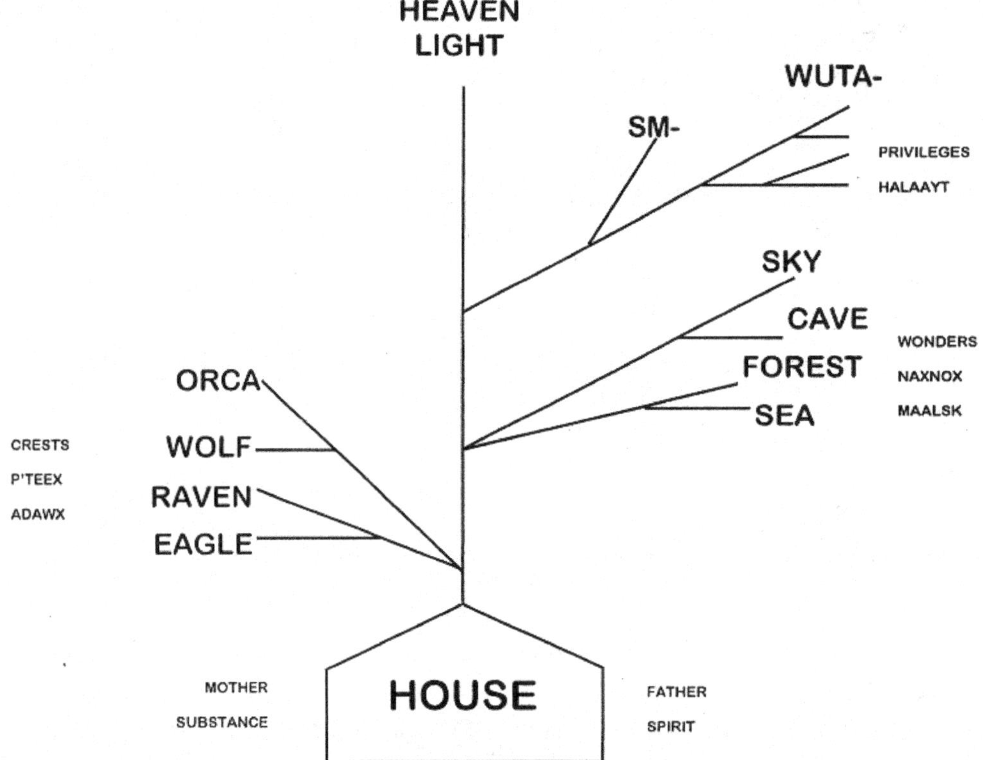

Figure 2. This three-dimensional diagram represents Tsimshian culture as a beam of light, with branches on four sides, focused on the house where the chief resides, using his own spinal column, poles, and canes to align chaotic power into culturally useful ways of benefit for his lands and household.

At the top front are the *halaayt* degrees and guilds eligible only to members of the elite or royal houses. To the right are the *naxnox* wonders, passed down through fathers according to *maalsk* epics and anecdotes; to the left the *p'teex* crests transmitted through the mother and validated by *adawk* histories. In the back behind, out of sight in shadow and dark, is the branch of sorcery *haldawgit*.

Overall, each of the branches points to a corner rather than a side of the house, further confining it in useful ways.

orders or guilds) of the ancient religion do not.[286]3 In other words, the realm of women, the basis for matrilineality, has survived well into the present, while the realm of men, the basis for traditional religious expressions, has not, except as sometimes recast in Anglican ways.

Through intermarriage these crests became shared by elite families in all Northcoast nations, regardless of language. Indeed, most royalty were multilingual. Nevertheless, Tlingits have been expanding to the north and south at the expense of neighbors, as have Wakashans along the central [661] coast. After a migration down the Skeena about 3,500 years ago (of the archaeologically designated Skeena complex), Tsimshianic seems to have developed along the sea, where it split into Coast and Southern dialects before Coast forms of language and culture spread back upriver, eventually influencing inland Athapaskans.

In general, the situation on the coast seems to have been dense and stable with prime lands long occupied by locals; while in the interior, with its varied terrain and climate, groups were highly mobile over time. On the coast, ancestral houses (in corporate sense) were more important, while resourceful heroes (in individualistic sense) appear more often in the interior. Indeed, given that the coast had much greater prestige and resources, a variety of peoples were drawn to (or borrowed from) it, in contrast to individuals in quest of adventure or trade (or both) who ventured upriver. For this reason, in seeming contradiction to this general pattern, when tracing one of three clusters of Wolf clan among the Tahltan, George Emmons (1911: 16) noted, "They came first and collectively from the interior, and later and individually from the coast."

For Tsimshians, each crest represents a cluster of houses sharing an ancestry that remained distinct within the larger grouping of a clan. For example, Coast and Southern Tsimshians recognize four paired clans (semi-moieties) called *Ganhada* (Raven) + *Laxsgiik* (upon Eagle) or *Gispwudwada* (Orca, locally called Blackfish or Killerwhale) + *Laxgibuu* (upon Wolf). The inland Gitksan and Nishga use Frog for Raven, and Grizzly ~ Fireweed for Orca.

Between the house and the clan are more than one cluster of house groups tracing a common origin from a different place or spirit. These clusters derive from epic *adaawx* and account for subsidiary crests within each clan, such as *Gispwudwada* (Orca, Grizzly, Grouse, Mosquito, Stars, Sun, Fireweed), *Ganhada* (Raven, Frog, Sculpin, Starfish), *Laxgibuu* (Wolf, Bear, Crane, Owl), and *Laxsgiik* (Eagle, Beaver, Halibut, Octopus) (Miller 1997: 54). Such a sterile listing, however, does not recognize the basis for these eight major crests in the epics, which validate the house clusters given below (epics 2-11) and thus enrich our understandings.

Religious law insisted that respect was due all forms of life. Thus, while humans might use parts and pieces of other beings, the entire body could only be used by members of that particular species. The *adaawx*, therefore, carefully interdict the abuse of living things or their articulated skeletons, their source of eternal vitality.[287]4 Indeed, a primary duty of any chief, as with the leader of a species, was to become so "evolved" as to channel such vitality down his spine (or its representation in totem pole or cane) to fructify the land of his people. [662]

Within these larger units Tsimshian remain organized on the basis of the household, once a distinct and decorated dwelling covered by adzed cedar planks. Each house owned a corpus of immortal names, passed down through that matriline, with the leading name serving as the title

---

[286] Indeed, William Duncan, famous missionary to the Tsimshian, was explicit: "I have never interfered with the crest business. It was very helpful to me" (quoted Usher 1974: 153 #14).

[287] For this reason, Tsimshian placed fish and animal bones in a fire to be consumed and reborn for the benefit of future life.

of the house chief, who had the sole right to recite its *adaawx* – the dense, distilled, and concentrated essences of world-shaking and world-making events involved with that name. Beginning in a stark and wet world that is obviously postglacial, the most ancient *adaawx* therefore span at least ten thousand years. Yet, as with the temporal sense of the Iroquois mentioned below, all these events do not happen simultaneously in a chaotic jumble, but, instead, sort themselves out as episodes in relative terms of what happened before and after each one. Because of these glacial conditions, remaining in alpine situations, and the endemic watery environment, however, flood stories reappear throughout the full chronology.

More important, each *adaawx* is told from the perspective of that one house, so it is both personal and laudatory. Triumphs are therefore always reported, yet defeats rarely. To convey this highly localized sense of "grounding," I have added details from the Douglas Channel homeland of the *Gitga'ata* (People of the Cane) where I was named. Though distinctly coastal, the Ecstall River Valley provided access to this region from the Skeena River, where the Coast Tsimshian majority have been confederated for about two millennia.

Where I most vary from a native perspective is in trying to present an account which interweaves, over time, as many crests as possible instead of specifying only the crest(s) of the house, and of related houses in that cluster, while ignoring or overlooking other houses, other crests, or foreign peoples who may have been there but have no longstanding or overt "claims on" or "relations with" a narrator.

Because the highest-ranking name holders were and are invited to the most feasts and potlatches, they were in a position to hear all the major epics recited in a public context. Their role, however, was to witness rather than to record or judge these "other" *adaawx*, for only the master of a house had the unassailable right to recite its epic, personally or, with greater prestige, through a designated and "paid" narrator.

Those who have long avoided getting lost in the maze, as some have phrased it, of the *adaawx* have now been provided with a brilliant ball of thread in the work of Susan Marsden (1996) of the Museum of Northern British Columbia in Prince Rupert.[288]5 Building on her insights at unraveling a relative chronology for middle-level events involving major clusters regarded as most significant by Tsimshian themselves, her useful guidelines allow for the identification of fifteen overlays, at least, within Tsimshian traditions, each associated with the famous name of a person or place. [663]

In presenting thumbnail sketches of each level, my intent is never to trivialize nor to slight these very significant and complex events.[289]6 Instead, within this overall guide, each layer

---

[288] Susan Marsden was educated as a philosopher and thus is mercifully free of the academic baggage detrimental to understanding the *adaawx* in their own right and relational sequencing. Her greatest insight has been the recognition that this sequence fills thousands rather than hundreds of years of culture chronology and consists of actual "history," in the sense that these events involved real (biological) people, places, emotions, and motivations.

[289] At the core of each *adaawx* is one or more song (*liimk'oy*), often translated [672] "dirge" for its slow place, although "anthem" conveys more of its patriotism while "lamentation" suggests its religious tone. During moments of great crisis, such as a world cataclysm, an *adaawx* will specify that sages met briefly to compose a song in case anyone survived and needed a reference point to explain its impact, often a fatal lesson in showing respect for all other life forms. Most *adaawx* detail encounters with *naxnox*, spirits resident in the

represents a milestone along the route of Tsimshian narrative history. Each name should be regarded in the same way as anyone seeking to understand the "Matter of Britain" would regard the personage of Arthur as the key figure in events that also include Twelve Knights of the Round Table, with Lancelot, Guinevere, Merlin, Mordred, and a host of other named characters and places playing significant roles within the story of Arthur.

Similarly, the nearest Americanist equivalent is the "historic" chronology among Iroquoians recognizing three layers, each named for a foremost participant. Thus, the creation of the world after their mother fell from the sky involved Earth Grasper and his malevolent twin Flint. Next came the founding of the League of the Iroquois by *Degandawidah*, aided by *Hyanwentha* (Hiawatha, "comber") and *Jingonsasay* (the Peace Queen), now generally dated to a lunar eclipse of 1350. In about 1800, Handsome Lake rose from his deathbed to preach the Good Word and revitalize Iroquoian religion.

For Tsimshian, however, the layering of chronological episodes is much more complex.

Laxha ~ 1

This preexistence is and was inhabited by immortals known as *naxnonax* under the leadership of Heaven ~ *laxha*. Most *naxnox* were and are protean batrachian shape-shifters combining aspects of humans, fish, and frogs. Beings have names and families, but no institutional units larger than the house (*walp*).

Moreavian *naxnox* living along inland valleys included the Robins of Kitsumkalum (*Gitsmgeelm*) and the Wind Brothers, who traveled as Ducks from the Ecstall headwaters.

Txamsem ~ 2

A *naxnox* comes to earth as a shining youth born to a noble Haida couple. Changed from an ascetic to a glutton, he becomes 'Wiigyet = Big Man, also known as *Txamsem*, and goes to the Nass River, changing the world toward its present condition.[290]7 Coming upon a rock and an elderberry about to give birth, he quickened the bush so humans now die and these bushes grow on their graves. Only the hardness of fingernails and toenails reminds people that they might have lived forever like stones.

He stole the bentwood box(es) holding sun, moon, and stars from [664] Raven at the Head of the Nass and opened it with a blinding flash, creating present species and seasons, except for those who escaped to remain *naxnox*.[291]8 In recognition of his acts, the *Ganhada*

Tsimshianic landscape embodied in masks. In general, if the human were a male, he will acquire access to strengthening power; whereas if a woman, she will have a child with divine powers and the right to pass on crests associated with these and subsequent events.

[290] According to Neil Sterritt and others (1995), the Nass River is the most ancient and complex homeland of Tsimshianic peoples, since its mouth was once occupied by Coast Tsimshians, middle reaches by Nishga, and upper reaches by Gitksans.

[291] This epic of the theft of the Box of Daylight was and is shared throughout the North Pacific, both American and Asian, and regarded as the "big bang" of creation that began the current progression and dimensionality of both time and space. In consequence, Raven took over responsibility for finishing the work of the Creator with not always satisfactory results.

matriclan with the Raven Crest was instituted, along with its Frog variants. In particular, this Raven and Frog interlinkage is well illustrated on the Raven rattle so distinctive of North Pacific chiefship, particularly in its *halaayt* aspect.

Nagwinaks ~ 3

On the coast a canoe from the Southern Tsimshian was taken under the sea into the elaborately decorated house of a resident *naxnox*, the chief of the Orca known as *Gitnugwinaks*. After four years, thinking they had been gone four days, the crew returned home with the right to build, carve, and paint a duplicate house and assume the names of *naxnox* from this spiritual abode. They became the *Gispwudwada* of the *Laxmoon* cluster within the Orca Crest, closely associated with the Kitasoo (*Gidestsu*) at Klemtu, who have long intermarried with *Gitga'at*. As the Raven and Frog were interlinked in the interior, so, on the coast, were the Orca and Wolf, both social carnivores organized into pods or packs, with Grizzlies sometimes added to the mix.

Ts'ooda ~ 4

One of the first beings to travel up from the mouth of the Skeena into the Yukon and back through the Nass and Skeena was *Ts'ooda* and his slave *Haalus*. More *naxnox* than mortals, the behavior of each clearly indicated his class and rank. *Ts'ooda* was kind, considerate, and efficient, while Haalus was awkward, greedy, and insufficient. *Ts'ooda* and *Haalus* also appeared, respectively, as a brightly colored butterball duck and a dull one. Though primarily a Wolf, *Ts'ooda*'s coastal origins also associated him with Orca. *Txamsem* (as Big Wings) built the first coastal house for him, setting the posts and beams with his claws, before sending a sister down from Heaven to be his wife and teach other women useful domestic skills. Later, *Ts'ooda* taught his own children the smelting of copper to make them rich and famous.

Sats'aan ~ 5

One of the earliest gathering places in the interior was *Laxwiiyip*, on the plateau drained by the headwaters of the Stikine, Nass, and Skeena Rivers. An important name there was *Niislaganoos* (Grandfather + Tlingit [665] term for "hill of the chief"), using a hat topped with ten articulated disks symbolizing vertebrae.

Among the earliest out-migrants were a Raven group led by *Sats'aan*.[292]9 While crossing a lake on a raft during a storm, a man drowned. His mourning sister later heard two songs and saw a frog and what looked a raven flying in the water (actually, a dark fish called a bullhead). These laments and crests (Water Raven~Bullhead, Frog) were thereafter claimed by this cluster.

---

[292] Among the *Wet'suwet'sen* (Bulkley River Carrier), a Raven artist became wealthy enough to potlatch and claim a formal seat using the name of *Sats'aan* because it was so venerable among the Tsimshian at nearby Kitselas. While he remained something like one of the Kwakwaka'wakw parvenus called Eagles, ranked between commoners and nobility, his daughter and later descendants became fully noble (Jenness 1943: 489-90).

172

Gaw'a ~ 6

A prince of the Raven village on the upper Nass was having an affair with a married woman in a village across the river, ruining her husband's hunting luck so he died impaled on a beaver dam. In revenge, his brothers killed the lover(s) and hid the prince's severed head. When the Ravens realized what had happened to their prince, they razed the other town. Only a girl (*Gaw'a ~ Gawo*) and her mother escaped. Pleading "Who will marry my daughter?" the mother accepted a son of the Sun, who then placed the mother inside a tree branch to produce arboreal creaking sounds and then took the girl into the sky to father Heavenly Children, often four sons and two daughters, one of them crippled.

Quickening their maturity, their grandfather Sun sent these youngsters back to the upper Nass, each son in a house with the first painted fronts and specialized crests, along with miraculous weapons used to destroy the Ravens utterly. Unrestrained, these brothers kept on fighting and killing until they met the beautiful women of the Babine River, who brought with them the Loon Crest. The sisters of these tamed warriors became the *Gisk'aast* ~ Fireweed crest, after a miraculous encounter with this plant.

Temlaxam ~ 7

A city called *Temlaxam* (prairie town ~ good land) grew up at the forks of the upper Skeena River near modern Hazelton, and its refined governance instituted the full flowering of culture, complete with clans, clusters, potlatches, and the moral law respecting all life. Among male religious institutions, displays of *naxnox* wonders and *smhalaayt* shamanism were specifically mentioned. As *Temlaxam* was the Tsimshianic center, so neighboring *Dizkle* was the Athapaskan hub.

Over time, however, the vast and growing population became wasteful, careless, and disrespectful. Several divine punishments ensued before a final one dispersed everyone. First, some boys abused a goat kid so [666] mountain goats lured everyone into the path of a rockslide that killed most of them. Second, some maidens used articulated trout skeletons on hats, playing frivolously with this integral source of life until a huge grizzly emerged from Seeley Lake to ravage the area. Third, after a young man insulted a salmon run. Heaven sent a blizzard that raged all summer long, until a bird with a berry in its beak warned *Ts'ibasaa* and his brothers *'Wiiseeks* (Big Seeks) and *Seeks* to struggle, each in turn, to the coast.[293]10 Fourth, some youths insulted a run of trout, so Heaven sent a flood to drown all but a few of those wealthy enough to have huge canoes to keep them afloat. From *Temlaxam*, a cluster of Nishga, Gitksan, and Tsimshian royal houses took up their historic locations, moving into towns long occupied by locals but now bound into an extensive trade network through this dispersed royalty.[294]

---

[293] Relying on detailed ornithological knowledge, this bird is often identified as a bluejay because they are very localized. Seeing this bird with a berry, those trapped inside the house knew that it was now fall with real winter on the way.

[294] Viola Garfield (1966: 34) argued that these royal houses were the result of resettlements at the fur trading posts, but the *adaawx* insist that certain clusters arrived on the coast already royal because of the fame acquired via their lavish potlatching, stone crests, and international relations, much as members of the Russian nobility fled to Europe, keeping

Of particular note as corroboration toward dating these events, a massive Stikyooden landslide at Chicago Creek near Seeley Lake has been geologically dated to 3,500 years ago (Monet and Skanu'u 1992: 11).

Assembling as neighboring tribal winter towns along Metlakatla Passage, replacing *Temlaxam*, Coast Tsimshian thrived. Also, the various *Gisk'aast* and *Gispwudwada* royal houses, both inland and sea, conjoined. Some survivors also went to the Tlingit, Haida, and other tribes, where their common origin was indicated by shared crests, chiefly names, and cluster label as a *wilnaat'aał*, a house grouping providing a loyalty and identity intermediate between a clan and a house.

Near *Temlaxam*, the heavy snow of the summer blizzard crushed the log salmon trap of the royal Orca house of Nta'wiiwalp, who escaped near starvation with his wife down the Ecstall Valley. There she gave birth to a daughter who grew up to marry the local *naxnox* son of the North Wind. Because of the husband's affinity with ducks, the wife always gave birth to quadruplets, until these numerous offspring founded the first semihuman town at a protected river fork in the homeland, now known as Old Town.

Nta'wiiwalp's brother *Gaaymtkwa* briefly joined them there before moving on to settle at Kitkatla. Similarly, the Orca brothers *'Wa'moodmłk*, married a Raven woman, while *Gwinaxnuutk* went to Kitkatla and settled in that homeland. Later their sibling rivalry over the white Kermode Bear Crest led to the founding of Star House, where *'Wa'moodmłk* added the name of Raven Snare, while a war was averted by giving the crest to Gwinaxnuutk.

Gwisk'aayn ~ 8

Strife with Ravens in the upper Stikine set off an extensive migration of Wolf clanspeople intermarried with Eagles. Over time, in addition to the [667] layering of events, this cluster (called the *Gwinhuut*, meaning fugitives, refugees, displaced people) leapfrogged over space, claiming places not permanently occupied or away from Tsimshian settlements. One of their leaders was Gwisk'aayn, whose Wolves sought protected inlets throughout coastal Tsimshian territory where they could entrench in a fort or stronghold. Among their affines were Eagle royal houses later associated with the high chief named Ligeex and another cluster headed by Gitxon ~ Gyetxawn ~ Gyethoon ~ Salmon Man).

Throughout the region, native houses are recognized as either "owners" or "others" (Miller 1981). Owners are those who saw the advantages of a place and pioneered its settlement and use after being empowered by a local *naxnox* assumed as a crest.[295]12 Others include various affines, friends, or visitors who reside in that locale with the approval of the owners. Thus, these fugitives wandered the coast seeking productive places where each could establish ownership, however briefly. By this time, however, most of the Tsimshian area had long been claimed by houses, so bitter fighting frequently ensued until victories, compromises, and all-important

---

their "good names" if not always the family fortunes and treasures. Among Northcoast people, however, royalty was even more a matter of intermarriage, since fathers and sons belonging to different clans contributed a cosmopolitanism to each other's rankings in a way that uncles and nephews belonging to the same clan could not.

[295] In *sm'algyax* (real language, Coast Tsimshianic), the phrasing is that owners have a place "where they could work the land" ~ *ndega dm di wil ha'li hałeelst* (Ts'ibasaa 1916).

intermarriages settled these situations.

Of note, carbon dates from around Metlakatla indicate that more than twelve existing towns were abandoned in about AD100, suggesting a starting date for this exodus when embattled Coast Tsimshian retreated to their tribal territories along tributaries of the lower Skeena. Of note, these towns had been widely dispersed with houses of uniform size, while those reoccupied after AD400 were concentrated (confederated) along Venn Passage in the immediate vicinity of Metlakatla with houses of varying size and wealth. Clearly, conditions of warfare encouraged the rapid growth of a ranked society concentrated for its own defense (Archer 1996).

In the homeland, *Nta'wiiwalp* led an intertribal war expedition to clear the Wolves from Douglas Channel and then Lowe Inlet, albeit allowing intermarriage with the royal survivors.

Aksk ~ 9

Eventually, after a brutal Gwinhuut attack on the Ecstall River, only a boy and girl survived and, vowing revenge, married although both were *Gispwudwada*. Thus, though often avoided in the *adaawx*, *Aksk* married his mother's sister's daughter to father ten sons, more often called his "nephews," all trained to be skilled warriors.[296]13 By this time, many *Gwinhuuts* were being identified as Tlingit enemies, although still sharing a remote ancestry with Tsimshian house clusters from the Nass and *Temlaxam*. Their stronghold was near Dundas Island across from the mouth of the Nass. [668]

When his sons were grown, *Aksk* moved to Kaien Island and built a two-story fort. Wooden effigies were placed in the beds with kelp tubes to carry the sound of imitated snoring. Lured into the fort, attacking Tlingits plunged daggers into the manikins only to become trapped because the weapons, which were tied to their wrists, remained stuck deep in the wood. Victorious, *Aksk* and his family took all of the weapons, crests, and treasures of these slain enemies.[297]14

Metlakatla ~ 10

With the Tlingits driven north, the Coast Tsimshian tribes came out of the lower Skeena to resume winter festivities along Metlakatla Passage in territory now "owned" by *Aksk*'s tribe, the *Gitwilgyoots* (People of the Kelp), because they had successfully fought for and "invested in" that locale. By AD1200, the region was densely and diversely occupied, with rankings presumably derived from the preeminent standing of the Kelp People.

Niishaywaaxs ~ 11

A high chief of Temlaxam, *Niishaywaaxs*[298] of the Grizzly Bear ~ *midiik* Crest took his

---

[296] Since *aks* means "water" and *-k* particularizes the meaning of a word (such as *gsms* [hair] becomes *gsmsk* [thin]), his name may be "fetch water" with the sense of providing relief.

[297] Much earlier at this locale was the home of a chief whose daughter suckled a woodworm until it became a menace to the town and was killed. Though a Tsimshian epic set in their homeland, this crest is best known from the Whale House of the Chilcat Tlingit, where it is represented in an enormous carved feasting trough.

[298] The name means Grandfather of *Haywaaxs*.

people downriver to claim the Zymoetz River Valley and the gateway at Kitselas Canyon (Wright 1962), but they were bitterly opposed by local Ravens for many years. Recriminations were unceasing. Treachery and murder shattered brief truces or marriage alliances. One Grizzly princess was incinerated on her wedding night; one *Niishaywaaxs* was crushed to death in an elaborate show of hostility, and so on until these Wars of *Midiik* ended at a settlement feast where Ravens compensated for the initial death, and land claims were validated to confirm Grizzly control of the upper Skeena Canyon.

Ligeex ~ 12

Building upon a vast array of marital ties, an Eagle chief of the Gispaxlo'ots (People of the Elderberry) rose to primacy among the Coast Tsimshian after 1800 under the titled name of Ligeex. In about 1500, the name had come from the *Kitamaat* via a marriage between a Raven chief and a *Gwinhuut Gispaxlo'ots* princess, whose daughter married *Hamdziit*, high chief at Heiltsuk (Wutsdaa, Bella Bella) and source of many *'wiihalaayt* (great *halaayt*) privileges. Via access to these secret orders and through strategic marriages by nephew heirs, the name Ligeex became allied with important houses over a wide area for several hundred years. By then, these [669] Elderberry People were the most numerous of all Coast Tsimshian tribes. Bitter wars were fought for direct access to the Gitksan fur trade through Kitselas Canyon, until dynastic marriages by *Gwinhuut* Eagles established the necessary links. After a devastating defeat, one Ligeex maneuvered to have the victorious *Niistaxho'ok* of Kitselas lead his flotilla against the Haida. Under Old Ligeex (died 1840), the most famous, intermarriages involved European institutions like the Hudson's Bay Company, who built their second Fort Simpson on a portion of his own land in 1834.

Duncan ~ 13

Then, in 1857, a lay Anglican missionary named William Duncan arrived from England and spent a year learning to speak Tsimshianic from an Orca nobleman named Clah (*łaa*) before he began to preach and to convert. By 1862, he led fifty converts, soon joined by two hundred more, back to ancient Metlakatla to found one of the most successful cooperative Christian communities in the world. The continued importance of the power of "light," together with identifying Duncan as "the chief," indicate that Christianity fit quite easily within the template of the traditional culture.

Deciding to join with other Tsimshian, *Gitga'at* families left their homeland to join Duncan between 1863 and 1873. In 1874, Methodists began a mission at Port Simpson which became the base of Reverend Thomas Crosby for twenty-three years.

New Metlakatla ~ 14

A bishop was sent to Metlakatla to downplay the economic cooperative in favor of a religious community of avowedly Anglican form. Duncan refused both ordination for himself and the sacrament of communion for his converts, fearing that consuming the body and blood of Christ would be confused with the ancient cannibal *halaayt*. Conditions worsened until, in 1887, Duncan led about eight hundred Tsimshians to Alaska in quest of religious freedom under U.S. protection.

Deciding to return to their homeland, about thirty *Gitga'ata* canoed south and founded a new town along Christian tenets at their ancient fall camp, since affiliated with the United Church of Canada.

As a result, Tsimshianic speakers now continue to live as Gitksan along the upper Skeena; Nisga'a along the Nass; Southern at Klemtu, Hartley Bay, and Kitkatia; and Coast at New Metlakatla, *Lax Kw'alaams* (Port Simpson), Kitsumkalum, Kitselas, and Old Metlakatia, the ancient Tsimshian bastion where a few chiefs stayed behind with Bishop William [670] Ridley after everyone else had left. Today, of course, most Tsimshian, like others involved in the cash economy, have moved to Prince Rupert and other Canadian and American cities.

Delgamuukw ~ 15

Under their hereditary titled names to assert their lasting aboriginal rights, the chiefs of the Gitksan and Wet'suwet'en spent three and a half years (1987-91) in British Columbia provincial court to argue for their land claims, based in the *adaawx*, only to be told by the chief justice that the province holds title by "virtue" of discovery by European ships (Monet and Skanu'u 1992). A decision on appeal was only marginally less insulting. At present, most native peoples of British Columbia are actively engaged in research in preparation for either court cases or treaty negotiations, which have been denied or resisted by officials of the province since the 1860s.

Currently, traditional uses and ownerships of the homeland are being documented, along with *adaawx*, proving their ongoing vitality and strength. In the process, the *adaawx* are more alive than ever, a varied topic of and for reference, discussion, and even debate.

Conclusion

Tsimshian say that people are given to the names rather than the reverse became the names are immortal and each can convey benefits to its "holder," who treats it with respect by leading an honorable and generous life. Names that are "older" in the overlays can be more famous, but that is not always the case because considerations of class remain vital. Thus, a royal name from *Temlaxam* should be more prominent than a more ancient one associated with a more remote context.

Yet more than antiquity or rank, names provide the basis of and for Tsimshian history because they are not just remembered, they are inherited to "live again" by another mortal body. Such recursiveness interweaves past, present, and future within an overall context of the immortal, the wellspring for cultural significance and understanding. Thus native history is a repeated and progressive viewing of glimpses of the immortal in ways that benefit the ongoing community through public events like feasts, ceremonies, and potlatches. So vital is this mortal-immortal connection that during and after the devastating epidemics, in the absence of suitable heirs, names were passed on to pets such as dogs or to the arms, legs, and other body parts of already overburdened "holders."

Tsimshian also say that "names feed people" because each is firmly [671] grounded in a portion of the landscape, conferring rights to all its resources. These rights were and are witnessed and validated at public events to make them "legal," provided that the holder and name are further enhanced (not tarnished) by generous sharing of that bounty with members of the house and with many guests. In this manner, the immortal sustains the mortal, both benefiting in the resultant prestige.

In keeping with the cultural elaboration of the North Pacific Coast, the recall of a few significant and "mythic" ancestors by many Native American tribes, such as the Iroquois and others,[299]16 is more complexly expressed by Tsimshian and their North Coast neighbors in terms of names stretching back to their very beginnings as a nation and leaning forward into the distant future.

Thanks

Though I was not always entirely gracious during this ordeal, I remain inexpress-ably grateful to Susan Marsden, John Dunn, Christopher Roth, Jean Mulder, Tanya Stebbins, Marjorie Halpin, Margaret Anderson, and, most especially, the Clifton, Hill, Gamble, Brown, Leighton, Wilson, and Neasloss families.

Documentation for this chronology, of course, resides in the *adaawx* of the hereditary houses of the Tsimshianic chiefs, with relevant sources in the Tsimshian File assembled by Marius Barbeau of the Canadian National Museum with all-important help from William Beynon, a *Gitlaan* Wolf chief named for layer 5.

---

[299] Though largely discredited, the *Walam Olum* – purporting to be the Delaware account of their own migration from Siberia into the American Northeast – lists the sequence of chiefs who led them during various stages of this migration.

Tsimshian Religion in Historical Perspective
Shamans, Prophets, and Christ

Given the thousands of pages we have on Tsimshian myths, crests, kinship, and economies, we really have next to nothing on religion. If defined as a relation with transcendence, the supernatural, or the extranormal, then Tsimshian religion traditionally focused on shamans, together with chiefs in their priestly guise as the bestowers of supernatural power to noble youngsters at Winter Ceremonials. Yet Boas (1916: 473-77) devotes only four pages out of a thousand to shamanism, Garfield (1951: 46-48) adds a few more, and Barbeau (1958) includes thirty pages on Tsimshian shamans in his one-hundred-page booklet. More material can be found in the Beynon notes, but *in toto* these are not impressive percentages for such a central feature of Tsimshian life and culture.

Aboriginal religion focused on the crucial concept of haleyt augmented by that of *naxnox*. Vastly simplifying, haleyt refers to controlled supernatural power expressed through simulations of desired state, while *naxnox* is unwieldy supernatural power associated with chiefly might, antisocial acts, and distinctive tendencies intended to instill fear into onlookers. Haleyt had continuous, legitimate usage, while *naxnox* was limited to masked performance and dramatic events held during the winter season.

During initial stages of Euro-Canadian intrusion, these concepts were challenged and demeaned.   In their defense, several native prophets appeared who preached revisions, making the concepts more acceptable to the Evangelical Christianity that eventually superseded them. Of these prophets, the most famous was *Bini,~* Mind, a Carrier Athapaskan who founded a line of imitators who also used his name. While accounts of *Bini* among the Tsimshian have yet to [138] appear in print, Jenness (1943: 550-59) discusses him within the Carrier context as the younger brother of Sisteyel and nephew of Sami, earlier prophets. Some of the appeal of Bini related to his position as chief of the Beaver phratry, strengthened further when he gave a large potlatch to dedicate his Fireweed totem pole in Bulkley Canyon. In fact, during his life he was best known as *Kwiis*, the Beaver chiefly name, only taking the name of Bini, and later of Samtelesa, after successive visits to the sky. He died about 1870, apparently from water – which he used for a curing – that had been poisoned.

At present all the older Tsimshian and many of the younger ones are devout Christians, the result of missionary work by William Duncan, Thomas Crosby, and others less well known. With their conversion, the Tsimshian came to publicly reject their previous beliefs as pagan and, as they say, "low class." Their native medicoreligious specialists were hounded into abandoning then-practice by accusations that they were in league with the devil. Even now with a reawakened appreciation of their past greatness, the accepted translation of the word *swansk* (shaman, Indian doctor) is "witch doctor" or "devil worker." Of all the Tsimshian, only the Gitksan, somewhat insulated by their interior homeland, continue to recognize and patronize shamans who derive their power from the Christian God and who practice a Christianized shamanism.   The Coast and Southern Tsimshian urge that shamanism be forgotten and sometimes go as far as to say that shamans were never all that important in the past anyway. Yet no matter how strenuous the denials, the subject of shamanism is not easily discussed at all without making the participants uneasy. Attitudes toward shamanism continue to run deep and be emotional. This became clear to me when I was showing the testament summarized in the

"Conflict over Christianity" section of this chapter to several Tsimshian. Though they occurred in 1918, the events described in the testament could as easily have happened in the 1980s.

In homage to Viola Garfield, this paper is based on materials either collected by her in the field or sent to her by William Beynon and now stored in the Garfield Collection of the University of Washington Archives. These data have been sufficient to trace the history of religious change among the Tsimshian by describing the roles, duties, and privileges of specific shamans, by presenting two brief accounts of Bini, prophet-cum-shaman, and by summarizing the narrative of a woman brought to the brink of insanity by her personal conflict between her new Christian faith and her training to assume the shaman's power of her dead mother's brother. [139]

Traditional: Swansk

Garfield was fortunate to have among her principle ethnographic informants at Port Simpson a man called Niasgane (died 1935), who was the only shaman in the community. But she was unable to broach the specific subject of shamanism with him, since he was on court probation from a charge of witchcraft and had to avoid any reference to this activity. Other members of the community were willing to discuss his career with Garfield as a warning for her to be careful while they were working together.

Among the people of the Nass and Skeena, *Niasgane* had a reputation as a powerful curer, but they would call on him only in great secrecy. One woman he was treating said that he could see through her and would know if she disobeyed him, so she never did anything without his consent. He communicated with the dead who would send messages to their living relatives through him. On occasion, he was called upon to insure success in fishing and other pursuits.

Niasgane's uncle *Watimanloik* (Without-Rising) was also a shaman. Although the position of shaman was not strictly hereditary, it was more likely for a boy to become a shaman if there was someone in the family to instruct him. The power of a shaman was called *smhalaayt* (real power). This power came to a boy through a vision while he was isolated from the community. It was said that the house of Watimanloik and his mother has always possessed shamans of great power. As evidenced by the fact that both Watimanloik and his mother were initiated shamans, the Tsimshian recognized that both men and women could be shamans, although men more commonly filled the role. Before a shaman could be said to be with haleyt (power), he would have to be sick for such a long time that people became alarmed and sent for a shaman to find out what was the matter. The shaman would see that such a person was afflicted by the power and he would so inform the household. The father of the patient would gather in all the shamans, who would (each in turn) take the same rattle and begin the cure by singing a song that belonged to a former shaman of this house. Night after night they would continue to sing in order to strengthen the supernatural power of the patient-cum-shaman. These shamans received compensation for their labors every night of the cure.

Eventually the cure progressed to the point where the patient began to sing his or her own personal curing song. At this juncture, the initiate would be exhibited before his or her tribe. The [140] shaman-to-be would then parade around the fire four times, singing the personal song, and then retire to bed. An initiate's father would distribute gifts to the guests, and the household feasted everyone as public confirmation of the power of the new shaman.

In curing, the shaman always had a young male assistant to beat the drum for him. Like the shaman, the young man was also compensated by the family of the patient. When a patient died, however, the fees were returned. If a shaman was not satisfied with the amount of compensation, he would not touch it or leave the house until the family increased the amount. Once he began the cure, the shaman wore eagle down and a crown of grizzly bear claws, a neck ring inlaid with carved bones, a fringed dancing apron, carried a carved wooden rattle in the right hand and an eagle feather in the left one, and wore either black or red face paint.

Widəldal (Gispawadwada crest, Gitsəm-ge•lon tribe) was another great Tsimshian shaman. In his day, while the people were living on the Nass, there was danger of starvation. One of the important men of the Gilutsau tribe urged that they gather together gifts and give them to this shaman to see if the eulachon were going to come that year and provide salvation. The gifts were brought and placed before the shaman, who filled two vessels with water drawn from the Nass River. One bowl he placed at the entrance and the other at the back of the house, then he took a dried eulachon and cut it in two so there was a piece in each vessel, and finally he said to those watching, "When I start to dance around the house watch these vessels. As soon as any fish come to life call out." He danced three times around the house and called out, "If the fish do not come to life, then there will be no eulachon and the people will starve." Before he was half way around for the fourth time, one of the watchers called out, "The fish has come to life." The shaman then said to the Gilutsau people, "Get your eulachon nets and set them tomorrow, as there will be many eulachon," and there were!

Nisshaida (Grandfather of the Haida?), a great shaman of the Gitxała (Kitkatla) tribe was visiting the Ginax'angik living in the house of *Gamayam* (Only Mocks). At this time there was concern over some tribesmen of *Gamayam* who were missing in a boat. They brought the shaman many gifts, so he took out his best paraphernalia, used only when the fee was large. He filled a bucket with salt water, covered his head, and looked into the water. He said, "I see they are not dead and will soon arrive home." He called a man to him and gave him a ceremonial cane, saying, "Take my cane and place it at the edge of the water on the beach. Do not allow the [141] water to splash on the cane, but when it reaches this mark on the cane, look out toward the point, below the Eagle House, and you will see a canoe, then call out." The man went out and the shaman began to sing and dance until the man called out and announced the safe arrival of the lost men. The people rushed to the beach to welcome them.

A very powerful shaman was believed to have the power to avenge his own death. Kininook, a Tlingit shaman, was captured by a Tsimshian raiding party, which cut off his head. As blood spurted into the air, the body ran around until it became stuck in a stump and died. The Tsimshian took the head home fastened by its long matted hair to the crosspiece that held the sail of their canoe. They sneered at the face and spat at it. But then the head moved and fell into the water. Immediately, there was a storm that destroyed all but one of the war party, who reached home to tell the tale.

A shaman would never cut his hair because of the belief that his spirit helpers lived there and in the bone tube that was worn suspended about the neck. It was actually these spirit helpers who told the shaman about mishaps, the causes and cures for illness, and many things other people could not see or know.

Niasbiens, another powerful shaman, once came to the man called *Lagaxni'tsk* (To Each Side Looks) and said, "I was going along the creek at Gitsamge'lon when I heard a voice from underground. My spirit said to me. That is the soul of Lagaxni'tsk which he lost here while hunting. Take it back to him.'" But Lagaxni'tsk was by then a convert, so he replied, "Take my soul. I lost it long ago and it is spoiled now. Take it and use it, you will live a long time."

Niasbiens was angry, so he put the soul on his own head and kept it. Later Niasbiens died and this soul died with him, but Lagaxni-'tsk felt no differently.

While some shamans did practice witchcraft ~ *haldawgit*, anyone could use it to produce illness or death if they knew how. The only difference was that the witchcraft of a shaman was always more effective.

Personal belongings were the most potent means of producing ill effects. Hair, nail parings, or soiled clothes were secured and combined with plants and objects believed to have an evil influence. Incantations were said over these, and the specific evil intended for the individual was mentioned. For illnesses caused by witchcraft, the patient could only be cured if the shaman secured the personal belongings that had been used and washed them clean of the harmful intent. For this reason, until a few years ago, no washing was [142] left out of doors overnight because of fear that it might be used for witchcraft. Even now, pieces are sometimes cut from garments left outside by people attempting witchcraft. The owners of mutilated laundry accordingly become at least nervous, if not ill.

Transitional: *Bini*, the Prophet

It is presumed that sometime around 1800 a prophet-cum-shaman of the Carrier (Athapaskan-speaking) people named Bini preached an early revitalistic form of religion among the Tsimshian . After his death, he had several imitators who also used his name, which makes it difficult to sort out the different persons called Bini.

Bini's influence extended not only to the Tsimshian but also to other groups as far north as Haines, Alaska, and as far south as Vancouver Island and Rivers Inlet. His preaching was also known to interior Athapaskan tribes such as the Babines, Tahltans, and the Tinnehs.

Beynon thought that Bini might have found some inspiration for his sect from contact with a Catholic missionary at the Bear Lake Missions. Many of his teachings may be seen as related to the increased tensions and pressures brought on by initial Euro-Canadian settlement. The five commandments laid down by Bini were that his followers (1) be faithful to their home life, (2) not encroach on the hunting territory of another tribal member, (3) not murder, (4) respect the voice of the old people and chiefs, and (5) cease making war on one another.

According to one biographical account collected at Hazelton, Bini was a member of the Hagwilget village of Carriers, and he was known as a great hunter, gambler, and shaman. Many feats of magic were attributed to him, including the defeat of some very powerful witches. His hereditary hunting grounds were filled with all kinds of resources, so he was very wealthy. However, it happened that during one session of gambling he lost everything.

First he bet and lost his possessions, then his nephews, then his parents, and finally his wife and children. He had nothing, and so he left the village and entered the forest in deepest sorrow. His wife's family was very angry with him, therefore he hid and wandered around in the mountain forest without food for many days. At last he became so tired that he dropped from exhaustion and slept.

He slept for a long time and a vision came to him. A person dressed in shining white came to him and said, "You will come with me up [143] into the hills, for I have much that I want to show you." Bini got up and, leaving his clothes behind, followed him. When they had gone some distance the man spoke again, "You will return to your people, tell them I have been sent down by the Chief of the Skies – you must teach your people to be good." As the person

182

spoke, he made a motion of touching his forehead, then each shoulder, and then the middle of his breast. At each gesture, he repeated a foreign word. This he did many times. Then, turning to Bini, he said, "You will do this saying the same words when meeting with your people. You will speak to them in a strange tongue, which will be interpreted by one of your nephews." After saying this, the stranger went away and Bini fell forward upon the ground.

Meanwhile, people were searching for Bini. They found where he had left his clothes, but as it was a very cold time of the year, they had no hope of finding him alive. Yet they did find him barely alive, lying on the ground with his head buried in snow. They carried him to the village, laid him by a fire, and a shaman worked on him for two days before he showed strong signs of life. When he did revive, he spoke to the people in a strange language and acted differently. He taught the people new songs and dances, which the people repeated until they dropped from exhaustion. They were able to learn because Bini's nephew interpreted the strange language. Some people danced and rolled on the floor until they fell asleep from sheer exhaustion. Other people brought food to Bini's house for everyone. After many days of this, Bini delivered his five commandments and moved on to visit other villages. He always used an unknown language that was interpreted by his nephew. Bini went to the mouth of the Skeena, where others imitated him and spread the religion everywhere.

According to another biographical account collected by Beynon at Port Simpson, Bini came from the Hagwilget people before the arrival of Reverend Duncan among the Tsimshian. Bini was noted for the use of a strange tongue and a strange manner of singing. While singing and dancing, he carried a cross and made something like the sign of the cross over his head and breast. After visiting the old Tsimshian camp at Metlakatla, he returned to the upper Skeena. It was the Coast Tsimshian themselves who spread the religion when they went up the Nass for eulachon and met Tlingits, Haidas, Niska, and other tribes. Beynon's source felt that this was actually not a new religion, but rather it was a new form of *halaayt* dance which also included unintelligible songs, dancing, and rolling on the floor. [144]

Conflict over Christianity

In Garfield's notes is a testimonial taken from a woman at Port Simpson who during 1918 fought a personal battle between the part of herself that wanted to be a good Christian and the part that wanted to fulfill her traditional obligation to assume the spirit power of a shaman who had been her mother's brother. A probable strong influence on this conflict was its occurrence in 1918, the year of the great influenza epidemic throughout Canada that had such a devastating effect on the population. The woman appears to vacillate between the belief that as a Christian she could pray for her friends and loved ones during the epidemic but that as a shaman she could actually do something for them. The angst expressed by this woman reflects the pathos affecting many tribal peoples after contact.

As a girl, this woman accompanied her shaman uncle when he was called to cure patients. As his assistant and heir apparent, she would carry the box in which he kept his paraphernalia so that she and the power objects could gradually become familiar with each other. But one day her uncle had a vision of angels with wings pulling on ropes that made mighty bells ring. When the angels told him to pull the ropes, the bells would not ring. Then he knew he had done wrong, so he became a Christian, and was baptized "Samuel." Four years later he died. Some years after, his spirit came to the niece one night. She sent it away. A year later it came again and she heard her uncle's song, the most powerful expression of his power, and saw her uncle as a boy and as a baby. She prayed to God and the spirit and visions again went away. But about this time her husband died and she was alone. The spirit next made her desire a man: "The evil spirit sees me; no sweetheart, no man, no husband; a widow woman has a hard time." She was able to hold off the urge and continued to pray and read the Bible.

Over the next fifteen years she would sometimes hear the sound of a shaman's rattle in her dreams, but that was about all. In 1918 while she was working at the cannery at Kumeen, she was out alone on a trail when a wren flew into a stump and killed itself. The stump became a human face moving from side to side, and a nearby mountain became a giant grizzly bear.

She managed to make it home to her cabin before she collapsed, remaining delirious for the next nine days. The devil spirit tormented her in her dreams by taking her out in small boats or up the Skeena River to drown her. She managed to regain her composure [145] by the ninth day and had her son take her to the hospital at Port Simpson. After four days in the hospital, she was given some rig white pills that kept away the spirit for some time.
But it returned again. She actually had to wrestle the being around the floor of her cabin before she could throw it out. Another time, three children all dressed in red appeared to her and the eldest one said, "You are going to become a shaman or you will die." She said, "No, I have my own chief. God, and my own witness, the Bible." They grabbed and twisted her arms until she passed out. She revived and began to sing "I Am Coming to the Cross," but then lapsed into delirium for the next four days, during which islands, fish, seagulls, and a cat spoke to her. When the Evil One, the Devil, or the spirit came, it told her to take up shamanism and threatened her with drowning if she did not. Once her left hand became paralyzed. Another time, the spirit said: "You are a poor woman. Your sisters' children and your daughters' children will die because you don't take the power."

She received some help from the white man who supervised the cannery and had employed her as a net mender. When she went to his home, a caged bluejay there spoke to her, warning her that while she was away from her cabin every possible spirit would crowd into it. The bluejay offered to help her if she would ask the white man to release it, because, it said, "I do not want to speak English i to the white man." Later the white man and his family invited her i to supper. The wife read to her from the Bible and told her: "In my Father's house are many mansions. He will prepare for you. I don't want you to die with some crazy spirit. I am in the church. I am a Catholic and my husband is Presbyterian, so we each take one of our two sons into our own religion." The woman baked some Catholic bread with square marks on it, which everyone ate up. Not one crumb was left in the pan. The woman felt better by the time she got home.

During the night she had a vision of a man with long hair standing straight up. He tormented her until the floor of her cabin split open to reveal a glimpse of Hell. Her right hand spoke to her left hand about taking up the Bibles that the woman kept on each side of the head of her bed. At this the visitor left and the woman wept. That Sunday she awoke to see tiny angels standing on the window curtain ruffle. Behind the angels stood women wearing nurses' caps. Soon she was strong enough to go back to the hospital in Port Simpson. Even while in her hospital room, she saw tiny devils everywhere; on the window, in the room, on the caps of the nurses. [146]

These devils were, she said, "Marking all of the people we are taking from all over the world." She said of her meals, "The cook made me meat and to me it was mud; another dish was

184

a boy; bread and butter was a flat fish like halibut; and peas were rats. One time there was a frog in my dish. The Evil Spirit caused me to see these things."

Visitors came to see her in the hospital with prayers and good wishes, but there were times she did not know they were even there. The doctor gave her pills and more pills. Yet still she was tormented by spirits, demons, and apparitions. Once the spirits demanded her to have intercourse with a specific man because she had led too pure a life. Again she was consumed by a desire for a man, but she prayed to God and kept control of herself. The doctor and other people tried to find a husband for her. The doctor said, "You are sick because no man has touched you since your husband died and your blood is too watery. A man changes a woman's blood and she his. You need a husband. You are sick because no man has touched you and changed your blood."

Finally, after further torment, she had a vision of a bright, shining youth who took her to Heaven where she saw the headdresses and white gowns worn by the Christian Tsimshians. With this she truly began to recover, but when she was released from the hospital and went to visit people in the community, she learned that many of the people whom she had recently seen in her vision of Heaven had actually just died in the 1918 flu epidemic.

She went back to the cannery to collect the money she had earned before her difficulties and reported: "I made over three hundred dollars in the cannery. God was good to me because He used me and I repented."

After this awesome experience, she remained afraid of drowning, as do most people who live along the coast, and she occasionally heard singing, but this always happened just before there was to be news of someone close to her.

Summary

Through the years, Tsimshian religion has undergone some very significant changes but the belief in haleyt = power has been maintained consistently by the traditionalist elders. While not all Tsimshian recognize the role and abilities of shamans, some still do consult practicing shamans in the inland villages. As shamans have thus continued to coexist with Christianity, so aspects of traditional Tsimshian culture have survived within the context of Euro-Canadian [147] society. An accommodation has been achieved between the old and the new – an accommodation initially attempted by prophets like Bini. The revitalistic haleyt of Bini has faded from memory, but the two traditions (native and white) that he tried to syncretize live on.

First Salmon Ceremony
of the Nass River Tsimshian

Roger Ernesti[300]

4/14/12

When the spring run of salmon is due, several canoes go out fishing. When a man catches the first salmon, he paddles toward the village singing. When the fishing camp hears him coming, the people know the first salmon had been caught. Everybody is happy and puts on his best clothing, (see props 18-23 inclusive) – even old people and children.[301] All go out in front of the house to the river so that they may see the man come in, singing as he paddles. When his canoe lands at the beach, all raise their hands above their heads, palms forward, and cry "He-e-e-y," (Thanks,) (see Rule 1), in order to send thanks to their "grandfather" for sending food up the river. The canoe comes to the shore and is held in the water parallel to the bank by the man in the bow. It is pointed upstream. (See Fig. 4 attached). The head shaman goes down towards the canoe. The other three shamans remain in the house with the mat. (prop 1) The three shamans who remain in the house get the mat from the woman shaman, whose duty it is to keep the mat stored in a box (prop 17) on the large storage shelf (see prop 14). Her ceremonial right to care for the mat is inherited. When the head shaman sees the fish, he looks back to the people, all dressed up. Then he calls, "Bring out the mat," (prop 1). The three shamans pick up the mat, two of them at the two corners at one end of the mat, one of them holding the two corners at the other end. They go outside the house, carrying the mat [2] at about waist height. They stop just outside the door. All the people cry "He-e-e-yi," and the three shamans lift the mat up as high as they can reach. As the cry ends, they lower it slowly to the ground and straighten up, hands held in front of them in reverential attitudes, palms forward, at shoulder height, arms bent.

The head shaman calls, "Come down with the mat." They pick it up and walk slowly to the beach; one shaman walks backward. They lay the mat down at the head shaman's command. It is put on the beach a few feet from the canoe, and is laid on top of a common mat (prop 4a), in order to avoid getting the special mat dirty. It is laid so that the salmon's head will be upstream. (See prop 1, also Rule 2.)

The head shaman looks back at the people and says, "Ready now. I am going to pick up the salmon." Then he steps into the canoe. The man in the stern of the canoe hold up his spear

---

[300] Jay Miller learned from Roger Ernesti in November 2000 that MGM financed this work at Warm Springs Reservation with Alex Morrison, a Nishka married to an enrolled member there, in 1936 for a film on Alaska called *Silver Horde* [*Spawn of the North*]. In 1937, Mel Jacobs worked with him on transcriptions. The artifacts should be at the Burke, unless they were discarded after use in the film.

[301] They have been warned of the approach of the catch by one of the other canoes which was present at the catch. Visitors from upstream have come previously, knowing it is time for the salmon. People from nearby fishing camps are called by messenger after the fish is caught, or come when they hear singing. They come in large canoes 30-40 feet long, similar to prop [#] 15 but with decorated bows on many of the canoes. {Footnotes are continuous herein, though in the original manuscript each page starts with 1.}

so that all may see what was used to catch the first salmon. The head shaman lifts up the salmon, faces the people, and all cry, "He-e-e-y," (see rules for ceremonial procedure, # 1). Head shaman says in an oratorical manner: "This is the first gift of our grandfather. We must take good care of it. We must not waste the bones. If we dry fish, we must dry bones, gills, and all of it. If there is any part of the fish not to be used, it must go into the fire. The salmon doesn't like the flies to be on it. Now we're "going to take the salmon into the house and cook it, and we'll sing a song while it roasts."

After saying this, the head shaman steps out of the canoe. The mat is all laid out with the three shamans at 3 corners. As the head shaman steps out, all cry "He-e-e-y." He walks to the mat with the fish, lays the fish on the mat, and, as he does so, all the people cry "He-e-e-y." (See Fig. 4 attached) [3] the head shaman calls to the doorman, "Open the door, we're coming with the salmon." To the people he says, "Line up by the door." The head shaman takes his place at the northeast corner of the mat. All 4 shamans take the corner of the good mat, (See Fig. 4 attached), and walk to the house with the salmon's head forward, its tail last. All 4 shamans face the mat as they carry it, so that 2 of them must walk backward and two forward. As they walk between the two rows of people, all the people cry "He-e-e-y," 4 times. (See Fig. 5). The 4 shamans enter the house and put the special mat on another (common mat, prop 4b), on the door side or east side of the fire. The fish's head is to the north. After the mat is put down, then the 2 lines of people come in. The highest ranking people have been closest to the door outside, (see Fig. 6 attached), and the lowest farthest from the house, so that as each line files in and walks along its side of the house (on either side of the fire,) the highest ranking people lead and are seated at the center of the back opposite the door. All sit quietly.

The 4 shamans lift the mat by its corners. All cry "He-e-e-y." The shamans, with the mat, walk counterclockwise around the fire to the southwest corner of the fire, set it down; all lift their hands and cry, "He-e-e-y!" (See Fig. 7 attached.) Then shamans pick up the mat and go to the southeast corner of the fire, set it down, and all cry "He-e-e-y!" (See Fig. 8.) Then to the northeast corner, then to the northwest corner of the fire, crying "He-e-e-y" at each corner. The assemblage says "He-e-e-y" sixteen times. This completes one circuit; there are four such circuits, ending at the northwest corner of the fire. Then it is moved to the middle of the west side of the fire, set down with the fish's head to the north, (see Fig. 9 attached), and all cry "He-e-e-y". Then the head shaman calls a woman shaman and tells her to cut the salmon. She takes the specially marked mat from beneath the fish and puts it [4] west of the fire for future use. The fish is now on a common mat (prop 4a). The woman shaman kneels on the west edge of the common mat, facing north, with the fish to her right. (See Fig. 10 attached.) Just as the knife (prop 3) touches the salmon, all the people start to sing. (Song # 1; see Rule 3). As the woman cuts the two halves of the salmon apart, the head shaman, standing at the northwest corner of the fire, takes the prepared roasting stick (prop 5) and paints it. Then he holds the stick at arm's length, slanting slightly forward, with hands slightly above shoulder height, and walks slowly around the fire (counter clockwise). As he comes back to the mat, the song ends, and, as all cry "He-e-e-y!", he slowly lets the stick down and lays it on the mat. The woman shaman takes it and inserts it longitudinally in the port side of the salmon, starting from the head end. All cry "He-e-e-y!" Then she takes the skewers, (prop 6) and puts them in, (Rule 4), twelve on each half of the fish. As she finishes one side of the salmon, she lays it on the fire side of the mat. The head shaman takes the roasting stick with the salmon and hold it up. All say "He-e-e-y!" As the cry ends, he brings the stick down into a hole, (prop 5), which has been made previously, on the west side of the fire.

Exactly the same procedure is followed for the second half of the salmon . It is put on the east side of the fire, opposite the first half. (Follow procedure from [blank]).

While the salmon roasts all the people sing, (Song # 1). The song is sung four times, after which there is about a half hour rest. This pattern is repeated four times, so that sixteen renditions of the song are completed.

During this time a bowl (prop 7) has stood beneath each piece of salmon, catching the juice which runs off. When these bowls are full, the salmon is done.

The head shaman stands, cries "He-e-e-y", grasps the roasting stick [5] from the west side of the fire, raises it, and lowers it, crying "He-e-e-y!"

The special mat, which has been to the left or west side of the woman shaman, is picked up by her and passed to the head shaman. He puts a half fish on the mat and the woman shaman removes the roasting stick. Twelve plates of hemlock bark are ready. (Prop 8). The woman cuts across the fish halfway between each pair of sticks so that there is a stick in each piece. As each section is cut off, the head shaman holds it up and calls the name of the man who is to get it, starting with the chief and calling the others' names in order of their rank. Each piece is put on a bark dish, and the 3 assistant shamans distribute the 12 dishes, starting to the right (north) of the door and proceeding counter clockwise to the halfway point opposite the door.

Exactly the same procedure is followed for the second half of the fish, except that other names are called, until twenty four of the important men have received plates of fish.

Before the people eat, the head shaman says oratorically: "This is the rule we shall follow as long as this river flows, according to what Salmon Boy has told us of how to care for the salmon we have caught. Even for a big run of fish, we must take good care of each fish that is caught. When we finish talking, I will raise my hands; all of you must do the same. I will say "Haw---n" (to rhyme with lawn), (Salmon), and all of you say the same. When I take a piece of the cooked salmon and take a bite of it, you do so at the same time."

The head shaman and all his assistants eat from one dish. As the head shaman takes a bite, all take one. Everyone present must eat a little, so each of the important men who have received pieces distributes his share among those sitting near him.

When everyone has swallowed the first bite, the head shaman says, [6] "All right, you people may eat."[302] When all have eaten, he directs his assistants to collect all the bones and scraps, which they bring to him. He puts all the scraps on one hemlock bark plate, stands at the east side of the fire, raises the plate, and says "He-e-e-y". He repeats the cry as he lowers the plate and throws the scraps into the fire.

He says, "Get water." Any young man gests it in a bucket (prop 10a), brings it to one of the assistant shamans, who passes it around with a drinking cup (prop 10b) so that everyone gets a drink. This is so that the salmon can go back to its country.

The head shaman says, "What we have done is the rule which must be followed; no one is to waste any fish or let it lie around."

This terminates the part of the Salmon Ceremony proper which takes place on the first night. After this, the people remain in the house for the rest of the evening and do their

---

[302] [#1] Meaning that the first bite was taken ritually; the rest is eaten in the customary fashion.

individual guardian spirit singing and dancing. For this part the lower class people, who have not come near the salmon ceremony, are permitted to come into the dance house.

On the second and third nights, guardian spirit songs are sung. Only one man sings each night, assisted by all the people. The shamans have no special part of this. These songs are highly individual, and are sung on ceremonial occasions. Because they do not pertain to the salmon ceremony directly, only owl spirit song which follows was obtained from the informant; more may be obtained if desired.

A man whose guardian spirit is an owl sings songs "which the spirit has taught him," and soon a live owl appears at the smoke hole in the roof, flies down int the house, where it circles a few minutes, finally lighting on the hands of the man who owns the owl spirit. He sings over it for a while, [7] and as he sings, it appears to grow smaller, until it is small enough to fit into his hands, one of which is cupped over the other so as to hide its contents completely. He sings faster and louder and has the people beat upon planks (prop 11) with sticks to keep time with the song. He keeps time with his cupped hands, together with his whole body, but does not dance. Finally, as the people watch, he "throws" the "owl" which he has been holding into the air. It is now invisible to the people; only the owner can see it. The end of the song terminates his performance, only one man performs each evening.

On the third night another man who has a different guardian spirit performs, this many take an entirely different form.

On the fourth night the salmon ceremony is resumed. The head shaman starts to sing, (Song # 1) and the people sing with him. As he sings, he circles the fire, walking slowly. When he completes one circuit of the fire, he stops the song with a signal, (see Rule 5,) and stands in place and talks to the crowd, not about the first salmon, but "of other things".[303] Then he resumes the song and repeats the process of circling the fire while singing, then stopping to harangue the audience. This is done 4 times in all. At the end of the fourth circuit, the head shaman tells the people to beat the planks, (prop 11) very hard and fast with their sticks. He calls the 3 assisting shamans to the west side of the fire, where the decorated mat (prop 1) has been placed before the evening's ceremonies began. This mat has been covered with as many tiny downy eagle feathers (prop 12) as it will hold. The 4 shamans take it by its corners, meanwhile marking time with a sort of rapid shuffle in place, keeping time with the beating of the planks, and raise it as high as all can reach, keeping it level. It is lowered to waist height; all cry "He-e-e-y" as it descends. Three times this is done; on the fourth raise, [8] the leader gives a signal and they flip the mat up so that all the feathers go into the air. The feathers fly all over the house, landing on the audience. Everyone upon whom a feather alights is considered to be blessed.

After this, the head shaman puts the mat (prop 1) before the woman shaman, who has been in her regular place west of the fire since the evening's ceremonies began. She rolls it up, ties it in two places with buckskin thong or cedar bark[304] (prop 10), and under each of the bow knots she inserts a large fluffy eagle plume (prop 13). She hands the rolled mat (prop 1) to the leader, who raises it in the air 4 times, each time saying "He-e-e-y!" He returns it to her, and she immediately takes it to its storage place on a large shelf or platform which runs around three sides of the room at a height of about six to ten feet. It is put in a carved box, and will be kept until next year.

---

[303] [#1] The informant did not know what subject the shaman talks about.
[304] [#1] A buckskin thong is preferred.

She returns to the fire and stands to the right of the head shaman, who faces west, his back to the fire, and recites in an oratorical tone the rules for handling salmon:

"This fish is the first gift of our grandfather, we must always take good care of the salmon. We must not waste the bones, if we dry the fish, we must dry bones, gills, and all of it. If there is any part of the fish not to be used, it must go into the fire, not lie around and get flies on it. When we have eaten salmon we must drink water so that the fish may return to its home."

After reciting the rules, the head shaman turns and faces the east, raises his hands and lowers them four times, each time saying "He-e-e-y!", after which he says the following prayer:
"We bless our great grandfather because He gives us
What we are going to live on this spring.
This is his first gift
We are all very glad because we ate His first gift."

After he has recited this prayer, the ceremony is done, and all the people go out of the house. Visitors return home next day.

List of Properties [10]

1. Special salmon mat for first salmon
2. Fish spear
3. Mussel shell knife
4a, b, c. Common mats
5. Roasting stick for salmon
6. Skewers [24]
7. Bowls for salmon drippings [2]
8. Plates for eating salmon [24]
9. Head shaman's rattle
10a. Water bucket. b. Dipper
11. Planks
12. Small downy feathers
13. Large downy feathers
14. Houses [model]
15a. Canoe. b. Paddles
16. Thong to tie mat
17. Drum [text says Box ?]
18. Dance apron
19. Head-ring
20. Shirts
21. Blankets
22. Woman shaman's outfit
23. Common people's outfits

salmon
Description Of Properties
Used In First Salmon Ceremony [11]

1. <u>The Special Mat</u> This is made of split cedarbark in a checkerboard weave. It is rectangular, approximately two feet by three feet. The designs were sometimes woven in, and sometimes painted on after the mat was made. (See Fig 1, attached.) The chevron or herringbone design should be parallel to the ribs and spines of the salmon. Whenever the mat is laid down, the chevrons on the center of the mat should point upstream or north. (See Goddard, p. 46, for details of weaving.)

2. <u>The Salmon Spear or Harpoon</u> This is made of a thin, rounded shaft of rough wood about 15 feet long, with two or more tines at the end. The points, which are detachable from the tines, are fastened to a string which runs along the shaft, so that when a fish is struck, the man can play him and avoid breaking the spear (See Goddard, p. 61, for illustration.)

3. <u>The Fish Knife</u> This is an ordinary butcher knife with a steel blade. (In the old days, a mussel shell was used.)

4a, b, c. <u>The Common Mats</u> The mats on which the special mat (prop 1) is laid are of split cedarbark, and are of the same checkerboard weave, but have no decoration. All are alike, but a separate, new mat is used at each phase. They are larger than the special mat, being approximately four feet by six feet.

5. <u>The Roasting Stick</u> This is about three feet long or a little longer, is pointed and tapering at both ends, and is thicker between the middle and the lower end. This bulge is to keep the salmon from sliding to the ground, [12] which would be an omen of a smaller fish run. In cross section, the stick is flattened; this flatness keeps the fish from twisting on the stick. At its widest point, it is about 2 inches wide and 1 inch thick; it tapers to very sharp points. Red chevron or herringbone designs are pointed toward the upper end of the stick. However, the half-fish is suspended head downward while roasting. Before the ceremony begins, the head shaman prepares the hole in which the roasting stick is set. He drives a common roasting stick into the ground. He is careful to see that the ground is tightly packed around the stick. Then he removes the stick, leaving a hole just the width of the stick and just deep enough to hold the fish's weight on the roasting stick, with the stick on a slant of about 45 degrees toward the fire. One such hole is made on the east, and one on the west side of the fire.

6. <u>The Skewers</u> There are 24 skewers which hold the halves of salmon on the stick (prop 6) while roasting. They are very thin, flat cedar sticks about one half inch wide, from one eighth to one fourth inch thick, and about a foot or a little over in length. One end is very sharp.

7. <u>The Bowls</u> for catching the juice of the salmon are carved from the tap-root of an elder tree, and are about the size of a teacup. Each bowl has two salmon carved on it, one on each side, so that for two bowls there is the magic number of four. See Goddard, p. 43. They are placed below the salmon while it roasts.

8. <u>The Plates</u> of hemlock bark are flat, rectangular pieces cut out of hemlock bark (<u>Tsuga heterophylla</u>). Second choice is spruce. They are about nine inches wide and twelve inches long. The fish is served on the inner side [13]

.

9. <u>The Head Shaman's Rattle</u> Is of wood, usually alder. It is round with a straight handle, all unadorned. See Fig. 2, attached.

10a. <u>The Water Bucket</u> is of cedar, about nine inches square by twelve inches high. (or larger in about that proportion.) The handle is a wooden bar abut ¼ to ½ inch thick, a reddish brown color. This is attached to opposite sides of the bucket. See Goddard, p. 42.
b. <u>The Dipper</u> This is used with the water bucket. It is a large spoon, made of horn or wood. See Niblack, Fig. 218, Pl XLI.

11. <u>The Planks</u> These planks, upon which the people beat time with sticks, are split from cedar and are hand hewn. They are an inch or a little over in thickness, a foot or two in width, and as long as desired – ten to twenty feet. They are painted and sometimes both carved and painted with clan totemic designs. (See Goddard, p. 153, for designs on a board.) The people sit in clan groups in the house, so that all who beat on one clan plank are members of that clan. The plank is raised from the ground to give it resonance by being set on small blocks. The sticks used to beat the plank are 12 to 18 inches in length, one half to one inch in thickness, and are not decorated.

12. <u>The Down Feathers thrown from the mat</u> These are as small as can be obtained. None should be longer than an inch and a half, and if possible they should have no quills, so that they will be very light. Feathers of any bird may be used, but they must be white.

13. <u>The Large, Downy Feathers</u> These are stuck under the thongs (prop 16) which tied the special mat (prop 1). They are white, very fluffy, and from four [14] to nine inches long. This type may be obtained from the tail of an eagle or hawk.

14. <u>Ceremonial House</u> There is only one ceremonial house in the group of fishing camps along one creek, and it is usually located in the camp furthest downstream. The house, which is 40 feet wide by 80 feet long, faces east toward the stream which runs from north to south. At the two front corners of the house are totem poles facing the stream. The entire house-front may be decorated by painting. The only door is in the east end. The roof is gabled and has a square hole in the center to allow smoke to escape. Inside, the house has a hard-packed dirt floor, no benches or chairs of any kind, and a big fire in the middle. A storage platform or shelf runs around three sides, (all but the door side), at a height of six feet. It is supported by round posts six inches thick. For ceremonial houses see Niblack, Pl. XXXV; Goddard, p28.
     The other houses of the fishing camp are very plain, (see Jenness, p47; Goddard, p30) in them the people lived and, after the arrival of the salmon run, cured the fish so that it could be kept for winter use. The women cut off the head of each fish, slit it down the back, remove the backbone and entrails, and cut off the tail and fins. Then they put three or four skewers similar to prop 6 in the fish to keep it spread out flat. The skewer across the tail end of the salmon of fish is slightly larger. In the house, numerous poles about an inch or two inches in diameter are

192

laid across between two roof beams so that the poles are about eight inches apart. The slab of fish is hung between two poles with each end of the tail skewer resting on one pole. Each family has a section with many fish, so that almost the whole house is hung with fish just above [15] the heads of the people.

15a. <u>The Fishing Canoe</u> This is big enough for two men. It is NOT the birch bark canoe commonly thought of as Indian. It is made from one piece of cedar, with a high bow and stern, and has a very graceful shape. See Niblack, Figs 169 to 172, Plates XXXIII and XXXIV.
  b. <u>The Paddles</u> These are of wood, carved in distinctive shape, sometimes decorated. See Niblack, Fig 165.

16. <u>The Thong to tie the special mat</u> This is made from tanned skin of almost any animal. It is buckskin or light tan color.

17. <u>The Drum used by the third shaman to accompany all singing</u> This is of the tambourine type, about four inches deep and from fifteen to twenty-eight inches in diameter. (See Niblack, Fig 302, Pl LVII.) The single head is of rawhide with the hair removed. The drum is grasped in the left hand by the thongs which cross the back, and beaten with a stick held in the right hand. The head of the stick is padded with a little soft buckskin or fur.
     The third shaman carries the drum during the ceremony, never setting it down.

18. <u>The Shaman's Dance-apron</u> This is made of tanned skin. It reaches from the waist to just below the knees, and does not quite meet in the back. The design is painted on with red and black. (See Goddard, p162.) The ornaments at the bottom of the fringe are deer toes which have been carefully hollowed out. Pig, sheep, goat, or the toes of any other ruminant may be used if they are black and not too large. The rattling of these toes is a constant accompaniment of the ceremony. [16]

19. <u>The Head-ring of claws</u> (Fig. 3, attached) This is worn by the head shaman only; other shamans wear other types of headgear such as cedar bark rings and fur caps. (Goddard, p90). The base of the head shaman's ring is of fur, and the claws are from a grizzly bear.

20. <u>The Shirts worn by the shamans</u> These are simple tunics, with or without sleeves, but are decorated a great deal. (Goddard, p158)

21. <u>The Blankets worn by the shamans</u> These may be of several types: the best, which is worn about the shoulders by the head shaman, is a "Chilcat" blanket. (Niblack, Fig. 33, Pl. X) The next best blanket-type is of tanned skin, (moose, elk, large buck,) which has designs painted on it. The last type is a dark wool trade blanket with appliquéd red flannel designs outlined with commercial white buttons. (Niblack, Figs 175 a and b, Plates IX, X, XIX).

22. <u>The Woman Shaman's Costume</u> This is a skirt of shredded cedar bark, (see Goddard, p80), and a blanket decorated as elaborately as any of the male shamans'. She may wear earrings of long (10 inch) bunches of shells and wool yarn, white, yellow, or blue-green, (Goddard, p80), and a head-ring of cedar bark.

23. <u>The Costumes of the Common People</u> These are much like the shamans' costumes, but less elaborate. Goddard, p90 and p125, gives some pictures which will be helpful IF the time of the ceremony is to be after the advent of white traders, except that all neck-rings in the pictures should be left off. If the action is to take place before the advent of white traders, no cloth save the native-woven mountain-goat wool blankets and shirts [can be used.]

Rules For Ceremonial Procedure [18]

1. The head shaman lifts his hands to arm's length above him with his palms forward, and as he lowers them cries "he-e-e-y!" very slowly. Only the arms move; the body remains erect. All the people do the same thing at the same time except where otherwise noted.

2. The salmon's head is always toward the north, which is upstream. When carried, it should go head first.

3. Cutting the salmon. The woman-shaman who cuts the fish kneels with her buttocks on her heels, facing north, on the southwest corner of the (common) mat (prop 4c) which is on the west side of the fire.   She holds the knife (prop 3) in her fist so that her thumb is at the top, and the blade points down. She cuts from south to north along the belly of the salmon, beginning at the vent. She cuts it into two separate halves. To do this, she must cut to one side of the bones. She cuts to the side nearest her, so that, since the fish is lying on its back, the bones are left in the salmon's own left or port side. The port side is cooked first. The skin is left on the salmon, and the inside, meaty part of each half is cooked first. There is no prescribed method for removing the entrails, which are put in the hemlock bark container (prop 8) and disposed of with the bones [in the fire.]

4. The skewers (prop 6) are thrust into the fish laterally. As they are inserted, they are worked over and under in such a way as to have alternate skewers above the roasting stick, the others below. A little of each end of a skewer is left sticking out at the sides of the fish, as these ends later afford convenient handles for the pieces of fish. Protruding ends are broken off (at the point end, which is dangerously sharp.) The skewers hold the [19] fish flat and keep it on the roasting stick.

5.   To stop the song, the head shaman holds his index finger pointing upward, above his forehead, and moves his hand and forearm slowly from left to right during the last part of the song. As it comes to the end of a phrase, he lowers his hand straight down the front so that the finger describes a 180 degree arc in front of him. It starts pointing upward and ends pointing downward.

Books Cited For Reference [20]

Goddard, PE Indians of the Northwest Coast American Museum of Natural History, Handbook Series # 10, 1934 $.75

Jenness, Diamond   The Indians Of Canada.   National Museum of Canada, Bulletin 65, Anthropological Series # 15 $2.00

Niblack, AP The Coast Indians Of Southern Alaska and Northern British Columbia. Annual Report, U.S. National Museum, 1888 Washington, 1890.

E-Mails

"Bill Holm" bholm@u.washington.edu
 jaymiller4@juno.com
Subject : RE: Roger
Date : Sun, Apr 22, 2012 11:04 AM
Subject : RE: Roger

Roger's movie research couldn't have been for "The Silver Horde," since that film was made in 1930, when Roger was 16 years old. It must have been for *Spawn of the North*", as I remembered him telling me, which was made in 1938, when Roger was 24, and a student at UW. His research was probably done a year before that. I met him either in 1938 or 39, but he probably told me about his film research some time after that. I guess I will have to get a video of the film and see just what they did with his information! Roger was adamant that they distorted his information, not only that the sequence was so short. I also remember that he was annoyed that they used a Japanese actor to portray the main Indian part!

From: "Bill Holm" <bholm@u.washington.edu>
To : <jaymiller4@juno.com>
Subject: RE: Roger
Date: Mon, Apr 23, 2012 11:52 AM

Jay, I guess I'd like to know what your project with the Ernesti, etc. material is! As for the "list of properties," there are no such things at the Burke. As far as I know, Roger never assembled such material for the film, his list was only suggestions and sources in the literature, and not actual collected specimens. I doubt that Annis knows a lot about Roger's early activities. She was a good and patient wife for him in his old age, but was not deeply involved with his special interests, as Avie, his first wife was. I knew all his wives and his mother, his father, Richard, died before my time. Both his father and his mother, Ethel, were painters. Roger's father had a sizable collection of Indian material and painted Indian subjects as well as landscapes. His mother mostly painted landscapes as far as I know. I one time did some drawings for here for a little children's book she planned to do on the 18th century painter Benjamin West. I don't think anything ever came of it.
I'd like to know more about your project. Bill

From:"jaymiller4@juno.com" jaymiller4@juno.com
To : bholm@u.washington.edu
Subject : RE: Roger
Date : Mon, Apr 23, 2012 01:27 PM

It is convoluted and complicated, with Roger a side interest. For over a decade I've been working with 3 notebooks at UW from Jerry Meeker with the most detailed info we have from a single village in Puget Sound, at Minter across the Narrows Bridge, where Jerry's mother's family were the leaders. The scribe of the notebooks never put his name in them. Years ago I set a goal to ID him, and eventually I did, thru Arthur Ballard stuff. Along the way, i asked everyone I could think of who this guy might be. Wayne was alive and interested, but had no clues. When I asked you, somehow it led to Roger. Vi had old, old friends in Yakima so I drove her over to visit them while I went to visit Roger, and, while he could not help with the ID, he asked me to look for his Nass mss, which we found and sent to him. I transcribed it a decade ago and got feedback that became the first note. I'm still working on the Minter book, but as I told Vi, when she passed I'd clean up and finish up various projects we started, and Roger is a holdover from that. Now I have to wonder if he let me tape our interview. It will take a search. How would you feel about letting me tape you about Roger to add to the value of this mss? best

Moieties and Cultural Amnesia:
Manipulation of Knowledge in a Pacific Northwest Coast Native Community

Abstract

The privileged, possession and manipulation of knowledge help to maintain and. perpetuate the status of elites in a society. The mixed Tsimshian + XaiXais Kwakiutl village of Klemtu, British Columbia, provides a vivid example; over the past three generations, its elite has managed to transform two co-existing tribal divisions into exogamous, matrilineal moieties, suppressing and modifying traditional knowledge and symbols to accord with recent and present needs and conditions. Recent fieldwork documents these processes and the concurrent ethnogenesis of Klemtu as a community.

The possession and transmission of knowledge are cornerstones of every human culture. Once laid, however, many different structures can be built upon it. Field, workers are particularly likely to become familiar with the manipulation of knowledge.[305] Whether they are consciously aware of the process as it is happening, in hindsight it becomes quite obvious. Nevertheless, the fragmented character of many North American tribes has precluded in-depth studies of not only this manipulation but also of the more general features of any Native sociology of knowledge. My own experience suggests that throughout Native America, knowledge, especially supernatural and esoteric knowledge, was and is equated with power. The kind of power was both religious and public power and the latter was and is equated with life, especially a long and successful life. For Caddoan-speaking Great Plains tribes. Holder (1970: 42, 43) found that the knowledge associated with village bundles or power packs was retained by a priest. As his life lengthened, the priest transferred his knowledge to an apprentice over a considerable period of time. As the priest did so, his power was expected [b] to wane until the last of the information was transferred and he died. Suttles (1967: 171) reported that among some Coast Salish peoples, members of the elite had honorable family trees, a repertoire of respectable hereditary names, and wealth reflecting successful ties to guardian spirits which were all incorporated in a body of closely guarded knowledge, usually called "advice" that was passed on within these elite families.

Among the Owikeno or Rivers Inlet Northern Kwakiutl, severe population losses left many hereditary names, crests, and privileges in abeyance, fostering a "black market" in them among neighboring tribes. However, names, crests, and privileges as such could not be sold to those not related to the Owikeno. Hence, what was sold were not the items themselves but rather the necessary knowledge to claim them successfully. For tribes of the northern Pacific Coast, this kind of knowledge takes the form of hereditary sagas which "contain much detail such as names, descriptions and events which supposedly only a rightful heir could know. Above all they contain detailed references to local places which no alien or false claimant could conceivably duplicate" (Olson 1967: 110). Some Owikeno are said to have sold such sagas

---

[305] For help and cooperation during my past and present research, I thank Chief Tommy Brown and Chief Johnny Clifton and the Neasloss and Hill families. Partial funding for my fieldwork came from the Melville and Elizabeth Jacobs Fund, University of Washington.

which authenticate some prominent but not paramount names. The new owners then validated their claims by potlatching to an assembled group of guests and reciting the sagas. The Owikeno "sellers" would often use their gains to bring out and potlatch other ranking family names for their own use. [25]

Figure 1 ~ Klemtu Village and surrounding area

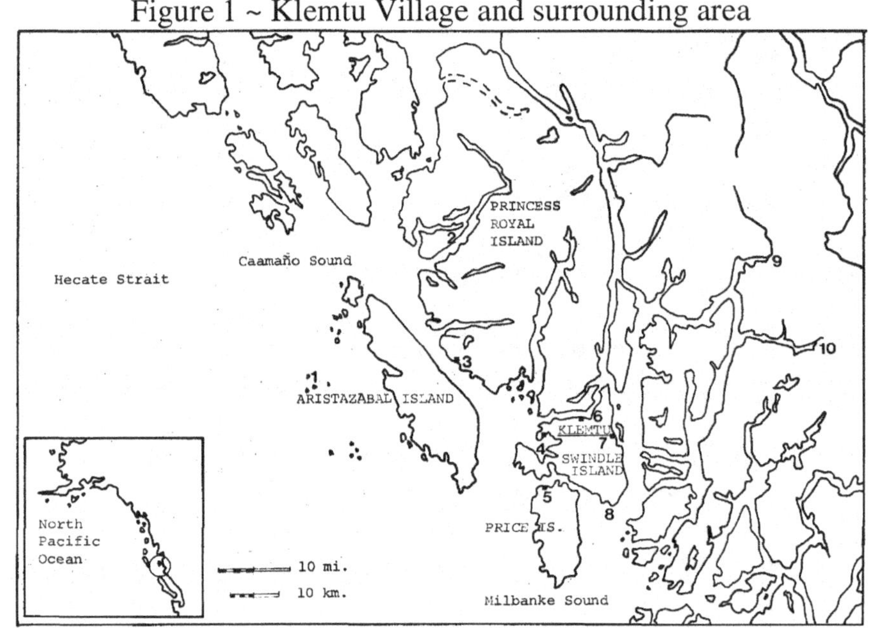

MAP KEY: A ~ Aristazabal Island = *Kndıs* B ~ Princess Royal Island
C~ Swindle Island D ~ Price Island = *'Kjidu*

1 *ıngʷınaks* = "there~where you are taken down", a bay in the Moore Islands beneath which is the underwater house of the Chief of all the Blackfish ~ Killer Whales.

2 Surf Inlet, border between the Gitisdzu tribe and the Gitqa'at tribe of Hartley Bay.

3 *Kdisdzu* village site on Laredo Channel, location of the grand house "ten steps down".

4 *Kınmʌxł* = "there~where you go over", village site at the head of Parsons Anchorage on Kitasoo Bay from which there is an easy portage into Higgins Passage.

5 *Kuxʷi* = village site on Higgins Passage.

6 *Klubʌłxk* = village site in Meyers Narrows, with the place called *Wılubʌkʷs* = "there~where there are Sasquatches" at the sandy beach in the narrowest part of the passage with high cliffs on each side.

7 Klemtu = contemporary village on Trout Bay, Swindle Island.

8 Jorkins Point = *Kındu•lalʌsk* in Southern Tsimshian , *mali•t* in XaiXais, a sacred area where there is a hole in the rock through which people who are ill or unfortunate can pass for four consecutive days to be totally cured or lucky..

9 Poison Cove on Mussel Inlet, the site of a XaiXais village.

10 Kynoch Inlet = the site of the other XaiXais village.

These Caddoan, Salishan, and Kwakiutl examples serve to illustrate how the manipulation of knowledge, through traditional and untraditional means of transference, sustains the maintenance of elites in a society. The formal stratified societies of the Pacific Northwest rely heavily on the privilege possession of knowledge, particularly as mythological information.

Recently, I have encountered yet another example of the manipulation of knowledge to perpetuate the status of an elite. This Pacific Northwestern example, drawn from the mixed Tsimshian and XaiXais Kwakiutl community of Klemtu, British Columbia, is especially fascinating because the manipulation was intended to forge rather than to maintain a tribal continuity. Such an intent is particularly characteristic of the Pacific Northwestern culture area and, thus, provides further insights into the cultural dynamics of the entire region.

Klemtu Village

Klemtu (# 7) is a village of about 250 inhabitants drawn from at least two XaiXais villages (# 9, 10, map) and from at least four Kitisdzu Tsimshian villages (# 3, , 5, 6, map). The XaiXais are a division of the Northern Kwakiutl. Both they and the Kitisdzu had been much reduced in numbers by the time that they settled together at Klemtu. Olson (1955: 344) sets the data of settlement at about 1875. The location was selected because it was a harbor sheltered by Cone Island, and on the steamship route, so that the early inhabitants could earn, at first, vouchers, and then money by supplying firewood for the steamship boilers. The conical shape of the island inspired the village's earlier name, China Hat. The name Klemtu is derived from The Tsimshian name for the site: Ktemdutxk, "concealed, blocked, or hidden passage". This is said to refer to an earlier practice of passing along the outer shore of Cone Island until someone discovered that Cone Island was separated from Swindle Island by Klemtu Passage. The native terms for some of these features will be given as part of a discussion of the mythological issues involved in the inter-tribal rivalry.

Despite visits from linguists and anthropologists over the years, Klemtu has appeared only in distributional studies. No one previously has visited Klemtu to learn its functioning as a community in its own right. Its role as the meeting place between the matri-llneal societies of the northern coast and the ambilateral societies of the central area has [b] not been fully appreciated, although it has been consistently mentioned by several of the fieldworkers who have visited the village in the past (Olson, Drucker, Rigsby). More importantly, however, is the fact that these researchers and others visited the village without learning that it is the last refuge for an unreported Tsimshian language, called *Sküüks* by the Tsimshian and Southern Tsimshian by the linguist John Dunn.[306]1 During 1976, I was with Dunn in Hartley Bay, the southernmost completely Tsimshian village. At that time the teachers in the Hartley Bay Tsimshian language program arranged for Dunn to meet a Southern Tsimshian speaking woman from Klemtu. In June of 1977, I was able to visit Klemtu and renew contact with her. I was interested in learning the social context of Southern Tsimshian. I collected contrastive Coast and Southern Tsimshian vocabularies from her and met informally with four of her close relatives. Southern Tsimshian currently survives as the privileged heirloom of these five individuals.

---

[306] Actually Dunn and I have found that earlier scholars introduced the term Southern Tsimshian, sensing a distinctiveness about the communities of Klemtu, Hartley Bay, and primarily Kitkata that my research has borne out. Among those using the term were Barbeau, Benyon, and Olson. Simonsen (1973) uses it in his archaeological report at a site near or at my map location # 5.

While my contact was initially through the Hartley Bay school, it proved extremely serendipitous. I had suspected that this woman was a member of the hereditary class of Tsimshian nobility, but, after a few days in Klemtu, I began to realize that she was a member of a rather more exalted elite. Her sister was married to the hereditary Kitisdzu Tsimshian leader of the village, while she herself was married to the possessor of what is probably the ranking XaiXais name. My contacts were thus with the elite members of both the Kitisdzu and XaiXais tribes. Especially helpful throughout my research was a close XaiXais relative who was an ordained United Church minister and a knowledgeable source on Klemtu history and traditions.

Working closely with these informed people of high rank gave me a model of Klemtu very different from that in the available literature. I began to ask myself how other field-workers could have missed an entirely new Tsimshian dialect and have overlooked some profound changes in Klemtu social organization. An answer presented itself with sudden clarity. I had entered Klemtu under the aegis of the Tsimshian, but all other fieldworkers had gone to Klemtu specifically to seek out and interview a remarkable XaiXais man who was [26] widely known up and down the coast as a reliable and prolific source on the traditional culture. His repute is actually international since he has worked with American, Canadian, and Dutch researchers. I too was referred to him by the XaiXais in the village, and I found him to be a superb professional informant.[307]2 But like all professionals he has a bias, which is to present XaiXais in the most favorable way possible. He has devoted his life to the task of collecting and dispersing data about his culture and society. In 1923 he watched Franz Boas record information on the Bella Bella from the equally venerable William Gladstone (who continues in 1977 to be a repository for Bella Bella traditional knowledge). This experience gave him his first awareness that an Indian language could be written down or that his "culture could be preserved on paper". He was unable to go to a boarding school, which he still regrets, but given the hostile and repressive attitudes such schools had toward Native traditions, it is perhaps fortunate that he was spared his education. Instead, he left Klemtu and went to live with relatives in Bella Bella from whose home every day he rowed across to the community school. There he learned to read and write, and there, too, he was affected by the Boas-Gladstone consortium.

He later returned to Klemtu where he did some fishing, in addition to interviewing the elderly at all opportunities. He seems to have memorized the information rather than written it down. He has published several brief accounts of the local culture in newspapers. His closest ties were with Bella Bella (Heiltsuk), XaiXais, and Owikeno peoples of the Northern Kwakiutl. Although he is related to many Tsimshian, they seem to have guarded much information from him. He was evidently unaware of the existence of Southern Tsimshian in his own village; even so, he provided me with both the XaiXais and Coast Tsimshian names for many in the vicinity of Klemtu. He asserted that the XaiXais had prior claims to the area on Swindle Island and farther east, but he recognized prior Kitisdzu claims to the islands in the vicinity of Laredo Channel.

---

[307] As he is now dead, I am at liberty to reveal that this XaiXai man was the remarkable William Freeman. He is long overdue for tribute which should include an obituary in some scholarly journal.

Northern Kwakiutl and Tsimshian
Tribal Locations and Crest Groups

According to Olson (1955: 344), the Bella Bella term "XaiXais" means = "people of the down (north) coast," and they occupied at least two winter villages: Kai'net in Kynoch Inlet [b] (# 10, map), and *Le'yuk* in Poison Cove (# 9, map). They also used several summer camps or villages: *Kwi'ıtu ~ Kuwi'h* in Marmot Cove across the channel of the modern town of Butedale at the northern limit of XaiXais territory; *Kʌtsu'ɬ* in a bay on Sarah Island across the Swindle Island; and *I'xwʌh* in Hikish Narrows. Olson also mentions an unnamed summer camp on Ivory Island and a possible winter village called *Sxayala'x* = "rapids full of kelp on which the animals run" on James Island just north of the narrows in Griffin Passage.

Boas (1916: 480) and Olson (l955: 344) report three XaiXais matrilineal crest groups:

Raven:
>Crests: raven, starfish, sun, sun's box.
>Chiefly Names: Tcau't, Kuwi'h = "raven"], Tsu'tsʌLawʌh = "black like dead
>>embers", A'tgaiyʌhah.

Eagle
>Crests: thunderbird, large dancing-hat.
>Chiefly Name: Ni'nkmasuh = "people going by in the night". A tale in Boas
>>(l932: 143) links this name with Kynoch Inlet.

Blackfish:
>Crests: killer whale, Sea Being ~ Blackfish chief, sea lion.
>Chiefly Name: Gʌ'sxʌ= "sour", Gun<u>x</u>not, which means in Tsimshian
>>= "surreptitiously makes himself heard."

According to the founding myth or legend told to Olson in 1935 or 1949 and to me in 1977, after a disastrous raid, the XaiXais were re-established at Kainet village by a brother and sister pair of the Raven group. Incest has ever after been a XaiXais prerogative in times of distress and need. This myth is also the reason given for the occasional breaches of crest group exogamy.

The XaiXais source in Klemtu mentioned earlier specified Moss Pass as the boundary between XaiXais and Bella Bella territories and attributed specific chiefly names to particular localities. The summer camp of *ku-wih* was across the channel from Butedale (see *Kwi'itu ~ Kuwi'h* above). Its Tsimshian name was *ksid ks* = "diarrhea" for the red berries eaten there. The associated chiefly name was *nankumasu* = "traveling at night" because the original chief used to capture and kill travelers. ("He had the hobby of killing people, like Idi Amin," my source said.) As above, this is an Eagle name probably associated with Kynoch Inlet. The village is locally famous because a Sasquatch mother and child once lived there.

At *t'gək^was* on Swanson Bay the chief was called *tutu'ʌ* = "star". According to the [27] XaiXais version, a possessor of this name was the first to camp at Klemtu.

At *kai'net* the chief's name was always *če•čelawah* = "'blackness of the raven" and with it also went the stewardship of Kynoch Inlet and environs. This is the Raven name "black like dead embers" listed above.

All of my sources agreed that Surf Inlet (# 2, map) was the traditional boundary between the Gitisdzu and the Kitqa'at Tsimshian currently living at Hartley Bay on Douglas Channel. The Gitisdzu claimed the inlet and the Kitqa'at had the islands just north of it.

Boas (1916: 483), Garfield (1939: 173), and others have consistently reported four matrilineal crest groups for the Tsimshian:

> Gispudwadwa ("?"):
>> Crests: blackfish, grizzly bear, fire-weed, mountain goat.
>
> Ganhada ("?"):
>> Crests: raven, frog, starfish, bullhead, abalone bow, scalp with wings.
>
> Lasskik ("on the Eagle"):
>> Crests: eagle, beaver, halibut.
>
> Laxgibu ("on the Wolf"):
>> Crests: wolf, bear, crane.

I learned only two Gitisdzu chiefly names in current usage. Lʌgaxni'itsk = "looking from side to side" refers to the watchfulness of the original chiefly possessor of this name who also had the habit of waylaying travelers, "like Idi Amin". The possessor seems to have proprietary rights to the red berry patches at Butedale. *Nislɔ'ɔs* = "grandfather of *lɔ'ɔs*" is the highest ranking Gitisdzu name, associated with the primary winter village of Kdisdsu (# 3, map).

At Klemtu these two chiefly names did not seem to be associated exclusively with any of the four crest groups mentioned above, although on the basis of background knowledge and past experience I came to Klemtu expecting to find four Tsimshian and three XaiXais crest groups. I assumed this during much of my fieldwork, and thought it confirmed by two carved headstones in the cemetery representing a killer whale fin, grizzly bear, and eagle. Yet my Klemtu sources did not verify the existence of these crest groups, a fact which I at first attributed to a desire to protect or guard their hereditary privileges from outsiders. Such suspicion was unwarranted on my part, actually I had fuller cooperation from noble families than I realized. A very reliable source insisted that in Klemtu all Tsimshian were Blackfish and that XaiXais were Ravens. Tsimshian and XaiXais informants all agreed that this was the case.

Further inquiry eventually provided four kinds of evidence showing that the Klemtu elite has managed over the past three [b] generations to create exogamous moieties from the former tribal divisions. The evidence comprises: 1) data on genealogies and arranged noble marriages; 2) an incident that occurred just before the dedication of a new community hall in the fall of 1976; 3) the sweatshirt selection in the Cooperative Band Store; 4) the statements of members of chiefly families that they have been deliberately "forgetting" many of the former names, crests, and privileges in the interest of protecting them, while at the same time they have perpetuated the most important ones within matrilineal exogamous moieties. I will consider each kind of evidence in turn.

First, as my genealogies clearly indicate for noble families and suggest for other marriages, XaiXais have been marrying Tsimshian in Klemtu because the rule has been for

Ravens to marry Blackfish. Most of the older noble people I spoke to had had such marriages arranged for them several decades ago. Children would tell me that they were. Raven of Blackfish depending upon whether their mother was XaiXais or Tsimshian. Those who did not know their affiliations when I first asked about them, later said they belonged to the moiety and tribe of their mother. In one case, the mother had been adopted and so was not positive of her own moiety and tribe, but after reflection she said confidently that since her husband was a XaiXais then she had to be a Tsimshian Blackfish. Even in the absence of clear genealogical data she seemed to assume the existence of exogamous, matrilineal moieties.

The second line of evidence relates to events associated with the new community hall. Several people told me that the community came to the brink of disaster in the fall of 1976 when the new hall was about to be dedicated. The white contractor, wanting to protect an inside wall, had a local artist, who happened to be a XaiXais Raven, paint a large design on it. The man painted a blackfish because it best filled the available space. When local people visited the hall the day before the official opening celebration, many Ravens were outraged and threatened to boycott the event. With visitors about to arrive from far and near, the community would have lost "face" if it were found to be torn with dissension. The elected town chief, who holds the Tsimshian name of *Nislɔ'ɔs*, convened a band council meeting in the new hall and managed to diffuse the anger by appealing to everyone's civic pride. The Ravens intend to paint a raven somewhere in the hall, but as yet this has not been done.

The third line of evidence comes from the sweatshirt crests. It is currently fashionable on the Northwest Coast for Native children to wear T-shirts with their family crests printed on them. The school in Hartley Bay has had [28] such T-shirts made for the children of the four crest groups in the village. At Bella Bella, the Heiltsuk names for each of the crests are printed 'below the emblems on the T-shirts. The Cooperative Band Store in Klemtu offers only sweatshirts with Blackfish or Ravens on them. I was made decisively aware of the Klemtu moiety system when I noted the care with which my Tsimshian host made sure that I selected a sweatshirt with a Blackfish design on it.

The fourth bit of evidence presented itself only on the day preceding my departure when my Tsimshian host said that village nobles could recall many Tsimshian names but they were making a conscious effort to "forget" them so that "those Ravens" could not lay claim to them. Given the marriage situation in Klemtu, "those Ravens" would have Tsimshian Blackfish fathers and thus might have some valid claims to the names. As noted earlier for the Owikeno, it is not the names themselves which are coveted, but rather the mythic accounts that validate the names and proprietary rights to associated songs, dances, crests, and resource areas. As strong members of the United Church, the claimants are unlikely ever to activate the full array of associated privileges, but the link between names and resource areas has continued to have ethnic and economic value even though the Klemtu men have also been passing hereditary claims to traplines for fur-bearing animals through patrilineal inheritance. The conflict between matrilineal and patrilineal claims has created some interesting political solutions in Klemtu, the most intriguing of which was transmission of the Tsimshian *Nislɔ'ɔs* chiefly name to its current holder, who was adopted as a "sister's son" or "nephew" by his own biological father. The Tsimshian arranged this because he was a stronger and more effective heir than either of the actual "sister's sons." The action was decided while the son was quite young, because he initially held the boys' name of *Gwʌsday'is* = "? + kelp" which always precedes the later bestowal of

Nislɔ'ɔs. It is my impression that the Tsimshian are the slightly more dominant group in Klemtu, and that this manipulation of the rules of succession was intended to maintain their position. My assumption about Tsimshian strength is based largely on the ability of the Tsimshian town chief to create a dramatic dance enacting the moribund myth of the visit of his chiefly ancestors to the undersea home of the Blackfish Chief of Wealth (# 1, map) and to have it performed at the dedication of the new community hall.

Significance of Place Names near Klemtu

Because Klemtu fishermen use traditional place names over their radios to give their compatriots an edge over the white fishermen in locating salmon runs, I will refrain from being too specific about the names except to note that here too the data were manipulated during my inquiries.

From my earliest arrival, I was specifically interested, in place names because I wanted to know the geographical distribution of Southern Tsimshian. My initial plotting included at least six distinct localities with the same name and two other localities which also shared a name even though they were on different islands. When I located someone who could translate the two terms, I learned that they were respectively Tsimshian and XaiXais words, *KsaxʌSamn* (Tsimshian) and *aniuesʌ* (XaiXais), with an identical meaning, "place of spruce trees", because it had been noticed that spruce trees grow well and abundantly at sites of former human occupation. I originally assumed these were general descriptive terms applicable to any such site. As time went on, however, various people began to "remember" that these spruce groves had other names which were also descriptive – so descriptive, in fact, that I realized why they were initially withheld. Most traditional place names indicate with particular clarity the type of resource found there. A few examples of the score that I collected include the following Tsimshian names:

spʌkwhan = "deer trail"

xtɪlmasɔ• = "there~where they get sockeye"

kɪnbi•nts = "there~where they get wild rhubarb"

knmalid = "there steethead"

ktnwatsa = "there~where you get otters"

kta'ɪla = "?seal"

Other place names are generally descriptive of local terrain, such as

gɔ'ɔpsunʌx̲ = "double entrance")

gopsʌnsex̲ = "double mouth" both for Helmcken Inlet on Princess Royal Island.

lʌɫgɔ'ɔt = "little heart" for island # 220 near Cann Inlet.

Very rarely do the terms refer to events or experiences. I could learn of only three:

x̱ʌsmɫa'am = "block with the knees" refers to a small island in Higgins Passage across from the opening to the lagoon on the northern end of Price Island. When the island was attacked by enemies (Haida?), there were so many people that they sat around the shore of the island to form a human blockade touching knee to knee.

kɪnsahay•da = "there~where it is mad as a Haida" was given as an alternate name for

kɪnsahay•lp = " ? " which was called Steven Point on early charts and is Dallain Point on present ones. The older speakers [29] said this was not the proper Tsimshian name and preferred the latter one, but agreed that the turbulence in Laredo Sound might suggest such an etymology.

wɪlubʌk^{w}s = "where there are Sasquatches" in Meyers Passage (# 6, map) has complex associations. It is a sandy beach surrounded by high cliffs. As it was explained to me, the name refers to the whistle used during fall ceremonials at this location. I infer from this that it was the Gitisdzu *spaksuut* = "fall place" or a locus for autumn games and rituals much as Port Essington was for the Coast Tsimshian villages. This is not to deny that the Klemtu people believe in Sasquatches (the legendary Big Foot). On the contrary, they quite honestly regard, them as North American apes. No one has ever explained to them that there are no (reported) North American apes. Since Sasquatches are said to whistle, eat fish and shellfish, and reside locally, this place name served to warn away unwanted visitors. The reason the site was selected for the *spaksuut* was that the shrill whistle sounds could reverberate off the surrounding cliffs.

Myth and Ritual

This leads us to a consideration of surviving myth and ritual as well as new ritual in Klemtu. Since becoming Methodists -and members of the United Church of Canada, Klemtu people have forsaken potlatches, winter ceremonies, and masked dramatizations. They have replaced them with feasts, Sunday services, and athletic competitions (especially basketball games). A few of the more traditional noble families formerly would pay someone in the category of father's sister to pierce the ears of a young girl and give her a hereditary name. The last such occasion I was told about was 30 years ago. Today a family will sometimes give a token payment to a "father's sister" at the time that a girl has her ears professionally pierced by a doctor or a jeweler. Slightly more frequently a "father's sister" will give gifts to various people "to wrap up the animal" when her "brother's son" makes his first kill. Some modern Tsimshian nobles use their knowledge of the Bible to exalt their positions much as I suspect knowledge of hereditary stories, events, and myths was used formerly. An example of this is the use by a high-ranking woman of the Tsimshian version of "Amazing Grace" as a personal crest privilege.

The village of Klemtu now sponsors two annual events. In May it usually hosts Sports Days which encourage athletic competitions. Since 1976, the village has also selected a Salmon Queen in July, which seems to represent a secular revival of the earlier First [b] Salmon Ceremony. For these past and present fisherfolk, salmon has always played an important economic and symbolic role.

But probably the most striking aspect of Klemtu's links with its Pacific Northwest Coast past is in its inhabitants' pervasive use of traditional myths in the political arena. While there are Tsimshian names for their traditional island locations and XaiXais ones for their mainland and island sites, places immediately around Klemtu have both Tsimshian and XaiXais names. Both local tribes have their own versions of how their ancestors killed a sea monster in Finlayson

Channel with the help of some courageous mythic birds. After the victory, their ancestors' canoe capsized and turned to stone, becoming Cone Island. The bailer slipped from the canoe to become Jane Island just to the north: *laxhačixʌtsa* (Tsimshian), *xalkɛlis* (XaiXais) = "Jane Island" ~ "a bailer."

In traditional Northwest societies, such myths served to minutely describe the terrain and to confer access and privileges to property and resources that they mentioned by means of the names held by the myth characters and their unbroken line of heirs. The existence of both Tsimshian and XaiXais place names for the same sites (see also # 8, map) means that each tribe can assert its own prior claim. This has not led to much open hostility because of a tacit agreement that the Gitisdzu have rightful claims to certain areas around Laredo Channel (# 3, 4, 5, 6, map) and elsewhere (# 1, map), while the XaiXais claims are mainly on the coast (# 9, 10, map). In practice, everyone in Klemtu can and does use both areas.

The distinction between the Tsimshian and XaiXais descendants at Klemtu is perhaps most finely drawn with regard to their differing charter myths. The XaiXais as Ravens claim the ubiquitous cycle of the trickster-transformer called Raven. Everyone knows the myth, but it rightfully belongs to the XaiXais in Klemtu.

Of greater significance for the entire northern Pacific Coast are the Tsimshian claims to the epic story of a visit to the undersea home of the Killer Whale Chief in a bay of the largest of the Moore Islands (# 1, map). This myth is specific to the Gitisdzu and is considered to be the charter and the source for all of the Blackfish crests of the Coast Tsimshian (Boas 1916: 483). According to Tsimshian traditions, many of the Tsimshian once lived together in *Temlaxam* = "Prairie Town" on the upper Skeena River near the modern town of Hazelton, British Columbia. Most Tsimshian crests are thus traced back to common ancestors from Prairie Town. The distinctive nature of the Gitisdzu is indicated [30] by the independent origin they claim for the Killer Whale crests. The Tsimshian town chief currently has in his possession a tape recording made by an old woman who seems to have been the adopted daughter of the chief named *Nislɔ'ɔs* who first settled in Klemtu about 1875. The tape recounts the Killer Whale myth in Coast Tsimshian, naming only three of the four men in the canoe:

Tsʌqʌmsekɪsk = "to pull" as an anchor
Wi•dimas = a red, stringy seaweed that grows on rocks)
Q'ay'i•t = " ? "

From another source (XaiXais) I learned what may be the name of the fourth man:

Ni•smu•t = " ? "

Boas (1916: 846, 1932: 119ff) published several versions of this myth. The most informative one for our purposes (Boas 1932: 124) specifies a Gitisdzu origin, and includes names for three of the four canoemen can be related to the names on the tape:

Dzagamsi'kisk = "dragging along the shore"
Wungawat = " ? "
Txəgat = "man-eater"

206

These three men are called brothers while the fourth canoeman, when he is included in the myth, is an unnamed man claiming the Eagle crest. After the death of the sea monster these men return to a place called *A'ntas*. They recover their wives by killing the men who had married them during their absence, and then introduce the new dances, crest, and house pattern they had acquired from the adventure. Unless *A'ntas* is a Heiltsuk name, the closest Tsimshian equivalent to it that I know is a variant of the name for Aristazabal Island = *'Kndis ~ (k)ntɩs*, an unusually vague location for a Northwest Coast myth. I can, however, specify one place which was likely to have been associated with this mythic return, although it is known by another name.

All of the Tsimshian names of the canoemen are currently held by Gitisdzu men living in Klemtu or the nearby communities of Kitimat and Bella Bella. The intrepid crew of the myth had closely observed the style and construction of the house of the Blackfish Chief and built a replica of it on their own. The present Tsimshian chief at Klemtu insisted that the house was constructed on the northern shore of Laredo Sound. That may have been the case originally, but archaeological evidence is lacking.

Accounts of the myth in Boas (1932: 124) and as told to me, indicate that the house had ten levels or stepped tiers excavated into the floor and that grizzly bears were carved at the lower ends of the four support posts.

While the corner posts have fallen, the remains of a house "ten steps down" are the dominant feature at the abandoned village of Kdisdzu (# 3, map). It is possible to infer from this that the most important chiefly name given to the canoemen was that of *Nislɔ'ɔs*. It remains the ranking Gitisdzu chiefly name at Klemtu.

Conclusions

At this point it seems advisable to summarize the discussion so far. I had gone to Klemtu to investigate the social context of the unreported language called Southern Tsimshian, and found myself in the midst of a fascinating social process whereby two unrelated tribes, one Gitisdzu Tsimshian and the other, the XaiXais Bella Bella, were fusing through the creation or at least the reorganization of matrilineal exogamous moieties, one being Blackfish and one Raven. The mechanism being used is the suppression of certain kinds of knowledge by the members of elite families. From the evidence of previous ethnography and genealogies, at least three generations ago the Gitisdzu had four crest groups and the XaiXais had three. Over the past two generations, these distinctions have been reduced at Klemtu to the most common denominators of tribal identities. Given the evidence of known village rivalries, sweatshirt crests, and personal statements, it appears that all Gitisdzu now inherit Killer Whale membership matrilineally just as the XaiXais inherit Raven membership. Thus we are led to ask how and why the present situation came about in Klemtu. I will suggest answers for each of these in turn.

Most sources report four crest phratries for the Tsimshian, but ongoing work strongly suggests that these units are the outcome of the historic amalgamation of various Tsimshian tribes and villages into missionary communities. Among the upper Skeena Tsimshian (the Gitksan) who have remained in their pre-contact villages, Adams (1973: 23) reports moieties for each village composed of Frog-Raven and one other crest group. At Hartley Bay, the Wolf crest group is subsumed under that of the Blackfish. As indicated earlier, the terms for the Wolf and

Eagle crests are readily translatable, which suggests that they are more recent in origin than the largely untranslatable terms for the Killer Whale and Raven crests. Judging by the present status of the XaiXais Eagle chiefly name, it appears that at Klemtu, Eagle has been subsumed by Raven. The present holder of this formerly Eagle name (*Ninkmasuh*) told me that he did not know his crest. For these reasons, I think that rather than speaking of phratries [31] or moieties for the Tsimshian, it is more justifiable to speak of semi-moieties:

Blackfish-Wolf

Raven-Eagle

Further support for introducing the concept of these semi-moieties is provided, by the conventions for inter-tribal marriages on the northern coast. Thus, for purposes of marriage exogamy, Haida Eagle equates with Tsimshian Raven-Eagle and Haida Ravens equate with Tsimshian Blackfish-Wolf (Boas 1916: 480). In other words, the "how" question can be answered in terms of the semi-moieties which were already inherent in the crest system.

The "why" question is more complicated. The greatest traumas in the history of Klemtu were probably felt in periods of population loss. Unlike many other Native peoples, these groups experienced little interference from Euro-Canadian settlers. The Gitisdzu and XaiXais voluntarily moved to Klemtu and voluntarily embraced Christianity. Although the Reverend Thomas Crosby managed to have the trappings of traditional rank and religion destroyed, the stratified society was left intact, so that even now the leaders in the Klemtu United Church are also hereditary nobles. In addition, Klemtu has almost always had a native Tsimshian minister. Such men were much more sensitive to and understanding of the traditional mores than a white minister might have been. Lacking alien domination, the inhabitants of Klemtu could develop their own solutions to forming an integrated society. The mechanism adopted by the elite families was the expedient of judiciously' "forgetting" almost everything not congruent with matrilineal moieties.

Contemporary Klemtu is noted up and down the coast of British Columbia as a "tough" town. When I left, some people encouraged me to reinforce that impression. To some extent, the reputation is deserved. Klemtu has only an elementary and a junior high school. Students have only been going out of the community to high schools in Vancouver, British Columbia for the past few years. When they return to Klemtu for the summer, they introduce some disruptive ideas and behaviors. Also, hostility is always seething just below the surface in the community because of the latent antagonism inherent between descendants of the two former tribes. Like exogamous tribal groups elsewhere in the world, people in Klemtu sometimes remark that "we marry our enemies."

Because of the basic antagonism in Klemtu, I began to suspect that some outside agency was involved in forcing the Tsimshian and XaiXais to work very closely together in the interests of community solidarity. As part of the discussion over the wall painting in the new community hall, I was given some incidental details on earlier town halls that [b] seemed insignificant then, but have since assumed greater importance in my understanding of the "ethnogenesis" of Klemtu. Ethno-genesis refers to the process by which a new or distinct social group-cum-identity is created.

As I presently understand it, the ethnogenesis of Klemtu involved the severe depopulation of Gitisdzu and XaiXais villages and their joint settlement in Klemtu to take advantage of the firewood needs of early steamships. Through the late 1800s Klemtu thrived as an entirely Native community with a large public hall. Presumably the Gitisdzu and XaiXais functioned as separate tribal groups with their full complements of traditional chiefs and crest groups. This would have continued until 1918 when about half of the Klemtu population died in the great influenza epidemic. The depopulation was so severe that the Klemtu survivors, with the finely tuned sense of setting so typical of the Northwest Coast, decided to tear down their large community hall and build a smaller one so their reduction in numbers would be less noticeable during public events. Presumably it was during this period that changes began which shifted emphasis from tribal affiliation toward the matrilineal, exogamous moieties. Added incentive occurred a decade later when a cannery, which functioned between 1927 and 1968, was built in Klemtu. During the fishing season when the cannery was in operation, the population of Klemtu almost doubled due to an influx of Asian, Canadian, and Native workers. These outsiders occupied the northern end of Trout Bay near the cannery. Their presence in Klemtu must have done much to encourage the further fusion of the original Gitisdzu and XaiXais inhabitants by crystallizing the matrilineal moieties (if they were not already established). The population continued to increase to the point where a new large hall was built in 1933.

While this process of Klemtu ethnogenesis was going on, several fieldworkers were in and out of the village. They cannot be faulted for their interest in data on the past, but clearly we could have benefited from observations they might have made of the contemporary manipulation of knowledge, traditional and otherwise, in Klemtu, that created the present situation. For knowledge belongs to the survivors, who use it for their sustenance and profit. Those who use it well and wisely earn elite status over time. Throughout Native America, if not the world, there is a simple equation that often goes unspecified: "Knowledge is power is life". Someone with knowledge has power (supernatural and practical) enough to live long and well.[308]3

---

[308] The most chilling example I know in [32] confirmation of this equation is of Zuni man who told Ruth Bunzel (1932: 494 # 2a) that he had given her all his knowledge and had no way to protect himself. He died two days later.

Ligeex:
A Tsimshian Dynasty

The antiquity and character of chiefs, and, in particular the high chief, of the Coast Tsimshian of northern British Columbia have been largely misunderstood by academics.[309] Each

---

[309] Tsimshian is an ethnonym deriving from *ts'm* 'inside' and *ksyaan* 'the Skeena River'. Basic sources on the Tsimshian (including Southern, Gitksan, and Nishga) include tens of thousands of manuscript pages by the Tsimshian chief William Beynon (*Gwisk'aayn*), with a few published in Marius Barbeau and William Beynon, *Tsimshian Narratives* I: Tricksters, Shamans and Heroes; *Tsimshian Narratives* 2: Trade and Warfare, John J. Cove and George F. MacDonald, eds. Canadian Museum of Civilization. Mercury Series. Directorate Paper 3, 1987.

See also Jay Miller, *Tsimshian Culture* 1997), along with Miller's Moiety Birth 1978; Moieties and Cultural Amnesia1981; Tsimshian Moieties and Other Clarifications 1981; Introduction, Tsimshian Religion in Historical Perspective 1984; Feasting with the Southern Tsimshian 1984; An Overview of Northwest Coast Mythology 1989; North Pacific Ethnoastronomy 1992.

An important source on the Ligeex line is Homer Barnett, Data from Port Simpson and Hazelton. University of British Columbia Special Collections, 1940: 3 notebooks.

General sources include Franz Boas, Tsimshian Texts, Nass River Dialect. Bureau of American Ethnology, Bulletin # 27 1902); *Tsimshian Mythology*, Based On Texts Recorded by Henry Tate. (Bureau of American Ethnology, Annual Report 31 For 1909-10, 1916): 29-1037; Marius Barbeau, Tsimsyan Songs (with 75 song texts), *The Tsimshian: Their Arts and Music*, Proceedings of the American Ethnological Society # 18, 1951: 97-157; John Dunn, *Sm'algyax*. A Reference Dictionary and Grammar of the Coast Tsimshian Language 1995); Tsimshian Internal Relations Reconsidered: Southern Tsimshian 1979: 62-82; Viola Garfield, *Tsimshian Clan and Society* 1939: 167-340; Marjorie Halpin and Margaret Seguin, Tsimshian Peoples: Southern Tsimshian, Coast Tsimshian, Nishga, and Gitksan 1990: 267-284; Alfred Kroeber, American Culture and the Northwest Coast 1923: 1-20; John Adams, *The Gitksan Potlatch* 1973); George MacDonald, The Epic of Nekt: The Archaeology of Metaphor 1984: 65-81; Stephen McNeary, Where Fire Came Down, Social and Economic Life of the Niska 1976; Ralph Maud, *A Guide to BC Indian Myth and Legend* 1982); Edward Sapir, A Sketch of the Social Organization of the Nass River Tribes 1915); Margaret Seguin, *The Tsimshian*: Images of the Past, Views for the Present 1984).

Of special note are a series of books inspired by Vonnie Hutchingson and Susan Marsden for Prince Rupert School District 52 in 1992, with the approved spelling of Ligeex used herein. 1 ~ *Na Amwaaltga Ts'msiyeen*: The Tsimshian, Trade, and the Northwest Coast Economy. Teachings of Our Grandfathers (Suwilaay'msga Na Ga'niiyatgm) 2 ~ *Adawga Gant Wilaaytga Gyetga Suwildook*, Rituals of Respect and the Sea Otter Trade, Told by Henry Reeves, Teachings of Our Grandfathers (Suwilaay'msga Na Ga'niiyatgm) 3 ~ *Saaban*, The Tsimshian and Europeans Meet, Told by Dorothy Brown, Teachings of Our Grandfathers (Suwilaay'msga Na Ga'niiyatgm) 4 ~ *Fort Simpson, Fur Fort at LaxLgu'alaams*, The Teachings of Our

held and holds a hereditary name names that is regarded as immortal by Tsimshian and their North Pacific neighbors, but it is often difficult to separate out the series of actual human holders, although the actions of each served to exalt or tarnish the fame of that name.[310] For natives, however, the _adaawx_, a sacred history precisely told by the head of a "house" (matriline) possessing its leading hereditary name, indicate that the titled name of Ligeex was held by a succession of Eagle crest (matriclan) leaders of the Gispaxlo'ots (People of Elderberry), which, through his efforts, became the foremost tribe in historic times.[311]

This name is first mentioned in adawk referring to events about five hundred years ago, but the most famous bearer, known as Old Ligeex, was active about 1800-1840 during the peak of the land-based fur trade.[312] The impetus for this dynasty seems to have been the dispensing of membership in spiritual guilds or secret orders (known as _wiihalaayt_) inherited by the founder from his Wutsdaa (Bella Bella Heitsuk) father but wrongly attributed by Marius Barbeau to Old Ligeex of three hundred years later.

> A chief bearing the name of Ligeex, apparently about 1830, was the originator of the secret societies among his band. These fraternities of mutually helpful craftsmen and raiders were his own device to break down the resistance of hostile clan chiefs opposing him and to bring about his domination among the northern tribes. They progressed the more easily among the Kwakiutls for the lack of opposition, in the absence of clans. The potlatch, an ancient system of native transactions and social entertainment, everywhere became the vehicle of new ambitions of conquest, prestige, and power.[313]

In the normal course of North Coast diffusion, such guilds had been spreading from Bella Bella, speakers of a Northern Kwakiutlan or Wakashan language, to the south and to the north, where they had already been placed among the Southern Tsimshian. By intermarrying at

---

Grandfathers (Suwilaay'msga Na <u>Ga</u>'niiyatgm) 5 ~ _Ndeh Wuwaal Kuudeex A Spaga Laxyuubm Ts'msiyeen._ When the Aleuts Were on Tsimshian Territory, Teachings of Our Grandfathers (Suwilaay'msga Na <u>Ga</u>'niiyatgm) 6 ~ _Conflict At Gits'ilaasu_, Teachings of Our Grandfathers (Suwilaay'msga Na <u>Ga</u>'niiyatgm) 7 ~ _Na Maalsga Walps Nislgumiik_, The Story of the House of nisłgumiik. Teachings of Our Grandfathers (Suwilaay'msga Na <u>Ga</u>'niiyatgm).

[310.] In keeping with its importance, the name Ligeex has no easy translation. Among Tsimshian, the more important a name, the more interpretations it has to consume time and energy. According to native sense, it means "impassability, invincibility, impenetrability, what cannot be overcome." The Ligeex spelling used herein was approved by literate Tsimshian for publications used in tribal schools and by the Tsimshian Language Authority. Europeans have spelled this name as Legaic, Legeek, Ilegauch, Illgayauch, Legaeek, or, recognizing its cohesiveness, the Illegaich Gang, but all versions have been standardized in this article.

[311.] See Susan Marsden, ms., Controlling the Flow of Furs: Northcoast Nations and the Maritime Fur Trade; Susan Marsden and Robert Galois, The Tsimshian, the Hudson's Bay Company, and the Geopolitics of the Northwest Coast Fur Trade 1995.

[312.] In a generally garbled account of this dynasty, Michael Robinson, _Sea Otter Chiefs_, Old Ligeex is called Legaik 2, but IV would be more like it.

[313.] Marius Barbeau, _Totem Poles II_ *: 765.

Kitamaat and Wudsdaa, Ligeex was able to bring these orders into the Tsimshian heartland to add to the prestige and fame of his house.

However, the murder of Old Ligeex's designated heir in May of 1839, precipitated a bitter rivalry between his own brother and nephew (sister's son, later baptized as Paul), both with claims to matrilineal succession.

Several academics, however, mostly relying on the records of the Hudson's Bay Company (HBC) trading at Fort Simpson, though built on land donated by Old Ligeex, have denied evidence of his primacy. Behind their arguments, moreover, lurks a misunderstanding of Tsimshian leadership, wrongly assuming a consistent royal imperiousness appropriate mostly to European monarchs. While impetuous and ambitious, the Ligeex line were neither tyrants nor autocrats, but rather successful negotiators skilled in the selective use of force.

For Tsimshian, a chief has, minimally, two contrasting management styles. Inheriting an unblemished pedigree from a long line of prior chiefs in the matriline, each holder of a famous name was expected to be "skilled in all things, energetic and ambitious."[314] Overall, chiefs were "able leaders, good speakers, haughty and proud before strangers, and humble and generous toward tribesmen. The ideal leader was an able organizer and speaker, and a model of good taste and conduct."[315] From a native perspective, a chief had to prove wisdom (*'wii ho'osxw*), kindness (*ammagoot*, "good heart"), and strength (*daxgyet*) in order to gain respect (*anttx'ooms*).[316]

The Tsimshianic language family is composed, in the interior, of Nishga ~ Nisga'a on the middle Nass River and Gitksan of the upper Skeena River and, downriver, of Canyon, Coast, and Southern Tsimshian. Since hard and fast boundaries are a convention only in state societies, as elsewhere in the world, Tsimshian border zones were, at least, bicultural and bilingual. Southern Tsimshian leaders were as fluent in Wakashan as Tsimshianic, while Gitksan knew Athapaskan and Nishga used Tlingit. Some of the Tsimshian chiefs spoke Haida and/or married there. Such dynastic marriages united the chiefly families along the entire coast, overarching differences of town, tribe, or parent language.

Viola Garfield, the classic Boasian Tsimshianist, estimated thirty Tsimshian tribal chiefs, each heading the major house of the tribal town.[317] While immortal names conferring rank were and are almost always male, however, in the absence of a close male heir, a woman could and did "carry" the name and was accordingly treated as a "man."

Before Christianity, each leader had four named spiritual aspects, often distinguished as sm "real." As *smgigyet* ("real people") house chiefs, they coordinated summer economic activities and conducted feasts and namings; as *naxnox* dancers, they sponsored and/or performed in fall masked ceremonials. As *smhalaayt*, with a carved frontlet on the forehead, a woven blanket over the shoulders, and a raven rattle in the hand, they initiated young people into ritual roles of the crest. As *'wiihalaayt* leader of one of the four secret guilds, they ritually confirmed the royal rank of children and adults."[318]

[314.] Viola Garfield, The Tsimshian and Their Neighbors 1966): 17.

[315.] Garfield, *The Tsimshian*, 27.

[316.] Gitsegukla History ~ *Anawkhl Gitsegukla* 1979: 37.

[317.] Garfield, *The Tsimshian*: 26.

[318.] Marjorie Halpin and Margaret Seguin, Tsimshian Peoples: Southern Tsimshian, Coast Tsimshian, Nishga, and Gitksan 1990: 279. Their Tsimshianic spellings have been updated.

Beneath these chiefs, several hundred lineage and house heads managed the societal routines and made up the nobility. Each tribal chief was advised by a council of these nobles, together with craft and resource specialists such as shamans, carpenters, carvers, painters, musicians, composers, herbalists, midwives and astronomers.[319] With the advice of these specialists, overall efforts were coordinated by the chief of the leading house of that town.

Since each Coast Tsimshian tribe functioned in terms of its constituent ranked houses, all territories and trade routes were controlled by the house chiefs. Both water and land routes were owned and defended by a house, although marriages among royalty forged trade alliances to provide access to a variety of desired resources.

In general, coastal towns specialized in various kinds of seafoods and marine goods (dried cockles, clams, grease, dried candlefish, seaweed, dried herring eggs, shells) traded to interior chiefs in return for prestigious furs, hides, and copper. Throughout the coast, potlatches relied heavily on such inland pelts, particularly of marmot.

Along with marital ties, such alliances were strengthened by exchanging names and privileges, by feasting, and by ceremonial displays. At strategic locations along inland trails, chiefs built feast houses where friendship-making (*ne-amex*) rites (a kind of *halaayt* ritual) could be held to warn against poaching.

The crucial importance of trade for Tsimshian society is further indicated by the use of seven numbering systems to readily specify the type and quantity of goods involved.[320] As merchants, Tsimshian were seasonally mobile, arguing against the proposition that seasonal rounds were post-contact phenomena in the Northwest. Based on archaeological surveys of Vancouver Island, Inglis and Haggarty suggest that the prehistoric density of town sites there indicated local control (ownership?) of all local resources, which were harvested by residents and circulated only through trade. After European epidemics and dislocations destabilized the Nuchahnulth population, however, survivors began a pattern of seasonal movements to harvest available resources in various locations.[321]

Extensive archaeology along the Skeena River and Prince Rupert Harbor indicate occupation for thousands of years leading to historic Tsimshian.[322] In particular, a dense concentration of town sites along Metlakatla Passage indicates a thousand years of joint winter residence by a dozen Coast Tsimshian tribes. In the spring people moved to the Nass for the candlefish run, rendering their trade mainstay of oolichan grease. In summer, towns moved to their territories along tributaries of the Skeena River until they all gathered together at Fall Place (*spaksuut*, Port Essington) for festivities before wintering back at Metlakatla.

Each year, summer was devoted to economic activities under the leadership of the chiefs of four crests – matrilineal clans forming semi-moieties of Orca-Wolf and Raven-Eagle.[323] Crest

---

[319.] See McNeary, Where Fire Came Down: 156, and Miller, North Pacific Ethnoastronomy.

[320.] These counting systems are distinguished as 1) general, 2) animal or flat (as pelts), 3) humans, 4) long objects, 5) canoes, 6) people in canoes, and 7) unit measures. See Dunn, *Sm'algyax*: 38-40.

[321.] Richard Inglis and James Haggarty, Cook to Jewitt 1987: 193-222.

[322.] See Gary Coupland, *Prehistoric Cultural Change at Kitselas Canyon* 1988); George MacDonald, Kitwanga Fort National Historic Site 1979; Richard Matson and Gary Coupland, *The Prehistory of the Northwest Coast*, 1995.

[323.] See Miller, Moiety Birth, Moieties and Cultural Amnesia, and Tsimshian Moieties and Other

celebrations, hosted by chiefs, were potlatches, when the *adaawx* of the household was recited and displayed on carved poles.[324] During the winter, chiefs assumed their priestly names and hosted dramatizations of their *halaayt* privileges, mostly elaborated visits to Heaven. The autumn gathering was devoted to presenting wonders, enactments of an encounter between an ancestor and a supernatural spirit (*naxnox*).

After 1830, Tsimshians relocated to a trading post and then an Anglican mission, adding to the three social classes of nobles, commoners, and slaves characteristic of the entire Northwest Coast Culture Area. Thus, historically, Tsimshian developed a fourth class of royalty, tribal chiefs who arose from the ranks of the former town leaders when heirs were placed in charge of either old or new locations. To reinforce their increased rank, royalty received initiation into one or more of the guilds and claimed new crests combining humans traits with fabulous creatures.[325]

During 1787 to 1805, the fur trade was ship-based and concerned with sea otter pelts, so coastal chiefs had the advantage, particularly the Kitkatla Orca named *Ts'ibasaa*, who served as Southern Tsimshian high chief. Another leader in an advantageous position was Txagaaxs ("World Raven," also named *'Wiiseeks*) who became a rival of Ligeex until killed during the 1836 smallpox epidemic. With the shift to beaver pelts during 1805-1825, Old Ligeex came into his own by maximizing his links with the interior.

Seeking a land base, the HBC built Fort Nass in 1831, but the site was too exposed to freezing winds. There, in particular, Ligeex benefited from the marriage of his daughter Sudaał to Dr. John Frederick Kennedy, physician and resident trader.[326] For two years, she talked to her father about a better locale until he offered his camp At The Wild Roses for Fort (Port) Simpson, built in 1834.[327] By 1840, when Old Ligeex vanished from the record, the other Coast Tsimshian tribes had each founded a neighborhood there in lieu of Metlakatla. By claiming a monopoly over the entire Skeena River, as well as ready access to the HBC, Ligeex rose to prominence

---

Clarifications.

[324] See Miller, Moiety Birth, Tsimshian Moieties and Other Clarifications and An Overview of Northwest Coast Mythology. A traditional chief had a moral and religious obligation to transform chaotic cosmic energy into socially useful power by conduiting it down his spine, ceremonial cane, or totem pole, which, above all, was the "deed" to "his" rank, name, house, and territory.

[325] See Marjorie Halpin, ms., Masks As Metaphors of Anti-Structure; The Tsimshian Crest System 1973; William Beynon, Ethnographer 1978; The Structure of Tsimshian Totemism 1984; A Critique of the Boasian Paradigm for Northwest Coast Art 1994.

[326] One source said that her mother was a Haida wife of Ligeex, but every other authority indicates that her mother was Nishga. If her mother (and very identity) had been Haida, the HBC records would have been very different. Instead, Haida traders at the fort often had to be guarded and escorted during their visits. Barnett (1940 1: 8) gives her name as Ashigiumk, with a son called Taawiis. Matthew Johnson (Barnett 1940 1: ??) recalled that Kennedy supplied his father-in-law with the first shingles, pants, and other trade specialties ever seen among the Tsimshian . At Fort Simpson, Ligeex was "boss" of the young men cutting firewood and gardening for the traders (1940 1: ??).

[327] See Helen Meilleur, *A Pour of Rain* 1980; Robert Grumet, Changes in Coast Tsimshian Redistributive Activities 1975; Managing the Fur Trade 1982.

214

over all the Tsimshian royalty, based not on his might but rather on his generosity by sharing these resources with his fellow chiefs.[328]

Outsiders, of course, saw mostly his imperious aspect, particularly his brilliant military strategies. As Chief Heber Clifton noted

> Ligeex was a most ferocious warrior and he had no respect or feeling for anybody, just like his Eagle warriors, mostly all Gispaxlo'ots. He was dreaded by all. Women from other tribes used his name in their nursery songs to instill fear into their children. The Ligeex warriors were a vicious group.[329]

Among the Tsimshian themselves, however, the Ligeex title was specially honored because of its succession of able managers, potlatch hosts, *halaayt* initiators, dynastic marriage brokers, and war lords.[330]

In contrast, academics have consistently misread statements from Henry Tate to Franz Boas about the history of the Ligeex line,[331] which need to be reconsidered carefully. In particular, because it fit with European notions of chronology, a false link was made between the Kitamaat origin of the name and the Ligeex six generations back from 1888 who painted his claim on a Nass River cliff. Therefore, the introduction of the Ligeex name, probably about five hundred years ago, was distinct from the momentum provided by the European fur trade, about 1750, to move that name into primacy. What Boas actually wrote was this:

> "Thus the highest in rank among all the Tsimshian chiefs was Ligeex, the chief of the Eagle group of Gispaxlo'ots. His family alone had the right to perform certain ceremonials corresponding to the highest secret societies of the Kwakiutl. Tradition says − and it is undoubtedly correct − that an Eagle woman of the Gispaxlo'ots tribe eloped with a Kitamaat chief (the tribe of Kwakiutl affinity inhabiting Gardner Channel), whose family assumed membership in the highest ceremonial society. After her return to the Skeena River, the woman was given the name *K'amdmaxł* ("ascending the mountain with a costly copper"). The name Ligeex is said to be a

---

[328.] In the most explicit statement about the nature of this monopoly, Matthew Johnson told Homer Barnett, notebook 1: +27, "Ligeex made a law that only one canoe per house, to control trade with Hagwilget." In other words, Ligeex regulated the trade for all the Tsimshian, specifying that each house, roughly a crest-based matriline, could send one and only one canoe to trade upriver along the Skeena with the Tsimshianic Gitksan, who in turn traded with the Athapaskan Wet'suwet'en (Bulkley River Western Carrier) whose towns included Hagwilget. Each house and canoe, of course, paid a tariff to Ligeex for this regulated access.

[329.] Barbeau and Beynon, *Tsimshian Narratives* 2: Trade and Warfare: 69.

[330.] The enormity of a full blown Ligeex potlatch is described in Garfield, Tsimshian Clan and Society: 201-204 and summarized in Miller, *Tsimshian Culture*: 86-87; while his vital role in the *halaayt* initiations of elite children appears in Volume 12, text 179, The Halait and All The Different Kinds of *Halait*, taken by William Beynon{ "Beynon, William" } in 1937 from Julia White and Mrs R Tate, now at the Butler Library of Columbia University, also Reel 3 of the set by Microfilming Corporation of America, 1980.

[331.] Boas, *Tsimshian Mythology*: 510.

Kitamaat name (perhaps from la "to go," -eg.a "behind" ?**).[332] The chief of the tribe took it after the previous hereditary chief's name, Nisbalaas , had lost its standing, because the bearer had been killed by a chief of the Raven clan and his head put up in the house of the latter."

Three paragraphs later − after describing Ligeex intermarriage with the Kitkatla royal Orca house, links with the Gitando, and remarking "I have also been told that the Gispaxlo'ots had the privilege of trade with the Gitksan, which they maintained successfully against the Hudson Bay Company until the later purchased it in 1866" − Boas added "The Ligeex who ruled about one hundred and fifty years ago (the sixth back from the year 1888) had his figure painted on a vertical precipice on Nass River, a series of coppers standing under his figure."

With greater precision, Matthew Johnson,[333] chief advisor to the Ligeexs in the early 1900s, told Homer Barnett that the grandmother of Ligeex I married the Kitamaat chief, while their daughter married *Hamdziit*, a leading Heiltsuk (Wutsdaa, Bella Bella) chief.[334] Thus this matriline became doubly empowered from the south by a Kitamaat name and Wutsdaa guilds from fathers whose paternal role in this matrilineal society was to extravagantly advancing the public career of his children.[335] Moreover, Heiltsuk chiefs had a tradition of memorialized their fame by having a "portrait" painted on a rock face.[336] Through his mother's Eagle crest, Ligeex was also allied with the Gwinhuut Fugitive Eagles of the Alaskan Stikine and Tlingit, along with the legendary Haida princess named Omen. His crests included both the Frog Hat, held on his head by two members of his father's clan, and a cane topped by a Frog, together with the Beaver Hat, which was held on Ligeex's head by a member from each of the four crests to show that Ligeex "was the highest in rank among all the clans."[337] For Tsimshian, this public act of cooperation among the four crests is regarded as proof of his primacy.

Moreover, Ligeex had many *naxnox* and *halaayt* privileges uniquely his own. One *naxnox* involved two enormous hands that reached down from the roof and lifted a man toward Heaven, while another, called Crack of Heaven, was a mask the made the house divide in two, move apart, and rejoin. His *halaayt* names included *txagaxsm laxha* (Heavenly Body),

---

332. According to Chief Gordon Robinson of Kitamaat 1956: 24-26, the name Ligeex means "overland traveler" and was assumed by Jasee (*ts'si*), a Gwinhuut Raven chief at Kitamaat whose own name had been given by his Eagle father and means "Eagle Claws."

333. Johnson was born 5 November 1855 and so was 85 when he worked with Barnett in 1940.

334. Barnett, notebook 1: 44.

335. Dr Emmon Bach, a linguist formerly at the University of Massachusetts at Amherst and now at the University of Northern British Columbia, worked on the Kitamaat version of Northern (Kwakiutlan) Wakashan with Jeffrey Legaik, who died in 1976.

336. A Beynon text (microfilm reel 2: 111-128) places this painting on the Nass, but another or duplicate also exists on the Skeena across from Port Essington, most likely sponsored by Old Ligeex to assert the claim to his Skeena trade prerogative. The original Skeena artist's name was Dzumks, although Gaya of Gitlaan later refurbished it. The basket *Dzumks* stood in and the rope used to suspend it were purchased from a Skidegate Haida chief, who made the trip home and back in eight days, for five coppers and five slaves.

337. See Boas, *Tsimshian Mythology*: 267, 272, 512.

hanatana, and *gaguliksgaax*.[338] Needless to say, these feats were spectacular beyond those of other chiefs.

The men called Ligeex participated in dynastic marriages; Old Ligeex married very well.[339] Before 1800, he wed *Maskgaax* (Meksgaax) of the House of *Saxsa'axt* of the royal Gitwilgyoots, who had sea otter beds and traded with the Masset Haida. One of their sons married into a Raven house of the Gits'iis. Next he married *A'maa'tk*, a sister of *Nisnawaa*, a leading chief of Kitselas from the House of *Senaxaat*, trading with Kaigani Haida and Gwinhuut Tlingits. One of their sons married a royal Gitzaxłał Raven with trading privileges into the Tongas Tlingit. After 1800, Old Ligeex allied with *Nts'iitskwoodat*, a niece of *Sgat'iin*, a Wolf chief of the upper Nass River. One of their daughters was *Sudaał*, who married Kennedy of the HBC, and another wed *Txagaax*, the former rival. This third wife lived well as a trader until dying in the 1836 smallpox outbreak, when the HBC provided her coffin and grave. At his apogee, Old Ligeex married *Nasełiyoontk*, also known as *Ksmgyemk* (Lady Sun), of the Kitkatla royal Orca house of *Ts'ibasaa ~ Hale*, who, in turn, wed Ligeex's eldest sister (named *K'amdmaxł* for their mother), and their Eagle son, Ligeex's heir, was named *Hatsksnee'x* (Long Fin).[340]

Through trade and ritual exchanges, the Ligeex received enormous cedar canoes from *Haida Gwaii* (Queen Charlotte Islands noted for huge cedar trees) to transport large loads of trade goods along the Skeena.

The keepers of the gateway to the furs of interior Gitksans and Athapaskans were the Kitselas at the Canyon of the Skeena. Their royal house was founded by a Fireweed from legendary *Temlaxam* (Prairie Town) with extensive kin ties. Later Githawn (Githɔn ~ Githoon ~ Salmon Man), a famous chief, founded an Eagle royal house there, fostering alliances with Ravens upriver among the Gitksan. Each spring, the Kitselas formally opened the annual trade with the Gitksan; only then could Old Ligeex impatiently begin his monopoly.

To circumvent this ritual requirement, Ligeex several times tried to vanquish the Kitselas and upriver towns. During one foray, he arrived in front of Kispayaks using the first umbrellas as a *naxnox* display to lure these townspeople into an ambush, which was brutal but indeterminant. Instead, over time, Ligeex used his own and other marriages, along with feasts, to regularize a successful alliance with the Kitselas.[341]

---

[338]. Boas, *Tsimshian Mythology*: 513, 556. See also Barnett, 1940, notebook 2: 20-21, listing five wonders and eight masks; Applied Anthropology in 1860 1942.

[339]. These marriages are contextualized in Marsden and Galois, The Tsimshian, The Hudson's Bay Company, and the Geopolitics, particularly in Figure 2 of Ligeex's prerogatives 1787-1830.

[340]. Today, Northwest natives are well aware of such parallels between the dynastic marriages of European and of Tsimshian noble houses. Royal Tsimshians specifically equate their own houses with others like the English House of Windsor, although their own, of course, are far older. It is to their benefit that Canada, unlike the US, honors such noble statuses.

[341]. Similarly, *Tsimshian Narratives* 2: Trade and Warfare has several texts about Ligeex, including the origin of his crests of the Gunhuut (Gwinhuut "fugitives", including Tlingit) branch of the Eagle semi-moiety from a conflict with the Ravens at Laxsail, Alaska (31-35), the origin of the Ligeex name and halait privileges from the Kitamaat and Bella Bella Heiltsuk (62-65, 69-75), his revenge against the Haida (66-68), conflict with the Kitselas (84-85), series of four

Yet, for all his preparations, Old Ligeex's well laid plans went awry just before he died about 1840. From 22 to 29 May 1839, a skirmish between Tsimshian and Skidegate Haida rocked Port Simpson. Among the many casualties was probably the designated heir to Old Ligeex, leaving the succession uncertain. When the old chief died a year later, his own brother (Hatsksnee'x, the proper name for the heir) and nephew (probably a boy) vied for the position with equal matrilineal claims.[342]

During this fierce rivalry, *Ts'ibasaa* tried hard to humiliate the boy, who was sagely protected by *Xiyoop*, his Eagle spokesman and guardian who once purchased the Cormorant Copper from the Haida with his own resources to best the Kitkatlas.

In time, the boy himself seems to have taken the name *Xiyoop* and continued to prove he measured up to his responsibilities. In keeping with family tradition, he married a Kitselas woman named wałk,[343] who had lived for four years in Victoria and could advise him about the ways and supplies of European fur traders.[344] He became a skilled warrior and plotted to confirm himself as Ligeex by massacring Skidegates in revenge for the lost heir. As Ligeex, he had a special house built where these Haida would be invited to a feast, trapped, and killed. Instead, however, at its completion, Niswiksunash, Gitlaan chief, threw eagle down on him in public, thereby forcing him to remain peaceful.[345] In 1865, his rival uncle was taken by the Gitando to be the Eagle chief named Sgagaweet.

Meanwhile, other major changes were taking place. Sponsored by the Church Missionary Society, Evangelical Anglicans, in 1857, William Duncan, a lay missionary, arrived from England. After devoting a year to learning Tsimshianic from Clah inside the fort, he began

---

ascendancy potlatches (92-94), chiefly contests (95-111, 118-126), staged cremation halaayt (116-117), and attempted murder of William Duncan (206-209). Other texts refer to actions by Gispaxlo'ots royal houses (213-235).

342. Old Ligeex, his brother, and his nephew should have all been Eagles through their mothers (who was also the sister of the brothers in terms of the nephew), yet this Uncle has what appears to be the Orca name of the heir to the royal house of Kitkatla, whose name is Ts'ibasaa, until he exchanged this name with a ship captain for that of Hale. Such a link to this foremost Orca house is reinforced by intense rivalry between Ts'ibasaa and the boy Ligeex in the 1840s.

343. Barnett 1940 1: + says she was the daughter of *Eks*.

344. Barnett, notebook 1: 27. While Wałk was on a visit to Port Simpson, the future Paul Ligeex decided to marry her, but she was warned that he was "mean" when drinking so she refused and escaped on the Beaver, the Hudson Bay Company steamship to Victoria, founded in 1849, where she stayed for four years, benefiting from contact with Sir James Douglas, first governor after a long career in the Hudson's Bay Company. When she returned north, Ligeex had reformed so they married. He called together the other chiefs and reported what his wife had told him about Victoria, proposing an expedition there, which took a month in 1854, opening a whole new trade network that, unfortunately, provided the route for the rapid spread of the 1862 devastating smallpox pandemic. See also, Clarence Bolt, *Thomas Crosby and the Tsimshian* 1992.

345. The downy white feathers of eagles or swans were and are scattered at native gatherings to enforce peaceful intent. Such eagle down was a pledge of legal and moral action free from any treachery. Antonia Mills aptly titled her book on the Wet'suwet'en Athapaskan neighbors of the Gitksan , *Eagle Down Is Our Law*.

preaching in Ligeex's own house until they had an angry falling out when Duncan persisted in ringing his bell during the enforced silence of the *halaayt* initiation of a Ligeex daughter. In 1862, to protect his converts, they founded a wealthy cooperative community back at Metlakatla, where Ligeex joined them and was baptized Paul Legaic.[346]   After two decades of success, however, differences with an imposed Anglican bishop drove Duncan and most of his converts to New Metlakatla in Alaska, seeking religious freedom under United States protection.

Frustrated and shamed after his Haida plot went askew, his councilors advised the soon-to-be Paul to join Duncan's community of Christian converts, where his primacy was still valued. At Metlakatla, all the houses looked the same so everyone would be equal before God, yet Paul had a house larger than the others because of his rank. Named *Walp Hawhaw*, it bore a lion head carved at its ridgepole end, and a sign written by Duncan, "This is the Lion House."[347]

While Paul played a prominent role in the Christian community until his death, over time, Duncan himself usurped the primary role of Ligeex, as evidenced by his oratorical fluency in the native language, his care and welfare for the community, and his constant industry − all traditional marks of chiefly status.[348]   Indeed, he was explicitly called "Chief."

After Paul joined Metlakatla, his councilors at Fort Simpson made his nephew Awx his surrogate among the traditional chiefs until inheriting the Ligeex name in his own right when Paul died in 1869. As Ligeex, Aux married a Kitkatla woman and potlatched a new-style milled lumber house when their first child was born in 1872. After his wife died, he moved to Victoria, where he died, perhaps also known as Paul. The Ligeex title then passed to *Marite* (Martha, Wułish), a niece, who died of measles two years later. In 1895, through his mother *Diiks*, sister of Paul I and wife of Taylor Dudoward, William Kelly inherited the Ligeex name until he died 29 September 1933. In lieu of a clear succession, the Gispaxlo'ots formed a committee of fourteen members to perform the powers of this chiefship[349] until in 1938, his son William Kelly assumed the name by right of his father adopting him as a nephew (sister's son).[350]

Against this historic native record and continuing Tsimshian regard for this great chief, several academics have argued against any primacy of the Ligeex line nor any claims to a Tsimshian chiefdom, despite two thousand of years of interactive winter occupation by allied tribes at Old Metlakatla. In particular, written reports mentioning other natives trading along the Skeena are taken as denials of any Ligeex monopoly, but this view is ethnocentric. Native sources are clear that anyone could trade along the Skeena, provided that they paid a tariff to

---

346.   See Peter Murray, *The Devil and Mr Duncan* 1985; Jean Usher, The Long Slumbering Offspring of Adam 1971; *William Duncan of Metlakatla* 1974.

347.   Barnett (1940, notebook 1: 53). Since Matthew Johnson (notebook 1: 46) also reported that Duncan jailed natives who cut down their totem poles because they attracted tourists, he may have had a similar reason for labeling such a "curio," although respect for Paul was such that he was one of the few partners Duncan allowed into his private trading company.

348.   Usher, *William Duncan*: 109.

349.   The Gitando also laid claim to some of these Ligeex powers because they had buried two prior Ligeexs.

350.   See Barnett (1940) notebooks 1: 55-58; 2: 6-10, 16. Johnson explicitly said (Barnett 1940 1: ??) that George Kelly was the fourth Ligeex he knew, listing as prior Paul, Aux, and Mather (?), which accounts for a present rival claim.

Ligeex for this privilege. Thus, while these other traders may have been seen, their payments to Ligeex were not.

In one *adaawx*, a Nishga Wolf Chief named *litux* went overland and traded so successfully with the Gitksan that he had to attempt to come down the Skeena after the spring thaw. Forewarned, Ligeex sent word to his Eagle clansmen at Kitselas that this Wolf "was eating out of my food box." Intercepted, Ⱡitux's canoes were smashed and his goods confiscated. Later, in consequence, revenge battles were fought on the Nass until peace was restored.[351] Yet, this Nishga's offense was not that he traded, but that he had the bravado to evade the tariff.

Nevertheless, Donald Mitchell, relying on existing records from Fort Simpson, has argued that the Tsimshian had "a tribal level of social complexity and that to characterize it as a chiefdom is to misinterpret its significance for an understanding of cultural evolution."

> These 13 years record at least 32 different trading excursion up the Skeena River. Seven refer only to Tsimshian trading; ten identify the traders as Gispaxlo'ots... and 15 make specific reference to Ligeex as the trader.... It seems clear that Ligeex and his group, the Gispaxlo'ots, did monopolize the Skeena River trade and that they did so for at least 30 years.... It seems undeniable that Ligeex and his people − the Gispaxlo'ots − had some kind of exclusive right to carry the fur trade up the Skeena River and into the interior. It also seems obvious that Ligeex was or became the individual of highest rank among the Metlakatla Tsimshian lineage heads. In this sense he was the "principal chief" of the Tsimshian although he may not have attained this status until the 1840s.
>
> But the contemporary observations of Fort Simpson traders make it seem most unlikely that Ligeex headed a political unit that could in any useful sense be termed a chiefdom. He ruled over no group but his own, and even there his hold seems fragile. In short, there was no chief and I would argue that the Tsimshian case provides us with no evidence of a Northwest Coast chiefdom.[352]

Similarly, after another intensive study of the written record, Jonathan Dean determined that at Fort Simpson three chiefs were most prominent: Neshoot of the Gitzaxłaał, Txaqaaxs (Wiiseeks) of the Ginaxangiik, and Ligeex of the Gispaxlo'ots, but only Ligeex survived the 1836 smallpox epidemic, in part because he was vaccinated by the HBC. As noted above, however, Old Ligeex finally coopted these very chiefs through strategic marriages.

> While Ligeex reportedly enjoyed a 'monopoly' in this time, this cannot be understood in Western terms, as a complete shutdown of all but Gispaxlo'ots commerce, but <u>might</u> have consisted of nominal control. Even after the rise of Ligeex in 1840, strangers from the Interior continued to use the Skeena to bring trade down to the fort, and the Nass river valley also continued as a very important venue. Beginning in the 1850's, the managers at Fort Simpson employed *Neshaki* − a Nishga noblewoman − to conduct the trade and transport furs from her village at Caxatan,

---

[351]. See *Conflict at Gits'ilaasu* Teachings of Our Grandfathers ~ Suwilaay'msga Na G̲a'niiyatgm # 6 1992.

[352]. See Donald Mitchell, Tribes and Chiefdoms of the Northwest Coast 1983: 60, 64.

and she continued to freight for the Company on the Nass after Ligeex left to join William Duncan at Metlakatla in 1862. By the middle 1860's *Neshaki* was even operating on the Skeena River, in Ligeex's 'backyard.'[353]

More specifically, in an unpublished study of the career of Ligeex, Dean suggested that Ligeex became more famous in memory after the name lapsed and the Gispaxlo'ots would not reciprocate with feasts, gifts, and potlatches, using past glory to justify present inactivity.[354]

Yet living memory among all the Coast Tsimshian, particularly as enshrined in the *adaawx*, makes it clear that the matriline of Ligeex high chiefs contributed to their overall cohesion during the trying times of the fur trade, Duncan's mission and flight from the Anglican bishop, and the imposition of Anglo-Canadian law and bureaucracy. Today, as all British Columbia First Nations prepare for their long overdue land claims and treaties, the name of Ligeex continues to be invoked as reminder of the superior leadership so characteristic of the Tsimshian from ancient times.[355]

Motivation

Lastly, the Ligeex climb to the top should be considered. While all chiefs were driven to excel, this line did more. Several hints indicate why. First, they were vastly and well connected. Hamdziit, the father of I, was a high ranking Heitsuk, a tribe so known for their supernatural powers that they are sometimes called wizards or enchanters. Second, the Gwinhuut Eagles were a royal house but small, so they probably tried harder. Third, the primary Gwinhuut Eagle chief among the Gispaxlo'ots before Ligeex was *Nisbalaas* , who became eclipsed. Boas wrote that a later Nisbalaas had been beheaded by Ravens.[356] Thus, to overcome this shame, the Ligeex

---

[353.] Jonathan Dean, "Those Rascally Spakaloids 1994: 77-78; ms., "My Canoe Was Full of People - But It Capsized - & all the People Lost but Myself..."

This woman (*Neshakx*, *Neshaki*, or Martha) aptly illustrates the abilities of high ranking women. She was married to *Sagewan*, the Nishga compliment to Ligeex until she left him to marry William McNeill, a Chief Trader of the Hudson's Bay Company. Her sister was married to Clah, Duncan's language teacher. His pride damaged, *Sagewan* undertook to shame *Neshaki*, sending her marten skins, accompanied by a taunting song. Not to be outdone, she sent him a fine Haida canoe. In return, *Sagewan* held a potlatch to renounce his wife. She countered by erecting a memorial pole for her deceased brother, elevating herself to the status of a Wolf chief above the pettiness of her former spouse. So there.

[354.] Dean, My Canoe was full of people: 20, made that charge that during the 1862 smallpox outbreak, "Had Legaic been the international specialist and the foremost chief as often portrayed, he should have taken steps to stabilize the situation (in spite of, or perhaps, because of, the smallpox) as semo'iget [smoogyet, real person, chief] and wihalait ['wiihalaayt, great priest], whose *raison d'etre* was to master temporal and natural powers." The *adaawx* indicate, however, that the Ligeex succession was then in disarray from smallpox and rival claims.

[355.] During my twenty years of fieldwork, Ligeex was always mentioned with such respect that people say the title is "too heavy" for anyone alive now to carry. The man most currently making a claim for this name died in January of 1997.

[356.] Boas, *Tsimshian Mythology*, 355-70. This disaster may have included the massacred of

name was advanced at a time of great stress and managed to overtake all rivals. Four, like Chief Seattle, the early Ligeexs served as an intertribal war lord for concerted Tsimshian engagements. Over time, military success led to loyalties that advanced this name among all the other chiefs.

At apex, Ligeex provided an orderly system to channel the flow of furs, power, and largesse so that these other chiefs could expect to benefit from his generosity and skill as an effective manager. Other chiefs had other prime specialties, such as *Ts'ibasaa* opening the winter ceremonial season or Sgagaweet leading the cannibal *halaayt*. Yet when outsiders were involved, all united behind Ligeex.

Acknowledgements

Study of these disparities between academic piecemeal and Tsimshian holistic treatments of Ligeex owe much to conversations with Susan Marsden, Viola Garfield, John Dunn, Christopher Roth, Ernest and Lynne Hill, Ray Fogelson, Marjorie Halpin, Jonathan Dean, and Chiefs Tom Brown and John Clifton.

---

virtually all Gispaxlo'ots chiefs, giving Ligeex even greater incentive to advance.

Ligeex, Tsimshian Chief:
A Reconciliation of Native and Scholar Views

The publication of a superb set of textbooks for use in Tsimshian schools in northern British Columbia (Prince Rupert School District 52) again raises the issue of native versus academic interpretations of history and culture. In particular, the role of Ligeex as Tsimshian "high or foremost" chief needs to be reexamined.

Ligeex, a hereditary chiefly name + title among the Eagle crest of the Gispaxlo'ots, passed matrilineally from maternal uncle to nephew, is, in particular, the subject of disagreement among scholars and natives. Scholars, thinking and writing in terms of European notions of politics, deny that Ligeex was anything like a high chief.

In recent decades, the academic understanding of the Tsimshian has improved (Miller and Eastman 1984, Seguin 1984) so the study of Ligeex involves larger issues. Generally, Tsimshian includes four divisions along the north Pacific coast and the Nass and Skeena Rivers. Near the shore were the Coast Tsimshian, ten tribes (of whom nine survive) who, for thousands of years (Matson and Coupland 1995, Coupland 1988), had summer locations along tributaries of the lower Skeena and winter neighborhoods along Metlakatla Pass. Southern Tsimshian (three tribes) lived on offshore islands and Douglas Channel (Dunn 1979, 1979a, Miller 1984b). Along the upper Nass were the Nisga'a, who moved downstream in recent centuries, and along the upper Skeena were the Gitksan.

Summer was devoted to economic activities under the leadership of the chiefs of four crests, matrilineal clans associated with Orca Killerwhale, Raven, Eagle, and Wolf. In practice, these crests formed semi-moieties of Orca-Wolf and Raven-Eagle (Miller 1978, 1981, 1981a). Crest celebrations, hosted by chiefs, were potlatches, when the adawk (sacred history) of the household was recited and shown on carved poles (Miller 1981, 1989). During the winter, chiefs took on their priestly names to host displays of their privileges known as *halaayt*, which were elaborate dramatizations of visits to Heaven. Fall, when people regathered from summer dispersal before returning to their winter homes, was devoted to the presentation of wonders, enactments of an encounter between an ancestor and a supernatural spirit (*naxnox*).

In the 1830s, the Hudson's Bay Company founded a fort on the Nass, then moved it to Coast Tsimshian lands controlled by Ligeex (Grumet 1975, 1982). In 1857, William Duncan, a lay missionary arrived from England and converted most of the Tsimshian, reestablishing a wealthy cooperative community at Metlakatla (Murray 1985, Usher 1971, 1974). Later, differences with the Anglican bishop forced a move to New Metlakatla in Alaska, seeking religious freedom under United States protection.

These relocations – to fort, trading post, and mission – fostered an elaboration of the three social classes of nobles, commoners, and slaves of the Northwest Coast Culture Area. Historically, Tsimshian also developed a class of royalty, tribal chiefs who arose from the ranks of the former town leaders. Foremost among these royalty was Ligeex.

Scholar Views

Donald Mitchell (1983), relying on existing records of the Hudson Bay Company at Fort Simpson from 1836-1866, has argued that the Tsimshian had "a tribal level of social complexity and that to characterize it as a chiefdom is to misinterpret its significance for an understanding of cultural evolution."

These 13 years record at least 32 different trading excursion up the Skeena River. Seven refer only to Tsimshian trading; ten identify the traders as Gispaxloats [Gispaxlo'ots] – the local group to which Legaic belonged of which he was head; and 15 make specific reference to Legaic as the trader.

It seems clear that Legaic and his group, the Gispaxloats, did monopolize the Skeena Rive trade and that they did so for at least 30 years (1983: 60).

> It seems undeniable that Legaic and his people – the Gispaxloats – had some kind of exclusive right to carry the fur trade up the Skeena River and into the interior. It also seems obvious that Legaic was or became the individual of highest rank among the Metlakatla Tsimshian lineage heads. In this sense he was the "principal chief" of the Tsimshian although he may not have attained this status until the 1840s.

But the contemporary observations of Fort Simpson traders make it seem most unlikely that Legaic headed a political unit that could in any useful sense be termed a chiefdom. He ruled over no group but his own, and even there his hold seems fragile. In short, there was no chief and I would argue that the Tsimshian case provides us with no evidence of a Northwest Coast chiefdom (1983: 64).

Similarly, after his intensive study of the written record, Jonathan Dean (ms.a) determined that at the site of the second fort, though the land was donated by Ligeex, three chiefs were most prominent: Neshot of the Gitzaxłaał, Tsa-qaxs of the Ginax'angiik, and Ligeex of the Gispaxlo'ots, but only Ligeex survived the 1836 smallpox epidemic.

While Legaic reportedly enjoyed a 'monopoly' in this time, this cannot be understood in Western terms, as a complete shutdown of all but Gispaxloat commerce, but might have consisted of nominal control. Even after the rise of Legaic in 1840, strangers from the Interior continued to use the Skeena to bring trade down to the fort, and the Nass river valley also continued as a very important venue. Beginning in the 1850's, the managers at Fort Simpson employed *Neshaki* – a Nishga noblewoman – to conduct the trade and transport furs from her village at Caxatan, and she continued to freight for the Company on the Nass after Legaic left to join William Duncan at Metlakatla in 1862. By the middle 1860's *Neshaki* was even operating on the Skeena River, in Legaic's 'backyard' (ms a: 33).

More specifically, in a study of the career of Ligeex, Dean (ms b) suggested that Ligeex became more famous in memory after the name lapsed and the Gispaxlo'ots did not reciprocate with feasts, gifts, and potlatches.

Homer Barnett (1940) collected information on the later history of the Ligeex line and the reasons behind the conversion of most famous name holders, who joined William Duncan at the Christian cooperative community of Metlakatla after being compromised by a rival for the title. He was baptized as Paul Legaic. At Metlakatla, all the houses looked the same so all would be equal before God. Only Paul Legaic was allowed to have a house larger than the others because of his rank.

After his conversion, Ligeex played a prominent role in the Christian community, but, over time, to a large extent, Duncan himself replaced the name-title of Ligeex as the paramount leader among the Tsimshian. Duncan's oratorical fluency in the native language, his care and welfare of the community, and his constant industry were all marks of chiefly status (Cf. Usher 1974: 109). Indeed, the Tsimshian explicitly called him "Chief."

Viola Garfield (1939: 169) reported the death of the last Ligeex in 1933, although the family generally acknowledged to hold this name occasionally mentions passing it on. They continue to discuss this possibility with the other hereditary Tsimshian chiefs because their agreement or consensus will be vital to the success of the transfer.

Reviewing only written sources, scholars agree that Ligeex did have economic, social, and ritual precedence, but not paramountcy. Yet politics, as such, was never elaborately developed on the coast (Kroeber 1923).

Native Views

After several years of consultation with Tsimshian chiefs and elders, along with scholars, the first book produced by the Prince Rupert School District 52[357] (1992: 70) says "The Gispaxlo'ots were led by several chiefs of different housegroups of different clans, but, of them all, the Eagle housegroup of Ligeex was considered the most powerful. Because of this, the House of Ligeex was considered the leading House of all the Maxtakxaata Tsimshian."

Book 4 in the series, *Fort Simpson, Fur Fort at laxLgu'alaams* (1992), explains how, after the first Fort Simpson was build on the Nass River in 1831, Sudaał, the eldest daughter of Ligeex and a Haida wife, married Dr John Frederick Kennedy, physician and trader of the Hudson Bay Company. After two years at the exposed site, Sudaal complained to her father, who offered the site of one of his camps for the second fort, built in 1834. By 1840, the winter home of all (nine of the original ten) Coast Tsimshian tribes had relocated to Simpson from Metlakatla in Prince Rupert Harbor.

It was control of the upriver trade, "combined with Ligeex's influence over who had access to the fort, that gave this group their monopoly of the Fort Simpson fur trade from approximately 1840 to 1860" (1992: 55).

During this time, the Gispaxlo'ots were the main link the people of the interior had with the new traders. Ligeex's wealth allowed him to purchase the best Haida canoes, and the largest. It was these canoes and the riches they brought from the interior that allowed the fort to thrive" (1992: 56).

Similarly, the second volume of Tsimshian Narratives: Trade and Warfare (1987a), collected by William Beynon and Marius Barbeau, has several texts about Ligeex, including the origin of his crests of the Gunhut (Tlingit) branch of the Eagle semi-moiety from a conflict with the Ravens at Laxsail, Alaska (1987: 31-35), the origin of the Ligeex name and *halaayt* privileges from the Kitimat and Bella Bella Heiltsuk (1987: 62-65, 69-75),[358] his revenge against the Haida (1987: 66-68), conflict with the Kitselas (1987: 84-85), series of four ascendancy

---

[357.] These books have now provided an "official" spelling of this name as Ligeex. Earlier records include Legaic, Legeek, Ilegauch, Illgayauch, Legaeek, and Illegaich Gang.

[358.] This text says that after being married to the Kitimat man, thereby legally entitled to his crest inheritances, the Gispaxlo'ots woman was captured and married to Humchitt, a great Raven chief at Bella Bella, the center of the wihalait or secret society priesthoods so important among the international royal families. Humchitt became the father of the first Ligeex, an awesome pedigree.

potlatches (1987: 92-94), chiefly contests (1987: 95-111, 118-126), staged cremation *halaayt* (1987: 116-117), and attempted murder of William Duncan (1987: 206-209). Other texts refer to actions by Gispaxlo'ots royal houses (1987: 213-235).

Today, Tsimshian themselves agree that Ligeex had "first say" among chiefs, indicating that he was foremost. Yet, because he was so "high," people criticized him and his line of heirs because chiefs should not get too haughty. For the same reason, rival traders delighted in thwarting his claim to the Skeena trade, as detailed in book 6 (1992) about how Litux, a Wolf chief of the Nass, tried to bypass Ligeex but got caught and plundered at Kitselas. The next year, he took his revenge when everyone came to render candlefish for oil on the Nass River.

Chiefly Styles

At base, this disagreement about the importance of Ligeex comes down to a misunderstanding of chiefly management styles. Unlike European monarchs, Tsimshian chiefs persuaded rather than ordered. The more effectively they managed the economic and religious routines of their town and tribe, the more quickly people did their bidding. By all accounts, the holders of the Ligeex name were very skilled managers. For this reason they do not fill the records of the traders or missionaries because when things go smoothly, there is little to report. Instead, what comes though the various adawk and anecdotes about the Ligeexs is that, foremost among historic chiefs, they were particularly ingenious, innovative, and ingratiating. For that reason, the name of Ligeex has a special place in Tsimshian culture to this day. Judged not by ledger entries but by involvement in Tsimshian institutions like the potlatch and *halaayt*, Ligeex was indeed great.

Chiefs

Some changes among Tsimshian began when the ship based trade arrived on the coast in the mid-1700s, but the major ones occurred when the land based forts were build in the 1830s. Tsimshian left the sites of their winter villages along Metlakatla Pass and moved to the trading post at Fort (later Port) Simpson, run by the Hudson's Bay Company (Meilleur 1980). Town chiefs appointed heirs to manage either the new neighborhood or the old town, thus elevating themselves into the role of tribal chiefs. These new ranks had to be confirmed in the old way by lavish generosity at witnessed public displays called potlatches, which now took on aspects of rivalry and confrontation so as to sort out the rankings of chiefs and their tribes.

From this melee emerged Ligeex, of the Gispaxlo'ots Eagle crest. The previous title for this tribal chief, Nisbalas, had been shamed when its holder was beheaded for insulting members of the Raven crest. An earlier disagreement with the Wolf crest has started the Gunhut migration from the Tlingit to the Tsimshian. Through potlatching, a foreign name from the Kitimat, inherited through a (captured ?) Gispaxlo'ots Eagle wife, was substituted as the tribal chiefly name (Boas 1916: 357). In the course of establishing the name of Ligeex in place of that of Nisbalas, the Gispaxlo'ots tribe moved to the forefront of the Coast Tsimshian and its chief became the high chief.

During the process whereby royalty emerged from nobility, the secret societies or *wutahalaayt* orders were borrowed from neighboring tribes and influenced by the older *smhalaayt* or "real *halaayt*" emblems of chiefly rank. In this way, the earlier triads of class and cult common to other North Pacific nations became the fourfold pattern of the Tsimshian. New crests involving humans and fabulous creatures, called combination monsters, were also being created to distinguish emerging royalty (Halpin 1984: 33).

Moreover, during these times of stress and instability, Coast Tsimshian gained confidence from their enhanced leadership. Such was the context for the angry response a Gitksan directed at John Adams (1973: 112).

When I discussed my model of the conflicts created in Gitksan society by imbalances of population and the problems of succession which result, one of my informants became furious with me: Who was I to accuse the Natives of having such problems? Didn't Whites have these same problems, too? Weren't the deaths of Martin Luther King and both Kennedys due to jealousy? Why couldn't Whites learn what the Natives had learned: that to avoid such problems it is necessary to install a king who is so high above everybody else that nobody can touch him.

Garfield (1966: 26) estimated thirty tribal chiefs for Coast, Nisga'a, and Gitksan. Each had an unblemished pedigree from a long line of chiefs, and was expected to be "skilled in all things, energetic and ambitious" (1966: 17). As a group they were "able leaders, good speakers, haughty and proud before strangers, and humble and generous toward tribesmen. The ideal leader was an able organizer and speaker, and a model of good taste and conduct" (1966: 27). Among the Gitksan, the Gitsegukla History (1979: 37) states that a chief had to prove wisdom (*wii ho'osxw*), kindness (*amma'gawd*), and strength (*dahx'get*) to gain respect (*an thlx'ooms*).

Each leader had four named spiritual aspects, distinguished as sm "real." As smgigyet or house chiefs, they conducted feasts and namings; as *naxnox* dancers, they performed in masked winter ceremonials. As *smhalaayt*, they wore a carved frontlet and robes, and "with the raven rattle as symbol of power, they initiated young people into ritual roles. The final formal named role for a leader was the *wiihalaayt* ~ 'great dancer,' the leader of the four secret societies, into which many of the people were initiated" (Halpin and Seguin 1990: 279).

There were several hundred lineage and house heads, who managed the societal routines and made up the nobility. Together with craft and resource specialists, they formed the advisory council that served each town and tribal chief. Their occupations included shamans, carpenters, carvers, painters, musicians, composers, herbalists, midwives (McNeary 1976: 156), and astronomers (Miller 1992). Each specialist had responsibility for an aspect of the world, but the overall system was coordinated by the chief of the town, assisted by heads of houses.

Since Coast Tsimshian tribes and towns functioned in terms of their constituent ranked houses, territories and trade routes were controlled by the house chiefs, who were responsible for maintaining the vitality of the traditional sacred histories. Both water and land routes were owned and defended by the house, while trade alliances were confirmed by royal marriages between households resident at the extremes of the rivers and tribal territories.

In addition to marital ties, alliances were also strengthened by the bestowal of names and privileges, by feasting, and by ceremonial displays. Thus, the name of Seeks, a relative of *Ts'ibasaa* when everyone lived at *Temlaxam* (mythical Prairie Town near modern Hazelton, British Columbia), was given to a Tlingit chief who became known as Shakes. Similarly at strategic locations along inland trails, chiefs built feast houses where friendship-making (ne-amex) *halaayts* could be held. Though based on clan and kinship solidarity rites, these particular *halaayts* were characterized by mistrust. At this ritual, a stranger was invited in, seated on a woven cedarbark mat, and entertained by a display of the host's *halaayt*, by feasting, and by gifts. Of course, in addition to forging an new alliance, the rite was also a warning about the consequences of the theft of local resources.

International Contexts

Tsimshian border zones were, at least, bicultural and bilingual. The Southern Tsimshian at Gitisu neighbored the Kwakiutlan Xaixais, before they moved together at Klemtu (China Hat). Tlingit and Nisga'a were north of Coast Tsimshian, with Gitksan to the east. While widely separated by Hecate Strait, particular Tsimshian towns nevertheless had close ties with Haida communities. In turn, some nations forged alliances with Athapaskan hunters further inland. Thus, the Gitksan traded with the Wet'suwet'en, who traded with the Kaska; the Nisga'a chief named Mountain monopolized trade with the Tsetsawt; and Tlingit chiefs contacted the Gunana (their term for Alaskan Athapaskans).

The Kitselas at the Canyon of the Skeena had a distinct identity which was fostered by their crucial position along the river. Their royal house was founded by a Fireweed lineage which departed *Temlaxam* and had extensive kin ties with royalty along the lower Skeena and at Kitkatla. Later Githawn (Githoon ~ Githɔn), a famous chief, founded an Eagle royal house there and established alliances with Ravens upriver among the Gitksan. Each spring, the Kitselas opened the annual trade with the Gitksan.

Such trade became the monopoly of the Gispaxlo'ots and Ligeex, who several times tried to vanquish the Kitselas and the Kispiox. During one foray, Ligeex arrived in front of Kispiox with umbrellas, which he used as a *naxnox* display to lure the townspeople into an ambush, but, though the attack was brutal, his victory was not complete. Over time, Ligeex used feasts and intermarriages via his daughter-in-law and other relatives to regularize alliances with Kitselas.

In general, coastal towns specialized in various kinds of seafoods and marine goods (dried cockles, clams, grease, dried candlefish, seaweed, dried herring eggs, shells) traded to interior chiefs in return for prestigious furs, hides, and copper.

Ligeex

For Tsimshian, Ligeex had a special position because of his success as a manager, host of potlatches, initiator into *halaayt*, broker of dynastic marriages, and war leader.

Boas (1916), based on fieldwork in 1888, provided important details on Ligeex, whose important crests included both the Frog Hat and a cane topped by a Frog, together with the Beaver Hat, which was help on Ligeex's head by a member from each of the four crests to show that Ligeex "was the highest in rank among all the clans" (1916: 512, 267, 272). Ligeex also claimed descent from the Haida princess known as Omen miraculously saved from the destruction of the town of *Dji'gua.* Boas (1916: 510) reported that by 1888 six men had held that title for over 150 years. The first memorialized his fame by having a portrait painted above a row of coppers on a cliff.[359]

---

[359] A Beynon text (Reel 2: 111-128) places this painting on the Nass, but either the location is wrong or it is a copy of the one that still exists on the Skeena across from Port Essington. The original artist's name was *Dzumks*, and *Gaya* of Gitlaan later refurbished it. The basket *Dzumks*

His mother, GandmaxL ("ascending the mountain with a costly copper") of this first name holder eloped with (or was captured by) a man from Kitimat,[360] whose family belonged to the highest ranked of the Wakashan secret societies. This name and privilege passed to family members of her Eagle crest.

Ligeex had many *halaayt* privileges uniquely his own. One *naxnox* involved two enormous hands that reached down from the roof and lifted a man toward Heaven (Barnett 1940: book 2: 2), while another, called Crack of Heaven, was a mask the made the house divide in two, move apart, and rejoin (Boas 1916: 556). His *halaayt* names included *txagaxsm laxha*, *hanatana*, and *gaguiksgax* (Boas 1916: 513).

The men called Ligeex participated in dynastic marriages. Each Ligeex's primary wife was a woman named *Ksmgamk*, the sister of the Blackfish chief at Kitkatla, the foremost leader of the Southern Tsimshian. In turn, this man, *Ts'ibasaa* ~ Hale, married the Eagle sister of Ligeex named after the mother Gandmaxł. Their son, Ligeex's heir, was named Hatsksneex.

Ligeex had other prominent wives from the Haida, who provided him with enormous canoes from *Haida Gwaii* (Queen Charlotte Islands), which he used to transport goods along the Skeena.

The basis for the prestige of Ligeex was his exclusive claim to trade with the Gitksan, after the Kitselas at the canyon. Among the populous coastal tribes, he dictated the trade along the Skeena River and had a boundless source of revenue.

Ligeex protected these prerogatives in various ways. He provided the land for the second Hudson's Bay Company post at Fort Simpson and his daughter married the chief factor. Yet when the company built a trading post at Lake Babine, Ligeex led warriors upriver to destroy it. The company only began to trade effectively with the inland tribes after it purchased the privilege to do so from Ligeex in 1866, providing funds probably used for his elaborate potlatch.

Ligeex's Potlatch, 1860s

One of the Ligeex hosted a potlatch, which was notable for the formality and dignity which was required because it included so many chiefs (Garfield 1939: 201-204).

A year before the event, Ligeex feasted his own Gispalo'ots tribe to announce his plans. Families offered to help and suggested which members should be named, elevated, or confirmed into higher ranks at the event. Next, he held a feast for members of his father's Raven crest to ask their help and to assign some of them to certain tasks, such as announcing, organizing, contributing particular foods, or commissioning a carving.

Meanwhile Ligeex amassed foods and gifts. When the date was set, tribesmen were sent as messengers, accompanied by a lesser chief to enhance their prestige, to invite chiefs on behalf of their towns and tribes. Arriving in front of the town, this visiting chief stood in the bow of the canoe, wearing a chilkat robe, using his raven rattle, and singing a *naxnox* song to the accompaniment of hidden whistles. He called out the name of the town chief three times,

---

stood in and the rope used to suspend it came from a Skidegate Haida chief in exchange for five coppers and five slaves, after his eight day trip home to retrieve basket and rope.

360. Dr Emmon Bach, a linguist at the University of Massachusetts, received data on Kitimat Northern Kwakiutlan Wakashan from the most recent holder of the Ligeex name there.

inviting him (and his people) to the potlatch. The fourth time, the chief responded by sending word to invite the visitors into his own house. He fed them and sent gifts back to Ligeex.

These chiefs then gathered their families and advisors to paddle to Ligeex's town, where each canoe waited in front of the beach until Ligeex's sister and other ranking women came down to greet them by dancing and singing. The sister, wearing a mask, acted as though she were grabbing one of Ligeex's *naxnox*, called All Calm Heavens, from the air and throwing it toward the guests. The arriving chief acted as though he caught it, wrestled with it, and threw it back to the sister.361 Then the canoes beached and the guests were welcomed. Chiefs, in particular, were escorted from the shore to their seat inside the house.

Inside the house, they witnessed displays of other names and spirits owned by Ligeex. After this dancing and singing, the guests were well fed. That night, chiefs stayed in homes of crest relatives. Other visitors camped on the beach, supplied with wood and food by the hosts.

The next day, a feast like a picnic was held on the beach. That night, a challenge feast was held with Ligeex boasting of his fame and belittling everyone else. Guests were seated by rank and some were singled out to receive huge ladlefuls of candlefish grease mixed with snow, brought from the mountain tops.

Ligeex's people came in dressed for war, with their hair bound up, but scattered eagle down everywhere to indicate their peaceful intent. After taunting songs and over-eating, gifts were distributed, accompanied by jokes about the shortcoming of the guests. Every item was counted out while a song was sung, the better to overwhelm the guests with the wealth of Ligeex. Many goods had been hidden behind a rear partition and these were now thrown into the room. Soon the pile was so high that the roof boards had to be removed. Ligeex taunted that he had thousands of items while other chiefs had only hundreds.

A Raven man, preassigned this task, then announced all of the names and histories that Ligeex claimed. All of his coppers[362] were shown and named. Children of Ligeex's crest were brought forward and named. Pregnant Eagle women were given the names of a boy and a girl to give to the newborn according to its gender.

While the guests relaxed, members of the tribe made a final tally of the remaining gifts. Bundles of sticks had previously been assembled to represent each group of guests, divided by house and crest. Quantities also varied by tribe, from most to least, according to a ranking from Kitkatla, the tribe of Ligeex's main wife, to the Gitlaan, a small group because most had converted and forsaken potlatching.[363]

The final day was spent giving out these gifts to chiefs, for the benefit of themselves and their tribes. Visiting chiefs and spokesmen gave speeches of thanks during a last feast. Then the hosts helped to pack all the canoes and the guests left.

Soon after, Ligeex feasted the Eagles to thank them for their help, providing gifts of food.

---

361. Among Nuchahnuulth and other nations, these greeting ceremonies seem to throw a crystal back and forth to show that powers of host and guest were equal, at least for that potlatch.

362. A copper had a rectangular lower half with a raised T shape down and across the middle. The top had a curved, flared convex surface decorated with a painted or engraved figure. Considered to be alive, coppers became emblems or wealth, vitality, and permanence after catastrophic epidemics took heavy tolls.

363. Garfield (1939: 204) gives this ranking, in her spelling, as Kitkatla, Gitzaklalth, Ginakangeek, Gitsees, Gilutsau, Gitwilgyots, Ginadoiks, Gitandau, and Gitlan.

230

Ligeex's Halaayt

In careful fieldnotes on a *halaayt* initiation, William Beynon (1937),[364] Tsimshian ethnographer and Wolf chief (Halpin 1978), was told by Julia White and Mrs R Tate how an initiate vanished at the sound of *naxnox* secret whistles and went to Heaven to "become elevated." Later, the child returned to town riding on a representation of a family crest. While this crest was inherited through the mother, the display itself was arranged by the father. Thus, the *halaayt* made use of both crest and wonder, mother and father, to create a new identity. Throughout his writings, Beynon described *halaayt* initiation as "elevation" and initiates as "elevated," calling attention to its celestial aspects.

These events were noteworthy because they involved Ligeex, the high chief of the Tsimshian during the historic period. During the first stage of initiation, called tsiik, the father of the child arranged for her or him to be elevated up (*m-nya*).

At the *halaayt* house of the Gispalo'ots, five children were cared for by paternal aunts until Ligeex arrived and threw his great *halaayt* power into them. Instantaneously, they disappeared, "ascending" to heaven (quickly hidden away by their aunts). Their parents then distributed much wealth to the guests, particularly to Ligeex.

On another occasion, as whistles sounded, a girl was led by her father's sister into the house of Ligeex, and formally seated. Ligeex came toward her singing and dancing, until, as he reached her, she disappeared. (Her aunt hid her in the back of her own house, where she was dressed in a small dancing garment with cedar bark rings around her neck and head.

Previously, craftsmen (*gitsontk*)[365] had made a big swan that could open its wings and had mounted it on a small canoe. The swan was one of the foremost crests of her father. Ligeex found a young girl to impersonate the initiate. The night before the girl came back from Heaven, the double was taken out in the swan canoe. Early in the morning, warned by blasts of *naxnox* whistles, people rushed to the beach to watch the girl's return from Heaven. Off shore, a huge swan appeared with the girl (her double) on its back, floated toward shore, opening its wings, and then suddenly sank out of sight. As the canoe vanished, the girl and paddlers swam underwater and hid behind boulders near shore.

Then, as whistles came from the hills, Ligeex, wearing a chilkat robe went into the forest and came back with the naked girl. Dancing and singing, they visited all the homes in the village, before going to the *halaayt* house of Ligeex. There, her parents gave away wealth, while the girl went into seclusion. Eventually, the whistles were heard outside of her father's house. Ligeex went inside, took the cedar bark rings off the girl, and received many gifts from her father. The girl went back into seclusion, until the woven rings were removed a second and a third time, after which the girl was free to resume normal life and play.

---

[364] Beynon (Text 179, 1937) Microfilm, Interview with Julia White and Mrs R Tate, Reel 3, Volume 12: 74-106 (Halait of Legaix).

[365] Crests, wonders, and halait each had its own type of artists. Those for the crests worked in public, but those for the naxnox spirits, both wonders and halait, worked in secret and were called *gitsontk*, people secluded. The punishment for seeing the unfinished art or laboring artist was execution.

Chiefly Allies and Rivals

The arrival of trading ships after the 1750s led to the rise of four war leaders, three of them chiefs, among the Tsimshian. Guns, clothes, and iron pots became coveted items. While Sabaen (Book 3, 1992), a Raven from Kitkatla, had the first reported encounter with a European ship near the southern end of Pitt Island, the most famous leader of the early era was *Ts'ibasaa*, a Kitkatla Blackfish chief and Ligeex's brother in law, who spent a year on a trading ship and learned to speak some English. *Ts'ibasaa*, by extension, chief of the Southern Tsimshian, eventually traded names with one of the first ship captains to visit his territory, taking the name of Hale ~ Hail, which still reigns in that town.

When he returned safely, he potlatched the new name of Hale and created a *halaayt* in which he wore a top hat, cutaway coat, and pants. He correctly realized that such "fancy" attire had prestige among Europeans and so adopted it as his own. He acquired a gun very early in the trade and used it to intimidate the Nisga'a at Fishery Bay on the Nass in order to retain the Tsimshian camp at Red Bluff for rendering candlefish oil (Marsden ms).

Early chiefs of the *Ts'ibasaa* line were haughty, as Mitchell (1981) showed in his reconstruction of the Kitkatla seasonal round for 1835, based on three diaries kept by employees of the Hudson's Bay Company. At least two Haida crests, Grizzly and Moon, were given to these chiefs by *Ts'ibasaa*, a powerful means of forging an alliance with foreigners.

Among the Gitksan, Neqt was also known for his haughty belligerence (MacDonald 1978, 1984b), but he did not survive long. From his ingenious fort among the Gitksan, he raided and terrorized widely. Known as Kitwanga Fort, a natural stone knob was artificially mounded and palisaded to protect several houses. Excavations date these constructions "from about the seventeenth century until the early part of the nineteenth century" (MacDonald 1979: vi), in other words, the fort overlaps the rise of the name Ligeex and its destruction coincided with the arrival of the Hudson Bay Company forts and the ascendancy of Ligeex. Coastal towns also had such forts where people took refuge from attackers. Often they were the cones of extinct volcanos (Dunn 1978: 97 #1873), whose rich soil was later used to grow potatos, introduced by traders, for lucrative sale to the Haida and Fort Simpson.

Neqt's mother was a Frog ~ Raven from the Nass, captured and married to a Haida chief. Later, she beheaded him, escaping as her son was quieted by sucking on the tongue protruding from his father's head. Reckless and cunning, Neqt controlled trade over a large region.

For the Nisga'a, *Sagewan* ("Mountain") arose among the lower Nass River during the 1860s. He was an Eagle and lived at Gitiks near the mouth of the Nass along the commercial routes. Eventually, he controlled the Nass River trade with the interior Athapaskans, particularly the Tsetsawt. Among Nass chiefs, rivalry focused on the height of their poles. The Wolf and Orca Killerwhale chiefs were in such fierce competition that the Killerwhale man was shot and killed. For protection, the Wolf chief allied himself with the leader of the Laxluutkst branch of the Eagles, whose chief was *Sagewan*. To mark his ascendancy, Sagewan commissioned the tallest pole on the coast, now at the Royal Ontario Museum in Toronto (McNeary 1976: 52, 141).

Later, one of Sagewan's wives deserted him to marry William McNeill, Chief Trader of the Hudson's Bay Company. She was the famous *Neshaki*, whose sister was married to Clah or Tamuks, baptized as Arthur Wellington, the man who taught Tsimshian to William Duncan. Her Christian name was Martha, but it was seldom used. Usually, she was called Mrs McNeill in the records. After her marriage, she maintained her own trading network on the Nass, extending the reach of Fort Simpson into the interior.

To shame *Neshaki*, *Sagewan* sent her a gift of marten skins, accompanied by a taunting song. Not to be outdone, she sent him a fine Haida canoe. To recover prestige, Sagewan potlatched to renounce his wife. She replied by erecting a memorial pole for her deceased brother, elevating herself to a Wolf chief above the pettiness of her former spouse (1976: 188).

Maud (1982: 55-59) mentioned that Chief Mountain converted to Christianity after his privileged ability to handle fire and red hot iron failed him. Barbeau (1951: 124, Song 27), who purchased Chief Mountain's pole after his death, records the song used to shame the former wife, *Neshaki*, although Barbeau gives her name as Weeyae and that of her brother as Neeskinwaetk.

Regrettably, these all too human qualities of great men and women are too often missing from he available literature. The highest ranking Nisga'a chiefs were left out of Sapir (1915), while Boas (1902) merely noted that Chief Mountain provided him with some Nishga texts.

In all, then, Ligeex has yet to be properly treated as "the" Tsimshian leader, nor have the leaders of the other three divisions. Ligeex may not have been as famous as Seattle, Tecumthah (Tecumsah), or Pontiac, but he too might have mobilized a chiefdom, if not a confederacy. Certainly, like them, the holders of the Ligeex name rose to preeminence as war leaders during times of threat from outsiders. His military successes offered protection to would-be allies. Moreover, the rise of the name to replace one that had been shamed certainly bespeaks a native, not an European, context for its beginnings.

As Heber Clifton noted (Barbeau and Beynon 1987: 69)

> Legaix was a most ferocious warrior and he had no respect or feeling for anybody, just like his Eagle warriors, mostly all Gispaxloats. He was dreaded by all. Women from other tribes used his name in their nursery songs to instill fear into their children. The Legaix warrior were a vicious group.

Finally, those who doubt the historical existence of a Tsimshian confederation should be reminded of the thousands of years Coast Tsimshian shared on Metlakatla Pass, when their constant interaction would have required some means of dispute resolution, particularly a leader who was the court of last resort. Such was the context in which a man grew to cosmopolitan influence among the Coast Tsimshian royalty. His Gunhut Eagles has originated from the Tlingit, his name was from the Kitimat, his *halaayt* privileges were confirmed at Bella Bella, his wives and kin belonged to the Haida, Southern Tsimshian, Gitksan, and other nations, and, most particularly, he was lavish and generous to the Gispaxlo'ots and other Coast Tsimshian.

Tsimshianic Oral Literature

Probably the oldest continuing traditional literature in Canada if not the world, Tsimshian epics-recorded by native scholars such as William Beynon and Henry Tate working with academics − have been vilified in provincial court, then, most honourably, redeemed by the Canadian Supreme Court in a 1998 legal case involving land claims (see Leslie Hall Pinder). The experience has been unique in the humanities, though not in the annals of colonialism.

The Tsimshianic language family, speakers of a linguistic isolate, perhaps related to the Penu-tian stock, consists, in the interior, of Nishga ~ Nisga'a on die middle Nass River, and of Gitksan (Gitxsan) on the upper Skeena R, and, near the ocean, of Coast and of Southern Tsimshians. Coastal Tsimshians recognize four paired clans (semi-moieties) called *Ganhada* (Raven) and *Laxsgiik* (On Eagle) or *Gispwudwada* (Orca, locally called Blackfish, Killerwhale) and *Laxgibuu* (On Wolf). Inland Gitksan and Nishga use Frog for Raven, and Grizzly ~ Fireweed for Orca.

Neighbours to the north were Tlingit, to the west Haida, to the south Wakashan speakers, and to the east various Athapaskans. For millennia, these nations interacted through trade, warfare, ceremonial exchanges, and royal intermarriages, effectively overarching differences of town, tribe, or parent language to blend oral motifs and themes:

Tsimshianic distinguishes two basic narrative types known as *maalsk*, 'tellings,' or *adaawx*, more culturally dense, rich, nuanced, and owned accounts that Natives call history, although 'sacred history' better conveys their many other-worldly aspects, as Claude Levi-Strauss made famous with the minor example of Asdiwal.

Stylistically, both narratives use repetition to underscore a main theme; to build momentum, rhythm, balance, or suspense; and to lull an audience while the narrator plans ahead. While the plot is familiar to listeners, subtleties in the word choice, along with rephrases and refrains, have provided the basis for aesthetic judgments. Text has sometimes varied with song, particularly when claiming privileges to music.

Tellings have no restrictions on time, manner, or person speaking or hearing them. They are general tales that can have moral as v/ell as entertainment value. Many involve their trickster Raven (*txamsn*), also known as Giant (*wiigyet*), who does good by both intent and mistake as well as by providing a singularly negative example. Ravenous in his appetites, he tricked the original owners out of the sun, moon, stars, tides, freshwater, and other necessities.

Indeed, ownership has been a primal feature of the Tsimshian universe and distinguishes these tellings from sacred histories, where many details of place, creativity, and individuals are manifested as the hereditary property of a noble house, the basic unit of North Pacific cultures. A house is simultaneously a cedar plank building, its membership traced through mothers and sisters, its landed estate frequented by named ancestors, and its crests − artistic treasures consisting of hats, masks, regalia, songs, dances, and other means of display − specifically explained in terms of a name in a sacred history.

Each name serves in the way that 'Arthur' does for the 'Matter of Britain,' providing a tag for events, neither solitary nor unique as with Euro-Canadians, but, according to first nations, as exemplary and worthy of repeated emulation , through subsequent generations.

Tsimshians say that people are given to names rather than the reverse because the names are immortal and each benefits a 'holder' who treats it with respect by leading an honourable and generous life. Moreover, names are said to 'live again' in another mortal body, recursively interweaving past, present, and future within an overall context of immortality. Thus, Native history is a progressive viewing of glimpses of the divine to benefit an ongoing community through public events such as feasts, ceremonies, and potlatches. So vital is this mortal/immortal connection that during and after devastating European-derived epidemics, in the absence of suitable heirs, names were passed on to pets such as dogs or to arms, legs, and other body parts of overburdened 'holders.'

Tsimshians also say 'names feed people' because each is firmly grounded in a portion of the landscape, conferring rights to all its resources. These rights were and are witnessed at validating public events to make them 'legal,' with a new totem pole providing that 'deed,' as long as that holder and name generously share that bounty with .household members and with many guests. In this manner, the immortal sustains the mortal to benefit their shared prestige.

Because the highest-ranking name holders were and are invited to every feast and potlatch, they were in a position to hear all the major epics recited in public. Their role, however, was to witness rather than to record or judge these 'other' *adaawx* for only the master of a house had the unassailable right to recite its epic, personally or, for greater prestige, via a 'hired' narrator.

While sacred histories primarily validated ownership to crests, many of these were shared among a duster of houses whose ancestors participated in die same epic events, setting them off as a subset within a clan to create clusters such as *Gispwudwada* (Orca, Grizzly, Grouse, Mosquito, Stars, Sun, Fireweed), *Ganhada* (Raven, Frog, Sculpin, Starfish), *Laxgibuu* (Wolf, Bear, Crane, Owl), and *Laxsgiik* (Eagle, Beaver, Halibut, Octopus).

Native moral and religious law demands respect toward all forms of life. Thus, while humans might use parts and pieces of other beings, the entire body could be used only by members of that particular species. *Adaawx*, therefore, carefully interdict any abuse of living things or their articulated skeletons, their source of eternal vitality, which were burned to assure reincarnation. Indeed, a primary duty of any chief, as with the leader of any species, was to become so 'evolved' as to channel such vitality down his spine (or its representation in totem pole or cane) to fructify the land of his people.

Beginning with the actions of divine Heaven ~ *laxha* in a stark and wet world that is obviously post-glacial, the most ancient *adaawx* span at least 12,000 years. Later ones sort themselves out as overlying episodes that happened relatively close to each other. Because of the past glacial conditions and present watery environment, flood stories reappear throughout the full chronology.

Any version is told from the perspective of one house so it is both personal and laudatory. reporting triumphs always but defeats rarely. Each is thoroughly 'grounded' in its claimed, consumed, and imagined landscape.

By about 8000 BCE, obsidian was being traded from Mt Edziza, north of the Stikine River throughout northern British Columbia and the Alaska panhandle. Established towns and trails (c 3000 BCE), today paved as modern highway, spread trade goods throughout the region. This trade included exotic goods supporting a ranked society much like that of modem Tsimshian.

Armour, weapons, and fractured bones from graves indicate increasing warfare. Trophy heads and rod armour imply ripples of influence from the Old Bering Sea complex (c1000 BCE) on both sides of the Pacific, which in turn had connections with Shang China (c1600 BCE), suggesting an ancestral foundation for the cultures of the Inuit, Aleut, and northern Northwest Coast.

Abroad range of foods began to narrow toward the use of shellfish (c 2000 BCE), then salmon (c 500 BCE). Coinciding with this specialization, concern with ranking restricted access to any resource as corporate property and encouraged its more intensive production, under the supervision of that leader, to benefit not just individual but also house, town, and clan prestige.

Plank houses and towns grew larger (c 500 BCE), indicating population increase, and complex woodworking tools elaborated the formline art style for which Tsimshians are famous. Social rank was indicated by differences in house size and imported goods, with the greatest house in the centre of the front row, as in historic times.

Tlingit ancestors (c AD 200) in the shadow of Asian military strategies applied them to Tsimshians, who in turn used them on Haida and various Wakashans. Slavery was almost surely one of the motivations for these attacks, adding extra labour for the elaboration of chiefly prestige.

Particularly significant among the 15 or more overlying episodes are the descent of Raven, the visit undersea to *Nagwinaks*, the revenge of the Heavenly Children leading to the founding of the great city of *Temlaxam*, the wars of *Medeek* ~ Grizzly over hundreds of years, and the rise of Metlakatla from 1,800 years ago until the 1830s, when Tsimshians moved to the trading post at Port (later Port) Simpson run by the Hudson's Bay company, entrenching strong tribal chiefs by lavish generosity at potlatches to intensify rivalry and confrontation so as to sort out overall chiefly rankings. From these tests, the Eagle crest of the Gispaxlo'ots tribe elevated the Kitimat-derived name of Ligeex to Coast Tsimshian 'high chief.'

Religious beliefs shifted when, about AD 1800, a series of Athapaskan prophets called Bini ('mind') preached a blend of European and traditional beliefs, until William Duncan, an Anglican lay missionary, settled among Coast Tsimshian, learned their language, and created a cooperative Christian community that still exists in Alaska.

Today, *adaawx*, as a basis of clans (*p'teex*) and heraldic crests, continue, while *naxnox* (masked wonders) and *halaayt* (elite privileges vested in four guilds) do not. In other words, the realm of women survived well through the power of narrative, while the realm of men did not, except as recast in biblical, Christian, particularly Anglican, ways.

Further reading: Marius Barbeau and William Beynon, Tsimshian Narratives I: Tricksters, Shamans and Heroes; Tsimshian Narratives II: Trade and Warfare, John J Cove and George F MacDonald, eds, Canadian Museum of Civilization, Mercury Series, Directorate Paper 3, 1987; Franz Boas, Tsimshian Mythology, Based on Texts Recorded by Henry Tate, Bureau of American Ethnology, Annual Report 31: 29-1037 1916; Jay Miller, Tsimhian Culture ~ A Light through the Ages, Lincoln: U Nebraska Press 1997.

2002 Encyclopedia of Literature in Canada.
William Herbert New, ed.
University of Toronto Press.

The Paideuma of 'Yankee' American Culture[366]

Abstract

Reviewing previous theories by Schneider and Hsu about the core values and categories of American culture, this paper argues for Independence (Love) Dependence as the axiomatic, dialectical opposition for this culture. The argument rests on a semiological analysis of various signs which play a prominent part in American life. The discussion also includes a consideration of the place of women in the overall system.

As alienated members of their natal cultures, anthropologists are much better at analyzing and understanding cultures other than their own. Yet, if anthropology is to claim successfully to be comparative and catholic, anthropologists must look inwardly as well as elsewhere. Not only our creditability as individuals, but also the validity of our theories demands at least this much. In this essay I will not only look but try to illustrate what is to be seen within the popular expressions of American culture, not as it is defined in various regional or racial contexts, but rather as it is defined by the dominant constituent, variously called Yankee American (as in the study of kinship) or, more recently, McWasp (middle class, white, Anglo-Saxon, Protestant).

Because anthropology has become increasingly fragmented and particularistic, the holistic perspective for which anthropology is justifiably famous needs a renewed interest. Like Humpty-Dumpty, the egg shell of culture has become scattered as everyone takes a piece for myopic analysis. However, culture is more than an adaptation, more than a set of institutions, and more than an assortment of ideas. It is a conceptual framework for structuring all of these and more. It is well and good to show this for other cultures, but very few American anthropologists have attempted to do this for their own. American culture expresses itself through them, their work, and in a myriad other ways in terms of national holidays, heroes, monsters, values, divinities, and so forth.

These external expressions, these signs or objectivized ideas, provide the subject matter for this analysis, expressing as they do the structuring of American culture. The intent is not to be exhaustive, but rather to illustrate the range of the most prominent expressions in order to substantiate their internal consistency. With these as the strongest cases, the others should eventually fall into place.

Others have made attempts in this direction, but their work has been more intuitive, psychological, or impressionistic. By focusing on common, well known expressions reflective of an underlying system, this analysis should have greater creditability with a broader spectrum of scholars. Not surprisingly, the most astute analysts of American culture in the past have been foreign born. Like all anthropologists, their position as initial outsiders gave the advantages of novelty and freshness, with a greater detachment and openness. However, once they provided

---

[366] While my inspiration was Native American, the motivation for this paper came from long, provocative conversations with Robert Odle, a master in his own right. Help was also given by Drs Larry Epstein, Koko Horikoshi Roe, and Marilyn Richen. Finally, this one is for Annie and Harry, to cite mastery.

the insights, some astute culture bearers are able to marshall more and better data for the support or refutation of their findings. The present work is intended to do just that.

The most recent and compelling motivation for all anthropologists to seek the axiomatic principle(s) guiding a culture has been provided by the work of Claude Levi-Strauss. For Levi-Strauss, the axiomatic opposition patterning all of Human Culture is that continuum with Culture and Nature as the opposite extremes. Culture is the domain of human control and expectability. Nature is the domain of disorder, if not chaos; the universe beyond the bounds of human control or understanding. Paz (1970) has poeticly characterized Culture as order and Nature as accident.

Unifying the disparity between Culture and Nature is the mediation supplied by the concept called Mind, composed of both brain and thought, of physiological processes and cultural learning. The relationships among these three notions display the characteristics of the so-called Struckon Model (Miller 1979). Analogous to the linguistic feature of "marking", mental constructs form themselves into enclosive, inclusive, and exclusive categories. In reverse order, the exclusive is the most constrained, marked, delimited, and definite of the set. The typical example of the exclusive is the concept of Culture discussed above. The inclusive is a higher order category that both includes the exclusive and contains information unique to itself. As shown above, Nature is inclusive. Finally, the enclosive is a subsuming and mediating category illustrated by the concept of Mind.

These, then, are the universal features of any human culture, irrespective of local distinctions; characteristic of all human endeavors, but distinctive of none. In order to arrive at some understanding of the organizational integrity of a culture, we need to introduce the concept of the *paideuma*, borrowed in modified form from the work of Leo Frobenius (Miller 1979). The paideuma is the apical opposition in the hierarchy of distinctive cultural features. Such paideuma are of limited number and reflect the inclusive (enclosive) exclusive relationship exhibited by Nature(Mind)Culture, Within each of these relationships, the enclosive is shown in parentheses to indicate its mediating character: I(O)E.

Without using the term "paideuma", several authors have developed models of its American representative. After summarizing their arguments, I will present a synthesis and refinement on their attempts. These presentations essentially fall into those following David Schneider and those with Francis Hsu. I will treat each group in the same sequence, moving from the leading model to an illustrative application of it, in keeping with the requirement of structuralist methodology that the Structure derive from the data rather than the reverse (Rossi 1974). Although analysis builds from data, it should never be constrained by ethnography because this functions on the conscious level and the aim of such analysis is to reach a more subliminal level, keeping in mind that to explain the facts it is necessary to rethink them in their logical order. After the previous models are summarized, I will present and "explain" a diagram substantiating such a logical rethinking of American culture in terms of its paideuma.

Schneider Congeners

Focusing on the domain of kinship from a culturological position, Schneider (1968: 52) asserts that the American manifestations of Nature (Mind) Culture are blood love) aw. The kinship opposition is between a relationship of biogenetic substance (blood) and a code for conduct(law), mediated by love as enduring, diffuse solidarity. Love, specifically as sexual intercourse within a marriage or culturally defined union, also underpins the uniting of blood and law that defines a family unit.

Moving tangentially and wide of the mark, Garretson claims inspiration from Schneider, but nonetheless keeps her analysis on the universal Nature / Culture level. While good on the historical context of the development of American ideology, she errs in treating only transformative processes in the creation of Culture from Nature: "Nature transformed by rationality results in Culture" (: 3). For example, she asserts that science transforms wilderness into abundance, work changes sinful idleness into salvation, and the US Constitution created democracy from anarchy. She virtually ignores enclosive mediators, or, as in the case of rationality, slights its function as an aspect of Mind. Love is disjointed as "two distinct kinds ... one appropriate for kin and one for nonkin" (: 19).

More to the point is the study of a midwestern town by Varenne (1977: 206), who found a dialectical tension between individualism and community, with neither dominant. This tension is diffused by the mediation of love, "an individual sentiment directed toward another person" (: 207). A child begins as all substance and no relation, but over time learns to balance these. Similarly, a group of friends begins as all relation and no substance until marriages occur within it and families are started. In this way, love creates small homogeneous groups, displaying among themselves diversity so characteristic of America in the eyes of the world.

Of these three Schneiderian studies, that of Schneider himself is the most detailed, and that of Varenne the most general, Garretson achieves a sweep of the topic in her little book that nevertheless fails to add any new insights. Yet, all these studies maintain a peculiarly limited focus that runs counter to the work of Hsu.

Hsu Congeners

The flaw in the previous work is an over-concentration on individualism. Individualism is a European development growing out of a demand for political equality. It entered America with the colonists, but has gone in its own direction. "The result is while a qualified individualism, with a qualified equality, has prevailed in England and the rest of Europe, what has been considered the inalienable right of every American is an unlimited self-reliance and an unlimited equality" (Hsu 1972: 249). (Of course, within the Yankee mold, this lack of limitations applies most directly to white males above the age of 21.) In opposition to self-reliance, Hsu places dependence as the pole that has been given the strongest negative evaluation in America.

This self-reliance / dependence relationship was also confirmed by a study of the "Little Orphan Annie" comic strip by Rhoads (1973), suggesting the vast utility of these concepts for understanding American culture and social forms.

Paideuma

Based on the preceding discussion, my cultural competence as an American, and the diagram to follow, the cultural importance of the concepts of love and of dependence can be accepted without question. The greatest danger to America, individually and collectively, is dependence, either from being lost in a crowd, on the dole as just a number, or from reliance on Arab oil, to cite only a few examples. Conversely, the triumph of America in the world stems from the scope and implementation of love as defined by Americans, to gift the world with obligations, to receive obedience ~ respect as Best and Brightest, or to submit to Ugly American.

The opposite pole is not individualism, although this is clearly a crucial value derived from an European ancestry. As noted by Dumont (1970: 4, 13) "our two cardinal ideals are called equality and liberty. They assume as their common principle, as a valorized representation, the idea of the human individual ... In England there is liberty with scarcely any equality. America has largely inherited liberty and has developed equality. The French Revolution took place entirely under the banner of equality."

Nor is self-reliance a satisfactory concept. It too expresses more widespread notions. For example, the Swahili term Harambee (literally: "pull together") is often translated as self-reliance but "The concept embodies ideas of mutual assistance, joint effort, mutual social responsibility, community self-reliance" (Mbithi and Rasmusson 1977: 12). As a word, "self-reliance" is not frequently used or emphasized in ordinary American conversation, indicating that it is not a significant category conceptually, emotionally, or linguistically, whether applied to individuals or to communities.

Having noted the axiomatic status of love and of dependence, it is only logical to assume that the opposite of dependence is its antonym of independence, but an independence with a structured context. Independence usually means privacy, options, and the freedom of choice to Americans. As Lee (1959: 75, 57) perceptively noted, an American "will brook no interference and no encroachment. He will spend his wealth installing private bathrooms, buying a private car, a private yacht, private woods and a beach, which he will then people with his privately chosen society. What incites the American individual to an answering engagement in the situation is definiteness, caliber, <u>within</u> the situation, a strong framework, "guts". Unstructured freedom, whether fenced in or not, is still namby-pamby ... Randomness, the unplanned and unscheduled, are like the despised jellyfish, and perpetuate or evoke inertia."

The profound insight in this quote, from a woman born and raised in Greece, rests on the recognition of the basic opposition between the definitions of Culture and of Nature by Americans. Culture is based on independence within a calibrated domain, on choice between structured options, on precision of a mechanical kind. Nature is the arena of dependence, lack of structure, randomness. The image she uses of a jellyfish, a formless, vague, repulsive, vegetative, mindless mass," provides the characteristics of the American definition of dependence and of Nature. This definition evokes terms like scum, slime, mob, swarm, herd, crowd, and other references to mindless, indiscriminate, amorphousness. In origin, the notion may be English, but in expression it is definitely American. Huxley (1971: 346, 350) provides a cogent statement about this "disgusting vice of herd-intoxication − of downward self-transcendence into subhumanity by the process of getting together in a mob ... Being in a crowd is the best known antidote to independent thought." In short, Nature at its most extreme is swarming, amorphous, and victimizing for Americans.

This then is the paideuma of American society and culture: Independence (Love) Dependence, where independence is exclusive like Culture and dependence is inclusive like Nature. Love is the mediator, but it has an important aspect that has been slighted previously. Love involves free choice. Ideally, "all you need is love", since "God is love," setting the role model. Love can be defined as a binding commitment based on a conscious choice, so that someone can love books, broccoli, cats, or a spouse. In fact, the need for calibrated choice that defines independence means that one must choose whom, what, and when to love.[367] Without sacrificing independence, someone can decide to restructure (but never demolish) a situation such as to create a family where love can flourish. For this reason, a married couple is not in a dependency relation, ideally. Rather, in all honesty and cultural consistency, they decide to marry and to have children. This process is what defines the character of American kinship. Similarly, we choose a president, or neighborhood, or career without fear of approaching the lack of substance or structural integrity at the dependency extreme.

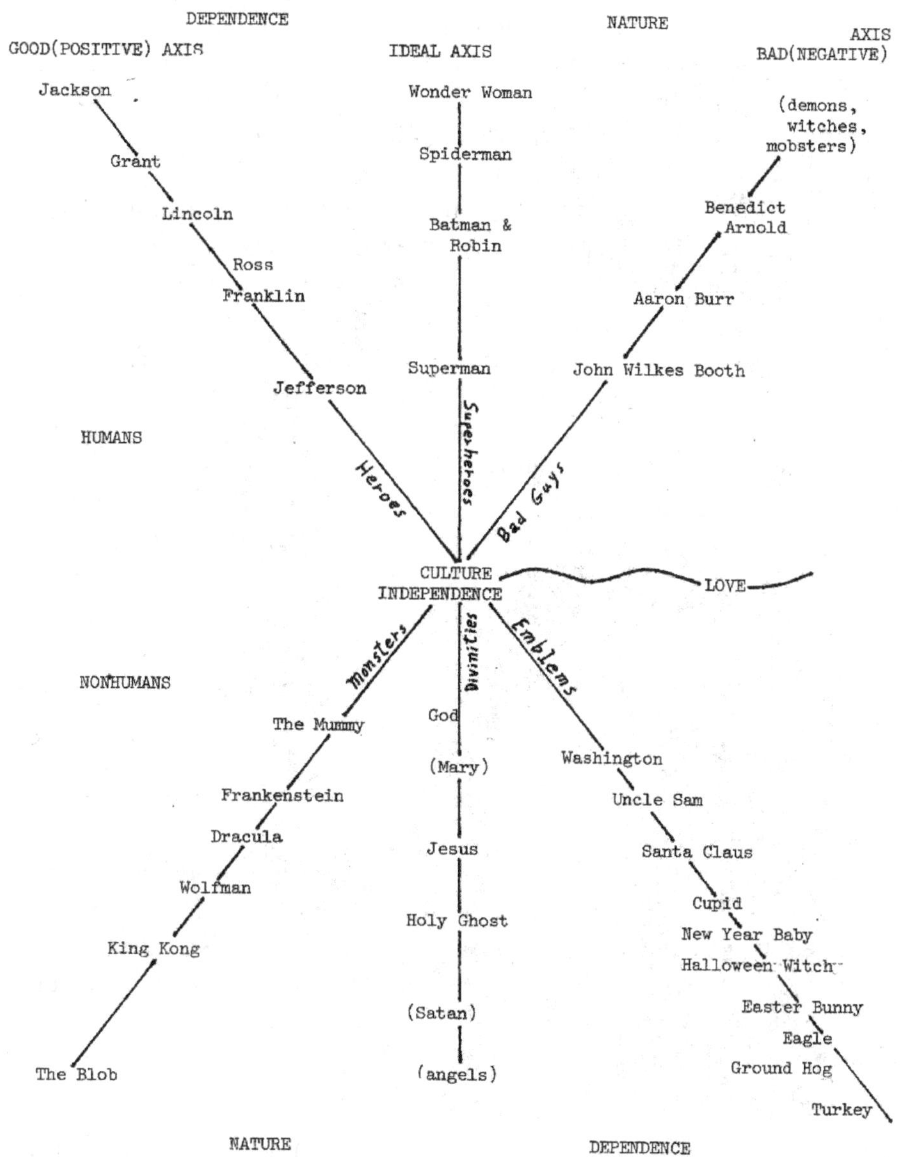

---

[367] The mediation of love actually rests on its dual character, always involving conscious choice. On a more cultural level, is love in its most refined sense, highest human(e) quality, but at the dependency natural extreme, it is nameless, faceless, ephemeral. Only Newton (1972: 112, Chapter Six title) gives this aspect of love its crude form "The Fast F--- and The Quick Buck."

As confirmation of this paideuma, we will now turn to a semiotic consideration of a diagram of some important American signs. A sign is a concrete manifestation of a concept to which it has an intrinsic relationship, herein as a way of illustrating its relative independence / dependency in American terms.

Diagram

Heuristicly, these signs can be arranged as four intersecting axes, with that of Love perpendicular to the others. These other axes consist of Bad, Good, and Ideal contexts, each with Arms on either side of the common nexus. Their shared nexus represents the domain of Culture while the vanishing extremes are form-less Nature. The cultural end coincides with Independence and the natural one with Dependence.

The position of each sign along an Arm is calibrated according to its relative state of Independence / Dependence. The Dependency extreme is characterized as formless, vegetative, mindless, viscous, and victimized. That of Independence at the extreme is the ability to make rational choices, most especially to articulate oneself within the structured choices. Most specifically, such articulation means, primarily, the recognition of the power of language for defining the world, second, the character of kinship recognition and choices, and third, an appreciation of technological precision. The data indicate that technology ranks lowest as a criterion, unless it is joined with the other attributes of language facility and kinship.

A corollary to this research has been the discovery that signs with intermediary positions along each Arm are intensely antagonistic. In efforts to control these tensions, therefore, these middle range signs receive greater prominence. Such a concern with transitional stages probably reflects the overall concern with axiomatic, impersonal, mechanistic calibration expressed throughout American culture.

The diagram developed from my attempts to duplicate the logical order of American culture in the interest of rethinking it. After listing all the signs that appeared in American culture, they were arranged into logical sets. Regardless of where or when they were used contextually, all of them together have been treated as a text. More personally, the overall model has grown out of an earlier interest in the American definition of monsters and, as a consequence, of humanity (Miller 1978). This has led to a bias toward animate signs, since apple pie as such and the flag are missing from the diagram.[368] However, these details mesh with the model and so are implicit in the analysis. Also implicit is that many (in fact, most) of these signs are European in origin, their frequency in the States is prime evidence that they are now Americanized. The placement of a sign along each Arm is based on its signature, intrinsic attribute(s) that are distinctive enough to usefully illustrate its position between the extremes.

---

[368] Although it is inanimate and outside this analysis, the American flag does have a contribution to make to our understanding. It consists of white stars on a blue field set in an upper corner with the rest of the flag filled with alternating red and white bands. The red evokes red blooded Americans and the white, Euro-American supremacy. Blue is associated with sea or sky, the edges of the continent. Within the blue, each of the identical stars represents a state in the Union. In short, the states are confined, excluded, and dependent, while the symbolism of the red and white is open ended and they are independent of each other.

The Bad Axis, Monsters Arm

As it was the first worked out, we begin with the Monsters side of the axis with Bad qualities. Most of these monsters have fictional origins in Europe, some in Africa, a few have been borrowed from Native Americans (Big Foot), but all are now Americanized. While each of them is positioned according to the signatures, as a group they all reflect negative aspects of the American definition of humanness. They are each something that a human should not be − hairy, fanged, vengeful, bloody, impulsive, or mystical (Miller 1978: 15). In addition to representing such reversals, each monster also has its own distinguishing signature.

The fate of the Mummy was sealed linguistically: his suspended state was the result of a spell intoned by members of an ancient Egyptian priesthood. His crime was choosing to love above his station in life. Frankenstein's signature is a mechanical one, as he is often likened to a machine or a weapon (Tropp 1977: 53, 92, 99, 147). His Americanization came when Hollywood directors added the famous scene in which a defective brain is sewn into the head (T77: 87), but nevertheless claimed the monster was "able to be redeemed by human love" (T77: 100, 151). Frankenstein emphasizes technology and fictive kinship with his creator and would-be bride, but the creature of both the novel (Shelley 1976) and films is doomed from the beginning by lack of choices or cogent understanding of them.

Dracula dominates this Arm because of the complex potency of his signature. He is the best known of all vampires, a nobleman, a shape-shifter, a defiler of virgins, and a blood sucker. For all of his cultural elitism, his signature is base natural, particularly since blood is the most natural substance of American kinship according to Schneider, as discussed above. The strongest attribute is the abuse of power, over men, over women, over fate, and over wealth. His link with vampires and bats is especially telling of American concerns. Vampires are the undead, leeches after blood, dwellers of the underground. They rise from the grave, and do harm. As an American indigene, the vampire bat has long had a strong commensal relation with humans. This competition has been well captured in fiction by Smith (1977: 214ff), "Bats are more widespread over the earth than any other mammal, except man ... And the closest of all bats to man is the vampire ... the only one that mates the year round, like humans ... the only bat that can jump and run ... the only bat unafraid of man."

The Wolfman is positioned more toward Nature, as an individual representative of his werewolf kindred (Russell and Russell 1978). His signature is a monthly transition from kindly Culture to beastly Nature, a hyper-macho equivalent to menstruation. As a human, he is meek and mild, but as a wolf he is an aggressive brute.

Beyond these monsters are increasingly more natural ones: Zombies to King Kong to mutant ants and swarming insects. The key signature here is an increasingly more amorphous state toward that most uniquely American monster: The Blob.

As monsters are inherently negative examples, their danger must be neutralized. In all cases, the antidote is an application of the opposite pole to the monster. Hence, the Mummy is sucked into Nature, either a swamp, bog, or sewer. Frankenstein is burned, and fire is a culturally controlled part of Nature. Dracula has a stake, a slightly modified artifact, driven through the heart. The Wolfman is vanquished with a silver bullet, which requires greater technology than a sharpened stake, King Kong falls off a skyscraper which requires greater technological precision to build. And so it goes, with each of the others, especially when the full complement of technology comes to the rescue in the form of the Army or atomic bombs. The Blob is refrigerated by the military and flown to the North Pole for safe keeping.

Of all these monsters, the ones to receive the most attention from films, novels, and children are also the most intermediate ones, Frankenstein and Dracula (Tropp 1977). This is not accidental. Mary Shelley began the novel as part of a contest with Percy Shelley, Lord Byron, and Polidori, all of whom began to write stories of vampires (Tropp 1977, Shelley 1976). Also, in the recent series made by Hammer Films, the Frankenstein movies have been assimilated to the Dracula story by making the creator an aristocratic baron, abusing his power and training (Tropp 1977, 125). The result has been to portray the tension and the double image of both of these monsters simultaneously. The only difference is one of signatures, Frankenstein remains more a blend of cultural-technological and Dracula more of a natural-elitist.

The Bad Axis, Bad Guy Arm

Under this rubric are included a host of villains, murderers, traitors, and other people who have behaved in such a way or committed such an act as to make them bad examples. They have been limited to early America for the sake of illustration. Nearest to the nexus is John Wilkes Booth, who was driven out of a sense of liberty to murder Lincoln. As an actor, he had a remarkable facility for language and speaking that was characteristic of his entire Thespian family. Next is Aaron Burr who tried to set up his own country in the West and who killed Alexander Hamilton in a duel, His signature was being sly, devious, and glib. Benedict Arnold was a hero until he attempted to betray West Point to the British in the Revolution. Interestingly, he is famous for losing his leg at the Battle of Saratoga because a monument was erected in honor of the leg to recognize Arnold's valor in the battle even though he became a traitor. Its wooden replacement made him somewhat dependent. At the far extreme are the hordes of evil variously expressed in America as witches at Salem, mobsters in Chicago, and demons in Hell.

The Good Axis

Emblems

One Arm of this axis is populated by the various "totemic" representations of our national holidays. Here the progression from Culture to Nature can be seen clearly, despite historical manipulation of the signs to assign them to particular holidays.

While he may have personally been a dullard, Washington's birthday was one of the earliest national holidays. Among his linguistic accomplishments is the Farewell Address, reminding America to stay independent. The axe and silver dollar are also associated with him. These items of technology reinforce his career as a surveyor. His kinship attribute distinguishes him as Father of the country. While Washington is a lineal relative, Uncle Sam is a collateral. Next in line would be Santa Claus, not a kinsman, but known for his technological ingenuity in producing toys. Wolf (in Spain 1975) has nicely summarized the Americanization of this figure by several prominent New Yorkers in the first third of the 1800s.[369] However, he did miss the

---

[369] For this process of Americanization, Wolf mentions the roles specific gifted individuals played in finding or creating acceptable signs for fledgling America. John Pintard made Washington's Birthday and July 4th into national holidays and fostered belief in St Nicholas. Clement Moore wrote the poem about the night before Christmas in 1822. Robert Weir drew

biography of Santa Claus done by Baum in 1902.[370] Beyond Santa are the less helpful Halloween Witch, the Cupid of Valentine's Day with his bow and arrow, and the less socialized New Year Baby who matures into Father Time with his scythe. We enter the realm of Nature with the Easter Bunny, whose concerns are cultural even if his form is natural. As a signature, the Easter Bunny is white, with a basket making technology and an artistic sense. He joins other solitary animal figures like the American Eagle, who conveys the virtues of strength, bravery, and courage, or the Ground Hog, who has the very natural purpose of indicating the change of seasons. At the amorphous extreme of Nature is the turkey, a flightless bird with drab, autumn colors that lives in flocks. A native of the Americas, this creature is too stupid to avoid its fate as the ultimate victim at Thanksgiving. Nonetheless, Lee (1959: 159) noted that the turkey remains a potent sign for Americans. During World War Two entire turkeys were shipped to Europe, supposedly: "If the turkeys did arrive, they contributed strongly to Allied victory." Some may wish to extend the Arm even further to include the Christmas cactus and the Easter Lily, both senseless creatures with a multitude of constituents. Like turkeys, they are numerous but defenseless things, lacking independence.

Of all the emblems, Santa and the Easter Bunny receive the most attention culturally and commercially. Both are engaged in manufacturing, but one is human and the other animal. One makes toys and the other makes eggs for the benefit of children. One lives in snow and cold and the other is always shown in a spring like climate. Both are the subject of much concern. Children anticipate their arrival the year round, but who ever heard of a kid anxious for Ground Hog Day? Admittedly, children have greedy incentives that help them remember Christmas and Easter, but both creatures are equally "good to think" within the sweep of American culture. Similarly, attempts to replace the eagle, a sign of European origin, with the turkey, an American native, are greeted with laughter. While it may be indigenous, the turkey personifies those features of Nature which evoke the worst kind of dependency and victimization.

The Good Axis

Heroes

For purposes of illustration, the numerous American role models will be limited to prominent early Americans. At the cultural end unquestionably belongs Thomas Jefferson, savant, inventor, pro-agrarian, and author of the all important Declaration of Independence. As the most articulate spokesman of his age and of American abilities, he represents the ideal of

---

Santa in a chimney in 1837, and Thomas Nast gave Santa his present image by 1863, in addition to creating the Tammany Tiger, Democratic Donkey, and Republican Elephant. For monsterdom, the equivalent figure is Abraham (Bram) Stoker, who wrote a series of books that popularized not only Dracula (1897), but also a female Mummy (1912), a female pseudo-vampire (1909), and a Celtic witch-dragon (1911). He even anticipated a principle emphasized by structuralism, "All things, all thoughts, all emotions, all experiences, all doubts and hopes and fears, all intentions, all wishes seen down to the lowest strata of their concrete and multitudinous elements, are finally resolved into direct opposites" (1975 [1912], 210). Stoker seems to have intuitively grasped and played with the structure of English monsters much more skillfully and effectively that has Hollywood who Americanized them.

[370]. Frank Baum, better known for his OZ books, ran an anti-Lakota newspaper in South Dakota.

independence, of rational choice among options. Further along is Ben Franklin, best known for his practicality and experiments with lightning. Jefferson was wise in theories relating to people, but Franklin was wise in the ways of Nature, including human nature, The Franklin stove, bifocals, and other inventions display his technical know-how, Equally technological was the contribution of Betsy Ross in sewing the first flag, based on the stars and stripes in the Washington family coat of arms. Presumably as it was a domestic task, such sewing was suitably done by a woman. More toward the Nature pole are other figures of a later period, For example, US Grant was called an "animal" for his drinking and low morals, but the associations of Andrew Jackson with the "rabble" comes closer to fitting the characteristic of the natural extreme. At an earlier time this position may have been filled or left latent, only to be supplanted by figures of a later period who are more apt to fit the requirements of the pattern. The point is not the full historicity of these people, which is beyond doubt, but rather the way in which America has managed to code them in terms of distinctive signatures. Certainly, at present, Lincoln and Kennedy have come to occupy similar positions on this Arm, as has the historical Washington as contrasted with the mythic one who never told a lie. Both Lincoln and Kennedy were is victims, but Kennedy is more toward the cultural pole based on his oratory, heroism, wealth, and support of high technology in the Space Program. Lincoln was also an orator and author of the Gettysburg Address, but he had been a poor laborer, transforming logs into split rails. His more manual associations place him more on the side of Nature. Born to wealth, Kennedy had an assured independence, while Lincoln's poverty made for a certain dependence which he symbolically overcame by becoming President and freeing the slaves. As the more natural figure, it is fitting that Lincoln was killed in a theatre, a place of "culture", while everyone knows that Kennedy, the more cultural figure, was killed near a grassy knoll.

However, time forgets and, at different periods, historical figures go in and out of fashion, so the available heroes are coded accordingly. The position of Jackson with the rabble is duplicated by the opinion that some have of FD Roosevelt with the Common Man during the depression, when the extreme of mob dependence was realized.

Ideal Axis

Divinity Arm

Christianity severely limits the number of deities positioned along this Arm. Nearest the Culture-Independence pole is God the Father, source for the Old Testament or the Bible as the word of God, thus fulfilling both the linguistic and the kinship attributes while also being the Maker of the World, quite a technological feat. Next is Jesus, His son, who stands for all that is good and cultural. More natural is the Holy Ghost, the third member of the Trinity, usually represented as a dove or a flame. As a sign of fidelity, the dove serves as a faithful messenger between God and humans. As a bird, it represents one of the indistinguishable members of a flock, like one flame from a fire. Mary, the Mother of Christ, if she appears at all, seems to occupy a position below God and Jesus because of her distinct kinship relations with both of them. At the natural extreme is the Fallen Angel, Satan, with his cloven hooves and tail. In lieu of placing the Devil among the divinities, then the heavenly host of angels, virtually identical, would represent the natural extreme. If Adam and Eve are considered divinities, they belong between Jesus and Satan because they were pure humans who learned about the natural frailty of sex. After their Fall, they initiated technology, the tertiary attribute of discerning mastery.

The Ideal Axis

Superheroes

Quite recently, American culture has grafted a range of comic book characters into the pattern, possibly replacing earlier epic or mythic ones. At the most Independent cultural extreme is Superman, an alien from another planet with a strong sense of law and order. His greatest nemesis is a bit of his exploded planet, a section of this alien Nature, again illustrating the balancing off of Culture and of Nature. His linguistic ability is shown by his employment as Clark Kent, mild mannered reporter for a great metropolitan newspaper. Further along the Arm are Batman and Robin, men of enormous wealth, fictive kinship (Bruce Wayne, alias Batman, is the legal guardian of the youngster given to puns), and advanced technology. Yet their very nicknames link them with swarming, flocking creatures. Similarly, Spiderman has many of these same swarming attributes in addition to radio actively increased "natural" strength and agility. The most dependent of the superheroes is Wonder Woman, one of a race of identical Amazons living on Paradise Island, who works in America as a Women's Army Corps secretary. Her power resides in a belt and bracelets, both reflecting a technology that unites feminine ornamentation and practicality.

The noticeable lack of women and of females in these alignments, except for many feminine asexual figures, will be considered in the conclusion.

Conclusions

While individual details may be problematic, the validity of the analysis rests on the consistent patterning along these axes from Independence to Dependence and the reverse. The amazing redundancy makes the case much better than each analysis does. For each one, the evidence indicates that Independence is a manifestation of Culture as the articulate choice among options. This articulation relates first to the power of language as spoken or written, second, to the network of kinship, and, third, to the display of technology. Dependence is a manifestation of Nature as an inarticulate mass, a victimized and amorphous blob. Dependence has inevitable consequences because such vagueness stifles the possibility of choices. Even the Holy Ghost, taking the form of a dove or small pigeon, serves as a vehicle for God rather than a conscious, independent deity in its own right.

The basis for the positioning of these signs along the Arms of each axis rests upon the distinctive intrinsic attribute(s), signature, of each as reflecting a relative independence or dependence. The overall plan rests on this patterning, regardless of other considerations like historicity. In the words of Sir Edmund Leach (1970: 291) "For ordinary men the significance of history lies in what is _believed_ to have happened, not in what _actually_ happened. And belief, by a process of selection, can fashion even the most incongruent stories into patterned (and therefore memorable) structures ... as systems of patterned contradiction."

One striking incongruity of this pattern is the relative absence of women. Some might argue that since Man is inclusive for Americans, then Man already includes Woman. For the monster examples, Miller (1978: 15) has argued that monsters are men because the American definition of humanity is chauvinist. To be taken seriously, these signs must be men because only men are important ~ powerful enough to receive sustained attention. Women appear in weaker, domestic, and dependency roles. If there are women monsters, they prey on children or more helpless beings (Stoker 1975: 236). Male monsters prey on everyone with impunity.

In American culture, according to Newton (1972: 127) "at base, 'masculinity' is the principle of aggressive brute force in the world ... Femininity opposes male strength through manipulativeness and beauty ... the real woman is of necessity <u>both</u> beautiful and bitchy." In terms of this paper, she is a combination of Wonder Woman, Betsy Ross, and the Halloween Witch. From this perspective, women cannot be monsters or potent signs since as women they must appear "totally helpless and incompetent." Since women are expected to be beautiful but monsters are usually grotesque, they are mutually exclusive (Harwood 1976, Hastings 1951). Thus in a culture where mastery is the highest ideal, women end up as Dependent. Yet they are saved from the stereotype of being a mindless gaggle by their greater perceived ability to manifest love, the ultimate cultural mediator. Washington fought and slaughtered for the love of his country, but Betsy Ross gave it unity and continuity by sewing it a flag. Yet there were women who fought and loved in a masculine style, both during the Revolution and on the Frontier. However, their contribution has been negatively charged if not deliberately forgotten. They were less than men but more than women. They were anomalous and therefore close to the Nature extreme. Women are fine as mothers and domestics, but outside of the exclusive category, they signal danger and threat to the overall pattern.

While this has been the case, it need not be immutable. A paideuma of Independence ~ Dependence mediated by Love offers great hope for change and improvement. These categories define American culture, but the people are the ones who must apply and interpret them. Independence puts a burden on each individual to create society anew and to maintain it by constant activity. Varenne (1977: 92) saw this as "the most exotic aspect of American life," but this active recreation takes place in a framework that has just been outlined. Hence, American signs are not unique but redundant throughout the system. Such redundancy gives greater support to this model, but it also suggests the complexity and focus for the task of sorting out and eventually unfolding the full structure for its conscious manipulation.

Key Words: Configurationalism paideuma American culture signs holidays heroes

American Culture:
Echo, Matrix, Tensions, Holidays

Abstract

Reviewing models of American culture that assert a complexity of core values and relationships, another view is proposed emphasizing a threeway tension. After considering humanism / materialism, self-reliance / dependence, blood (love) law, individual / community, and substance (love) relation; we consider how all of these can be subsumed under a matrix and reverberating echo of mastery (love) dependency, Supporting data are drawn from case examples from five cities and from a diagram illustrating a range of emblems selected from public contexts showing the major features of this patterning. The conclusion deals with considerations of gender and of utilizing symbolic insights once they have been made manifest.

Anthropologists are notoriously better at studying cultures other than their own, both from personal preferences and from the ease with which a totally novel situation can be addressed analytically. Yet, if anthropology is to be comparative and catholic, our results must also be recognizably significant to astute members of these cultures.

As a test of such significance, it seems relevant to look at this assumption in the context of American culture, since it has direct bearing on all the theories and practices of the most viable anthropological community in the world. As I see it, such a test is also important because it serves to remind us again of what an important role culture plays in all human groups, despite the fact that most anthropologists have rejected any overall view of culture as a comprehensive, integrated system, except in lip service of the vaguest terms. As a consequence, the profession has become fragmented as everyone concentrates upon only a facet of the whole. This is, of course, in keeping with the canons of scientific method and neo-positivist philosophy. "As Descartes had already said, scientific thinking aimed to divide the difficulty into as many parts as were necessary in order to solve it" (Levi-Strauss 1979: 17). As we shall see, this goal of fragmentation into many small groups also has a corollary in the structuring of American culture. Nevertheless, unlike culture with its set assumptions, science actually allows for a second mode of analysis, often ignored. As the first is reductionist, seeking to deal with the fragments, so the second is structuralist, intending to understand the whole in its "quest for the invariant, or for the invariant elements among superficial differences" (LS79: 8). In this context, my purpose is structuralist in that I seek a framework systematizing diverse events and experiences into a coherent whole at a given time and place. It does not reject reductionism, however, for it too can account for the temporal dimension of change and for details within the larger whole.

Similarly, two definitions of culture have been used within the profession. In the reductionist view, culture is seen as built up from the smaller units of observable practices, revealed in the documentation of major institutions and rituals. It requires the interpretation of selective aspects of words and deeds. The structuralist position sees culture as a comprehensive model based upon a core "bundle of relationships" ordering and informing everything else in the society. It can be understood in terms of every facet of daily and extraordinary life. In short, a reductionist extracts from data what is measurable and concrete, but a structuralist absorbs the coherent framework within the rich texture of life and thought truly characteristic of a culture.

Assuming a structural-holistic perspective, I will present a range of case materials considered against previous interpretations of the structure of American culture. Because they deal more with mundane features of American life, they should provide useful tests of model reliability. In the second section, we consider data from the more public, institutional domain (sometimes called civil religion) of mythic, heroic, and holiday figures to expand the treatment.

As culture pervades all communal and individual action, it can be seen in the most mundane of experiences, as well as in the most elaborated. With this in mind, we can now turn to five disparate cases drawn from American life, chosen to express the greatest range of variation, to guide the discussion in the first section. So as to refer to them more easily, I have localized each example in a different city.

Selected Cases

1]. In Seattle, a physician who had decided to devote his career to service within the context of Health Maintenance Organizations (HMO) rather than in private practice, took the opportunity to help found a HMO in a large rural area. After several years, when it became clear that the dominant figure was determined to make a healthy income by mixing HMO and private consultations, the younger doctor left to join in a private partnership far removed from any degree of socialized medicine.

2]. In Chicago, a man was sent to prison after a life of crime noted for robbery, assault, maiming, and killing several people. After a short time, he himself was killed by unknown fellow prisoners who found him too obnoxious. During the testimony of a former wife seeking financial compensation for his death, she was asked to name something good or redeeming about the man. While hard pressed and after considerable thought, she was able to mention that he was usually good with children.

3]. In Miami, a woman was given a job as an alcoholism counselor solely on the basis that she was herself a reformed alcoholic, but otherwise had no training or experience in counseling. Other reformed addicts have received similar positions, always insisting that "You have to be one, or have been one, to know how to deal with others in the predicament." The important thing here is that other Americans find this a valid argument.

4]. Residents of Las Vegas like to describe it as the soul of America because their gambling economy brings out all that Americans hold dear. It fosters honesty, choice, and success "up front". Your cards are placed on the table in front of you, you make decisions about them, and then you abide by the outcome for better or worse. "You pay your money and take your chances." More than this however, seething just below the surface is an undercurrent of manipulation noted by Dr Gonzo when he searched for the American Dream there and found it typified by the owner of the Circus Circus Casino. "Las Vegas ... is like the Army, the shark ethic prevails–eat the wounded. In a closed society where everybody's guilty, the only crime is getting caught"... [The owner] ... "always wanted to run away and join the circus when he was a kid"..[Now he] ... has his own circus, and a license to steal, too ... he's the model" (Thompson 1971: 72).

5]. In Hollywood as described by Powdermaker (1950), the tension between the American values of humanism / materialism is constantly struggling during the making of a film.

In this highly collaborative enterprise, "There is an obvious dependency of each group on the other, and at the same time a constant struggle for control and domination. The overt verbal behavior in all these relationships is that of love and friendship" (P50: 29). All of this thinly veils an overwhelming hostility, hatred and lack of respect, all relations are basically manipulative and lacking in all dignity. Individuals strive hard to keep others in positions of dependency rather than oust them outright since future projects may require them. Once a film is in production, "the master is the front-office executive; and behind him are banks and financial interests with their goal of quick, sure, and large profits" (P50: 35, cf 107, 215). The contradiction between people and things must be balanced out if the film is to be successful. "Love is ... supposed to be the mainspring for all creative work, whether in science or the arts ... yet ... props were early used to produce emotional effects" (P50: 324, 282). Usually things have the larger or more crucial role, as actors. Scripts and talents become classed together as properties owned by a studio. Yet the possible rewards in money, friends, and prestige are considered to more than compensate for such indignities by most people.

Each of these cases is a reflection of American culture, so our goal becomes to seek the invariant from the superficial. Several scholars have previously indicated the route we must take, but lacked the semantic precision that we intend. In lieu of being exhaustive, we will rather illustrate the outline or framework that makes internal consistency possible, asserting the strongest position with the intention of having the others fall into place through contributions from reductionists. Not surprisingly, in what follows many of the most insightful contributors were foreign-born, such as Dorothy Demetracopoulou Lee, Francis Hsu, and Herve Varenne. We can only hope that others, especially Asian scholars, will soon add their own contributions, derived from their advantage of novelty and freshness as cultural outsiders.

Impetus for my work came from the theoretical contributions of Claude Levi-Strauss, significantly known as the Master to his followers, and from some difficult questions posed to me by Native American friends and relations.[371] According to Levi-Strauss, the axiomatic tension for all human apperception is a continuum with Nature and Culture as the extremes. Culture refers to aspects of the world under human control and characterized by expectable events, while Nature refers to accident, if not chaos or emptiness, outside the realm of human predictability. Poetically, Paz (1970) has equated Culture with order and Nature with accident. The resolution of these extremes is provided by Mind, composed of brain and of consciousness, integrating cultural learning with natural processes of physiology and biology. I have added to this model a dimension of internally consistent triadic relationships called the matrix, based on the Latin word for womb. The matrix has components that are inclusive – unmarked, conjunctive, integrative, indefinite, and open; exclusive – marked, disjunctive, segregative, definite, and closed as a special case of the former; and enclosive – mediating, pervasive, and encompassing because it has qualities of both other relations in addition to others unique to its class of permeating nexi.

While this formal matrix occurs in all cultures, its content varies according to features of internal development, external relations, and local environment. For each culture, it is possible

---

[371] While my inspiration was Native American, the motivation for this paper came from long, provocative conversations with Robert Odle, a master in his own right. Help was also given by Drs Larry Epstein, Koko Horikoshi Roe, and Marilyn Richen. Finally, this one is for Annie and Harry, to cite mastery.

to discover a predominant tension and set of mediators dependent on it that structure, influence, and inform all others. Leo Frobenius call a single such axiom the paideuma of a culture and Miller (1979) redefined it as a tension, but further thought leads me to characterize it simply as the echo of a culture, reverberating throughout its form and content. According to the universal human echo, Culture can be considered exclusive because it is a special case of Nature, often called human nature; while Nature is inclusive, having aspects of its own that include Culture. The Mind, especially as memory, is the enclosive that locks the entire system into place and time. In the following discussion, we adopt the conventions of presenting each inclusive / exclusive duality (sometimes with an enclosive mediator) as I (O) E.

Before presenting my interpretation of the distinctively American content of the matrix, I will briefly refer to other theories that have also recognized a complex, dynamic bundle of relationships for this culture. I begin with the early (1835, 1840) work of de Tocqueville to supply some historical depth before turning to the more recent work of Schneider and Hsu, together with some of their interpreters. History has shown de Tocqueville to have been a remarkably insightful observer and thinker. He is part of a series of French scholars that includes Levi-Strauss and Varenne who have added to our understanding of culture. Since the dominant features of American culture, variously called Yankee in the East and Anglo in the Southwest, have their origins in English (and Dutch) Protestantism, a Gallic viewpoint has been particularly effective for analytical purposes.

Alexis de Tocqueville

During his 1931 tour of fledgling America (1945 [I 1835; II 1840]), this nobleman called attention to several oppositions in regional life and philosophical tenets. Among these were a solemn Northeast / sensuous Southeast (I: 22, national sovereignty / state independence (I: 123), abstract truth aesthetics / immediate-practical rewards (II: 40), and, importantly, that lithe principle of equality begets two tendencies, the one leads men straight to independence and may suddenly drive them into anarchy; the other conducts them a longer, more secret, but more certain road to servitude" (II: 304). Elsewhere, he repeats that license leads to anarchy and tyranny to despotism (II: 388), adding that such mutability of possibilities rests on a taste for variety fostered by the strong belief in an individualism that even submits the truths of religion to private judgement (I: 213, 269). In the most revealing passage, he remarks (II: 104) "Individualism is a mature and calm feeling, which disposes each member of the community to sever himself from the mass of his fellows and to draw apart from his family and friends, so that after he has thus formed a little circle of his own, he willingly leaves society at large to itself" (my emphasis).

Many of these themes have reoccurred in the more recent scientific work of scholars who have followed this pioneer by a century or more. Of these, the significance of individualism, within the general context of equality, has received the greatest attention attempting to refine it, particularly by Hsu and others.

Francis Hsu

From a psychological perspective, Hsu has argued that the American core values are self-reliance / dependency, tracing their sources in European history and the notion of individualism,

252

"While a qualified individualism, with a qualified equality, has prevailed in England and the rest of Europe, what has been considered the inalienable right of every American is an unlimited self-reliance and an unlimited equality" (Hsu 1972: 249). This is the positive aspect of the core values, while any degree of dependency represents a negative condition much to be avoided. Hsu has based his analysis on observations of Americans and their attitudes toward home and family, where these tensions are most often played out in terms of the care of elderly parents.

Applying the Hsu model, Rhoads (1973) was able to show that the Little Orphan Annie" comic strip provided a concrete example of the strong value placed on self-reliance on the part of a clever girl.

While this model of self-reliance / dependence has utility for understanding American culture; in practice, self-reliance has been largely intended to apply only to white males over 21 years old. Now, it seems to imply an unlimited straining for success in material terms, a victory in the dog-eat-dog world or a frontier attitude of besting the wilderness in a situation of grave personal danger, Looking acutely at the larger realm of self and family, Schneider has shown that a more complex relationship is involved in the context of society, one that includes a mediation of these and other distinctions.

David Schneider and Associates

Focusing on that most anthropological of topics, kinship, Schneider (1968: 52) asserted that the American expressions of Nature (Mind) Culture are specifically blood (love) law. In other words, the tension involves a relationship between shared bio-genetic substance (blood) and a code for conduct (law), mediated by an enduring, diffuse solidarity (love). Especially as sexual congress within a socially-sanctioned union like marriage, love provides for the uniting of blood and law by means of the creation of children that define a family. Love is both a biological act and a cultural belief, binding people to each other and creating new people from the children of such unions.

Using only the Nature / Culture universal, Garretson (1976) claims inspiration from Schneider for her assertions of transformation and process in the history of America. She wisely indicates the role of education and law in turning immigrants into Americans, but her analysis remains too general and patent to also account for social relations and behavior. Her concern is process rather than structure, which is difficult without an appreciation of the forms that underlie and make possible these changes. She recognizes no mediators as such and pays little attention to the complex functions of Mind, unless her use of the term rationality is intended to imply both physiological and cultural aspects. Among her generalizations are that rationality transforms Nature to Culture, science transforms wilderness to abundance, work transforms idleness to salvation, and the Constitution changed anarchy to democracy. Love is disjointed in that there are two kinds, one for kin and another for non-kin. In all, hers is a sweeping schematic model, intended as a popular account for undergraduates, but it lacks a sense of structure and of ethnographic specificity.

More timely is a study of a Midwestern town done by Varenne (1977: 206) under the guidance of Schneider. This anthropologist is a native of France who found a strong tension between individual / community defused by the mediation of love "an individual sentiment directed toward another person" (V77: 207). He extends the blood / law tension of kinship to that of substance / relations for the community, recognizing that a baby begins as all substance and no relation but learns to balance these two through time. Moreover, a group of friends begins as all relation and no substance until marriages and children forge families that blend relation with substance. Hence, love functions to create small homogeneous groups, like those noted by de Tocqueville a century and a half the before, fostering great diversity among themselves which has served to characterize America in the eyes of the rest of the world.

Echo and Matrix

It is these diverse groupings which both individualism and self-reliance fail to account for, regardless of the intellectual background of the proponents of each theory. On the other hand, general consensus recognizes that both dependency and love are very pervasive concepts and values in American culture. In media, public speeches, and private conversations, the dangers and dread of dependency are constantly reiterated in expressions that evoke pity for homeless runaways, a child lost in a crowd, over-reliance on foreign oil, people on the dole reduced to numbers, and parents sent off to nursing homes. Conversely, love interjects into these situations a balm that balances out the negative aspects, The gift of America to the world is love, which demands immediate reciprocation in terms of accepting American dictates and desires in a similar spirit of affection. To reject American wishes is to reject love, concern, and devotion, making the rejector extremely suspect in future dealings.

Unlike the high frequency of usage given to love and dependency concepts, individualism and self-reliance have more specialized use, as in phrases like rugged individualism and high self-reliance − indicating an outdoor, wilderness, or basic survival orientation stressing skills applicable away from the human community and "civilization." The only communal expression of self-reliance of note is the Black idiom based on the Swahili value of Harambee (literally, "pull together"). "The concept embodies ideas of mutual assistance, joint effort, mutual social responsibility, community self-reliance" (Nbithi and Rasmusson 1977: 12).

The inclusive axiom of American culture, therefore, must relate more closely to more frequently expressed ideals, particularly relating to life, liberty, and the pursuit of happiness. My initial decision was that independence, as the direct antonym of dependence, was the best choice since it involves notions of privacy, options, and freedom held dear by Americans. After all, Lee (1959: 75, 57) perceptively noted that an American "will brook no interference and no encroachment. He will spend his wealth installing private bathrooms, buying a private car, a private yacht, private woods and a beach, which he will then people with his privately chosen society ... What incites the American individual to an answering engagement in a situation is definiteness, caliber, within the situation, a strong framework, "guts". Unstructured freedom, whether fenced in or not, is still namby-pamby ... Randomness, the unplanned and unscheduled, are like the despised jellyfish, and perpetuate or evoke inertia" (my emphasis).

While the reference to material possessions and privacy support the belief in individuality as a form of independence, the emphasis on the privately chosen society again indicates the importance of a social dynamic behind the axiom. The frequent use of epithets like jellyfish, scum, and slim, indicating an inert formless, vague, amorphousness, also bear this out. As dependency invokes the helpless, hopeless, despised, motionless, and repulsive; so the inclusive member must be the reverse of these. In human terms, such dependency ranges from the mob to the blob. More specifically, the danger of dependency includes the "disgusting vice of herd-intoxication − of downward self-transcendence into subhumanity by the process of getting together into a mob ... Being in a crowd is the best known antidote to independent thought" (Huxley 1971: 346, 350).

What gives character and form to counteract this downward tendency toward anarchy is the ability of an individual to make free choices in his or her own best interests on the basis of careful discernment. Those who can best make such decisions consistently are accorded special status as someone to be admired and emulated. In this regard, therefore, the missing member of the axiomatic echo of American culture is mastery, the ability to turn something to personal advantage and well-being. Unlike individualism, self-reliance, and independence, mastery both implies these and the public recognition needed to institute a group following based on established conventions. Indeed, the most obvious manifestation of mastery in American is the ability to initiate or pioneer in a new approach or a new field of endeavor.

The echo of American culture, then, is mastery (love) dependency, as commonly expressed in phrases like "Take charge of your own life to become master of your own fate," God is love and Jesus is Lord and Master, "Don't be dependent on others your whole life if you want success and happiness." Of significance, too, is the use of the term master as both a noun and a verb, suggesting that it has such overall importance for the culture that usual distinctions are blurred in its case.

Return to Cases

In terms of the five cases cited above, each shows the interplay of the echo in various ways. The Seattle physician exercised his options by assuming a more masterly position in a smaller partnership, despite previous training, philosophical position, and loss of income, because it was more conducive to his general well-being in the long run. The Chicago criminal was clearly a kind of master of his own fate and that of several others, but his excessive brutality made him unacceptable even in the prison situation. He was much the individual, but to the harm of those around him. His purported kindness to children was a sympathetic plea aimed at community sentiment, but it gives further evidence of the power of children as tokens of love in America. The fact that his killers went unpunished indicates that prison too has its small groups organized around canons of mastery. The Miami woman gained her mastery by personally experiencing alcoholism and its cure at first hand, presumably with enough consciousness of the process to articulate it to others. The Las Vegas attitude represents the simplest expression of mastery, with jockeying and manipulation based on the repeated luck of the draw and the skillful decisions made during bets and card choices. As expressed in a popular song, mastery at cards requires that you know when to hold them, fold them, walk away, and run. Success brings money, enjoyment, and friends, but loss means rejection since no body loves you when you're down and out. In Hollywood, the model is also clear since each contributor to a film is an acknowledged master in his or her own right, who then collaborates with others under the overall supervision of the master controlling the purse strings.

Further, these cases indicate that mastery is a complex process involving the skillful balancing of aspects of Nature, Culture, and Mind, specifically expressed in terms of innate ability, training or education, and luck. Here again, they are interrelated in that innate ability is inclusive and strongly valued, training hones what you already have, making it special and exclusive, and luck is enclosive because it combines these with mental recognition of same. In brief, luck − good luck − can be defined as being the right person at the right time and place who knows that he or she is all these. Bad luck is the reverse of these, leading to helplessness and the need to depend upon others for survival. Being alone is the worst kind of dependency because you lack ability, resources, or training to gain any advantages and influence anyone else.

Both love and luck involve thought, human interaction, and conscious decisions to arrive at any mastery. The consequences of this for American society is that as people cease to be masters of their means to livelihood, they turn to other areas, especially avocations to assert the mastery that provides a compatible set of conventions and a group fostering self-worth and happiness. The characteristics of such mastery are immediate gratification, speedy results in some tangible form such as awards, trophies, and finished products, and encouraging support from a small population of like-minded individuals.

The best avenues to recognized mastery balance the innate and the derived aspects of personality in contexts encouraging luck in such a way that one can honestly say that he or she loves what they are doing. These involve activities, usually away from work, where community approval and personal satisfaction set rules that do not leave a feeling of being trapped, but rather of functioning for the benefit of humane goals in teams, hobbies, and sports where one can display competency, satisfaction, and routine finesse. Then, love grows out of luck to become a binding commitment based on personal, conscious choice and discernment.[372] As a result, one can truthfully speak of loving some particular, such as golf, books, cats, broccoli, or a spouse. Ideally, a marriage represents another type of mastery since it involves the decision to marry legally and to have children, who then grow from dependent substance to masterful relations, balancing innate and acquired abilities of sex and parenting.

American culture emphasizes such balancing in terms of degrees of articulation blending natural and cultural factors. In rank order, the three most significant seem to be language facility first, kinship ties second, and manual-technological dexterity third. As language is a natural ability differentially, used, it is most characteristic of mastery because you must understand something thoroughly to teach or explain it. This applies equally to the great writer, the street poet, the punster, and the glib used-car salesman. The recognition of kinship as both an innate tie of blood and a relational bond of law, with a generous allowance for luck in getting agreeable relatives, involves great discernment and tact. The love and devotion given to a subject can result in someone being called the father or mother of it for the same reason, particularly if it required pioneering work. Thirdly, the skillful use of hands and machines sets humans apart from other animals, who may have rudimentary versions of the physical assets but lack the minds to develop them.

Support for these characterizations and the American echo can be seen in the public expressions used for history, holidays, and national events, especially since they are less personal reflections of the culture. These concrete expressions are arranged in the following diagram along three axes, representing the enclosive, inclusive, and exclusive contents of the matrix which are commonly called the ideal, good, and bad.

[372.] The mediation of love actually rests on its dual character. It always involves conscious choice, but on the more cultural level it is love in the most refined sense, the highest human(e) quality, but at the dependency natural extreme it is nameless, faceless, and ephemeral. Only Newton (1972: 112, Chapter Six title) has given this aspect of love its correct designation, "The Fast F--- And The Quick Buck."

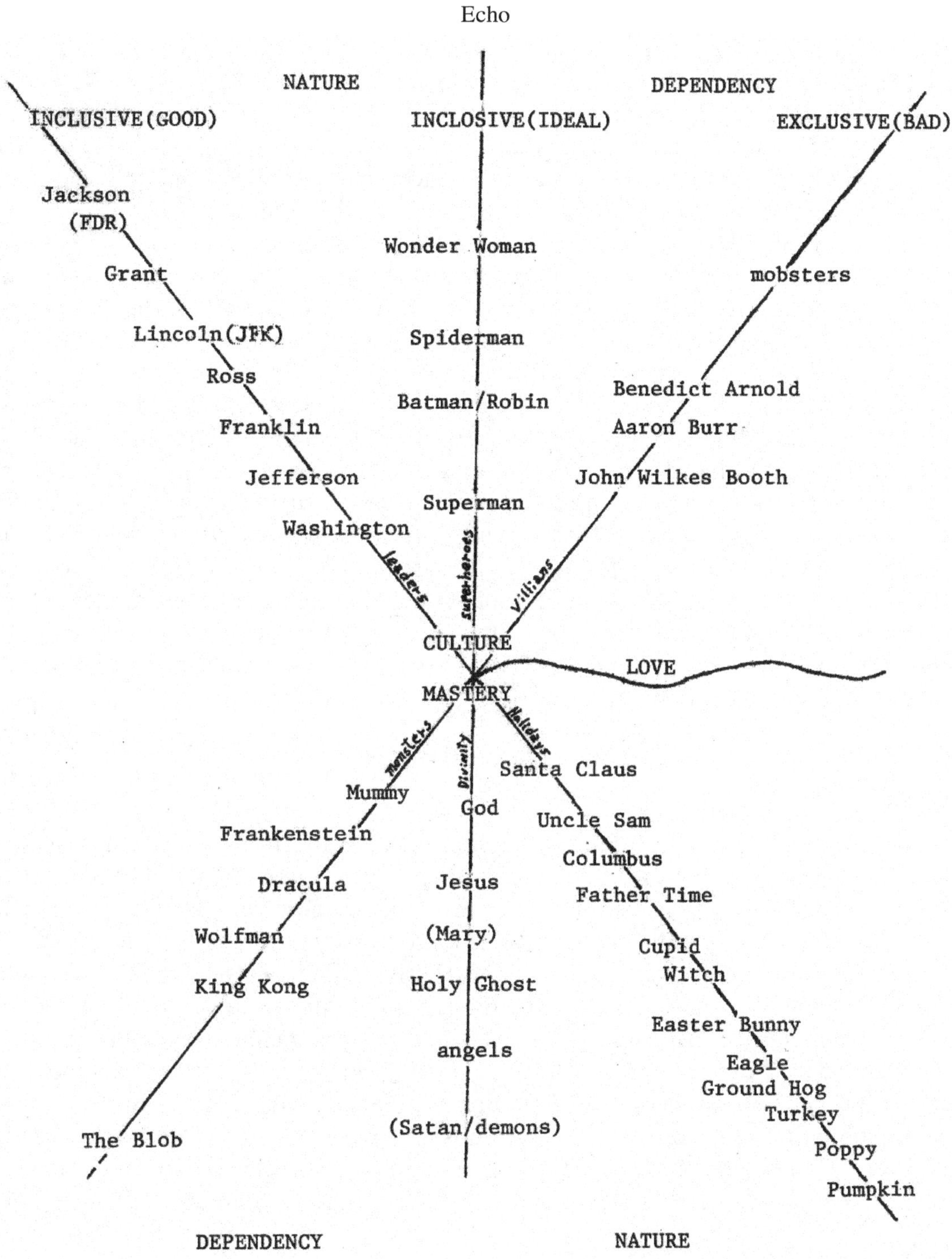

Diagram

In keeping with the special place of humans in the American cosmos, each axis has two arms, one for humans and one for non-humans. The emblems situated along each arm and axis are not intended to be exhaustive, but only to refer to possible positions along the range of variation each includes. Although many of the humans were historical figures, they are included here not as personalities but as history has remembered and emblemized them, often in a pithy sentence or two that serves to provide a characteristic signature or attribute relating to language, kinship, and/or technology to place them within the logical context of the culture. This history then is not a record of diachronic processes, but rather an expression of suitable examples over time that are memorable in terms of the echo and matrix of this culture.

A corollary of this recognized during the completion of this diagram was that the emblems in intermediary positions were under particular strain from the mastery / dependency tension and accordingly receive greater attention, concern, and elaboration in their expression and treatment. Often they are more strongly antagonistic or antithetical to others nearby, giving these more prominence than the diagram indicates.

While I will refer to these position fillers as emblems, they are more properly signs in the semiological sense: objectivized ideas with an intrinsic relationship between idea and emblem.

The diagram developed from my attempts to understand the logical order beneath American culture, following the structuralist canon that such understanding requires a rethinking of superficials and a sifting for invariant structure. More personally, the model grew out of an earlier interest in the American definition of monsters, and, as a consequence, of humanity (Miller 1978). This has given the research a bias toward more animate signs, hence apple pie and the flag (Old Glory) are missing from the discussion. Suffice it to say that they are extremely complex and potent summary emblems for much of the following discussion. They will require special treatment in the future.[373]

The Exclusive (Bad) Axis

Monsters

As it was the first worked out, we begin with the Monsters side of the axis with Bad qualities. Most of these monsters have fictional origins in Europe, some in Africa, a few have been borrowed from Native Americans (Big Foot), but all are now Americanized. While each of them is positioned according to the signatures, as a group they all reflect negative aspects of the American definition of humanness. They are each something that a human should not be – hairy, fanged, vengeful, bloody, impulsive, or mystical (Miller 1978: 15). In addition to representing such reversals, each monster also has its own distinguishing signature.

The fate of the Mummy was sealed linguistically: his suspended state was the result of a spell intoned by members of an ancient Egyptian priesthood. His crime was choosing to love above his station in life. Frankenstein's signature is a mechanical one, as he is often likened to a machine or a weapon (Tropp 1977: 53, 92, 99, 147). His Americanization came when Hollywood directors added the famous scene in which a defective brain is sewn into the head

---

[373.] Although it is inanimate and outside this analysis, the American flag does have a contribution to make to our understanding. It consists of white stars on a blue field set in an upper corner with the rest of the flag filled with alternating red and white bands. The red evokes red blooded Americans and the white, Euro-American supremacy. Blue is associated with sea or sky, the edges of the continent. Within the blue, each of the identical stars represents a state in the Union. In short, the states are confined, excluded, and dependent, while the symbolism of the red and white is open ended and they are independent of each other.

258

(T77: 87), but nevertheless claimed the monster was "able to be redeemed by human love" (T77: 100, 151). Frankenstein emphasizes technology and fictive kinship with his creator and would-be bride, but the creature of both the novel (Shelley 1976) and films is doomed from the beginning by lack of choices or cogent understanding of them.

Dracula dominates this Arm because of the complex potency of his signature. He is the best known of all vampires, a nobleman, a shape-shifter, a defiler of virgins, and a blood sucker. For all of his cultural elitism, his signature is base natural, particularly since blood is the most natural substance of American kinship according to Schneider, as discussed above. The strongest attribute is the abuse of power, over men, over women, over fate, and over wealth. His link with vampires and bats is especially telling of American concerns. Vampires are the undead, leeches after blood, dwellers of the underground. They rise from the grave, and do harm. As an American indigene, the vampire bat has long had a strong commensal relation with humans. This competition has been well captured in fiction by Smith (1977: 214ff), "Bats are more widespread over the earth than any other mammal, except man ... And the closest of all bats to man is the vampire ... the only one that mates the year round, like humans ... the only bat that can jump and run ... the only bat unafraid of man."

The Wolfman is positioned more toward Nature, as an individual representative of his werewolf kindred (Russell and Russell 1978). His signature is a monthly transition from kindly Culture to beastly Nature, a hyper-macho equivalent to menstruation. As a human, he is meek and mild, but as a wolf he is an aggressive brute.

Beyond these monsters are increasingly more natural ones from Zombies to King Kong to mutant ants and other swarming insects. The key signature here is an increasingly more amorphous state until the most uniquely American monster of all appears: The Blob.

As monsters are inherently negative examples, their danger must be neutralized. In all cases, the antidote is an application of the opposite pole to the monster. Hence, the Mummy is sucked into Nature, either a swamp, bog, or sewer. Frankenstein is burned, and fire is a culturally controlled part of Nature. Dracula has a stake, a slightly modified artifact, driven through the heart. The Wolfman is vanquished with a silver bullet, which requires greater technology than a sharpened stake, King Kong falls off a skyscraper which requires greater technological precision to build. And so it goes, with each of the others, especially when the full complement of technology comes to the rescue in the form of the Army or atomic bombs. The Blob is refrigerated by the military and flown to the North Pole for safe keeping.

Of all these monsters, the ones to receive the most attention from films, novels, and children are also the most intermediate ones, Frankenstein and Dracula (Tropp 1977). This is not accidental. Mary Shelley began the novel as part of a contest with Percy Shelley, Lord Byron, and Polidori, all of whom began to write stories of vampires (Tropp 1977, Shelley 1976). Also, in the recent series made by Hammer Films, the Frankenstein movies have been assimilated to the Dracula story by making the creator an aristocratic baron, abusing his power and training (Tropp 1977, 125). The result has been to portray the tension and the double image of both of these monsters simultaneously. The only difference is one of signatures. Frankenstein remains more a blend of cultural-technological and Dracula more of a natural-elitist.

Exclusive (Bad) Axis

Villains

Under this rubric are included a host of bad guys (murderers, traitors, thugs, and criminals of conscience) who behaved in such a way or committed such an act as to make them particularly bad examples for future generations. For sake of illustration, they are limited here to the early American period.

Nearest to the nexus is John Wilkes Booth, driven out of a sense of liberty to murder Abraham Lincoln, but noted as an actor, speaker, and master of language who came from an important theatrical family.

Aaron Burr tried to found his own country in the West, to "father" it so to speak, and was involved in many other schemes where he was noted for being sly and glib, if not outright dishonest. He killed Alexander Hamilton in a duel, using a gun, a manufactured weapon. Benedict Arnold was a national hero until he tried to betray West Point to the British during the Revolution. He distinguished himself at the Battle of Saratoga, where he lost a leg. Later, a monument was erected on the battlefield to the leg, as it was not part of Arnold's treachery. Ever after he wore a wooden leg, a product of technology.

At the far extreme are the hordes of nameless, faceless evil variously known in America as the witches of Salem and mobsters in Chicago.

The Inclusive (Good) Axis

Holidays

This arm of the axis consists of the various "totemic" signs used to represent our national holidays. Once they are rethought in logical order, their progression from cultural mastery to indistinguishable if populous dependency emerges clearly, regardless of the various historical accidents that associated each of them with a season or event in the year.

As the grandfatherly figure with long lists and a toy factory, Santa Claus is the most likely member of these emblems to be located at the culture nexus. Wolf (in Spain 1975) has traced the Americanization of this figure in the works of several New Yorkers of the early 1800s.[374]   To these, I would add the biography of Santa done in 1902 by Frank Baum, better known for his OZ series.

[374.] For this process of Americanization, Wolf mentions the roles specific gifted individuals played in finding or creating acceptable signs for fledgling America. John Pintard made Washington's Birthday and July 4th into national holidays and fostered belief in St. Nicholas. Clement Moore wrote the poem about the night before Christmas in 1822. Robert Weir drew Santa in a chimney in 1837, and Thomas Nast gave Santa his present image by 1863, in addition to creating the Tammany Tiger, Democratic Donkey, and Republican Elephant. For monsterdom, the equivalent figure is Abraham (Bram) Stoker, who wrote a series of books that popularized not only Dracula (1897), but also a female Mummy (1912), a female pseudo-vampire (1909), and a Celtic witch-dragon (1911).   He even anticipated a principle emphasized by structuralism, "All things, all thoughts, all emotions, all experiences, all doubts and hopes and fears, all intentions, all wishes seen down to the lowest strata of their concrete and multitudinous elements, are finally resolved into direct opposites" (1975 [1912]: 210).

Further along are Uncle Sam, a collateral relative personifying the country, and Christopher Columbus, who mastered technology enough to encounter the New World. Father Time and his New Year's Baby alter ego span the generations and the machines of time, Cupid has a bow and arrow to cause love to spring between individuals, blending technology with mediation. The Halloween Witch with her broom and brewing caldron represents female skills and techniques put to dangerous ends.

We come closer to Nature and diffuse dependency with the Easter Bunny, the white rabbit who gives colored eggs and chocolates in baskets to children. In many respects, he is the mirror opposite of Santa in that his equations are with spring, nature, and food rather than winter, culture, and toys. Beyond the bunny are various biota who are increasingly more helpless, amorphous, and scattered. These range from the solitary Eagle and Ground Hog to the Turkey, a flightless bird with drab, autumnal plumage living in flocks and the ultimate helpless victim at Thanksgiving. The Snakes of Saint Patrick are even more non-descript since they were successfully banished. Among plants, there are the Christmas Cactus, Easter Lily, and Memorial Day Poppy, each having many identical blooms that lack any individual character or quality. Perhaps the most perfect of natural emblems is the pumpkin, a vegetative blob that calls for some change to balance out its place in the framework. Accordingly, it receives a distinctively humanoid face and a candle (fire is the paramount accomplishment of culture) to compensate for its other wise offensive symbolism, since its very amorphousness also includes its cooking down into a mush and pie of bland texture, unlike apple pie where the slices keep at least some of their character.

The Inclusive (Good) Axis

Leaders

For purposes of illustration, the numerous American role models will be limited primarily to prominent early presidents and distinguished citizens.

As Father of the Country, author of the Farewell Address calling for America to keep its position of mastery and equality, and as user of false teeth, Washington has all the attributes of mastery to place him at the head of this arm. His use of the ax to chop down the cherry tree and the silver dollar thrown across the river give him further technical skills to complement his career as surveyor and soldier, a leader of man and master of dangerous situations.

Next would be Thomas Jefferson, savant, inventor, pro-agrarian, and author of the crucial Declaration of Independence. As the most articulate spokesman of his age, he represents the ideal of rational choice among options and the intelligent use of technology that have been used to characterize the quality and ability of America.

Further along is Ben Franklin, best known for his practicality and experiments with printing and lightning. As Jefferson was wise in the intellectual theories relating to people, so Franklin was wise in the ways of nature, including human nature. The Franklin stove, bifocals, and other inventions show his technical know-how and abilities.

Stoker seems to have intuitively grasped and played with the structure of English monsters much more skillfully and effectively that has Hollywood who Americanized them.

Equally technological was the contribution of Betsy Ross in sewing the first flag, basing it on the stars and stripes in the Washington family coat of arms. As it was a domestic task, it was appropriately done by a woman after a man had made the request.

More toward the pole of Nature are other figures of a later period. For example, U.S. Grant was called an "animal" for his drinking and low morals, but the association of Andrew Jackson with the popular "rabble" comes closer to fitting the attributes of the dependency extreme. Of course, as history supplies better examples of these positions, earlier figures become forgotten and replaced. For example, some have the opinion that Franklin Delano Roosevelt (FDR) better represents the dependency extreme because of his association with the Common Man during the Great Depression when the dependency of dole, down-and-out, and despair gave the American working class a uniformity the past generation learned to dread.

Also, at present Lincoln and John F Kennedy (JFK) have come to occupy similar positions on this arm, but they have been coded in such a way as to leave each of them in a unique position. Both Lincoln and Kennedy were victims of assassination, but Kennedy has been placed more toward the cultural end. Both were great orators, but Kennedy is associated with the high technology of the Space Program and Lincoln was a poor laborer who hand-split rails. Born to wealth, Kennedy was born to a position of mastery, while the poverty of Lincoln made his accomplishments all the more unique. As the more natural figure, it is fitting that Lincoln was killed in a theater, balancing Nature with Culture, while Kennedy was killed outside near a grassy knoll, with the same effect.

As can be seen with these most historical of people, our remembrance of them has more to do with a process of coding particular relationships than with any actual details of their lives. At an earlier period, the symmetrical reversals applied to Lincoln and Washington as can be seen from such minor details as having one shown with black hair and one with white, or more tellingly, that Lincoln decided to free the slaves while flowing down a river on a raft, while Washington, a slave holder, indicated his gentry membership by throwing a coin across a river. These are minor details in the events of their lives but history has chosen to remember them because they form parts of an intermeshed whole.

The Enclosive (Ideal) Axis

Divinity

Christianity severely limits the number of deities positioned along this Arm. Nearest the Culture-Independence pole is God the Father, source for the Old Testament or the Bible as the word of God, thus fulfilling both the linguistic and the kinship attributes while also being the Maker of the World, quite a technological feat. Next is Jesus, His son, who stands for all that is good and cultural. More natural is the Holy Ghost, the third member of the Trinity, usually represented as a dove or a flame. As a sign of fidelity, the dove serves as a faithful messenger between God and humans. As a bird, it represents one of the indistinguishable members of a flock, like one flame from a fire. Mary, the Mother of Christ, if she appears at all, seems to occupy a position below God and Jesus because of her distinct kinship relations with both of them. At the natural extreme is the Fallen Angel, Satan, with his cloven hooves and tail. In lieu of placing the Devil among the divinities, then the heavenly host of angels, virtually identical, would represent the natural extreme. If Adam and Eve are considered divinities, they belong

262

between Jesus and Satan because they were pure humans who learned about the natural frailty of sex. After their Fall, they initiated technology, the tertiary attribute of discerning mastery.

The Enclosive (Ideal) Axis

Superheroes

Quite recently, American culture has grafted a range of comic book characters into the pattern, possibly replacing earlier epic or mythic ones. At the most Independent cultural extreme is Superman, an alien from another planet with a strong sense of law and order. His greatest nemesis is a bit of his exploded planet, a section of this alien Nature, again illustrating the balancing off of Culture and of Nature. His linguistic ability is shown by his employment as Clark Kent, mild mannered reporter for a great metropolitan newspaper. Further along the Arm are Batman and Robin, men of enormous wealth, fictive kinship (Bruce Wayne, alias Batman, is the legal guardian of the youngster given to puns), and advanced technology. Yet their very nicknames link them with swarming, flocking creatures. Similarly, Spiderman has many of these same swarming attributes in addition to radio actively increased "natural" strength and agility. The most dependent of the superheroes is Wonder Woman, one of a race of identical Amazons living on Paradise Island, who works in America as a Women's Army Corps secretary. Her power resides in a belt and bracelets, both reflecting a technology that unites feminine ornamentation and practicality.

The noticeable lack of women and of females in these alignments, except for many feminine asexual figures, will be considered in the conclusion.

Conclusions

While some of the individual details may be uncertain, the validity of this analysis rest on the consistent patterning along the axes from a distinctive, character-rich mastery to a uniform, inert dependency. The amazing overall redundancy makes the argument more telling, regardless of the arms and axis. In each case, mastery is a manifestation of Culture, balancing innate, acquired, and lucky considerations, particularly in terms of language, kin relations, and/or technology. Dependency is a manifestation of Nature as an inarticulate mass, often a victimized, characterless blob. An inevitable consequence of such dependency is that such uniformity and vagueness stifles choices and possibilities. For example, the Holy Ghost, in the form of a dove, one of many in a flock, serves only as a vehicle for divinity rather than being fully a master in its own right.

The positioning of the emblems along each arm and axis rests on the signature of each in terms of its relative mastery or dependency. The patterning of these in terms of linguistic, kinship, or manual considerations has to do with consequences of coding rather than any historicity. As Sir Edmund Leach (1970: 291) has already noted "For ordinary men ... the significance of history lies in what is believed to have happened, not in what actually happened. And belief, by a process of selection, can fashion even the most incongruent stories into patterned (and therefore memorable) structures ... as systems of patterned contradiction."

The most striking incongruity within this pattern is the relative absence of women. Since Man is inclusive, some have argued, any reference to Man also includes Woman. For the monster examples, however, Miller (1978: 15) has argued that monsters are men because the

American definition of humanity is chauvinist. To be taken seriously, these signs must been because only men are important and powerful enough to receive sustained attention. Women appear in weaker, domestic, and dependency roles. If there are women monsters, they prey on children or more, helpless beings (Stoker 1975: 236). Male monsters prey on everyone and anyone with impunity.

In American culture, according to Newton (1972: 127) "at base, 'masculinity' is the principle of aggressive brute force in the world ... Femininity opposes male strength through manipulativeness and beauty ... the real woman is of necessity both beautiful and bitchy." In terms of this paper, she is a combination of Wonder Woman, Betsy Ross, and the Halloween Witch. From this perspective, women cannot be monsters or potent signs since as women they must appear "totally helpless and incompetent." Since women are expected to be beautiful but monsters are usually grotesque, they are mutually exclusive (Harwood 1976, Hastings 1951). Thus in a culture where mastery is the highest ideal, women end up as Dependent. Yet they are saved from the stereotype of being a mindless gaggle by their greater perceived ability to manifest love, the ultimate cultural mediator. Washington fought and slaughtered for the love of his country, but Betsy Ross gave it unity and continuity by sewing it a flag. Yet there were women who fought and loved in a masculine style, both during the Revolution and on the Frontier. However, their contribution has been negatively charged if not deliberately forgotten. They were less than men but more than women. They were anomalous and therefore close to the Nature extreme. Women are fine as mothers and domestics, but outside of the exclusive category, they signal danger and threat to the overall pattern.

While this has been the past pattern, it need not continue in the same fashion. The echo of mastery (love) dependency offers great flexibility for change and improvement. By making clear the obvious for the culture, the society can thus make the echo subject to reformulation and reanalysis in terms of the manipulations that can be instituted in old situations via a process of novel rephrasings and a new insight on mastery, making it open to all genders equally. While these are the categories and symbols that define American culture, they must be applied and interpreted by people. Mastery places the burden upon every individual both to maintain society as learned from the past and to recreate it anew in every generation by means of constant activity and reflection. In the process, small viable groupings are created to support and nourish the conventional and unconventional differences. It is this constant striving to recreate anew society it many different facets that Varenne (1977: 92) called "the most exotic aspect of American life."

Key Works: America, culture, Strucon, triads, echo, matrix, mastery, love, dependency

In her blindness – Aunt Susie

The little wild blackberry called sxagᵂəd in dxᵂləsucid ~ Lushootseed ~ Puget Sound Salish was and is the most important of our berries.

Dora Solomon gave us a story of its origin. Myrtle Woodcock gave us another story unbracing its power to invoke and portray precious emotion.

Louise Anderson required the family to pick 100 quarts of berries each year so that guests could be offered and served me choicest of desserts when they came to visit.

Every year, Aunt Susie made it her practice also to pick and preserve an ample supply for her family and friends.

ʔal sʔubadils, ƛ́ucut tsi siʔab gʷəqʷuĺcəʔ, xʷuʔələ ləq̓ʷələxᵂ kʷi sx̣əgᵂəd. ʔa xᵂuʔələ ʔuʔaʔsil, dxᵂcutəb tiʔəʔ cədił sx̣əgᵂəd, "ʔa ʔu kᵂi łuʔəƛ̓, c̓əbəbiluł, ʔa ʔu kᵂi łuc̓əbəb. łuʔa čəd ʔu ləskᵂədyalc gᵂəl xᵂi kᵂi gᵂat łuləc̓əbəb čəda x̣ᵂul łuxᵂit̓il."

As she aged, Aunt Susie slowly lost her vision. She depended on her sensitive fmgers to serve her as she continued to practice and provide for her own and her family's needs. She wove rugs out of worn out garments and she continued to knit sox and other apparel from wool cut from sheep.

As July and the warmth of summer approached, Aunt Susie could be heard addressing the berries that were ripening. With a voice choked with emotion and empathy, she voiced their feelings in Lushootseed she said: "Who will be coming to gather me? Will anybody be coming to pick me or will I just be hanging on these vines, wasting the purpose of my being!"

Aunt Susie gave us so many things, I thank her spirit for this memory and I shall forever honor and enjoy the gift of the little wild blackberry who ripens each year, hoping to be used joyfully by those who can and do appreciate the creator's most precious gift to us. Dora Solomon says, "this berry is the Blood of the Indian". Myrtle Woodcock reminds us that it reflects the pure and true love that is shared!

taqᵂšəblu shares these feelings with you that you also may anticipate the ripening of our special little blackberry and savor her beautiful gift of life.

Traditionally from taqᵂšəblu [Vi Hilbert] 6-15-99

Masks and Matrilineality Again

In her famous article, Elizabeth Tooker (1968: 1170) explored "an association between the use of masks in religious ritual and the presence of matrilineal institutions" in Native North America.

She recalled that Fritz Graebner noted an association between secret societies with masks and matrilineal moieties as part of his East Papuan or Matrilineal Two-Class kulturkreis, but when Alfred Kroeber and Catherine Holt tested for such an association, they found no correlation between masks and moieties.

Looking again at the Kroeber and Holt sample, Tooker factored for matrilineal moieties and found that "although masks are frequently found in societies that lack matrilineal moieties, it is of some interest that no society that has matrilineal moieties lacks masks." According to her Table 2, "Masks and Matrilineal Moieties in a Sample of North American Cultures," the five representatives were Haida, Hidatsa, Iroquois, Mandan, Tlingit.

Moreover, looking at the relationship between masks and general matrilineality, particularly among the Pueblos, she found support "that the more important matrilineal institutions are in the organization of a society, the more important masking will [2] also be in the religious ritual of that society." Her Table 3, "Masks and Matrilineality In A Sample Of North American Cultures," listed twelve representatives, the same five (Haida, Hidatsa, Iroquois, Mandan, Tlingit) along with seven others (Crow, Delaware, Hopi, Kutchin, Navaho, Tsimshian, Zuni).

While "no present anthropological theory adequately accounts for" this linkage, she suggested "it seems most likely that there is at least one intermediary variable that can be ascertained only through further study" as neither masking nor matrilineality is mutually causal.

As the source for this variable, she pointed to the role of male authority in matrilineal societies, where "Men do not propitiate the gods; they become the gods by the mere act of putting on the mask" and "men and spirits together work to keep the world in order."

To pursue this line of reasoning, we first need to correct for misinterpretations of some of the previous data. For example, while the Tsimshian have been described as having four clans, this is more a consequence of anthropologists working in resettled communities than of ethnographic reality (Miller and Eastman 1984). In Tsimshian terms, their society consists of moieties, each in turn divided into two semi-moieties. Traditionally, each town functioned with an Owner and an Other moiety which intermarried and performed social obligations for each other, particularly at funerals. Tsimshian society was organized in terms of households, each composed of inhabitants [3] from the classes of nobles, commoners, and slaves. Leaders lived in the well protected rear of the house, commoners along the sides, and slaves near the door, where they were most vulnerable during battles.

Each household had a double pose. During the summer, activities were economic, concerned with the harvesting of inherited resource locations under the direction of moiety leaders. During the winter, activities were religious, concerned with the display of wonderous abilities and dramatic incidents, under the management of the same leaders in their priestly aspect. Thus, summer was a time of moiety loyalties expressed in terms of potlatches hosted by the heraldic crests of the household, while the winter was a time of dramatic wonders displayed during winter ceremonials. Both crests and wonders were associated with hereditary names which were believed to be eternal, passed down through the reincarnating heirs of a household in each generation.

The emblems of moiety-based names were crests, art works of which the most important was a hat worn during rituals. The emblems of the wonder-based names were masks. Pursuing the analogies further reveals that crests were traced through the mother, while wonders were traced to a male, often a supernatural father in the sacred histories of the household. Even within the matrilines, regard was also accorded to the father^ side, a source of help, both financial and spiritual. According to Adams (1973: 39), "there are essential spiritual and physical [4] components of every Gitksan which come from the father as well as from the mother. A child who is living in his father's village will not be harmed because he has some of the look and character of his father's people, some of his spiritual qualities, in the literal sense, which will return to his fathers people eventually." Among the Tsimshian, therefore, there is an equation of moieties and masks, but with the twist that the masks are specifically equated with men.

In contrast to the hundreds of masks used by the Tsimshian until conversion to Christianity, the historic Delaware had only three (Miller 1979). Although the Delaware also had three clans, there is no clear association of masks with clans. Two masks were similar, made of braided cornhusk and worn by a pair of men acting as messengers to announce the date of the Green Corn Ceremony in the late Summer. During the dance, these Huskfaces led the line of male dancers. In all, these two masks were ritual specific and associated with men. The single mask was carved of wood and worn by a man costumed in bearskin outfit to embody a being called Masing, the patron of game and crops who lived in mountains floating just above the earth but who was often in the forests. During the fall, a specific rite was dedicated to Masing which lasted one night. As patron of hunters and guardian of children, Masing had associations with the role of father, reinforcing the link between masks and men in matrilineal societies.

Aside from Tooker's surmise about the linkage of masks with [5] men in a context of matrilineality, there have been few theories of masking. Among those most distinctive is that of Laura Makarius (in Crumrine and Halpin 1983: 195), who argues that "masks represent instruments of protection" from the violation of taboos, the most basic of which for her is the shedding of blood. In contexts fraught with ambivalence, masks themselves become sources of danger (same: 200) and, hence, treated with reverence and fear.

While Makarius may help to explain masking connotations, she does not address the intent of mask use in specific societies, particularly matrilineal ones. Fathers, standing outside the vital social fabric, become sources of power, aliens charged with energies from the limits of the known and related. Their connections with the body of the community are superficial since substance came from women, passed on matrilineally. It is just this superficiality that encourages the use of masks, the face of Otherness representing a link based on appearance, on analogy, but not of identity.

The clearest statement in the literature is not from the Americas, but from Papua New Guinea. According to Nancy Munn (1986: 143, 142) "Whereas the child's bond to the mother is an intrinsic one of material substance and continuity, the ideal relationship to the father is one of likeness to someone extrinsic to one's own bodily self ... Ideally, a child's face (*magi-*, a term that also denotes appearance) should resemble its father's." That such a statement does apply in the Americas is [6] supported by comments from the Tlingit reported by Ronald Olson and by Sergei Kan (1989: 67) with "reference to a resemblance between his or her face and those of his or her classificatory fathers." Olson (1967: 16) noted that "A special relationship holds between a person and his [sic] father's clansmen ... This relationship may also be on a joking plane. Thus a person might say to his fathers brother (or anyone he called by that term) ... child of Kagwantan, his face. This is making fun of the face of the person addressed, teasing him. If her resented it he might reply ... from among you, I look the same."

Since Tooker published her article, more has been written about American masking (Crumrine and Halpin 1983) and its various tribal contexts (Fenton 1987). These studies demonstrate that well-developed masking traditions were rarely simple. Raymond Fogelson (and Bell 1983:54) observed a distinction, common among Eastern tribes, between carved wooden masks and woven cornhusk or cut gourd masks. The former were associated with the forests and male activities such as hunting, while the latter were associated with clearings and female efforts such as farming. Even so, the husk or gourd masks were worn by men representing both men and women beings. Among Iroquois cultures, genders are reversed from those expected by Anglo-Americans. For Iroquois, female is the unmarked or general category, while male is the marked and specific. It is therefore entirely appropriate for Bushyhead husk masks to represent both men and women beings. Moreover, in keeping with their Otherness, the Bushyheads were believed to be [6] "a people from the other side of the world where the seasons are reversed" who taught humans "the arts of hunting and agriculture" (Fenton 1987: 54). Thus, even when the symbolic equation of the Bushyheads was with women, who were the Iroquois farmers, it was men who expressed the relationship.

Among matrilineal societies, women were substance and men were surface. For a child to admit kinship with a father, he had to rely on external characteristics. In the interest of saving face and claiming affection, masks were used to convey the complexities of such superficial images. In this instance, at least, masks had a profundity which was fully intended to be only skin deep. [7]

The Northwest Coast of What?

The NWC, the New World, and their inhabitants are well known for their diversity and relative isolation. However, we must not lose sight of the fact that from what we know at present. Native America was first inhabited by the most recent members of the Hominid line. Homo sapiens sapiens. This means that the cultural diversity in Native America is a recent phenomenon largely resulting from factors of ecological adaptation and of the universal constraints of human thought and behaviour. The NWC clearly subscribes to the constraints of ecology and universals like the rest of Native America. In addition the NWC is characterized by distinctive art styles and the potlatch. But how is one,to consider such distinctive traits?

In the past they have been used to separate the NWC as much from Native America as from the rest of the world. But is such a separation valid? Is it an artefact of professional anthropology, of the "real world," or of both? To answer such a question and to set the stage for the succeeding discussion, we, must turn to the background of American anthropology. [2]

Within the North American continent there were discrete zones of Native occupation consisting of similar patterns of technology, social organization, and religion which we have come to call 'culture areas.' Traditionally these culture areas are defined on the basis of their most distinctive traits, with little recognition given to the universal processes that shape human institutions. Nor has sufficient consideration been given to the fact that traits do not exist in isolation but rather as a part of some greater whole. We must remember that recognition, in and of itself, is culturally relevant. Beliefs and attitudes, whether folk or scientific, are derived from cultural systems. In American anthropology, no less or more than in other sciences, our system of beliefs has developed through a dialectic process. One side, represented by Lewis Henry Morgan, was concerned with evolutionary, cross-cultural studies emphasizing impersonal constraints such as sex, age, and technology. The other side, represented by Franz Boas and the Bureau of American Ethnology, was concerned with particular studies emphasizing constraints related to individual perceptions and cultural contexts.

As an area of research, the NWC has been molded by the Boasian tradition. My purpose in recalling our intellectual ancestry is to make us all the more aware that our set of professional beliefs was socially constructed in the past and has become sanctified as tradition in the present. As Boasians we are clustered and focused on the sacrament that is called data. [3]

Because ethnography functions as the Boasian mystical communion, the high quality of NWC descriptions has drawn scholars from all over the world to use (and abuse) them. It is not an exaggeration to say that the growth of anthropology toward a more rigorous, explanatory, predictive science can be measured by how well researchers at different times have been able to account for more and more of the empirical phenomena of the NWC. We know that anthropology has not yet reached maturity, but we will know when it does as much from what Thomas Kuhn would call a unified paradigm as from the final resolution of the various forms and interpretations of the potlatch into a single, coherent whole.

In the same way that diffusionism, functionalism, and historical comparison have each in turn affected our professional belief system, so now structuralism is providing new insights, relations, and coherence in NWC data. Each of these theoretical perspectives has been, and continues to be, important for various kinds of empirical facts and problems. It would be impossible for me to adopt a non-theoretical stance, however, I will try to keep my theory to a minimum. My own work in New Mexico, Oklahome, and New England has been influenced by structuralism. I have also been favorably impressed by some, but no means all, of the structuralist work being done in the NWC. With my theoretical bias made explicit, I must also acknowledge the importance of empirical evidence. Once again, the relationship between facts and theory has to be dialectical, one without the other is [4] inherently uninteresting and uneventful.

Having said there can be no final summation of anthropology, Native America, or NWC just now, allow me to turn to other concerns.

Intellectually, I am opposed to the type of thumb-nail areal sketches which expedience encourages me to present for the purposes of my argument. A culture should be presented as a whole, as a totality conferring order and meaning on the world. A proper discussion should begin with the origin myth of the particular society in order to determine how its world is chartered. The various social institutions can then be discussed as formally constituted systems of human beings inter-acting with the objectified ideas of this chartered cosmos. Comparisons of these local cultures as totalities would then establish culture areas, continental patterns, and the full complement of human cultures.

However, as an anthropologist, I am familiar with the discrepancy between the ideal and the real, so I can now proceed on the basis of heuristic considerations and available information.

The framework of the next section of my paper is drawn from the 1923 discussion of "American Culture and the Northwest Coast" by AL Kroeber. [5]

II

Kroeber separated Native America theoretically into 4 groups of "ingredients:" 1) those brought by the early immigrants, 2) those developed indigenously and widely diffused, 3) those developed and maintained locally, and 4)those introduced from the Old World at later times. I will not consider these ingredients in detail because I find his discussion of isolated traits and hypotethical time periods somewhat dated. However, by ignoring any diachronic considerations, his outline still has utility.

Included in the list of ingredients brought by Asiatic immigrants into Native America are shamanism, the spear thrower, life cycle rites, and (I would add) the guardian spirit cult and moieties as general features of both of the Americas.

The ingredients which were indigenously developed and widely diffused serve to give many of the culture areas their particular cast. Chief among these generic ingredients are the trinity of corn, beans, and squash; the use of pottery and of copper; the tending of turkeys, tobacco, and cotton; and the construction of earth and masonry mounds. Kroeber also implies that urbanization, bureaucratic leaders and priests, confederacies, and regulated offerings at shrines were independent New World developments. Recent research would concur with him on this, but at the same time underscore the importance of ecological factors limiting and permitting only a few human possibilities in the [6] Neolithic situation. In other words, while there were different domesticated crops in the Old World and the New World, the human adaptation to the Neolithic way of life was essentially the same. We will consider later how this observation has relevance for the NWC, even though the NWC shares none of these generic Native North American ingredients.[375]

The third group of strictly localized phenomena consists of specializations such as art styles, particular forms of dwellings, unique rituals or food habits, and scientific achievements like the concept of zero and glyphs among the Maya. While the NWC art style qualifies for this third group, I would prefer to exclude the potlatch in general because its redistributive aspects make it comparable to functional.equivalents in Native America, Melanesia, and elsewhere.

The Old World ingredients of the fourth group are quite small. Kroeber limits these to certain folktales, rod armor, and the composite bow. Over the intervening half century, there have also been arguments for the introduction of pottery from Japan, of sweat lodges from Asia (Driver; 129), of iron from China, and of various features from extraterrestrial sources. Wherever these items came from, it is vital that we always remember that each was incorporated into an on-going cultural system with its own manner of conferring order and meaning.

Since at least the work of Kroeber (1923: 20), it has been [7] generally accepted that "the outstanding characteristic of NWC culture is its seeming comparative aloofness from both Asia and America." However, before we tacitly accept such statements from our academic elders, let me call to your attention that it was also Kroeber (1923: 9) who said that "the NWC is substantially without officials, chiefs, government, or political authority." He meant by this that the NWC, especially toward the south, had leaders with only status and influence but no constituted authority. Leadership derived from possessions not from power. Even so, I doubt if anyone at present would agree with Kroeber. Just because the source of power is economic does not mean that the power is not also political.

In keeping with an significant tradition in NWC studies, encouraged by Vernon Ray and Joyce Wike (1957), for constructive re-evaluations of aspects, problems, and puzzles in NWC anthropology and their interpretation; it is fitting that we now turn to a discussion of the NWC and its relationships with the rest of Native America and the world.

III

---

[375] If I had access to Philip Drucker's unpublished PhD dissertation when I wrote this paper, some of my arguments could have been obviated by direct quotes from it, I especially like his argument for tracing the spread of possible NWC features throughout Native America by plotting the distribution of the trade in dentalia. Among the important parallels he noted are the functional equivalence of the NWC potlatch and the Beloved Child complex of the Plains. His most important observations can be summarized by direct quotation (Drucker 1937: 97, 110):

We have remarked interest in wealth as being a feature of Northwest Coast social life which set this area off against all others of North America. When we come to analyze the matter, we find wealth figured more or less in many other regions, more, for example, in the Plains.
The Northwest Coast cannot then be regarded as unique in content, but rather as an area sharing in widespread American complexes. The distinctiveness of the area resulted from a different accenting of such culture components. The differences were of degree rather than kind.

The NWC is distinguished by the combination of several features: 1) an ecology which is exploited by a marine adaptation best represented by the symbolic importance of salmon and whaling, 2) a high population density, 3) corporate resource holding groups [8] with Incumbent crest systems, specializations, and surplus of preserved foods, and finally 4) potlatch displays and winter ceremonials. I will consider each of these four features in turn.

As Kroeber (1963: 28) noted:

"the ecological correspondence is remarkably close for the Northwest Coast. The vegetational-climatic area of the Northwestern Hygrophytic Coniferous Forest tallies almost absolutely with the cultural one. This forest is generally considered as extending into northern California. The culture extends to Cape Mendocino and the lower Eel River, which lie about at the middle of the Redwood belt. This Redwood strip may be viewed as a specialized southern extension of the northwestern forest; its denser and more characteristic part is its northern half, which belongs clearly to the Northwest culture.

The areal types of the Northwest culture can be formulated only tentatively. While this is one of the more intensively studied regions of the continent, interest has been away from classificatory and developmental problems."

More recently, Wayne Suttles (1968: 67-68) has argued for perceived and real "seasonal and local variations in the amount of food offered by their habitat" and that such variation required successful means for organizing labour, for redistributing the population and resources over the habitat, for motivating and encouraging labour, and for maintaining an adequate technology. The orientation of the NWC infrastructure was much more to the water than to the land (as we all know).

This marine adaptation has been treated in considerable detail by Suttles, Philip Drucker, and others. I have chosen to [9] focus on the ceremonial and social aspects of this adaptation. In its most general form it was expressed by the First Salmon Ritual, while one of its most distinctive forms as whaling.

Erna Gunther (1926: 1928) has given us two comparative studies of the First Salmon Ceremony. As expected, the occurrance of the ritual coincides with the seasonal run of fish, but not exclusively salmon runs. Gunther (1928: 156) noted the functional equivalence of the rite with corn. Bear, and First Fruit rites in other culture areas. Recent ecological studies among the Ainu of Japan show even more detailed parallels.

According to Hitoshi Watanabe (1973: 159), the Ainu, Tungus, and NWC peoples are "related closely with their way of ordering nature in terms of spatial orientation." The Ainu held their Salmon Rites on the eve of the run, at the first catch, and at the close of the runs. The ceremony of the first catch seems closest to the NWC first salmon ceremony (Gunther 1928: 150ff, Watanabe 1973: 71ff). Shared aspects also include grouping the salmon of each river course under a salmon leader, attributing human form to the salmon in their homes under the sea, a general ritual welcome for the first salmon caught, and a return of some or all salmon bones to the sea so that the salmon will be reborn and willing to return the next year.

I have been able to find only slight evidence for similar fish rites elsewhere in Native America. Fish, shellfish, and sea [10] mammals were important resources along both coasts and the Great Lakes. Generally, throughout much of Native America, tobacco was offered to the first of any species that was appropriated for human use. More specifically, before their dispersal in the 1600's, Canadian Algonquians and Hurons had an annual spring ceremony in which two virgin girls were married to seine net to ensure a bountiful catch (Tooker 1964: 79). This is exactly analogous to the Katzie Salish belief, described by Wayne Suttles at this NWC conference, that these people have an affinal relationship with the sockeye salmon. The presence of two girls may be related to the equation of salmon and twins throughout much of the NWC. During the major fishing season in the fall, Huron fish preachers begged the fish to allow themselves to be caught and also promised the fish that the Huron would not burn the fish bones (Tooker 1964: 64). Throughout Native America such procedures seem to be closely related to beliefs that animals (and sometimes plants) have metaphorical human forms, immortal essences, and the ability to come and go of their own will. For this reason, animal bones are always properly treated. In the Southwest, deer and bear bones are collected together, sanctified by a hunting priesthood among the Pueblos, and then deposited in mountain shrines (Davis 1959). In sum, then, we can regard the First Salmon Ceremony as a combination of features shared widely in Native America and elsewhere, which are usually specifically focused on the peculiarities of the salmon. [11]

While the parallels are less with respect to salmon, the parallels in whaling between NWC and Northeast Coast are stronger.

Whaling occurred aboriginally in Siberia, the Arctic, the NWC, and very likely in the Northeast. We are already familiar with the North Pacific parallels. According to Adrian Linder (n.d.) the Northeast aboriginal whaling centers included Cape Cod and Nantucket, where in 1712 or 1712 whaling crews were still either half Indian or all Indian with a white captain. In the early 1700's Parliament passed laws making it illegal for Indians to drink or for whites to impede Indians during the whaling season. At even earlier periods, the parallels between the North Pacific and the North Atlantic whaling practices are clearer since European ships and equipment were not in use. For example in 1605 George Waymouth saw Indians around the Kennebec River in Maine, go "in the company of their king with a multitude of boats" to hunt a whale. After the whale was harpooned, killed, and dragged ashore; the people sang while their "chief lords" cut up the carcass and gave everyone a share of the meat.

Among the Indians of Rhode Island, it was the custom when a whale was cast ashore or killed within their jurisdiction to cut the flesh into pieces and send some to the neighboring tribes as a present of peculiar value (Starbuck quoted in Linder.)

At the risk of being obvious, I will only note that these incidents of Algonquian whaling had direct parallels in Nootka practice [12] on the West Coast of Vancouver Island. Furthermore, the sharing of meat is an important social phenomenon in all native societies. Rather than call whaling a distinctive NWC trait, we might do better to compare occurrences of Native American whaling to the purpose of showing its function among available resources, or of the influence of the intervening Eskimos, or Inuit Peoples rather than of any cultural uniqueness.

The NWC is also said to have had one of the highest population densities in Native America. This density was related to the richness of marine and land resources in addition to the techniques developed to harvest and store them. There is also a very significant but overlooked feature of NWC population distribution. The population could only be localized within favorable resource and beach area, which themselves were circumscribed between the shore and the coast mountain ranges. The denseness and bramble of the land vegetation limited penetration into the interior with the exception of available corridors were the river valleys which cut through these mountain ranges.

Robert Carneiro has argued that state systems are most likely to develop in such circumscribed areas, hemmed in by mountain walls, as is the NWC, or by deserts, as in the Old World. The high rate of individual mobility on the NWC has been noted, but it is also important that we recall that such mobility was actually constrained by settlement location and overall terrain. When [13] individuals and groups can move out of a given area, levels of social complexity remain minimal. However, in circumscribed areas, social complexity increases. Populations become differentiated as access to resources becomes regulated. Concommitently, these differentiated social groups are held together by developed forms of mutual inter-independence relying on specializations and redistributive networks. In other words, I believe that the exploitation of the resource potential, the development of a high population density, and the circumscription of the area go a long way toward explaining the social complexity not only of.the NWC but also of the Southwest and the Southeast culture areas. Similarly, in the early historic period, a more complete exploitation of the resource potential of the Great Plains grasslands which was permitted by the introduction of the horse, which made bison hunting more efficient. The ownership of horses encouraged the development of pastoral societies in which differential access to horses was fostering an emerging class system.

Much earlier, probably with the retreat of the Ice Age, a similar sorting out of people and resources began on the NWC. Simplistically, we can view NWC social organization as a gradient from the matrilineal, moiety-based societies of the north to the more loosely patrilineal, task group-based societies of the south. The northern societies also emphasize time depth through their focus on ancestors as the sources for the matrilines and [14] of the crest systems. Toward the south, the emphasis, seems to be upon the immediacy of individual action and choices. A similar gradient, but in reverse order, characterized the East Culture area: matrilineal, moiety-based societies of the Muskogeans of the Southeast graded into the loosely patrilineal, task group-based kindreds of the Northeastern Subarctic. To better understand this similarity, I would suggest looking into the possibility that the greatest areas of circumscription and of resource exploitation might coincide with those areas where the sorting out process was rigorous enough to create stratified, matrilineal societies.

Ronald Olsen (1933: 395) once suggested that the moieties of the East, Southwest, and NWC culture areas had a common origin because all of them could be interpreted as based on an earth/sky duality. However, the recent theoretical work on moieties by Claude Levi-Strauss, David Maybury-Lewis, and Alfonso Ortiz makes me more willing to view such similarities as the result of universal human processes rather than of diffusion. As a Tewa Indian and an anthropologist, Alfonso Ortiz (1965) has contributed significantly to our understanding of moiety inter-relationships in the southwest. Such studies should now be done for the moieties of the Southeast and NWC. These are functionally equivalent. For example, the White moiety of the Creek Indians parallels the Tlingit Ravens in that both are conceived as homogeneous or "all on one side," while the Creek Red moiety and the Tlingit Eagle-Wolf moiety are [15] alike in that they are regarded as heterogeneous. These are expected to incorporate alien peoples into the moiety system by 2 making them Reds or Eagle-Wolves.[376] As Levi-Strauss has reminded us,

---

[376] In checking the literature, I found that the Creek-Tlingit moiety parallels exist in more complex form than I described them. It is true that the Creek White moiety is usually called

moieties are important for the study of human social organization because they are logically the simplest example of something that indeed can be more complex (Boon: 76). In structuralist terms, binary oppositions stand in relation to systems in general, just as dual organization, especially when formalized as moieties, stands in relation to social organization generally. In the reciprocal and hierarchical inter-action of two elements we can see the fundamental workings of all social systems.

Allied with the theoretical importance of moieties is the unexplained observation of Elisabeth Tooker that "although masks are often found in societies lacking matrilineal moeties, no society that has matrilineal moieties is without masks" (Barnouw 1975: 326).

This reference to masks brings us to a consideration of the potlatch and winter ceremonials of the NWC. Both events involve crests, which can be defined as = inherited art forms; such as songs, dances, designs, etc. I will regard the potlatch as a formalized redistribution of crests, privileges, people, and resources before a body of witnesses, who validate changes in the social fabric of NWC societies. While crests and potlatches are a hallmark of the NWC, they are not unique in the human record. [16]

Stylistic and functional equivalents for each can be found in that type of communal event which has such an integrative character that Marcel Mauss called them "total social phenomena."

---

by a term which translates as "White people," "Those who stick or adhere together (Swanton 1928:157) analogously to the Tlingit Ravens. Similarly, the Creek Red moiety and the Tlingit Eagle-Wolf are "Those of Different Speech" or heterogeneous origins. However, while the Tlingit Eagle-Wolf moiety does incorporate aliens (Oberg: 44), among the Creek "the White or Peace side was that which usually took in foreign communities (Swanton: 250, also 266, 53). Swanton (274) himself saw this Creek and Tlingit evidence as "suggesting a foreign origin for one of the two moieties" in each case. In addition, the Tlingit Raven crests are said to largely consist of non-predators, and the Eagle-Wolf crests of predatory totemic animals (Oberg: 47). Similarly, the White moiety and its clans are said to represent Peace and the Red moiety and clans, War.

The attributes are as I originally reported them but these structural transformations were not noted. I still believe that these attributes and their complex equivalences are much more a function of human thought and social usage than of any historical factors.

After working both in the NWC and the Southeast, Swanton (725) concluded that on the SE coast

Although in modified form, we discover a tendency toward the social condition so characteristic of the North Pacific, a system resting on wealth rather [22] than birth or warlike prowess, widespread commercialism giving rise to a medium of exchange and affecting basal laws. We find an analogy also in the use of wooden armor, though there does not seem at first sight any necessary connection between it and a property system. In any case a complete development after the northwest coast pattern was prevented by the absence of a lofty range of mountains which might have defended the dwellers by the ocean, and the relative richness and hence greater power of the interior Indians.

In all, a hint of the circumscription hypothesis I have proposed elsewhere in this paper.

Each of the culture areas was characterized by its own total social phenomenon. The East had the Green Corn rite, the Plains had the Sun Dance and now has the Native American Church, the Southwest has calendrical world renewals, and the various culture areas in western Native America have First Fruit observances. While all of these integrative rites are different in form and content, they are similar in function.

IV

It is time now to summarize my argument and to offer some new directions to NWC research based on developments in anthropology and in Native American studies.

My argument has been close to that of Levi-Strauss for anthropology generally although the ideas are not uniquely his. He has said we can best show the commonalities of humans globally by accounting for their local differences. With this point in mind, the important focus for NWC research is not to show its uniqueness, but rather how this uniqueness (if we can validly call it this) is related to the totality of forms, contents, functions, and meanings in other societies of Native America and of the world. To help orient the way, let me suggest some recent work that might [17] help. I will particularly address developments in aesthetics, social organization, and cosmology.

In the area of aesthetics, scholarship best knows the NWC and its art from the work of Bill Reid, Wilson Duff, Paul Wingert and Bill Holm. But art is not limited to painting and sculpture. The beauty and richness of NWC music and dance has all but ignored in publications. I realize that the crest system and ownership rights might impede such research, but the need is great for an integrated presentation in this realm of art. I especially have in mind the co-operative venture of native initiative and full native participation with professionals as a way of recording for posterity NWC music and dance. There is also the example of the co-operative work which Gertrude Kurath has done with Iroquois music and dance (1964) and with Tewa music and dance (1970). Her publications provide not only an analysis of the music but also careful Laban notations of the accompanying dances.

In the area of social organization, relevant developments range from work in New Guinea to work among Pueblos. New Guinea might seem a strange place to look for insights into the NWC, so let me explain. New Guinea is one of the few areas of the world where anthropologists arrived at about the same time as the settlers. In other worlds, we have a particularly accurate view of the aboriginal conditions, especially of Highland New Guinea. Anyone interested in comparative data on individual mobility and on the contact situation might do well to consult the continuing discussion in New [18] Guinea ethnography which characterizes society as organized flow (Watson 1970), A specific focus on such research should also include an investigation into the patterns of adoption and fosterage as a means of regulating the flow, especially of NWC commoners.

Also relevant to the study of NWC social organization is work done by Alfonso Ortiz (1969) and myself (1974) on the symbolic reversal of important cultural principles across ethnic boundaries. One example is the reversal of the definitions and of the associations of the sexual and seasonal categories between the Tewa and the Keres Pueblos of New Mexico. Such reversals serve as vital boundary markers between Societies which frequently interact. The analogous but unanalyzed example for the NWC would probably be the .reversal of the crests of the Eagle and the Raven moieties between the mainland tribes and the Haida (Garfield

276

1939:231). The results of an in-depth analysis of this NWC reversal should be theoretically quite exciting in terms of our understanding of cultural transmission and ethnic boundaries.

It is in the area of cosmology that the greatest lack exists in NWC studies. Given the wealth of material on mythology, on the location of supernaturals, and on geographical terminology; I find it puzzling that no one has presented a well-rounded picture of the various NWC cosmologies. I think the reason lies more in the theoretical orientation of fieldworkers than in the quality of [19] the data. It will take a thorough grounding in symbolic theory and a more sophisticated model, but I do believe that such a presentation is possible. Relevant work has already been done on this topic in South America (Reichel-Dolmatoff 1971) and, to some extent in Australia (Meggitt 1972). In the past, the cosmological data has been viewed as piecemeal, but by using insights from other areas and by shifting our perspective on the data, I believe that a search for inter-relationships and integration will provide the necessary breakthrough.

As I said in the beginning, NWC research is what all of us make it. If we look for underlying patterns of similarity behind the differences, anthropology as a whole will benefit. The future will tell, as will the past.

"BOOK WATCH"
Sam D Gill, *Mother Earth*, An American Story. University of Chicago Press 1987

This is a polemical work, a version of the "dozens" where Blacks take turns insulting each other's mothers, only here it is played upon our collective Mother Earth. Much rests on the manner in which Gill constructs his argument, insisting on a distinction between metaphor and theology. While he acknowledges the metaphorical existence of Mother Earth, he denies She had a theological status as a goddess, until this century. All of this is argued from a range of Euro-American historical and academic sources: He would have done well to be more skeptical of the documents and more open to native testimony.

This work is an exercise within a European tradition dedicated to debunking the status of Mother Earth in classical religions. Thus, Gill is engaged in an intellectual dialogue apart from Native America, seeking to broaden it by treating Americanist data.

Using quotes attributed to Tecumsah (*Tekumtha*) and Smohalla, he states that these constitute the flimsy evidence for the existence of Mother Earth. He also considers the reports of her existence among the Zuni and Luiseno.

He discusses historical evidence for a meeting between Tecumsah and William H Harrison at Vincennes, suggesting that Tecumsah stated that he chose to repose on his mother's bosom, the ground, not for religious but for political reasons, to create "a hitch in the negotiations" (p17). He traces the use of the quote in various newspapers, plays, and histories, finding slavish copying from one to another.

In a brief consideration of Shawnee religion, he cites work from the 1930s on "Our Grandmother," their deity. Gill plays dense with Her, the focus of Shawnee rituals and prayers to this day, arguing that Her eminence is historic. (Incidentally, the wide availability of Gill's books and his reliance on only the published record has irritated some native people, who read therein about their surviving rituals and religion in the past tense.) He ends the discussion of the Shawnee with a consideration of the importance of Indians, especially Tecumsah, for defining an American identity. Considering the Euro-American image of Indian America as a girl, as Pocahontas, and Euro (white) America as man, he relates these to motifs in European folklore.

For Smohalla, he considers treaties and land loss throughout the Plateau. He argues that likening the earth to a mother helped natives express their sense of dismay over the loss of their homelands. In considering the various prophet cults throughout the region, he decides that the mythic combination of characters, such as Coyote, Jesus, and Mother Earth in the same story, suggests that the last is probably "very recently acquired in the context of a highly creative and dynamic historical situation" (p61), but this is being overly selective.

He next considers Zuni belief, where Mother Earth and Father Sky have long been reported by scholars, particularly Frank Cushing, who supposedly composed his own summary of Zuni creation to include a "Metamother Earth." Gill slights data from other Pueblos, such as the Keres where Iatiku and other primordial women do equate with a maternal earth.

The Luiseno of southern California are famous for the poetic complexity of their origin saga, a creation of order from chaos by means of brother/sister incest. Reviewing all the versions and their collectors only complicates the issue further, particularly because Gill does not evaluate their relative merits.

In the two final chapters, he discusses how scholars and Indians have contributed to the deification of Mother Earth. He becomes indignant that EB Tylor, H Haeberlin, M Eliade, and A

Hultkrantz have espoused Mother Earth from what Gill regards as little evidence. For Indians, he has to accept the current importance of Mother Earth, but he attributes it to recent events and the appeal of Her image for both red and white. Tracing this image to the writing of Charles Eastman (*Ohiyesa*), he finds that it invokes the nobility of primitivism and environmentalism, allows white to be criticized obliquely, and focuses an identity that has both continuity and creativity.

The book compels the reader because Gill persists in being dense and literal with the data. He does not control the literature on the various tribes and regions (e.g. regarding the Nespelem as Northern Okanagan (p57)), and evidently has never talked to natives of these traditions. By relying only on documents — and denying other interpretations and insights, he builds his case. He is raiding across disciplines, without being grounded in them. Most profoundly, he can deny Mother Earth because he ignores the significance of "Man"/ "Woman" symbolism throughout the Americas. His division of metaphor from theology is artificial, as is his concern with gods and goddesses. These categories are not appropriate for the Americas, where attention focuses on the paradoxical and the culturally multi-faceted. Someone as fundamental as Mother Earth, the foundation for the life of growers, two-legs, and four-footed, is so obvious and accepted as to require hardly any special mention.

Deified Mind among the Keresan Pueblos

Abstract
The Keresan belief in a supreme deity, who has been called Thought Woman in the literature, is explored here. The belief revolves around many dimensions with symbolic oppositions involving Man / Woman, Sacred / Secular, and Nature / Culture. As an androgynous being, with the potential to assume any form but particularly that of a spider, this creator truly presides over a rational universe.

Stanley Newman did not introduce me to the literature on the Keresan Pueblos, but he certainly made me more aware of its complexities. As my undergraduate advisor, he had the difficult task of guiding me through shifting loyalties to archaeology, linguistics, and symbolic anthropology. My rudder through it all was a fascination with the Keres that was continually reinforced by my exposure to their prehistory as a member of the Anasazi Origins Project, their ethnography through reading, their public rituals as an observer, and their language via examples used by Newman from his fieldwork with Laguna.

Eventually, the Keres took me to graduate school and provided a dissertation. They continue to fascinate me, but now in comparison with other Native American tribes where I have done more sustained Held work (Miller 1980, 1985).

Yet one aspect of Keres culture stands out above all others. This is their belief in a high god or supreme deity who has been often called Thought Woman in the literature. Recently, several authors, themselves belonging to Laguna Pueblo (Parsons 1923), have also provided commentary on this being. Among the things that impressed me in Newman's classes was his interest in the more subjective side of linguistics, particularly his interest in the sound symbolism and psychiatric dimensions of speech.

Assessing both the older literature on this deity and modern commentary, our understanding of this "female" deity should improve. It is not that such a being is unique to the Keres, after all the Shawnee pray to Grandmother and the southern Numic to Ocean Woman.
[152]
The earliest account in this century occurs in the curious volume by Gunn (1917:89):

> Their theory is that reason (personified) is the supreme power, a master mind that has always existed, which they call *Sitch-tche-na-ko*. This is the feminine form for thought or reason. She had one sister, Shro-tu-me-na-ko, memory or instinct. Their belief is that *Sitch-tche-na-ko* is the Creator of all, and to her they offer their most devout prayers, but never to *Shro-tu-me-na-ko*. They say it is bad to do so. This shows that they know of the two divisions of the mind, reason and instinct, and also that they are aware of the apparent uselessness, and possible evil consequences, of cultivating the subjective mind.

While there is much in his book which is questionable, as in some of this paragraph, his basic statement does hold. The creator at Laguna is something like personified thought or reason. This was confirmed a few years later in the work of Parsons (1920:114), where she names the four sisters who figure in the Origin Saga: *iyetiku, tsichinnako, naustiti, ushstiti.* In a

280

footnote (1920: 114 #3) she adds, for the second, "The etymology given is *tsichu*, think, *chinnaku*, femaleness."

Again from Laguna, Boas (1928:7, 276), building on the fieldwork of Parsons, makes reference to *ts'its'i.'na.k'o* and to "Thought Woman (the Spider?)." He includes the only available text in Keresan (Keresic) making reference to her role as creator of the universe.

At the end of their discussion of the ceremonial calendar at Laguna, Dutton and Marmon (1936: 20) call attention to "Reason, a great power — the Great Spirit, we might call it — had created earth, the sun, the stars, and all living creatures." This is again the deity in the guise of an English equivalent.

The most careful statement, however, has come from a member of the pueblo, attempting to compare Keres and Christian notions of the deity (Purley 1974). For him, the hallmarks of Thought Woman are the concepts of a supreme being, a female, a fused godhead, and a denial of human dominion over the world.

In the course of this, he reports

> *Tse che nako* is all-comprehensive and in no need to be worshipped, therefore she does not demand worship for herself to satisfy "Her Own." "Her Own" includes all life possibilities within herself (p.30).

> The Keres people believe that *Tse che nako* has more female than male attributes: therefore she is referred to and approached as if she is female (p30). [153]

> *Tse che nako* is not limited to a female role in the total theology ... she is both Mother and Father to all people and to all creatures. She can function in whichever role she chooses and very often does ... (p30).

> She did not restrict the process of creation only to herself. Tse che nako included the power to create individual thought in all human beings and all creatures. In other words, all living things can create, although it is a matter of degree (p31).

> Keres holy men hesitate to mention *Tse che nako*'s name, especially for purely secular discussions. Thought Woman's name is reserved for use only in sacred ceremonies. In secular discussions and teachings, *Tse che nako* is often symbolically referred to as Old Spider Woman or Spider Woman (p31).

> ... evil, while it is a separate, recognized force, is not so strong that it must be blamed for mankind's wrongdoing. Mankind is responsible for its own behavior (p32).

Curiously, Purley does not mention that aspect of the Christian tradition which is closest to Keresan notions of divinity, namely Sophia as Wisdom and feminized Mind.

Lastly, we have the poem that begins the famous novel by Silko (1977), herself of Laguna ancestry, paying homage to "*Ts'its'tsi'nako*, Thought-Woman" (line 1), Thought-Woman, the spider (line 10), who is "sitting in a room" (line 14) thinking the story we are about to be told.

Laguna is one of seven contemporary Keres pueblos in central New Mexico, and, to some extent, the most divergent. About 1870, after the railroad came through their lands, the pueblo split into different groups. While all of the other Keres are nominally Roman Catholic, Laguna had a sizeable Protestant segment, the outcome of intermarriage with American men of authority. The more traditionally conservative and Catholic party left Old Laguna and settled at Isleta, a Tiwa Pueblo just south of Albuquerque. After a few years, many of them came back to Laguna land and built the town of Mesita, although their religious paraphernalia, or much of it, stayed at Isleta (Harvey 1963).

As I have reconstructed it, Keres social organization is binary at many levels, all of them pervaded by an axiomatic concern with gender. Thus, of the seven modern towns, three (Cochiti, Santo Domingo, and San Felipe) are manly, characterized by leaders drawn from the priesthoods and by the initiation of only boys into the cult of the masked Katsina. [154]

The other four (Santa Ana, Sia, Acoma, and Laguna) are womanly, with leaders selected for both matri-clan and priesthood and the Katsina initiation of both boys and girls. Further, there is also something like an intensity scale in which Cochiti and Santa Ana are the most strongly consistent with this ideology and Santo Domingo and Laguna, both of which have many external links with other cultures, are the most diffuse.

Hence, we need to consider the belief in this deity among other Keres before we can properly appreciate all of these references from Laguna.

To date, the best published statement on this deity appears in the last volume of Leslie White's (1962:113) comparative study of the Keresan towns.

The most important deity in Sia cosmology is *Tsityosti.nako*, "Prophesying Woman" ... This deity is found at Santa Ana ... and at Laguna ... also. But everywhere the conception appears to be unclear and even inconsistent. Stevenson treats this deity as a male, but in her emergence myth *Sussistinnako* is addressed as "our mother" (in Keresan pueblos the cacique, a man, is ceremonially addressed as "mother"). The ending *-nako* means 'woman.' But at Laguna she "looked like a man" (Boas 1925: 221, 228). Stevenson says that *Sussistinnako* was a spider; my informants, that *Tsityostinako* "had the shape of a certain kind of spider."

Tsityostinako is called Prophesying Woman because "she knows [rather than deciding or determining] what is going to happen;" one informant added: "when a person is thinking about something that is *Tsityostinako* expressing herself in him."

Tsityostinako lives at *Shipop* in the Yellow world, "but she is everywhere, like God," one informant said. She is the creator in Sia cosmology as she is at Laguna (Gunn 1917: 89). She bore two daughters, *Utctsiti,* the mother of the Indians, and *Naotsiti,* the mother of other races and peoples.

As this quote confirms, this deity is associated with thought in several modes, with spider, and with creation as an ongoing process. The 'thought' etymology is supported by recent grammars. For Santa Ana, Davis (1964: 170 #455) lists *c'idʸustA* as 'to think, to worry.' From Acoma, Wick Miller (1965:n84, 109) has *'ic'itistaan'i* 'mind, willpower' and *–'uc'itistaaN* 'to think'. In a text. Spider Woman gives aid to the War Twins (Miller 1965:2 53).

For the manner in which the original creation took place we must refer to two volumes dealing with the Acoma account. By a curious twist, the [155] account of the saga was published by Stirling (1942), but the most important aspect of the process, the songs which enabled creation to occur, was published by Densmore (1957).

Together, these versions make clear that thought has a pulsating vitality most like song. It is this parallel that has been overlooked in previous accounts of the saga, such as the summary by White (1960).

The spider attribute relates both to the form of the arachnid body and its web: a center with extensions. The web is a particularly apt metaphor for thought because the rhythmic pulse of thought waves mirrored in the songs of creation and curing flows out as ripples and rays from the source and summary which is this deity. The presence of two terms for this deity is a reflection of the important distinction between the ordinary Keresan language used by everyone and the ceremonial vocabulary used by men in the kivas, first reported for Laguna by Hrdlicka (1903) and since confirmed for all Keres (White 1944, Fox in Lange 1959: 558).

All of the evidence assembled indicates that Thought Woman, as Mind, is not so much an entity as a nexus of many important dimensions, the crux of a series of symbolic oppositions, involving Man / Woman, Sacred / Secular, and Nature / Culture. As a manlike being with female attributes, with the potential to assume any form but particularly that of a spider, this creator truly presides over a rational universe.

Struckon Model:
Comprehensive Anthropological Description

Anthropology has always been defined as the study of humans, but in actual practice, it has only approached this definition in terms of broad cross-cultural studies that depend upon data amassed from particular ethnographic societies. The necessary transition between Culture (as the singularly human attribute) and a culture (as a conceptual system for imposing order and meaning within the cosmos of a particular human group) has yet to be articulated in a manner that is efficient and parsimonious. While anthropologists are well aware of this so-called etic / emic distinction, this paper attempts such an articulation to bridge the distinction.

Struckon Model

The accompanying diagram outlines a model for the description of a structural configuration (a struckon) that fulfills requirements basic to any scientific endeavor: holism, parsimony, and coherence. The model itself is a unique blend that has been inspired by the German configurationalism of Leo Frobenius,[377] and the French structuralism of Claude Levi-Strauss,[378] and the theory of "marking" of the Prague Linguistic Circle as interpreted by Joseph Greenberg.[379] The model owes to Frobenius the recognition of the integrated coherence of a culture as derived from a shared, pervasive property called a "paideuma". By adopting this term from Frobenius, I also intend to separate my configurational model from the more diffuse, stylistic configurationalism of Ruth Benedict[380] and Alfred Kroeber. In keeping with a general structuralist orientation, the focus of the struckon model is upon relationships rather than objects. In terms of marking, the model recognizes the dyadic and inherently triadic, relationships that are universal for human conceptualization. To better express these relationships, the more strictly linguistic phenomena of marking are distinguished below from the cultural ones by introducing the terms "inclusive/exclusive" to apply to the cultural categories.

Throughout the discussion, "culture" is used to refer to an integrated conceptual system for bringing order and meaning to the world. "Society" refers to the behaviors and institutions which result from the dialectical interplay between culture and environment. A struckon is defined as an integrated system of relationships among concrete expressions, which I have called "emanations", linked to an apical, all-pervasive, logical opposition (paideuma).[2]

The model has two aspects: a universal etic one and a specific emic one. The etic aspect relates to the form of the relationships, while the emic one depends upon the content of relationships specific to a culture and its interplay with environment through the means of a

---

[377] J Honigmann, *The Development of Anthropological Ideas*. The Dorsey Press; Homewood, Illinois 1976.

[378] The Most Succinct Statement on Levi-Straussian's structuralism remains Ino Rossi's Structuralism As Scientific Method: 60-106 in a work he edited entitled *The Unconscious in Culture*; The Structuralism of Claude Levi-Strauss in Perspective. EP Dutton, New York 1974.

[379] J Greenberg, *Language Universals*, Mouton, The Hague 1966.

[380] R Benedict, *Patterns of Culture*, Mentor, New York, 1960. Originally published in 1934.

society. The etic relationships of form will be considered first, although this is strictly for purposes of exposition since the form and the content of any struckon are always dialectically related.

The struckon aspect of form is derived from the recognition of two basic types of relationships: hierarchy and reciprocity among binary contrasts.[381] The backbone of the model consists of a graded hierarchical sequence articulated by reference to the paideuma at its apex. The hierarchy itself is composed of paired metaphors which I call "emanations". Integrating these emanations at various levels are mediators, which serve to bridge some or all of the distinctions between the members of an emanation pair, in addition to having properties unique to themselves as mediators. The exact qualities of these mediators will be more fully discussed below after the term "inclosive" has been introduced to clarify the properties of triadic relationships.

Following Levi-Strauss, in terms of the etic form, the Human Struckon for all cultures recognizes the paideuma of Nature / Culture medicated by Mind. In particular, this recognition of Mind (Intellect) as the apical mediator establishes a fixed point of reference for a universal form hierarchy. Such a hierarchy serves as an "etic grid" from which alternative "emic" cultures are derived through a process of transforming or re-arranging the emanations within the overall hierarchical and [3] reciprocal relationships. In this way, it is possible to derive variable contents for specific cultures with different paideuma from this invariant form of etic hierarchy. The etic hierarchy can be usefully viewed as a sequence composed of three types of emanations.

With the Mind as point of reference and proximity as our criterion, these three types are hierarchically arranged in terms of what I have called sensory, interpersonal, and cosmic emanations. Sensory emanations are paired sets nearest to the apex because they relate to the mind of an individual culture-bearer, specifically to the sensory aspects of a person. Interpersonal metaphors are intermediate in the hierarchy in that they refer to the collective interactions of society members within the contexts of various social institutions. Furthest removed from the apex are those emanations concerned with the interplay of humans and their cosmos.

Each of these emanation types has some typical representations which can be usefully listed to further clarify our recognition of them. Sensory emanations, because they relate to mind-body interactions, include colors, sights, sounds, silences, smells, styles of cooking, foods, tastes, hand (laterality) priority (and by extension tactile expressions in shapes, textures, and manufactures), physiological states, and even pattern numbers since these are often used to bring order to sensory experiences.[382] Interpersonal emanations, since they represent the collective

---

[381] C Levi-Strauss, Reciprocity and Hierarchy, *American Anthropologist* 46: 266-268 1944.

[382] A useful scheme for organizing such sensory data has been provided by JB Watson and H Nelson in terms of their "Body-Environment Transactions: A Standard Model for Cross-Cultural Analysis," *Southwestern Journal of Anthropology* 23 (3): 292-309 1967. Their model works best for the etic level, but it can .be accordingly adapted for the emic aspects of a particular culture. in terms of our present understanding, we should expect particular emanations to have fairly standard etic associations with inclusive / exclusive attributes on the basis of their high frequency of co-occurrence in the ethnography. Thus, circular shapes are most usually inclusive and rectangular ones exclusive (see S Witkowski and C Brown "lexical universals" in the *Annual Review of Anthropology* 7: 451 1978, man is inclusive and

interaction of individuals, include various contexts of economy, polity, descent, life cycle, religion, and language. Cosmic emanations, as expressions of the relations among humans and their total environment, include symbolically charged aspects of biota, terrain, geography, meteorological phenomena, celestial bodies, myth characters, temporal progressions, philosophical conclusions, and abstract or other-worldly dimensions.[383] [4]

In addition to its relationship within the hierarchy, each of the emanation pairs is also characterized by a relationship of reciprocity. This reciprocity is defined in terms of the attribute of "inclusivity", which is related to the notion of marking for linguistic phenomenon. Because of the position of reciprocity within the struckon model, the aptness of the terms inclusive / exclusive for this reciprocal relationship, and the ability to pun with the terms "inclusive and inclosive", I prefer to use these terms and to reserve "marking" for reference to linguistic usages. Linguists already familiar with the use of the inclusive / exclusive for first person plural pronouns[384] might be initially confused by my terms, but the reasons given above serve to justify my choice. Greenberg discussed eight criteria for distinguishing marked from unmarked forms, of which the primary one is a much greater frequency of use for the unmarked. Similarly, a primary criterion for recognizing the inclusive from the exclusive relates to a greater frequency of occurrence for the former. This higher frequency seems to derive from an ambiguity inherent in the inclusive attribute.

In each reciprocal relationship, the exclusive member of a pair specifically asserts the presence of a certain property (X), but the inclusive ambiguously asserts either the absence of that property (not-X) in some contexts or the presence of both properties (X and not -X) in these and other contexts.

This relationship was nicely captured in the translation by JNB Hewitt of the terms for the Iroquois Great Beings as "Man-Beings" and "Woman-Man Beings."[385] In this example, Man is exclusive and Woman is inclusive. Before considering other Native American data, comparative [4a] examples from China and Western biology will illustrate the universality of inclusive/exclusive aspects of the human metaphor. In Chinese, the important opposition between yang/yin is also associated with light / dark and male / female. Closer investigation shows that while yang equates high, bright, male, sun, and the male sex organ; yin equates with dark, shadow, moon, female, and both the male and the female sex organs. Culturally, a Chinese man must constantly guard against any loss of his yang, while yin is considered to be boundless. In other words, in China yang is exclusive and yin is inclusive. Similarly, a Western biologist describes the chromosomes of the female as XX and of the male as XY. Whatever the physiological basis for this statement, it is nevertheless clear that conceptually the female is exclusive and the male is inclusive. The Chinese and biological examples illustrate inverse relationships of the inclusive / exclusive attributes of the Precopernican paideuma. In the

---

woman exclusive, and animals are inclusive and plants exclusive.

[383] Some researchers might prefer to subdivide the Cosmic Emanations into "Natural" and "Supernatural" components so that biota and meteorological phenomena can be distinguished etically from the less tangible myth figures and philosophical assumptions, whether or not these are personified.

[384] Mary Haas 'Exclusive' and 'Inclusive': A Look at Early Usage, *International Journal of American Linguistics* 35 (1): 1-6 (1969).

[385] JNB Hewitt, Iroquoian Cosmology, Bureau of American Ethnology *Annual Report* 43 1928.

Chinese example, Man is exclusive but woman is inclusive. Western biology reverses these associations, but the Iroquois duplicate them.

Greenberg did not provide different terms to specify this ambiguity, probably because the ambiguity is always inherent in the relationship and thus difficult to characterize. However, by using the term "inclusive", I am able to capture both of these ambiguous qualities by referring to the inclusive when it is specifically opposed [5] to the exclusive as simply the inclusive (as not-X) and to the inclusive when it generally refers to both the inclusive and the exclusive as the "inclosive". Further, this inclosive dimension remains latent in the Inclusive whether or not it is explicitly expressed. The distinction is necessary because the inclusive and the inclosive have different formal properties: The inclusive / exclusive is a dyadic relationship while the inclusive (inclosive) exclusive is a triadic one that admits the possibility of a mediator in the inclosive position. Based on this observation, it is also possible to consistently align the inclusive metaphors on one side of the hierarchy and the .exclusive ones on the other, with the inclosive mediators in the middle. This assortment permits the logical consistency of a struckon to emerge with a particular clarity that goes far beyond the confused surface of ethnographic data. In the words of Levi-Strauss, "If social phenomena are just objectivized systems of Ideas, to explain them is to rethink them in their logical order."[386]

Having introduced the inclosive, we are now prepared to examine the role of mediators. I have retained both the terms inclusive and inclosive, although indicating that the inclosive is inherent in the inclusive, because when the inclosive does emerge (or become recognized) from the inclusive it often seems to have a life of its own.

In other words, it becomes distinct from the inclusive in much the same way that mediators are distinct from metaphors. When mediators intrude on an emanation pair, they occupy the most inclusive (inclosive) position in that they neutralize the basis of the contrast between the members of the pair and stand for the entire relationship. For example, in the Hegelian dialectic, the thesis [6] states the presence of something, like the exclusive; the antithesis countervenes it, like the inclusive; and the synthesis mediates the entire pair, like the inclosive. Unlike abstract states, however, mediators are usually tangible and concrete. They share features with each member of the pair but also have properties of their own which link them with other mediators. For example, Delaware mediators always have their own independent associations with water, trees, and Mind regardless of the emanation pair they are mediating.

These features lead me to suggest that mediators can be said to "intrude" among emanations. Moreover, they can be said to be linked with other emanations which are specifically important within particular emic systems, most especially in terms of primordial properties introduced in the Origin Myth or redundant for all human cultures. The very presence of a mediator in a relationship identifies it as triadic, but not all relationships have mediators. A relationship characterized by only the inclusive / exclusive is open-ended and truly complementary in the same way that two points are sufficient to form an infinite line, which then provides the basis for more complex geometrical shapes. The triad of inclusive (inclosive) exclusive, however, has even greater coherence and integrity since three points are minimally sufficient to provide closure, to define a plane.

---

[386] Quoted in Rossi p79. See Note 2.

In most cultures, the more specific and significant emanation pairs appear to have intrusive mediators occupying the inclusive position. Many of these mediators have metonymic ties to the Origin Myth, as noted above. Other mediators draw upon redundant features common to human experience, such as reference to the number 3 with its ability to express closure. More to the point, also, are recurrent expressions of the importance of [7] Mind by means of various typical mediators. I interpret the predominant characteristic of these mediators as the ability to represent a "permeating nexus", as though Mind were conceived as a central point from which some sort of tendrils emanated to permeate and engulf everything else in the cultural realm. Such permeation is ambiguous, ubiquitous, and sometimes subtle enough to appear amorphous. Indeed, classic examples of such permeating nexi include references to spiders as important culture heroes, **to** a cross as defining the four cardinal directions, to a pole as *axis mundi*, to a shape like that of the six-pointed toy used in the game of jacks which conjoins the cross and pole, to a cube as delimiting the 3 dimensions of volume, and to water, the most ubiquitous permeator on a planet largely covered by this element. The significance of water is further indicated by references to amphibians and reptiles as important mediators. The World Turtle of the Delaware is but one of many examples that could be cited. Another recurrent mediator is the D-shape, a roughly triangularoid shape which also serves to conjoin linear and circular expressions. One example of it is the frequent description of the universe as a sky dome over on earth disk (a horizontal-D: ⌒). Because these mediators can be related to the pervasiveness of Mind, they all share a metonymical relationship which serves to keep them distinct from the particular emanation pair mediated by each of them.

On the other hand, the metaphorical emanations are related to each other by their shared inclusivity or exclusivity, their reciprocity, and their position within the hierarchy. While mediators have inter-relationships of contiguity and sequence (the syntagmatic), metaphors are related by A reciprocity and substitution (the paradigmatic). [8]

By way of summarizing the etic aspect of form within the struckon, we can again note the salience of an etic hierarchy composed of sensory, interpersonal, and cosmic emanations depending upon the paideuma of Nature / Culture mediated by Mind. In this etic paideuma, Nature is inclusive since it both includes Culture, the adaptation of the human animal, and is opposed to it as accident or chaos is opposed to order. Culture is exclusive, therefore, and uniquely human. Mind is inclosive because it is all-encompassing both as expressed in conscious thought and in physiological processes.

By and large, however, anthropologists have no familiarity with this etic grid of struckon form. Each professional has his or her own familiarities, but they relate to content and not to form. In terms of the struckon model, therefore, we must now shift to discuss the content aspect of the struckon in order to provide a procedure for sorting out the relative merits of emanations and paideuma for a particular culture. Which of the emanations of the potential etic form apply to a particular culture and how can we determine their relative rankings in order to establish the paideuma and the overall relationships of that particular struckon?

In initial stages, a struckonal analysis duplicates the four steps of a structuralist analysis[387]

---

[387] Outlined in Rossi.

288

1   Immersion in the data

2   Analyzing the data into abstract categories and relationships expressed as several alternative models.

3   Mental experimentation and manipulation of these alternatives in order to reject the weaker models that account for less of these data.

4   Assertion of the Structure as that model which best includes available data and recombines all the relationships into a meaningful whole. [9]

Like a Structure, a struckon must be characterized by holism, coherence, parsimony, and exhaustiveness.   In addition, a struckonal analysis includes two steps which distinguish the particular emic content of a culture from the etic form:

5   Determination of the relevant emanations of a society in terms of their content, their type, and their inclusivity.

6 Recognition of the pervasive redundancy of the paideuma as that emanation pair which apically subsumes the others for that culture.

While each struckon has to be explored, analyzed, and understood in its own terms, enough research has already been carried out to suggest three content pairs which are crucial for substantiating a paideuma.   In terms of analytical efficiency, the most informative Sensory emanation is right / left[388] that for the Interpersonal is men / women[389] and the Cosmic pair is animal / plant.[390]

While part of every etic form, these emanations are also sensitive indicators of the manipulations of hierarchy and reciprocity that are so important for understanding the content of a particular struckon.

As should be obvious, the struckon model is synchronic. However, once the paideuma is recognized and the struckon worked out in detail, it is possible to project the emic aspect into a diachronic study.   At present, archaeological and historical data are not sufficient in and of themselves **to** articulate a struckon model because so much of the relevant emic data cannot be recovered from these sources: "History does not reveal causes; it presents only a blank succession of unexplained events".[391]

In other words, the true reality is the least obvious and [10] often missed, although it should be even more readily apparent "in the care which it takes to evade our attention".[392]

In sum, a proper struckonal analysis requires the collection of data either from voluminous published ethnography or, best of all, from a planned program of concerted fieldwork always mindful of the dialectic between form and content.

---

[388] R Needham, *Right and Left*: *Essays on Dual Symbolic Classification.* University of Chicago Press 1973.

[389] M Douglas, *Purity And Danger*; *An Analysis of Concepts of Pollution and Taboo*o. Pelican Books, London 1970.

[390] J Fernandez, The Mission of Metaphor in Expressive Culture, *Current Anthropology* 15 (2): 119-145 1974.

[391] I Berlin, *The Hedgehog and the Fox*; *An Essay On Tolstoy's View of History.* Weidenfeld and Nicolson, London 1953.

[392] Quoted in Rossi: 64.

struckon

Because the true reality is meta-empirical, all social phenomena can only be understood through the use of models at various levels of removal from the actual description. In the words of Mary Haas

> the best solution for attaining reality and for narrowing the gap between own-culture and other-culture "is the use of models — not empirical models... but formal models, the more formal the better".[393]

However, purely formal models are also flawed because they are too static. They do not allow for the dialectic, which not only captures the order and meaning of cultural worlds but also"- allows for the manipulation of relevant relationships for specific emic purposes.

The advantage of the struckon model is that it more adequately accounts for more cultural data than previous attempts because it both provides for the etic aspects of form, hierarchy/reciprocity, and inclusive / exclusive, while at the same time recognizing the dialectical flexibility between these relationships and the emic content of paideuma / emanations.

The analysis itself must conform to four criteria which are sufficient to establish the verification of the paideuma. These are deduction, commutability, elegance, and inter-subjectivity. The analysis proceeds by means of deduction (movement from the known to the unknown by logical steps) in quest of relations which are commutable (producing the same results by variable sequences: $3+1 = 4$, or $2 \times 2 = 4$) and lead to a struckonal paideuma that is scientifically elegant (parsimonious, exhaustive, and coherent) and confirmable inter-subjectively (by like-minded researchers).

---

[393] M. Haas 'Other-Culture' vs. 'Own-Culture': Some Thoughts on L White's Query. *American Anthropologist* 67 (6): 1556-1559 1965.

290

Bibliography

Adams, John W
1973 *The Gitksan Potlatch*: Population Flux, Resource Ownership and Reciprocity. Toronto: Holt, Rinehart and Winston of Canada.

Adamson, Thelma
1934 Folktales of the Coast Salish. *Memoirs of the American Folklore Society* # 27. Lancaster.

Andrade, MJ
1931 Quileute Texts. *Columbia University Contributions to Anthropology* 12. New York.

Andrus, Cecil
1979 American Indian Religious Freedom Act Report (PL 95-J41). Federal Agencies Task Force.

Archer, David
1996   New Evidence on the Development of Ranked Society in the Prince Rupert Area. Twenty-ninth Annual Meeting of the Canadian Archaeological Association, Halifax, NS.

Aristotle,
1931 *De Portibus Animalism.* vol. 5 of The Works of Aristotle. WD Ross, ed. Oxford: Clarendon Press.

Bailey, Garrick, ed.
1995 *The Osage and the Invisible World*, From the Works of Francis La Flesche. Norman: University of Oklahoma Press.

Ballard, Arthur C.
1927 Some Tales of the Southern Puget Sound Salish. *University of Washington Publications in Anthropology,* 2: 57–81. Seattle.
1929 Mythology of Southern Puget Sound. *University of Washington Publications in Anthropology,* 3 (2): 31–150. Seattle.

Barbeau, Marius
1917 Review of Franz Boas: Tsimshian Mythology. *American Anthropologist* 19 (4):548–563
1929   Totem Poles of the Gitksan, Upper Skeena River, British Columbia. *Canadian Geological Survey, Bulletin* 61, *Anthropological Series* 12. Ottawa.
1951 Tsimsyan Songs: 97-157 (With 75 Song Texts). *The Tsimshian: Their Arts And Music.* Proceedings of the American Ethnological Society 18. New York: JJ Augustin.

Barbeau, Marius, and William Beynon [206]
1987a Tsimshian Narratives 1: Tricksters, Shamans and Heroes. John J Cove and George F MacDonald, eds. Ottawa: Canadian Museum of Civilization, Mercury Series, Directorate Paper #3.
1987b Tsimshian Narratives 2: Trade and Warfare. George F Macdonald And John J Cove, eds. Canadian Museum Of Civilization. Mercury Series. Directorate Paper # 3.

Barnes, RH
1984 *Two Crows Denies It*:   A History of Controversy of Omaha Sociology. Lincoln: University of Nebraska Press.
1990 A Legacy of Misperception and Invention ~ The Omaha Indians in Anthropology: 211-36. *The Invented Indian*: Cultural Fictions and Government Policies. James Clifton, ed. New Brunswick: Transaction Publishers.

Barnett, Homer.
  1940 Notebooks From Port Simpson and Hazelton. University of British Columbia Special Collections.
  1942 Applied Anthropology In 1860. Applied Anthropology 1 (3): 19-32.
Barnouw, Victor
  1975 An Introduction To Anthropology: Ethnology. Homewood, IL: The Dorsey Press.
Barrett, SA
  1917 Pomo Bear Doctors. University of California Publications in American Archaeology and Ethnology 12 (11): 443-65.
Baum, Frank
  1976 *The Life and Adventures of Santa Claus.* New York: Dover Publications. [1902]
Benedict, Ruth
  1923 The Concept of the Guardian Spirit in North America. American Anthropological Association Memoir # 29.
Berlandier, Jean Louis
  1969 The Indians of Texas in 1830. John Ewers, ed. Smithsonian Institution Press, Washington, DC.
Beynon, William.
  1937 The Halait and All The Different Kinds of Halait. Text From Mrs Julia White and Mrs R Tate. Volume 12, Text # 179, Aug-Sept. Reel 3. Microfilm of Beynon Manuscripts in Butler Library, Columbia University.
Birket-Smith, Kaj and Frederica de Laguna
  1938 *The Eyak Indians of the Copper River Delta, Alaska.* Copenhagen.
Blackburn, Thomas
  1975 *December's Child*, A Book of Chumash Oral Narratives. Berkeley: University of California Press.
Boas, Franz
  1894 Chinook Texts. *Bureau of American Ethnology, Bulletin* 20. Washington.
  1896 The Growth of Indian Mythologies. *Journal of American Folklore* 9: 1–11.
  1898a Introduction, to Traditions of the Thompson Indians of British Columbia. *Memoirs of the American Folklore Society* # 6: 1–18. Lancaster.
  1898b The Mythology of the Bella Coola Indians. *Memoirs of the American Museum of Natural History*, 2:25–127. New York.
  1901 Kathlamet Texts. *Bureau of American Ethnology, Bulletin* # 26. Washington.
  1902 Tsimshian Texts ~ Nass River Dialect. *Bureau of American Ethnology, Bulletin* # 27. Washington
  1905 Kwakiutl Texts. *Memoirs of the American Museum of Natural History*, 5: 1–532. New York.
  1906 Kwakiutl Texts, New Series. *Memoirs of the American Museum of Natural History*, 1: 41–269. New York.
  1910 Kwakiutl Tales. *Columbia University Contributions to Anthropology*, 2: 1–495. New York.
  1912 Tsimshian Texts (New Series). *Publication of the American Ethnological Society* 3: 65–284.

1914 Mythology and Folk-Tales of the North American Indians. *Journal of American Folklore* 27: 374–410.

1916 Tsimshian Mythology. *Thirty-first Annual Report of the Bureau of American Ethnology* 29–979. Washington.

1916a The Development of Folk-Tales and Myths. *Scientific Monthly*, 3: 335–343.

1918 Kutenai Tales. Washington, D.C.: Bureau of American Ethnology, Bulletin # 59.

1925 Contributions to the Ethnology of the Kwakiutl. *Columbia University Contributions to Anthropology*, 3:1–357. New York.

1928 Bella Bella Texts. *Columbia University Contributions to Anthropology*, 5: 1–291.

1928 Keresan Texts. Publications of the American Ethnological Society # 8 ~ 1 & 2: 1-300.

1929 Metaphorical Expressions in the Language of the Kwakiutl Indians. *Race, Language, and Culture.* Reprinted 1949: 232–239. The Macmillan Co., New York.

1930 The Religion of the Kwakiutl Indians. *Columbia University Contributions to Anthropology*, 10: 1-284. New York.

1932 Bella Bella Tales. *Memoirs of the American Folklore Society* 25.

1935 Kwakiutl Culture as Reflected in Mythology. *Memoirs of the American Folklore Society* 28: 1–190. Lancaster.

1935 Kwakiutl Tales, New Series. *Columbia University Contributions to Anthropology* # 26 (1): 1–230. New York.

1943 Kwakiutl Tales, New Series. *Columbia University Contributions to Anthropology* # 26 (2): 1–228. New York.

1966 *Kwakiutl Ethnography.* Helen Coder, ed. University of Chicago Press.

Bolton, Herbert Eugene
1987 *The Hasinais.* Southern Caddoans as Seen by the Earliest Europeans. Russell Magnaghi, ed. Norman: University of Oklahoma Press.

Boon, James
1972 From Symbolism To Structuralism. New York: Harper Torchbooks.

Broch, H
1977 A Note on Berdache Among the Hare Indians of Northwestern Canada. *Western Canadian Journal of Anthropology* 7 (3): 95-101.

Buchler, Ira and Henry Selby
1968 *Kinship and Social Organization*: An Introduction to Theory and Method. New York: The Macmillan Company.

Bunzel, Ruth
1932 Introduction to Zuni Ceremonialism, Bureau of American Ethnology, Forty-Seventh Annual Report 1929-1930: 469-544. Washington, DC.

Carter, Cecile Elkins
1995 *Caddo Indians: Where We Come From.* Norman: University of Oklahoma Press.

Cassirer, E
1944 *An Essay on Man.* New Haven: Yale University Press.

Chicago Anthropology Exchange
1981 *Native American Lands.* Special Double Issue. 14 (1-2): 1-218.

Chafe, Wallace
1976 The Caddoan, Iroquoian, and Siouian Languages: 213-235. Mouton, The Hague.

1979   Caddoan.   Languages of Native North America: A Historical and Comparative Assessment. Lyle Campbell and Marianne Mithun, eds. Austin: University of Texas Press.

1983   The Caddo Language, Its Relatives, and Its Neighbors: 243-250. *North American Indians: Humanistic Perspectives*. James Thayer, ed. Norman: University of Oklahoma, Papers in Anthropology 24 (2).

Chamberlain, Von Del

1982 When Stars Came Down to Earth: Cosmology of the Skidi Pawnee Indians of North America. *Ballena Press Anthropological Papers* # 26. Los Altos.

Chowning, Ann

1962   Raven Myths in Northwestern North America and Northeastern Asia. *Arctic Anthropology* 1 (1): 1–5.

Clark, Ella E

1953 *Indian Legends of the Pacific Northwest.* University of California Press, Berkeley.

Clutesi, George

1967 *Son of Raven, Son of Deer.* Sidney, BC: Grays.

Collins, June McCormick

1952 The Mythological Basis for Attitudes toward Animals among Salish Indians. *Journal of American Folklore* # 65 (258): 353–359.

Connaway, John

2007   Fishweirs ~ A World Perspective with Emphasis on the Fishweirs of Mississippi. Jackson: Mississippi Department of Archives and History, Archaeological Reports Series #33.

Cooper, John M

1934 The Northern Algonquian Supreme Being. The Catholic U of America, Anthropological Series, 2" 1-78.

Coupland, Gary.

1988   *Prehistoric Cultural Change At Kitselas Canyon.* Ottawa: Canadian Museum Of Civilization.

Cove, John

1985 A Detailed Inventory of the Barbeau Northwest Coast Files. *Canadian Centre For Folk Culture Studies, Paper* # 54. Ottawa.

Crapo, Richley

1976 Big Smokey Valley Shoshoni. Reno: Desert Research Institute Publications in the Social Sciences # 10.

Crumrine, N Ross and Marjorie Halpin, eds.

1983   The Power of Symbols ~ Masks and Masquerade in the Americas. Vancouver: University of British Columbia Press.

Curtis, E

1911 The Kutenai: 117-54. *The North American Indian* # 7. Norwood, Mass: Plimpton Press.

1926 Cochiti, Laguna, and Acoma. *The North American Indian* # 16. Norwood, Mass: Plimpton Press.

d'Azevedo, Warren

nd This Herb. Manuscript in possession of the author.

Dauenhauer, Nora Marks and Richard Dauenhauer
1987 *Haa Shuka, Our Ancestors. Tlingit Oral Narratives.* University of Washington Press, Seattle.

Davenport, William
1959 Nonunilinear Descent and Descent Groups. *American Anthropologist*: 557-69.

Davis, Irvine
1964 The Language of Santa Ana. Bureau of American Ethnology, Bulletin 191, *Anthropological Paper* 69: 53-190.

Davis, James
1960 An Appraisal of Certain Speculations on Prehistoric Puebloan Subsistence. Southwestern Journal of Anthropology 16: 15-23.

Dean, Jonathan
ms.a "Those Rascally Spakaloids ...:" ~ The Rise of Gispaxlot Hegemony At Fort Simpson, 1832 to 1840.
ms.b "My Canoe Was Full Of People - But It Capsized - & All The People Lost But Myself...": The Rise and Fall of Legaic 1840 to 1865.

Densmore, Frances
1939 *Nootka and Quileute Music.* Bureau of American Ethnology, Bulletin # 124. Washington.
1957 *Music of Acoma, Isleta, Cochiti, and Zuni.* Bureau of American Ethnology Bulletin 165.

DeMallie, Raymond and Alfonso Ortiz, eds.
1994 *North American Indian Anthropology*: Essays in Society and Culture. Norman: University of Oklahoma Press.

De Tocqueville, Alexis
1945 *Democracy in America.* Phillips Bradley, ed. New York: Vintage Books. [Volume I, 1835; Ii, 1840]

Demos, John
1994 *The Unredeemed Captive.* A Family Story from Early America. New York: Alfred Knopf.

Dewdney, S
1975 *The Sacred Scrolls of the Southern Ojibway.* Toronto: University of Toronto Press.

Dorsey, George
1904a Traditions of the Ankara. Washington, DC: Carnegie Institution of Washington Publication # 17.
1904b The Mythology of the Wichita. Washington, DC: Carnegie Institution of Washington Publication # 21.
1905a Traditions of the Caddo. Washington, DC: Carnegie Institution of Washington Publication # 41.
1905b Caddo Customs of Childhood. Journal of American Folklore 18: 226-228.
1906 The Pawnee: Mythology. Washington, DC: Carnegie Institution of Washington Publication # 59. .

Dorsey, James Owen
1884 Omaha Sociology. Bureau of American Ethnology Annual Report # 3.

Douglas, Mary
  1970 *Purity and Danger*: An Analysis of Concepts of Pollution and Taboo, London: Pelican Books.
Driver, Harold
  1961 Indians of North America. U of Chicago Press.
Dutton, Bertha, and Miriam Marmon
  1936 The Laguna calendar. *University of New Mexico Bulletin* 283. *Anthropological Series* 1 (2): 1-21.
Drucker, Philip
  1937 Diffusion in Northwest Coast Culture in the Light of Some Distributions. PhD, U of California at Berkeley.
  1950 Culture Element Distributions: XXVI Northwest Coast. *Anthropological Records* 9 (3): 157-294.
  1951 *The Northern and Central Nootkan Tribes*. Bureau of American Ethnology, Bulletin 144.
  1955 Indians of the Northwest Coast. Garden City: The Natural History Press.
  1965 Cultures of the North Pacific Coast. Scranton: Chandler Publishing.
Du Bois, Cora
  2007 The 1870 Ghost Dance. University of Nebraska Press, Lincoln. [1939]
Dumont, Louis
  1970 *Homo Hierarchicus*. The U of Chicago Press.
Dunn, John
  1978 A *Practical Dictionary* of the Coast Tsimshian Language. Ottawa: Canadian Ethnology Service Paper # 42.
  1979 A *Reference Grammar* for the Coast Tsimshian Language. Ottawa: National Museums Of Canada, Mercury Series, Canadian Ethnology Service, Paper # 55. 91pp.
  1979a Tsimshian Internal Relations Reconsidered: Southern Tsimshian: 62-82. *The Victoria Conference On Northwestern Languages*. British Columbia Provincial Museum, Heritage Record 4. Barbara Efrat, ed.
  1984 International Matri-moieties: The North Maritime Province of the North Pacific Coast. *The Tsimshian: Images of the Past, Views for the Present*. Margaret Seguin ed. Vancouver: University of British Columbia Press.
  1988 Aesthetic Properties of a Coast Tsimshian Text Fragment: 78–89. *Proceedings of the 23rd International Conference on Salish and Neighboring Languages*.
  nd The Tsimshian Calendars. Manuscript in possession of the author.
Edel, May M
  1944 Stability in Tillamook Folklore. *Journal of American Folklore* 57 (224): 116- .
Edmonson, Munro
  1958 Status Terminology and the Social Structure of North American Indians. American Ethnological Society Monograph # 30.
  1982 *The Ancient Future of the Itza*. The Book of Chilam Balam of Tizimin. Austin: University of Texas Press.
Ellis, Florence Hawley
  1983 Foreword: xxiii-xxxviii. *The Architecture and Dendrochronology of Chetro Ketl, Chaco Canyon, New Mexico*. Stephen Lekson, ed. Albuquerque: Reports of the Chaco Center # 6.

Emmons, George

1911 The Tahltan Indians. Philadelphia: University of Pennsylvania Anthropological Publications 4 (1).

1991 *The Tlingit Indians*. Seattle: University of Washington Press.

Eggan, Fred, ed.

1937 Social Anthropology of North American Tribes. Chicago: University of Chicago Press.

Eggan, Fred

1950 *Social Organization of the Western Pueblos*. Chicago: University of Chicago Press.

Eggan, Fred ed.

1955 *Social Anthropology of North American Tribes*, enlarged edn. Chicago: University of Chicago Press.

1966 *The American Indian*: Perspectives for the Study of Social Change. Cambridge: Cambridge University Press.

Elmendorf, William W

1960 The Structure of Twana Culture. *Washington State University Research Studies, Monographic Supplement # 2*.

1961 Skokomish and Other Coast Salish Tales. *Washington State University Research Studies* # 29 (1): 1–37, 29 (2): 84–117, 29 (3): 119–150. Pullman.

Ervin, Susan

1962 The Connotations of Gender. *Word* 18 (3): 248-261.

Facilitators

1980 MX Native American Cultural and Socio-Economic Studies Draft. Manuscript in possession of the author.

Farrand, Livingston and Theresa Mayer

1919 Quileute Tales. *Journal of American Folklore* 32 (124): 251–279.

Fenton, William N

1987 The False Faces of the Iroquois. Norman: University of Oklahoma Press.

Fienup-Riordan, Ann

1990 *Eskimo Essays*. Yup'ik Lives and How We See Them. New Brunswick: Rutgers University Press.

1994 *Boundaries and Passages*: Rule and Ritual in Yup'ik Eskimo Oral Tradition. Norman: University of Oklahoma Press.

Firth, Raymond

1957 A Note on Descent Groups in Polynesia. *Man* 57: 4-7.

Fletcher, Alice

1904 *The Hako: A Pawnee Ceremony*. Bureau of American Ethnology, Annual Report 22, part 2.

Fletcher, Alice and Francis La Flesche

1911 *The Omaha Tribe*. Bureau of American Ethnology Annual Report # 27: 17-660.

1972 *The Omaha Tribe*. Vol 1 & 2. Lincoln: University of Nebraska Press.

Fogelson, Raymond

1985 Night Thoughts on Native American Social History Newberry

1971 A Cherokee Ballgame Cycle: An Ethnographer's View. *Ethnomusicology* 15 (3): 327-338.

Fogelson, Raymond and Amelia Bell
1983   Cherokee Booger Mask Tradition: 48-69.   The Power of Symbols ~ Masks and Masquerade in the Americas.   Ross Crumrine and Marjorie Halpin, eds.   Vancouver: University of British Columbia Press.

Fortes, Meyer
1972 Kinship and the Social Order: The Legacy of LH Morgan. *Current Anthropology* 13 (2): 285-96 April.

Foster, George M
1944 A Summary of Yuki Culture. Anthropological Records 5 (3): 154-244.

Fowler, Catherine
1970 *Great Basin Anthropology ~ A Bibliography.* Reno: University of Nevada Desert Research Institute Publications in the Social Sciences # 5.

Fowler, Catherine, and Joy Leland
1967 Some Northern Paiute Native Categories. *Ethnology* 6: 381-404.

Fox, Robin
1967a *The Keresan Bridge*: A Problem in Pueblo Ethnology. London: Athlonc Press London School of Economics, Anthropological Monograph # 35. [152]
1967b *Kinship and Marriage* ~ An Anthropological Perspective. Middlesex: Penguin.

Frachtenberg, Leo J
1913 Coos Texts. *Columbia University Contributions to Anthropology* # 1: 1–216. New York.
1914   Lower Umpqua Texts and Notes on the Kusan Dialect. *Columbia University Contributions to Anthropology* 4: 1–156. New York.
1915 Shasta and Athapascan Myths from Oregon, Collected by Livingston Farrand. *Journal of American Folklore* 28 (109): 207–242.
1920   Alsea Texts and Myths. *Bureau of American Ethnology, Bulletin # 67: 1–304. Washington.

Friederich, Steven
2010 Artifacts found at Hoquiam. *The Daily World.* Saturday, May 29.

Galloway, Patricia
1995 *Choctaw Genesis*, 1500-1700. Lincoln: University of Nebraska Press.

Garfield, Viola E
1939 Tsimshian Clan and Society. University of Washington Publications in Anthropology # 7 (3): 167-340.
1966 The Tsimshian and Their Neighbors: 1-70. *The Tsimshian and Their Arts.* Viola E Garfield And Paul S Wingert, eds Seattle: University of Washington Press.
1953 Contemporary Problems of Folklore Collecting and Study. *Anthropological Papers of the University of Alaska* 1 (2): 25–37.

Garfield, Viola E and Paul S Wingert
1966 *The Tsimshian and Their Arts.* University of Washington Press, Seattle.

Garfield, Viola E and Linn A Forrest
1961 *The Wolf and the Raven: Totem Poles of Southeastern Alaska.* University of Washington Press, Seattle.

Garretson, Lucy
1976 *American Culture*: An Anthropological Perspective. Dubuque, Iowa: Wm. C. Brown Elements of Anthropology.

Gill, J
1933 *Gill's Dictionary* of the Chinook Jargon. Portland: JK Gill.

Gitsegukla History ~ *Anawkhl Gitsegukla*
1979 By The Band Council. 41pp.

Golder, FA
1907 Tlingit Myths. *Journal of American Folklore* 20 (76): 290–295.

Goldenweiscr, Alexander
1915 The Social Organization of the Indians of North America: 350-78. *Anthropology of North America*. Franz Boas et al, eds. New York: GE Stechert and Co.

Gearing, Fred
1962 *Priests and Warriors*. Social Structures for Cherokee Politics in the 18th Century. AAA Memoir 93.

Golla, Susan S
1975 Skidi Pawnee Religion: A Structural Analysis. DC: MA Thesis, George Washington U.

Goodwin, Grenville
1969 *The Social Organization of the Western Apache*. Tucson: University of Arizona Press.

Goss, James A
1972 A Basin-Plateau Shoshonean Ecological Model. *Great Basin Cultural Ecology*: A Symposium. DD Fowler, ed. Reno: Desert Research Institute Publications in the Social Sciences # 8: 123-128.

Graburn, Nelson
1971 *Readings in Kinship and Social Structure*. New York: Harper & Row.

Gregory, Hiram F.
1986 The Southern Caddo: An Anthology. Garland Publishing, New York.

Griffith, William Joyce
1954 The Hasinai Indians of East Texas as Seen by Europeans, 1687-1772. Tulane University, Middle American Research Institute, Philological and Documentary Studies 2 (3): 40-165.

Grumet, Robert
1975 Changes In Coast Tsimshian Redistributive Activities in the Fort Simpson Region Of British Columbia, 1788-1862. Ethnohistory 22 (4): 295-318.
1982 Managing The Fur Trade: The Coast Tsimshian To 1862: 26-39. *Affluence And Cultural Survival*. 1981 Proceedings of the American Ethnological Society. Richard Salisbury And Elisabeth Tooker, eds. St Paul: West Publishing Co.

Gunn, John
1917 *Schat-Chen: history, traditions and narratives of the Queres Indians of Laguna and Acoma*. Albuquerque: Albright and Anderson.

Gunther, Erna
1926 An Analysis Of The First Salmon Ceremony. American Anthropologist 28 (4): 605-617.
1927 Klallam Folk Tales. *University of Washington Publications in Anthropology* 1: 113– 169. Seattle.

1928   A Further Analysis of the First Salmon Ceremony.   Seattle: U of Washington Publications in Anthropology 2 (5): 129-173.

Haeberlin, Herman
1917 Mythology of Puget Sound. *Journal of American Folklore* 37 (144): 371–438.

Hale, Duane
1987 *Peacemakers on the Frontier*: A History of the Delaware Tribe of Western Oklahoma. Delaware Press, Anadarko.

Hallowell, AI
1926 Bear Ceremonialism in the Northern Hemisphere. *American Anthropologist* 28: 1-175.
1992   The Ojibwa of Berens River, Manitoba.   Ethnography into History.   Case Studies in Cultural Anthropology.   Jennifer SH Brown, ed.   Fort Worth: Harcourt Brace Jovanovich College Publishers.

Halpin, Marjorie
ms Masks As Metaphors Of Anti-Structure.
1973 The Tsimshian Crest System: A Study Based On Museum Specimens And The Marius Barbeau And William Beynon Field Notes.   PhD Dissertation, University of British Columbia. 469pp.
1978   William Beynon, Ethnographer. Tsimshian, 1888-1958:   141-156. *American Indian Intellectuals*.   Margot Liberty, ed.   Proceedings of the 1976 American Ethnological Society. St Paul: West Publishing Co.
1984 The Structure of Tsimshian Totemism: 16-35. Miller And Eastman 1984.
1994 A Critique of the Boasian Paradigm for Northwest Coast Art. Culture 14 (1): 5-16.

Halpin, Marjorie and Margaret Seguin
1990 Tsimshian Peoples: Southern Tsimshian, Coast Tsimshian, Nishga, and Gitksan: 267-84.   Handbook of North American Indians # 7 ~ *Northwest Coast*.   Wayne Suttles, ed. Washington, DC: Smithsonian Institution Press.

Hamell, George
1983   Trading in Metaphors: The Magic of Beads: 5-28.   Another Perspective upon Indian-European Contact in Northeastern North America.   Proceedings of the 1982 Glass Trade Bead Conference.   Charles Hayes III, ed.   Rochester Museum and Science Center Research Records # 16.

Handelman, Don
1967 The Development of A Washo Shaman. *Ethnology* 6: 444-464. [84]

Hann, John
1988 *Apalachee*: The Land Between the Rivers. Unversity of Florida Press, Gainesville.
1991 *Missions to the Calusa.* University of Florida Press, Gainesville.

Harkin, Michael
1988 Dialogues of History: Transformation and Change in Heiltsuk History, 1790-1920. PhD University of Chicago.

Harrington, Mark R
1920 Certain Caddo Sites in Arkansas. *Indian Notes and Monographs*, Miscellaneous 10.

Harris, Jack
1940 The White Knife Shoshone of Nevada: 39-166. *Acculturation in Seven American Indian Tribes*. Ralph Linton, ed. New York: Appleton-Century.

Hartigan, Francis
1980 MX in Nevada: A Humanistic Perspective. Reno: Center for Religion and Life.
Harwood, Francis
1976   Myth, Memory, and The Oral Tradition: Cicero In The Trobriands. *American Anthropologist* 78 (4): 783-796.
Harvey, Byron
1963   Masks at a Maskless Pueblo: the Laguna Colony Katsina Organization at Isleta. *Ethnology* 2 (4): 278-289.
Hassick, Ross
1964 The Sioux Life and Customs of a Warrior Society. Norman: U of Oklahoma Press.
Hastings, James, Ed.
1951 Monsters (Biological) and (Ethnic). *Encyclopedia of Religion and Ethics.* New York: Charles Scribners and Sons.
HDR (Henningson, Durham, and Richardson)
1980   Environmental Characteristics of Alternative Designated Deployment Areas: Native American Concerns in Nevada and Utah, prepared by Katherine Martin. MX-ETR 21. Manscript in possession of the author.
Heizer, Robert, and Martin Baumhoff
1962   *Prehistoric Rock Art of Nevada and Eastern California.* Berkeley: University of California Press.
Henry, Jules
1973   A Theory for an Anthropological Analysis of American Culture. *On Sham, Vulnerability and Other Forms of Self-Destruction.* New York: Vintage Books.
Hickerson, Nancy
1994 *The Jumanos*: Hunters and Traders of the South Plains. Austin: University of Texas Press.
Hilbert. Vi
1985 *Haboo: Native American Stories from Puget Sound.* University of Washington Press, Seattle.
Hillerman, Tony
1976 *The Spell of New Mexico.* Albuquerque: University of New Mexico Press.
Hilton, Susanne, and John Rath
1982 Objections to Franz Boas's referring to eating people in the translation of the Kwakwala terms baXwbakwalnuXwsiwe and hamats!a.:   98-106, *Working Papers of the 17th International Conference on Salish and Neighboring Languages.* Portland State University. 9-11 August.
Hindle, Lonnie, and Bruce Rigsby
1973 A Short Dictionary of the Gitksan Language. Northwest Anthropological Research Notes 7 (1): 1-60.
Hoebel, E Adamson
1935 The Sun Dance of the Hekandika Shoshone. *American Anthropologist* 37: 570-581.
ms Subjective Aspects of Shoshone Religion. Manuscript in tht author's possession.
Hoffman, W. J.
1884 Selish Myths. *Bulletin of the Essex Institute* # 15. Salem, MA.

Holder, Preston
   1970 *The Hoe and the Horse on the Plains*: A Study of Cultural Development among North American Indians. Lincoln: University of Nebraska Press.
Hrdlicka, Ales
   1903 A Laguna ceremonial language. *American Anthropologist 5:* 730-2.
Hsu, Francis
   1972 American Core Value and National Character. *Psychological Anthropology*. Cambridge: Schenkman Publ. Co.
Hughes, Jack
   1968 Prehistory of the Caddoan-Speaking Tribes. PhD, Columbia University.
Hulse, Frederick
   1935 SRRA-Inyo: Owens Valley Fieldnotes. Berkeley: Bancroft Library.
Hultkrantz, Ake
   1966 An Ecological Approach to Religion. *Ethnos* 31: 131-150.
   1976 Religion and Ecology Among Great Basin Indians: 137-150. *World Anthropology*: The Realm of the Extra-Human, Ideas and Actions. A Bharati, ed. Mouton: The Hague.
Hunt, George
   1906 The Rival Chiefs, a Kwakiutl Story: 108–136. *Anthropological Papers Written in Honor of Franz Boas*. GE Stechert and Co, New York.
Huxley, Aldous
   1971 *The Devils of Loudon*. New York: Harper and Row. [1952]
Hymes, Dell
   1953 Two Wasco Motifs. *Journal of American Folklore* 66 (259): 69–70.
   1965 Some North Pacific Coast Poems: A Problem in Anthropological Philology. *American Anthropologist* 67: 316–341.
   1968 The 'Wife' Who 'Goes Out' Like a Man; Reinterpretation of a Clackamas Chinook Myth. *Social Science Information (Studies in Semiotics)*, 7 (3): 173–199.
   1975a Breakthrough into Performance: 11–74. *Folklore and Communication*, edited by Dan Ben-Amos and Kenneth Goldstein. The Hague.
1975b Folklore's Nature and the Sun's Myth. *Journal of American Folklore* 88: 147–369.
1976 Louis Simpson's 'The Deserted Boy'. *Poetics* 5: 119–177.
   1981 *"In Vain I Tried To Tell You." Essays in Native American Ethnopoetics*. University of Pennsylvania Press, Philadelphia.
   1985 Language, Memory, and Selective Performance: Cultee's "Salmon Myth" as Twice Told To Boas. *Journal of American Folklore,* 98 (390): 391–434.
Inter-Tribal Council of Nevada
   1976a *Nuwuvi*: A Southern Paiute History. Salt Lake City: University of Utah Press.
   1976 *Newe*: A Western Shoshone History. Salt Lake City: University of Utah Press.
   1976c *Numa*: A Northern Paiute History. Salt Lake City: University of Utah Press.
Jacobs, Melville
   1940 Coos Myth Texts. *University of Washington Publications in Anthropology* # 8. Seattle.
   1949 Kalapuya Texts. *University of Washington Publications in Anthropology* # 11: 1-394. Seattle.
   1952 Psychological Inferences from a Chinook Myth. *Journal of American Folklore* 65 (256): 121–137.

302

1959a A Few Observations on the World View of the Clackamas Chinook Indians. *Journal of American Folklore* 68: 283–289

1959b *The Content and Style of An Oral Literature*: *Clackamas Chinook Myths and Tales.* Viking Fund Publications in Anthropology 26: 1–285. New York.

1959c Folklore. In Anthropology of Franz Boas. *American Anthropologist* 61 (5) [part 2]: 119–138.

1960 *The People Are Coming Soon, An Analysis of Clackamas Chinook Myths and Tales.* University of Washington Press, Seattle.

1962 The Fate of Indian Oral Literature in Oregon. *Northwest Review,* 5: 90–99.

1966 A Look Ahead In Oral Literature Research. *Journal of American Folklore* 79: 413–427.

1967 Our Knowledge of Pacific Northwest Indian Folklores. *Northwest Folklore* 2 (2): 14–21.

1972 Areal Spread of Indian Oral Genre Features in the Northwest States. *Journal of the Folklore Institute,* 9 (1): 10–17.

ms. A Popular Account of Oral Literature in the Northwest States.

Jacobs, Elizabeth Derr

1959 Nehalem Tillamook Tales. *University of Oregon Studies in Anthropology,* 5:1–216. Eugene.

Jenness, Diamond

1935 The Saanich Indians of Vancouver Island. Canadian Ethnology Service Archives, # VII-G-8M, Ottawa.

1943 The Carrier Indians of the Bulkley River. Their Social and Religious Life. Bureau of American Ethnology, Bulletin 133, Anthropological Paper 25: 469-586.

1955 The Faith of a Coast Salish Indian. *Anthropology in British Columbia, Memoir* 3: 1–92. Victoria.

Kan, Sergei

1989 *Symbolic Immortality.* The Tlingit Potlatch of the Nineteenth Century. Smithsonian Institution Press.

Kelly, Isabel

1964 Southern Paiute Ethnography. University of Utah Anthropological Papers # 69.

Kenyon, Susan

1980 The Kyuquot Way: A Study of a West Coast Nootkan Community. National Museum of Man, Mercury Series, *Canadian Ethnology Service* # 61.

Kinietz, W

1940 *The Indians of the Western Great Lakes* 1615-1760. University of Michigan, Museum of Anthropology, Occasional Contributions #10.

Kinkade, MD

1975 The Lexical Domain of Anatomy in Columbian Salish. Peter de Ridder Press Publications on Salish Languages # 1.

1983 "Daughters of Fire:" Narrative Verse Analysis of an Upper Chehalis Folktale. University of Oklahoma, *Papers in Anthropology* 24 (2): 267–278. Norman.

Knack, Martha

1976 Social and Economic Roles of Contemporary Southern Paiute Women. Paper presented at the 1976 Great Basin Anthropological Conference, Las Vegas.

Kniffen, Fred B., Hiram F. Gregory, and George A. Stokes
   1987 *The Historic Indian Tribes of Louisiana*, From 1542 to the Present. Baton Rouge: Louisiana State University Press.
Knight, Vemon
   1989 Symbolism of Mississippian Mounds: 279-291. *Powhatan's Mantle* ~ Indians in the Colonial Southeast. Peter Wood, Gregory Waselkov, and Thomas Hatley, eds. University of Nebraska Press, Lincoln.
Kroeber, Alfred
   1909 Classificatory Systems of Relationship. *Journal of the Royal Anthropological Institute* 39: 77-84.
   1919 Sinkyone Tales. *Journal of American Folklore* 32 (125): 346–351.
   1923 American Culture and the Northwest Coast. *American Anthropologist* 25 (1): 1-20.
   1963 Cultural and Natural Areas of Native North America. Berkeley: U of California Press.
Kroeber, Alfred and Edward Gifford
   1949 World Renewal: A Cult System of Native Northwest California. Berkeley: University of California, *Anthropological Records* 13 (1): 1-156.
Kurath, Gertrude
   1970 Music and Dance of the Tewa Pueblos. Santa Fe: Museum of New Mexico Press.
Lafitau, Joseph-Francois
   1724 *Moeurs des sauvages ameriquains, comparees aux moeurs premiers temps*. Paris: Saugrain l'aine.
de Laguna, Frederica
   1972 *Under Mount Saint Elias*. Yakutat Tlingit. Smithsonian Press, Washington.
Laird, Carobeth
   1974 Chemehuevi Religious Beliefs and Practices. *Journal of California Anthropology* 1 (1): 19-25.
   1976 *The Chemehuevis*. Banning: Malki Museum Press.
   1980 Chemehuevi Shamanism, Sorcery, and Charms. *Journal of California and Great Basin Anthropology* 2 (1): 80-87.
Lamb, Sydney M
   1958 Linguistic Prehistory in the Great Basin. *International Journal of American Linguistics* 24 (2): 95-100.
Landes, R
   1968 *Ojibwa Religion and the Midewiwin*. Madison: University of Wisconsin Press.
Lange, Charles
   1974 The Caddo Treaty of July 1, 1835. Caddoan Indians II. Garland Publishing, New York.
   1968 *Cochiti* ~ A New Mexico Pueblo, past and present.. Carbondale: Southern Illinois University Press.
Lawton, Harry, Philip Wilke, Mary DeDecker, and William Mason
   1976 Agriculture Among the Paiute of Owens Valley. *Journal of California Anthropology* 3 (1): 13-50.
Leach, Edmund
   1970 The Legitimacy of Solomon. *Introduction To Structuralism*. Michael Lane, ed. New York: Basic Books.
Lee, Dorothy

1959 *Freedom and Culture.* New York: Spectrum Books.

Leiber, Michael
1964 Field Report. Reno: Desert Research Institute Ethnographic Archive # 6.

Levi, Jerome Meyer
1978   Wii'pay: The Living Rocks-Ethnographic Notes on Crystal Magic Among Some California Yumans. *Journal of California Anthropology* 5 (1): 42-52.

Levi-Strauss, Claude
1945   French Sociology. *Twentieth Century Sociology.* G Gurvitch and WE Moore, eds. New York: Philosophical Library.
1962 Totemism. R Needham, translator. Boston: Beacon Press.
1967 The Story of Asdiwal: 11–74. Nicholas Mann, trans. *The Structural Study of Myth and Totemism.* Edmund Leach, ed. *ASA Monographs* # 5. London.
1968 *The Savage Mind.* U of Chicago Press.
1969 *The Raw and the Cooked.* New York: Harper and Row.
1969   *The Elementary Structures of Kinship.* James Harle Bell, John Richard Von Stunner, and Rodney Needham, trans. Boston: Beacon Press [original French publication 1949].
1971 *L'Homme Nu.* Mythologiques 4. Plon, Paris.
1972 Structuralism and Ecology. Barnard Alumnae Magazine.
1978 *The Origin of Table Manners.* John and Doreen Weightman, translators. New York: Harper Colophon.
1981 The Naked Man. Introduction to *The Science of Mythology* Volume 4. John and Doreen Weightman, trans. Harper and Row, New York.

Liljeblad, Sven
1962 The People Are Coming Soon: A Review Article. *Midwest Folklore* 12 (2): 93–103.
1969 The Religious Attitude of the Shoshonean Indian. *Rendezvous* 4 (1): 47-58.

Linder, Adrian
nd   Aspects of Aboriginal Whale Hunting in the Northwest Coast Cultural Area of North America.

Linton, Ralph
1940   Editor's Summary: White Knife Acculturation: 117-118. *Acculturation in Seven American Indian Tribes.* Ralph Linton, ed. New York: Appleton-Century.

Losey, Robert
2009 Animism as a Means of Exploring Archaeological Fishing Structures on Willapa Bay, Washington, USA. *Cambridge Archaeological Journal* 20 (1):17-32.

Lounsbury, Floyd
1964a The Structural Analysis of Kinship Semantics: 1073-93. *Proceedings of the Ninth International Congress of Linguists.* Horace G Lunt, ed. The Hague: Mouton.

Lounsbury, Floyd
1964b A Formal Account of Crow- and Omaha-Type Kinship Terminologies. *Explorations in Cultural Anthropology.* Ward Goodenough, ed. New York: McGraw-Hill Book Company.

Lowie, Robert
1924   Notes on Shoshonean Ethnography. American Museum of Natural History Anthropological Papers 20 (3): 183-314. [85]
1936 Lewis Henry Morgan in Historical Perspective. *Essays in Anthropology,* Presented to AL Kroeber. Berkeley: University of California Press.

1948 *Social Organization.* New York: Holt, Rinehart & Winston.
Lurie, NO
1953 Winnebago Berdache. *American Anthropologist* 55: 708-12.
McClellan, Catharine
1963 Wealth Woman and Frogs among the Tagish Indians. *Anthropos* 58: 121–128.
1970 The Girl Who Married the Bear. *National Museums of Canada, Publication in Ethnology* # 2: 1–58. Ottawa.
Macdonald, George
1979 Kitwanga Fort National Historic Site, Skeena River, British Columbia. Historical Research And Analysis Of Structural Remains. Parks Canada: Manuscript Report # 341.
1984 The Epic Of Nekt: The Archaeology of Metaphor: 65-81. Seguin 1984a.
MacDonald, George and John Cove
1987 Tsimshian Narratives I: Trickster, Shamans and Heroes II: Trade and Warfare. *Canadian Museum of Civilization, Mercury Series, Directorate Paper* # 3. Ottawa.
McFeat, Tom
1966 Indians Of The North Pacific Coast. Seattle: U of Washington Press.
Mcllwraith, Thomas
1948 *The Bella Coola.* 1 & 2. University of Toronto Press.
McNeary, Stephen
1976 Where Fire Came Down. Social and Economic Life of the Niska. PhD, Bryn Mawr.
McNeley, James Kale
1981 *Holy Wind in Navajo Philosophy.* Tucson: University of Arizona Press.
Malouf, Carling
1974 The Gosiute Indians. American Indian Ethnohistory. California and Basin-Plateau Indians. Shoshone. New York: Garland Publishing.
Marsden, Susan
1996 Defending the Mouth of the Skeena: Perspectives on Tsimshian Tlingit Relations. Twenty-ninth Annual Meeting of the Canadian Archaeological Association, Halifax, NS.
  ms Controlling the Flow of Furs: Northcoast Nations and The Maritime Fur Trade.
Matson, Richard, and Gary Coupland
1995 *The Prehistory of the Northwest Coast.* San Diego: Academic Press.
Maud, Ralph
1982 *A Guide To BC Indian Myth and Legend.* A Short History of Myth-Collecting and A Survey of Published Texts. Vancouver: Talonbooks.
1989 The Henry Tate-Franz Boas Collaboration on Tsimshian Mythology. *American Ethnologist*, 16 (1): 158–162.
Mbithi, Philip And Rasmus Rasmusson
1977 *Self-Reliance in Kenya* ~ The Case of Harambee. Uppsala: The Scandinavian Institute of African Studies.
Meggitt, Mervyn
1972 Understanding Australian Aboriginal Society: Kinship Systems or Cultural Categories: 64-87. Kinship Studies in the Morgan Centennial Year. Priscilla Reining, ed. DC: Washington Anthro Society.
Meilleur, Helen
1980 *A Pour Of Rain.* Stories from a West Coast Fort. Victoria, BC: Sono Nis Press.

Miller, Jay

1972 The Priority of the Left. *Man* 7: 646-47.

1974 The Delaware As Women: A Symbolic Solution. *American Ethnologist* 1: 507-14.

1974 Why the World is on the Back of a Turtle. *Man* 9 (2): 306-308

1977-78 Sanpoil Fieldnotes.

1977   Delaware Anatomy: With Linguistic, Social, and Medical Aspects. *Anthropological Linguistics* 19 (4): 144-66.

1978 Moiety Birth. Northwest Anthropological Research Notes 13 (1): 45-50.

1978 American Humanity and Other Monsters ~ A Structuralist Analysis Of Frankenstein, The Mummy, Dracula, and The Wolfman. Anthropolgy of the Unknown, International Conference On Humanoid Monsters. U of British Columbia. May 10-13.

1979 A Struckon Model of Delaware Culture and the Positioning of Mediators. *American Ethnologist* 6 (4): 791-802.

1979 Delaware Language and Culture: 23-31

1980a The Matter of the (Thoughtful) Heart: Centrality, Focality, or Overlap. *Journal of Anthropological Research* 36: 338-42.

1980b High-Minded High Gods in North America. *Anthropos* 75: 916-19.

1981   Tsimshian Moieties and Other Clarifications. *Northwest Anthropological Research Notes* 16 (2): 148-64.

1981 Moieties And Cultural Amnesia: Manipulations of Knowledge in a Pacific Northwest Coast Native Community. *Arctic Anthropology* 18 (1): 23-32.

1984 Introduction. Miller and Eastman 1984.

1984a Tsimshian Religion in Historical Perspective: 137-147. Miller And Eastman 1984.

1984b Feasting with the Southern Tsimshian: 27-39. Sequin 1984b.

1985 Shamanism in western Native America: Numic, Salish, and Keres Pueblo. *Woman, Poet, Scientist:* Essays in New World Anthropology, honoring Dr Emma Louise Davis. Compiled and edited by the Great Basin Foundation. Los Altos, California: Ballena Press.

1988 *Shamanic Odyssey*: A Comparative Study Of The Lushootseed (Puget Salish) Journey to the Land of the Dead in Terms of Death, Power, and Cooperating Shamans in Native North America. Ballena Press Anthropological Papers # 32.

1989 An Overview of Northwest Coast Mythology. *Northwest Anthropological Research Notes* 23 (2): 125-141.

1990 *Mourning Dove*. A Salishan Autobiography. University of Nebraska Press, Lincoln.

1992 Earthmaker. Tribal Stories from Native North America. Putnam Perigree, New York.

1992 North Pacific Ethnoastronomy: 193-206. *Earth And Sky*. Visions of the Cosmos In Native American Folklore. Ray Williamson and Claire Farrer, eds. Albuquerque: University Of New Mexico Press.

1997 *Tsimshian Culture*: A Light through the Ages. Lincoln: University of Nebraska Press.

1997 Back to Basics: Chiefdoms in Puget Sound. Ethnohistory 44 (2): 375-388.

1998 Middle Columbia River Salishans: 253-270. 12 ~ *Plateau*. Smithsonian Handbook of North American Indians. Deward Walker, ed. Washington, DC: Smithsonian Institution Press.

1999 *Lushootseed Culture and the Shamanic Odyssey*: An Anchored Radiance. Lincoln: University of Nebraska Press.

Miller, Jay, and Carol Eastman
1984 *The Tsimshian and Their Neighbors of the North Pacific Coast.* Seattle: University Of Washington Press.
Miller, Jay, with Warren Snyder
1999 Suquamish Traditions. *Northwest Anthropological Research Notes (NARN)* 33 (1): 105-175, Spring.
Miller, Robert
1952 Situation and Sequence in the Study of Folklore. *Journal of American Folklore* 65 (255): 29–48.
Miller, Wick
1965 *Acoma Grammar and Texts.* Berkeley: University of California Publications in Linguistics 40.
Mitchell, Donald
1981 Sebassa's Men: 79-86. Abbott 1981.
1983 Tribes and Chiefdoms of the Northwest Coast: The Tsimshian Case: 57-64. *The Evolution Of Martime Cultures On The Northeast And Northwest Coasts Of America.* Ronald Nash, ed. Simon Fraser University, Department of Archaeology Publications # 11.
Monet, Don, and *Skanu'u* [Ardythe Wilson]
1992 *Colonialism on Trial*: Indigenous Land Rights and the Gitksan and Wet'suwet'en Sovereignty Case. Gabriola Island, bc: New Society Publishers.
Moore, Clarence
1912 Some Aboriginal Sites on Red River. *Journal of the Academy of Natural Sciences of Philadelphia* 14 (5): 483-644.
Morgan, Lawrence
1980 Kootenay-Salish Linguistic Comparison: A Preliminary Study. MA, Vancouver: University of British Columbia.
Morgan, Lewis Henry
1851 *League of the Ho-de-no-sau-nee, or Iroquois.* Rochester: Sage and Brothers.
1870 *Systems of Consanguinity and Affinity of the Human Family.* Smithsonian Contributions to Knowledge XVII. [153]
1877 *Ancient Society*, Researches in the Lines of Human Progress from Savagery through Barbarism to Civilization. New York: Henry Holt and Company.
Morison, O
1889 Tsimshian Proverbs. *Journal of American Folk-Lore* 2: 285-86.
Munn, Nancy
1986 The Fame Of Gawa ~ A Symbolic Study Of Value Transformation In A Massim (Papua New Guinea) Society. Cambridge University Press.
Murdock, George Peter
1949 *Social Structure.* New York: The Free Press.
1960 *Social Structure in Southeast Asia.* Viking Fund Publications in Anthropology # 29.
Murie, James
1914 Pawnee Indian Societies. NY: American Museum of Natural History Anthropological Papers # 11: 543-644.
1981 *Ceremonies of the Pawnee.* Part I: The Skiri; Part II: The South Bands. Washington, DC: Smithsonian Contributions to Anthropology # 27.

Murray, Peter
1985 *The Devil and Mr Duncan*. A History Of The Two Metlakatlas. Victoria, B. C.: Sono Nis Press.

Needham, Rodney
1973 *Right and Left*: Essays on Dual Symbolic Classification. Chicago: University of Chicago Press.

Neuman, Robert
1974 Historic Locations of Certain Caddoan Tribes. Caddoan Indians II. Garland Publishing, New York.

Newcomb, William
1984 *The Indians of Texas*. From Prehistoric to Modem Times. University of Texas Press, Austin.

Newkumet, Vynola Beaver, and Howard Meredith
1988 *Hasinai*: A Traditional History of the Caddo Confederacy. Texas A & M University, College Station.

Newton, Esther
1972 *Mother Camp*: Female Impersonators in America. Englewood Cliffs: Prentice-Hall.

Newton, Norman
1975 On Survival of Ancient Astronomical Ideas among the Peoples of the Northwest Coast. *British Columbia Studies* 26: 16-38.

Olofson, Harold
1979 Northern Paiute Shamanism Revisited. *Anthropos* 74: 11-24.

Olson, Ronald
1933   Clan and Moiety in Native America. U Of California Publications in American Archaeology and Ethnology # 33 (4): 351-422.
1936 The Quinault Indians. University of Washington Publications in Anthropology 6 (1): 1-190.
1954 Social Life of the Owikeno Kwakiutl. Anthropological Records 14 (3): 213-260.
1955 Notes on the Bella Bella Kwakiutl. Anthropological Records 14 (5): 319-348.
1967 Black Market in Prerogatives Among the Northern Kwakiutl: 108-111. Indians of the North Pacific Coast, edited by Tom McFeat, Seattle: University of Washington Press.
1967 Social Structure and Social Life of the Tlingit in Alaska. Anthropological Records 26: 1-126.

Ortiz, Alfonso
1965 Dual Organization as an Operational Concept in the Pueblo Southwest. Ethnology 4: 389-396
1969 *The Tewa World*: Space, Time, Being, and Becoming in a Pueblo Indian Society. University of Chicago Press.

Ortner, S
1974 Is Female to Male As Nature Is to Culture?: 67-87. *Women, Culture, and Society*. M Rosaldo and L Lamphere, eds. Stanford: Stanford University Press.

Park, Willard Z
1938 *Shamanism in Western North America*: A Study of Cultural Relationships. Evanston: Northwestern University Studies in the Social Sciences # 2.

Cultural Succession in the Great Basin: 180-203. *Language, Culture and Personality ~ Essays in Memory of Edward Sapir*. Leslie Spier, Irving Hallowell, and Stanley Newman, eds. Menasha, Wi: Sapir Memorial Publication Fund.

Parks, Douglas

1977 *Caddoan Texts*. International Journal of American Linguistics, Native American Texts Series 2 (1).

1991 *Traditional Narratives of the Arikara Indians*. Stories of Alfred Morsette: English Translations. Volume 3. University of Nebraska Press, Lincoln.

Parks, Douglas, and Waldo Wedel

1985 Pawnee Geography, Historical and Sacred. *Great Plains Quarterly* 5 (Summer): 143-176.

Parsons, Elsie Clews

1920 *Notes on Ceremonialism at Laguna*. Anthropological Papers of the American Museum of Natural History 19 (Part 4): 85-131.

1923 *Laguna Genealogies*. American Museum of Natural History, Anthropological Papers 19 (5): 131-282.

1941 Notes on the Caddo. Memoir 57, American Anthropologist 43 (3, pt 2).

Paz, Octavio

1970 *Claude Levi-Strauss*: An Introduction. New York: Delta Books.

Penicaut, Andre

1953 *Fleur de Lys and Calumet*. Being the Penicaut Narrative of French Adventure in Louisiana. Translated by Richebourge Gaillard McWilliams. Louisiana State University Press, Baton Rouge.

Perttula, Timothy

1992 *The Caddo Nation*: ArchaeologicalandEthnohistoric Perspectives. University of Texas Press, Austin.

Pierce, William Henry

1933 *From Potlatch to Pulpit*. Vancouver, British Columbia: Vancouver Bindery.

Powell, John Wesley

1971 *Anthropology of the Numa*: John Wesley Powell's Manuscripts on the Numic Peoples of Western North America, 1868-1880. Don D Fowler and Catherine S Fowler, eds. Washington, DC: Smithsonian Contributions to Anthropology # 14.

Powers, William K

1977 *Oglala Religion*. Lincoln: U of Nebraska Press.

Prince Rupert School District 52

1992 *Na Amwaaltga Ts'msiyeen*: The Tsimshian, Trade, And The Northwest Coast Economy. Teachings Of Our Grandfathers (Suwilaay'msga Na Ga'niiyatgm) 1.

1992a *Adawga Gant Wilaaytga Gyetga Suwildook*. Rituals Of Respect And The Sea Otter Trade. Told By Henry Reeves. Teachings Of Our Grandfathers (*Suwilaay'msga Na Ga'niiyatgm*) 2.

1992b *Saaban*. The Tsimshian and Europeans Meet. Told By Dorothy Brown. Teachings Of Our Grandfathers (*Suwilaay'msga Na Ga'niiyatgm*) 3.

1992c Fort Simpson, Fur Fort At Laxlgu'alaams. The Teachings Of Our Grandfathers (*Suwilaay'msga Na Ga'niiyatgm*) 4.

1992d *Ndeh Wuwaal Kuudeex A Spaga Laxyuubm Ts'msiyeen.* When The Aleuts Were On Tsimshian Territory. Teachings of Our Grandfathers (*Suwilaay'msga Na Ga'niiyatgm*) 5.

1992e *Conflict At Gits'ilaasu.* Teachings Of Our Grandfathers (*Suwilaay'msga Na Ga'niiyatgm*) 6.

1992f *Na Maalsga Walps Nislgumiik*: The Story of The House of Nislgumiik. Teachings Of Our Grandfathers (*Suwilaay'msga Na Ga'niiyatgm*) 7.

Purley, Anthony
1974 Keres Pueblo Concepts of Deity. *American Indian Culture and Research Journal* 1 (1): 29-32.

Radin, Paul
1970 The Winnebago Tribe. Lincoln: University of Nebraska Press.

Randall, Betty Uchitelle
1949 The Cinderella Theme in Northwest Coast Folklore: 243–285. *Indians of the Urban Northwest.* Marian Smith, ed. . Columbia University Press, New York.

Ray, Verne F
1932 The Sanpoil and Nespelem: Salishan Tribes of Northeastern Washington. University of Washington Publications in Anthropology #5: 1-237.

Reagan, Albert B.
1935 Some Myths of the Hoh and Quillayote Indians. *Transactions of the Kansas Academy of Science* 38. Topeka.

Reichard, Gladys
1974 Navaho Religion, A Study in Symbolism. Princeton: Bollingen Series #18. [b]

Reichel-Dolmatoff, Geraldo
1971 *Amazonian Cosmos*: The Sexual and Religious Symbolism of the Tukano Indians. Chicago: University of Chicago Press.

Reining, Pricilla ed.
1972 *Kinship Studies in the Morgan Centennial Year.* The Anthropological Society of Washington.

Rhoads, Ellen
1973 Little Orphan Annie and Levi-Strauss: The Myth And The Method. *Journal Of American Folklore* 86 (342): 345-55.

Ridington, Robin and Dennis Hastings
1997 *Blessing for a Long Time*: The Sacred Pole of the Omaha Tribe. Lincoln: University of Nebraska Press.

Riley, Carroll
1955 The Story of Skalaxt, a Lummi Training Myth. *Davidson Journal of Anthropology,* 1 (2): 133–140. Reprinted *Northwest Anthropological Research Notes* 21: 141–148.

Rohrbaugh, Charles
1982 An Hypothesis for the Origin of the Kichai: 51-63. *Pathways to Plains Prehistory*: Anthropological Perspectives of Plains Natives and Their Pasts, edited by Don Wyckoff and Jack Hoffman. Oklahoma Anthropological Society, Memoir # 3.

Rossi, Ino
1974 Structuralism as Scientific Method. *The Unconscious in Culture.* New York: EP Dutton.

Rooth, Anna Birgitta
  1957 The Creation Myths of the North American Indians. *Anthropos* 52: 497-508.
Russell, WMS, and Claire Russell
  1978 The Social Biology of Werewolves. *Animals in Folklore.* Joshua Porter and William Russell, eds. Totowa, NJ: Rowman And Littlefield.
Sabo, George
  1987 Reordering Their World: A Caddoan Ethnohistory: 25-47. *Visions and Revisions*: Ethnohistoric Perspectives on Southern Culture. George Sabo and William Schneider, eds. Southern Anthropological Society Proceedings # 20.
Said, Edward
  1978 *Orientalism.* New York: Random House
Saint Clair, HH, and LJ Frachtenberg
  1909 Traditions of the Coos Indians of Oregon. *Journal of American Folklore* 22 (83): 29–41.
Sapir, Edward
  1909a Wishram Texts. Publications of the American Ethnological Society 2: 1–314.
  1909b Takelma Texts. University of Pennsylvania Museum: Anthropological Papers 2: 1–267. Philadelphia.
  1915 Abnormal Types of Speech in Nootka. Canada Department of Mines, Geological Survey, Anthropology Series 62 (5).
  1915 A Sketch Of The Social Organization Of The Nass River Tribes. Canadian Geological Survey, Museum Bulletin # 19, Anthropological Series # 7: 1-30.
  1919 A Flood Legend of the Nootka Indians of Vancouver Island. *Journal of American Folklore,* 32(124):351–355.
  1929 Central and North American Languages. Encyclopedia Britannica 5: 138-141.
  1930 Texts of the Kaibab Paiutes and Uintah Utes. American Academy of Arts and Sciences Proceedings 65 (2): 297-535.
Sapir, Edward and Morris Swadesh
  1939 *Nootka Texts.* Linguistic Society of America, Philadelphia.
Schaeffer, C
  1965 The Kutenai Female Berdache: Courier, Guide, Prophetess, and Warrior. Ethnohistory 12: 193-236.
  1966 Bear Ceremonialism of the Kutenai Indians. Browning, Montana: Museum of the Plains Indian, Studies in Plains Anthropology and History # 4.
Schambach, Frank, and Frank Rackerby
  1982 Contributions to the Archeology of the Great Bend Region. Arkansas Archeological Survey Research Series # 22.
Schmidt, Wilhelm
  1933 *High Gods in North America.* Oxford: U Press.
Schneider, David
  1968 *American Kinship*: A Cultural Account. Englewood Cliffs, NJ: Prentice-Hall.
Seguin, Margaret, ed.
  1984 *The Tsimshian : Images Of The Past, Views For The Present.* Vancouver: University Of British Columbia Press.

Sharp, Henry

1988 *The Transformation of Bigfoot.* Maleness, Power and Belief among the Chipewyan. Washington, DC: Smithsonian Institution Press.

Shaul, David

1982 The "Ave Maria" in Piman. *International Journal of American Linguistics* 48 (1): 87-88.

Shelley, Mary Wollstonecraft

1976 *Frankenstein or The Modern Prometheus* (The 1818 Text). Edited, With Variant Readings, An Introduction and Notes, by James Rieger. New York: Pocket Books.

Silko, Leslie Marmon

1977 *Ceremony.* New York: New American Library.

Simonsen, Bjorn

1973 Archaeological Investigations in Hecate Strait – Milbanke Sound Area British Columbia. Ottawa: National Museums of Canada, Mercury Series. Archaeological Survey of Canada, Paper # 13.

Skinner, Alanson

1914 Bear Customs of the Cree and Other Algonkin Indians of Northern Ontario. Ontario Historical Society Papers and Records 12: 203-9.

Smith, Foster Todd

1995 *The Caddo Indians.* Tribes at the Convergence of Empires, 1542-1854. Texas A & M University Press, College Station.

Smith, Martin Cruz

1977 *Nightwing.* New York: Jove Books.

Spain, David

1975 *The Human Experience.* Readings In Sociocultural Anthropology. Homewood, IL: The Dorsey Press.

Speck, Frank

1915a The Family Hunting Band as the Basis of Algonkian Social Organization. American Anthropologist 17 (2): 289-305.

1915b The Eastern Algonkian Wabanaki Confederacy. American Anthropologist 17 (3): 492-508.

1917a Malecite Tales, # 2. Malecite Version of the Water-Famine and Human Transformation Myth. Journal of American Folklore 30: 480-481

1917 Game Totems among the Northern Algonkians. American Anthropologist 19 (1): 9-18.

1935 Abenaki Clans – Never. American Anthropologist 37 (3): 528-30.

1937 Oklahoma Delaware Ceremonies, Feasts and Dances. Philadelphia: Memoirs of the American Philosophical Society # 7.

Spencer, Robert F.

Spencer, Robert

1940 A Preliminary Sketch of Keresan Grammar. University of New Mexico, MA Thesis.

1952 Native Myths and Moderneligion among the Klamath Indians. *Journal of American Folklore* 65 (257): 217–226.

Spencer, Robert, Jesse Jennings, and others

1965 The Native Americans. New York: Harper and Row.

Spier, Leslie

1925 The Distribution of Kinship Systems in North America. University of Washington Publications in Anthropology 1 (2): 69-88.

1931 Historical Interpretation of Culture Traits: Franz Boas' Study of Tsimshian Mythology: 449–457. *Methods in Social Science, a Case Book.* Stuart Rice, ed. University of Chicago Press, IL.

1933 Yuman Tribes of the Gila River. Chicago: University of Chicago Press.

Spier, Leslie and Edward Sapir

1930 Wishram Ethnography. *University of Washington Publications in Anthropology* # 3 (3): 151–300. Seattle.

Sterritt, Neil, Susan Marsden, Peter Grant, Robert Galois, and Richard Overstall

1995 Tribal Boundaries in the Nass Watershed. Gitanmaax, bc: Gitxsan Treaty Office. [674]

Stewart, Hilary

1982 Indian Fishing. Early Methods on the Northwest Coast. University of Washington Press, Seattle.

Steward, Julian

1933 Ethnography of the Owens Valley Paiute. Berkeley: University of California Publications in American Archaeology and Ethnology 33 (3): 233-350.

1937 Myths of the Owens Valley Paiute. Berkeley: University of California Publications in American Archaeology and Ethnology 34 (5): 355-440.

1938 Basin-Plateau Aboriginal Socio-Political Groups. Washington, DC: Bureau of American Ethnology Bulletin # 120.

Stirling, Mathew

1942 *Origin Myth of Acoma and other records.* Bureau of American Ethnology Bulletin 135.

Stoker, Bram

1975 *Dracula.* New York: Dell Publ. Co. [1897]

1975 *The Lady of The Shroud.* London: Arrow Books. [1909]

1975 *The Lair of The White Worm.* London: Arrow Books. [1911]

1975 *The Jewel of Seven Stars.* London: Arrow Books. [1912]

Strong, William Duncan

1929 Cross Cousin Marriage and the Culture of the Northeast Algonkian. *American Anthropologist* 31: 277-88.

Suttles, Wayne

1967 Private Knowledge, Morality, and Social Classes Among the Coast Salish: 186-179. *Indians of the North Pacific Coast.* Tom McFeat, ed. Seattle: University of Washington Press.

1968 Coping With Abundance: Subsistence on the Northwest Coast: 56-68. Man The Hunter. Richard Lee and Irven Devore, eds. Chicago: Aldine Publishing Co.

Swanton, John R.

1905a Haida Texts and Myths. *Bureau of American Ethnology Bulletin* # 29. Washington.

1905b Types of Haida and Tlingit Myths. *American Anthropologist* 7 (1): 94–103.

1905c Contributions to the Ethnology of the Haida. *Memoirs of the American Museum of Natural History* 5 (1): 1-300. New York.

1908 Haida Texts. *Memoirs of the American Museum of Natural History* 14: 273–812. New York.

1909 Tlingit Myths and Texts. *Bureau of American Ethnology*, Bulletin # 39. Washington.

1928a   Social Organization and Social Usages of the Indians of the Creek Confederacy. Washington, DC: Bureau of American Ethnology - Annual Report 1924-1925 #42: 23-472.

1928b   Religious Beliefs and Medical Practices of the Creek Indians. Washington, DC: Bureau of American Ethnology - Annual Report 1924-1925 #42: 473-672. .

1942   Source Material on the History and Ethnology of the Caddo Indians. Bureau of American Ethnology, Bulletin # 132.

Tanner, Adrian

1979 *Bringing Home Animals*: Religious Ideology and Mode of Production of the Mistassini Cree. New York: St Martin's Press.

Tantaquidgeon, G

1972   Folk Medicines of the Delaware and Related Algonkian Indians.   Harrisburg: Pennsylvania Historical and Museum Commission, Anthropology Series # 3.

Tax, Sol

1955 From Lafitau to Radcliffe-Brown: A Short History of the Study of Social Organization: 443-81. *Social Anthropology of North American Tribes*. Fred Eggan, ed. Chicago: University of Chicago Press.

Thompson, Hunter S

1971 *Fear and Loathing in Las Vegas*, A Savage Journey To The Heart Of The American Dream. New York: Popular Library.

Thompson, Stith

1966 *Tales of the North American Indians*. University of Indiana Press, Bloomington.

Thwaites, Reuben Gold, ed.

1897a Hurons: 1636. Jesuit Relations and Allied Documents. Travels and Explorations of the Jesuit Missionaries in New France 1610-1791. Vol X: 167-168. Cleveland: The Burrows Brothers.

1897b Hurons and Three Rivers: 1639-1640. Jesuit Relations and Allied Documents. Travels and Explorations of the Jesuit Missionaries in New France 1610-1791. Vol XVII: 197-201. Cleveland: The Burrows Brothers.

Tooker, Elisabeth

1964   An Ethnography of the Huron Indians, 1615-1649.   DC: Bureau of American Ethnology, Bulletin # 190.

1968 Masking and Matrilineality in North America. American Anthropologist 70 (6): 1170-1177.

Trigger, Bruce

1969 The Huron Farmers of the North. NY: Holt, Rinehart and Winston.

Tropp, Martin

1977 *Mary Shelley's Monster*, The Story of Frankenstein. Boston: Houghton Mifflin Co.

Ts'ibasaa, Joshua

1916   The *Adawx* of Garment of the Lightnings.   Recorded and transcribed by William Beynon. Orthographic and poetics interpretation by John Asher Dunn. Manuscript.

Turner, Victor

1964   Betwixt and Between:The Liminal Period in Rites De Passage. *Symposium on New Approaches to the Study of Religion*. Proceedings of The 1964 Annual Spring Meeting of The American Ethnological Society. U of Washington Press.

Turney-High, H

1941   Ethnography of the Kutenai. Memoirs of the American Anthropological Association # 56.
Umiker-Sebeok, D and T Sebeok
  1978   *Aboriginal Sign Languages of the Americans and Australia.* The Americas and Australia, vol. 2. New York: Plenum Press.
Usher, Jean
  1974   William Duncan of Metlakatla: A Victorian Missionary in British Columbia. Publications in History #5. Ottawa, ON: National Museums of Canada.
Van Valkenburgh, Richard
  1976   Chemehuevi Notes. American Indian Ethno-history, California and Basin-Plateau Indian, Paiute II: 225-253. New York: Garland Publishing.
Varenne, Herve
  1977   *Americans Together* ~ Structured Diversity in a Midwestern Town. New York: Teachers College Press, Columbia University.
Velten, H.V.
  1939   Two Southern Tlingit Tales. *International Journal of American Linguistics* 10 (2/3): 65–74.
  1944   Three Tlingit Stories. *International Journal of American Linguistics* 10 (4): 168–180.
Voegelin, Erminie
  1938   Tubatulabal Ethnography. *Anthropological Records* 2 (1): 1-48.
Wallace, A
  1949   The Role of the Bear in Delaware Society. *Pennsylvania Archaeologist* 19 (1-2): 37-46.
Watanabe, Hitoshi
  1973   The Ainu Ecosystem. Seattle: U of Washington Press for American Ethnological Society Monograph # 54.
Waterman, Thomas T
  1914   The Explanatory Element in the Folk-Tales of the North American Indians. *Journal of American Folklore* 27 (103): 1–54.
  1920   Yurok Geography. Berkeley: University of California Publications in American Archaelogy and Ethnology 16 (5): 177-314.
Waterman, TT, and AL Kroeber
  1938   The Kepel Fish Dam. University of California Publications in American Archaeology and Ethnology 35 (6): 49-80.
Watson, James
  1970   Society a Organized Flow: The Tairora Case. Southwestern Journal of Anthropology 26 (2): 107-124.
Wedel, Mildred Mott
  1978   La Harpe 's 1719 Post on Red River and Nearby Caddo Settlements. University of Texas at Austin. Texas Memorial Museum, Bulletin 30.
Wedel, Waldo
  1979   Toward Plains Caddoan Origins: A Symposium. *Nebraska History* 60 (2).
Weltfish, Gene
  1971   *The Lost Universe.* New York: Ballantine Books.
  1977   *Lost Universe.* Pawnee Life and Culture. University of Nebraska Press, Lincoln.

316

White, Leslie

1943 *New Material From Acoma.* Bureau of American Ethnology, Bulletin # 136: 301-59.

1944 A Ceremonial Vocabulary among the Pueblos. *International Journal of American Linguistics* 10: 161 —67.

1960 The World of the Keresan Pueblo Indians: 53-64. *Culture in History ~ Essays in Honor of Paul Radin.* New York: Columbia University Press for Brandeis University.

1962 *The Pueblo of Sia, New Mexico.* Bureau of American Ethnology, Bulletin 184.

White, Leslie, ed

1959 *The Indian Journals* 1859-62 of Lewis Henry Morgan. Ann Arbor: University of Michigan Press.

1964 Introduction: xii-xlii. *Ancient Society* by Lewis Henry Morgan. Cambridge, MA: The Belknap Press of Harvard University.

Williams, Stephen, and John Goggin

1956 The Long-Nosed God Mask. *Missouri Archaeologis*t 18 (3). [259]

Whiting, Beatrice B

1950 *Paiute Sorcery.* New York: Viking Fund Publications in Anthropology # 15.

Wike, Joyce

1957 More Puzzles on the Northwest Coast. American Anthropologist 59: 301-317.

Willoughby, NC

1963 Division of Labor Among the Indians of California. Reports of the University of California Archaeological Survey 60: 7-79.

Witherspoon, Gary

1977 *Language and Art in the Navajo Universe.* Ann Arbor: The University of Michigan Press.

Wright, Walter *Niistaxo'ok*

1962 Men of Medeek. Will Robinson, ed. Kitimat, BC: Northern Sentinel Press.

Zigmond, Maurice

1972 Some Mythological and Supernatural Aspects of Kawaiisu Ethnography and Ethnobiology. *Great Basin Cultural Ecology*: A Symposium, Don D Fowler, ed. Reno: Desert Research Institute Publications in Social Sciences # 8: 129-135.

1980 *Kawaiisu Mythology*, An Oral Tradition of the South-Central California. Ballena Press Anthropological Papers # 18.

Help the Fight against Typo Gnomes!